U0509457

上海市人民政府
发展研究中心系列报告

国际智库咨询
系列报告

INTEGRATION OF THE YANGTZE RIVER DELTA FOR HIGH-QUALITY DEVELOPMENT

长三角一体化与高质量发展

2019 年上海国际智库咨询研究报告

Consultation Report of Shanghai International Think Tank, 2019

上海市人民政府发展研究中心　编

The Development Research Center
of Shanghai Municipal People's Government

上海远东出版社　　上海人民出版社

主　编	Chief Editor
王德忠	Wang Dezhong

副主编	Subeditor
徐　诤	Xu Zheng
周师迅	Zhou Shixun

编　辑　　　　　Editing Team
（以姓氏拼音排序）　（in alphabetical order）

董萍萍	Dong Pingping
杜　磊	Du Lei
娄蓉嫒	Lou Rongyuan
潘春来	Pan Chunlai
史　磊	Shi Lei
孙子阳	Sun Ziyang
谭　旻	Tan Min
唐一辰	Tang Yichen
王　妍	Wang Yan
肖维青	Xiao Weiqing
姚　治	Yao Zhi
叶文兴	Ye Wenxing
张明海	Zhang Minghai
郑钧庭	Zheng Junting
朱惠涵	Zhu Huihan

嘉宾合影
Group Photo of the Distinguished Guests

上海市人民政府秘书长陈靖作开幕致辞
Opening Address by Chen Jing, Secretary General of Shanghai Municipal People's Government

上海市人民政府发展研究中心主任王德忠作开幕主持
Opening Ceremony by Wang Dezhong, Director General of the Development Research Center of Shanghai Municipal People's Government

上海市人民政府发展和改革委员会副主任、长三角生态绿色一体化发展示范区执委会副主任
张忠伟作主题演讲
Keynote Address by Zhang Zhongwei, Deputy Director General of Shanghai Municipal Development
and Reform Commission, Deputy Director of the Executive Committee of the Yangtze River Delta
Ecologically Friendly Demonstration Area

波士顿咨询公司全球合伙人兼董事总经理朱晖作主旨发言
Keynote Speech by Zhu Hui, Managing Director and Partner of Boston Consulting Group

罗兰贝格高级合伙人、中国区副总裁许季刚作主旨发言

Keynote Speech by Alex Xu, Global Senior Partner and Vice President of Roland Berger Greater China

德勤华东主管合伙人、中国创新主管合伙人刘明华作主旨发言

Keynote Speech by Dora Liu, Managing Partner of Deloitte China Eastern Region and Leader of Deloitte China Innovation

戴德梁行华东区董事总经理黎庆文作主旨发言
Keynote Speech by Kelvin Li, Managing Director for East China at Cushman & Wakefield

麦肯锡全球董事合伙人张帆作主旨发言
Keynote Speech by Derek Zhang, Partner at McKinsey & Company

仲量联行华东区董事总经理吴允燊作主旨发言
Keynote Speech by Eddie Ng, Managing Director for Shanghai and East China at JLL

美中贸易全国委员会上海首席代表欧文作主旨发言
Keynote Speech by Owen Haacke, Chief Representative of US-China Business Council Shanghai Office

毕马威政府与公共事务、特殊经济区咨询服务合伙人刘明作主旨发言
Keynote Speech by Liu Ming, Partner of Government & Public Sector and Special Economic Zone
Service at KPMG China

世界银行社会、城市、农村和灾害风险管理全球发展实践局首席城市专家梅柏杰作主旨发言
Keynote Speech by Barjor Mehta, Lead Urban Specialist of Social, Rural, Urban & Resilience
Global Practice in the World Bank

穆迪投资者服务有限公司董事总经理、中国区总经理施浩作主旨发言
Keynote Speech by Shi Hao, Managing Director of Moody's Investors Service

上海发展研究基金会副会长兼秘书长乔依德作主旨发言
Keynote Speech by Qiao Yide, Vice Chairman & Secretary General of Shanghai Development Research Foundation

互动讨论一：国际区域一体化经验及其对长三角高质量发展的启示

Panel Discussion 1：Experience from International Integrative Regions and Its Enlightenment for High-quality Development of the Yangtze River Delta

科尔尼(上海)企业咨询有限公司全球合伙人王宇发言

Panel Discussion by Jefferson Wang, Partner-Head of ATK China Government & Economic Development Practice

野村综研(上海)咨询有限公司副总经理、合伙人朱四明发言
Panel Discussion by Zhu Siming, Deputy General Manager and Partner of NRI(Shanghai)

普华永道中国创新城市综合服务合伙人高骏杰发言
Panel Discussion by Ken Gao, Partner of Integrated Urban Services at PwC

日本贸易振兴机构上海所副所长船桥宪发言
Panel Discussion by Ken FUNABASHI, Vice President of JETRO Shanghai

上海财经大学长三角与长江经济带发展研究院执行院长张学良发言
Panel Discussion by Zhang Xueliang, Executive Dean of the Development Research Institute of the Yangtze River Delta and Yangtze River Economic Belt in Shanghai University of Finance and Economics

互动讨论二：长三角一体化与营商环境共建

Panel Discussion 2：Integration of the Yangtze River Delta and Co-construction of Doing-business Environment

毕马威中国董事合伙人杨洁发言

Panel Discussion by Tracy Yang, Partner of KPMG China Board Member

凯捷咨询(中国)有限公司首席执行官余煌超发言
Panel Discussion by Cliff Yu, CEO of Capgemini China

高风咨询创始人兼 CEO 谢祖墀发言
Panel Discussion by Edward Tse, Founder and CEO of Gao Feng Advisory Company

安永中国管理咨询总监、区域经济业务合伙人周亮发言
Panel Discussion by Bryant Zhou, Director of Business Advisory Services in Ernst & Young

印度工业联合会中国代表处首席代表马德武发言
Panel Discussion by Madhav Sharma, Head-Greater China & Chief Representative of the Confederation of Indian Industry China

上海社科院副院长王振发言
Panel Discussion by Wang Zhen, Vice President of Shanghai Academy of Social Sciences

毕马威中国董事合伙人杨洁作总结发言
Concluding Speech by Tracy Yang, Partner of KPMG China Board Member

论坛现场
Conference Site

PREFACE

序

在首届中国国际进口博览会开幕式上，习近平总书记宣布支持长江三角洲区域一体化发展上升为国家战略。2019年以来，随着《长江三角洲区域一体化发展规划纲要》和《长三角生态绿色一体化发展示范区总体方案》陆续发布，长三角一体化发展国家战略进入全面实施阶段。作为中国经济发展最活跃、开放程度最高、创新能力最强的区域之一，长三角三省一市政产学研各界紧扣"一体化"与"高质量"，从各自角度合力推动区域一体化发展。在上海市人民政府发展研究中心的倡议下，上海国际智库交流中心成员单位以"长三角一体化与高质量发展"为主题，开展相关决策咨询研究，并于2019年12月共同举办"2019年上海国际智库高峰论坛"。

麦肯锡、毕马威等国际智库围绕论坛主题，从国内外区域合作的有效途径和体制机制等宏观层面，以及交通、能源、创新、环保等产业层面，开展了系列专题研究；并聚焦"国际区域一体化建设经验""长三角城市群协同创新""长三角未来产业机遇""长三角一体化背景下的企业发展"与"长三角更高质量一体化"五个方面，探讨了区域一体化国际经验、长三角一体化进程中存在的问题和面临的挑战，提出了对长三角高质量一体化发展的意见和建议。国际智库专家普遍认为，长三角基础设施互联互通已加速落地，一体化市场体系初现雏形，但在体制、创新、产业和营商环境层面上，仍面临挑战，需要注重形成跨省市协调的长效机制、统一的市场体系和营商环境，强化数字技术在长三角一体化中的作用，从区域和产业两个角度实现城市群协同发展。在此基础上，他们提出了三方面的对策建议：一是上海在长三角一体化发展战略实施过程中，要当好龙头，在数据标准制定、产业制度创新和统一的营商环境方面发挥引领作用;二是长三角三省一市要深化区域内产业结构战略整合,构建利益共享机制,形成优势互补、互利共生的城市分工,完善产业链梯度布局;三是探索通过跨省市产业项目合作、打造超级产业集群、区域港务管理一体化创新、建立自下而上及多元参与的智库咨询机制等具体形式,推进长三角高质量一体化发展。

上海市人民政府发展研究中心高度重视国际智库专家的意见和建议,及时报市领导决策参考,同时,为扩大研究成果的国内外影响,现将国际智库相关决策咨询报告和本届论坛实录汇编成《长三角一体化与高质量发展——2019年上海国际智库咨询研究报告》,以飨读者。

本届论坛得到了上海市政府相关部门的关心支持,上海市人民政府秘书长陈靖出席了论坛并致辞,长三角区域合作办公室和东方网·东方智库作为支持单位提供了大力帮助,在此深表感谢。我们希望国际智库的国际化视野,及其前瞻性、系统性研究成果,能为关注和研究长三角高质量一体化发展的社会各界人士提供有益的思考与启示,也期待未来能有更多国际智库加入上海的决策咨询研究队伍,为上海经济社会发展和城市建设贡献力量。

上海市人民政府发展研究中心主任

2020 年 5 月 18 日

At the opening ceremony of the first China International Import Expo (CIIE), CPC General Secretary Xi Jinping announced the integrated development of the Yangtze River Delta as a national strategy. Since 2019, with the fresh release of the *Outline of the Integrated Regional Development of the Yangtze River Delta* and the *Overall Plan for the Demonstration Area in the Yangtze River Delta on Ecologically Friendly Development*, the integrated development of the Yangtze River Delta strategy has entered into the phase to be carried out in a comprehensive manner. As one of China's most economically active, open and innovative regions, the governments, industries, universities and research institutes of three provinces and one municipality within the Delta have been cooperating in their common endeavor to foster the region's "integrated and high-quality" development, and by their concerted efforts. Against this backdrop and in response to the initiative of the Development Research Center of Shanghai Municipal People's Government (SDRC), the members of the Shanghai International Think Tank Exchange Center took as the topic "Integration of the Yangtze River Delta for High-quality Development", conducted research on relevant decision consultation, and co-organized the "2019 Shanghai International Think Tank Summit" in December 2019.

According to the summit's topic, international think tanks such as McKinsey and KPMG have carried out a series of studies from a macro level, such as the effective ways and institutional mechanisms of regional cooperation at home and abroad, and from the industrial level, such as transportation, energy, innovation and environmental protection; they have also focused on five aspects of "International Experience of the Global Regional Integration Construction", "Synergistic Innovation in the Yangtze River Delta City Cluster", "Future Industrial Opportunities in the Yangtze River Delta", "Enterprise Development in the Context of the Yangtze River Delta Integration" and "Higher-quality Integration in the Yangtze River Delta", and have discussed international experience in regional integration, problems and challenges in the process of the Yangtze River Delta integration, and put forward opinions and suggestions on the development of high-quality integration in the Yangtze River Delta. Experts from international think tanks generally agreed that the infrastructure connectivity in the Yangtze River Delta has been put into practice at a rapid speed and the integrated market system is gradually taking shape, but it still faces challenges at the institutional, innovation, industry and business environment levels; therefore, it is essential to focus on forming a long-term mechanism for inter-provincial and municipal coordination, a unified market system and business environment, and strengthen the role of digital technology in the integration of the Yangtze River Delta, so as to achieve synergistic development of the city cluster from both regional and industrial perspectives. On this basis, they put forward three countermeasures: first, Shanghai should play a pioneering role in implementing the integrated development strategy of the Yangtze River Delta and in formulation of data standards, innovation of industrial systems and a unified business environment; second, the three provinces and one municipality in the Yangtze River Delta should deepen the strategic integration of industrial structures in the region, build a mechanism for profit-sharing, form a division of labor in cities characterized by complementarity and mutually beneficial coexistence, and improve the layout of industrial chain gradients; third, efforts should be made to explore applicable forms to promote the high-quality integrated development of the Yangtze River Delta through cross-provincial and municipal industrial project cooperation, the creation of super-industrial clusters, regional port management integration and innovation, and the establishment of a bottom-up and multi-participation think tank advisory mechanism.

The Development Research Center of Shanghai Municipal People's Government attached great importance to those opinions and suggestions from international think tank experts and promptly summarized and reported them to municipal leaders for decision-making reference. Meanwhile, in an effort to expand the impact of the research results both at home and abroad, we collected the relevant decision-making consultation reports by the international think tank and the proceedings of this Summit and compiled this "Integration of the Yangtze River Delta for High-quality Development-Consultation Report of Shanghai International Think Tank, 2019" for our readers.

The Summit was concerned and supported by the relevant departments of the Shanghai Municipal Government, particularly with Chen Jing, Secretary General of the Shanghai Municipal People's Government, who attended the Summit and delivered an opening speech. The Yangtze River Delta Regional Cooperation Office and the Eastday · Oriental Think Tank as supporting organizations also lent strong assistance, for which we would like to express our deep gratitude. We hope that the international perspective of international think tanks and their forward-looking and systematic research can trigger further thinking and serve as a source of inspiration for people from all walks of life who are concerned about the high-quality integrated development of the Yangtze River Delta, and we also hope that in the future, more international think tanks will join this decision-making, consulting and research team in Shanghai, contributing to Shanghai's economic and social development as well as its urban construction.

Wang Dezhong

Director General of the SDRC

May 18, 2020

CONTENTS

目 录

2019 年上海国际智库高峰论坛实录
Part 2　Record of the 2019 Shanghai International Think Tank Summit

Part 1

国际智库系列研究报告

Research Papers of International Think Tanks

International Experience of the Global Regional Integration Construction

国际区域一体化建设经验

借鉴"新世代东京计划",促进多元化共治,构筑面向未来的超大城市治理能力

科尔尼企业咨询公司

根据科尔尼 2019 年的"全球城市指数"排名结果,目前长三角地区的上海、南京、杭州、苏州、无锡、宁波 6 座城市被列入全球 130 个城市的榜单之中。对比全球上榜城市所在的城市群,长三角地区所涵盖的上榜城市数量令其当之无愧地成为世界顶级城市群之一。其中,根据全球综合城市排名,上海名列前茅,始终保持在前 20 名的位置。南京、杭州、苏州三座城市于 2015 年上榜,当前排名位列第 85—100 名之间。而后起之秀的宁波和无锡,也于 2018 年上榜,目前排名为第 116 名和第 124 名。这也是我们的"全球城市指数"报告自 2008 年发布以来,十多年间首次出现 5 个以上的同城市圈城市上榜,真正体现了长三角城市群的综合影响力与竞争力。

究其原因,这个成绩的取得除了得益于经济发展、商业活动方面的高竞争力以外,近年来也逐渐得益于对人力资本的关注。可以看到,人力资本取得长足进步,是推动长三角地区城市亮眼表现的核心驱动力。展望未来,科尔尼认为长三角地区发展仍需关注人力资本,聚焦"以市民为中心"。这不仅体现在宏观的人力资本的方面,更体现在微观层面居民幸福度的提升。

真正体现"以市民为中心",意味着不仅城市宜居、舒适,公共服务高效便民,更重要的是真正能将本地市民作为区域发展的主体。

结合近年提到的城市"高质量发展"要求和治理体系与能力现代化要求,我们认为包括上海在内的长三角各个主要城市,应该将探索"国际超大城市治理现代化"领域的引领性和示范性角色作为一个发展重点,而这离不开本地人才的积极参与。

结合科尔尼近期在东京开展的一系列工作,我们对这个话题做一个分享。

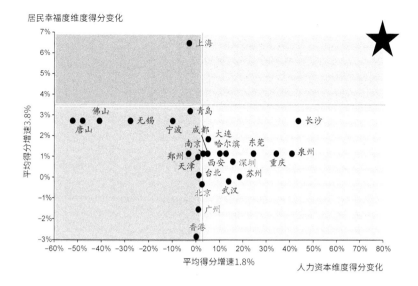

图 1　中国上榜城市的人力资本与居民幸福度得分增长（2015—2019）

注：其中长沙、宁波、无锡、佛山、烟台和唐山属于 2018 年新上榜城市，统计的是
　　2018—2019 年的增长情况

资料来源：科尔尼 2019 年全球城市指数报告

一、东京在双向城市治理方面的经验

从国际超大城市治理实践来看，政府、企业、市民之间如何充分协作，结合自上而下的统筹规划和自下而上的市民多元参与，是超大城市治理的一个关键。目前在这方面，国内各大城市已开始有所尝试，但是深度和广度都相对有限。

在这个方面，纽约、伦敦、东京等世界级超大型城市做出了很好的示范。

我们将以东京作为阐述国际超大型城市治理的最佳实践，并重点介绍"新世代东京计划"（NexTokyo Project）下的各项城市治理促进举措。该计划由科尔尼日本公司董事长梅泽高明先生于 2014 年提出，并发起成立了"新世代东京计划"社会贤达机构，希望借助该计划，帮助东京把握 2020 年奥运会的发展机遇，并实现城市的二次腾飞，成为世界上最具魅力的都市。

该机构吸引了来自建筑、城市规划、设计、艺术、体育、媒体，以及法律等各行各业的 12 名专家，基于专家小组对城市未来发展的意见与洞察，提出对未来城市的发展愿景，并向包括中央政府、地方政府、地产开发商和产业界在内的各层级人士提出东京城市的未来发展建议。

发起五年以来，"新世代东京计划"在各个层面都取得了良好效果，在社会层面广泛地引起了日本媒体和政界的关注，并引发一系列对东京未来的关键讨论。该计划主导发起推动的多项东京都政府立法,涉及国际人才吸引、夜间经济管理、民宿管理等各个方面,同时也亲自策划和发起多个项目落地,包括重点区域再开发、创新创业社区运营、国际教育机构引进等,无一不在推动着东京城市的发展。

二、"新世代东京计划"的关键成功因素

"新世代东京计划"的成功关键,在于在机制上充分动员、保障和鼓励东京本土的精英贤达人士对城市发展的热情与设想,对于上海乃至长三角区域各个大型城市来说,存在以下几个关键的借鉴经验。

1. 自下而上的对话机制,跨学科、多元化的意见输入,以复合知识解答城市发展未来

"新世代东京计划"采用新颖的城市发展思路,特别是集中于决策、建设两大层面。在针对城市发展决策时,不仅要实现中央及地方领导层自上而下的决策,更要重视来自民间的想法,为下情上达提供通畅的途径。在建设时,需特别重视修复再生(renovation)和改造(conversion)的手法,发挥现有资产的二次利用价值。

该计划注重吸引本地专家,给予本地意见领袖较大的发挥空间。来自"新世代东京计划"社会贤达机构的 12 人专家小组,其成员中不乏来自咨询公司和商业界的专家,来自科技和创业领域的企业家,推进多个公共立法的资深律师。此外,小组还拥有出身设计和艺术、来自东京大学的艺术家,来自 Time Out 东京的出版人、哈佛大学建筑系主任、知名城市规划专家以及前奥运会顶级运动员等等。由多元学科的专业人士来参与"新世代东京计划",避免了任何领域的知识垄断,通过跨学科、多元化的专家意见输入,建立多方共识,探索城市发展的关键问题。

2. 推动政策制定与本地立法,促进城市规划举措有效落地

在"新世代东京计划"的进展过程之中,总有各种各样的法律法规挡在面前。为了越过现有的规则和障碍,"新世代东京计划"团队充分利用国家战略特区计划,以求特定区域内规章制度的松动,抑或是推动全国范围内的法律改革。

该计划与东京都各级政府,乃至日本中央政府,建立了密切的沟通和交流机制,向政府的国家战略特别区域咨询会议工作小组,以及规章制度改革推进室等机构提交了多项提案。提案包括:针对创新人才放宽工作签证限制、废除针对休娱业态夜间经营的限制、增设民宿特区、开放市内公共空间。其中大多数提案都已经获得了法律的支持,并已进入实施阶段。尤其是"针对创新人才放宽工作签证限制"和"废除针对夜间营业的限制"这两个提案,已经获得政府通过,并由新世代东京团队深入参与到项目的执行过程之中。

从政策具体细节来看,举一个简单的例子。创新人才政策涉及高级人才签证及设计类毕业生工作签证条件放宽。其中,由新世代东京团队提案,在"高级人才积分制度"中纳入设计和艺术等创意领域关键人才,并设置具体加分指标。该政策已于 2017 年 6 月被正式纳入政府方针。

3. 作为"超级项目经理",发起与介入区域再开发和公共性项目

在区域层面具体落地的区域再开发和公告性项目,"新世代东京计划"团队也取得了一定成效,有两个案例。

第一个案例是联合英国皇家艺术学院和东京大学生产技术研究所,成立东京设计实验室。该项国际合作的主要内容包括英国皇家艺术学院向东京派遣教员和研究人员,并协同双方科学技术和设计技术,以项目的形式将人们对未来城市的设想一步步变成现实。

这一国际合作的实现,离不开"新世代东京计划"三位成员的努力,并通过日本内阁府战略推进会议,为这次国际合作提供了战略构想方面的全方位支持。该设计实验室未来也将作为国际化的前沿设计中心,与日本产业界相互扶持,专注于国际影响力的提高。

第二个案例是目前还在推进中的东京创业园区建立。"新世代东京计划"团队正努力与国际知名创业孵化基地 CIC 开展积极沟通,试图在东京设立 CIC Tokyo 分部。

在与 CIC 合作共建创业园区的计划中,其中一项被称为"冒险咖啡厅东京"的活动目前正进行初步试水。该活动于每个星期四晚虎之门之丘咖啡馆定期举办创新性社区活动。简而言之,这是在东京建立的更深入的创新社区的一次尝试,希望通过将"冒险咖啡厅"活动创建的社区作为开设东京创新中心的基础。

此外,由该机构提出的其他东京区域实践也纳入了政府层面的考虑,其中包括对筑地海鲜市场搬迁后的改造设想和 2020 年东京奥运会的社区拆建和区域交通改造,也由该团队提交相应提案。

特别要指出的是,这类具体项目的推进,并非"新世代东京计划"所独有的。事实上由精英市民发起,政府支持,公众团体和企业界深度协作的城市发展模式在东京并不鲜见。团队 12 人之一的楠本先生,过去曾多次发起和推动一系列类似工作,例如知名的涩谷"猫街"再开发、"东京丰收节"(Tokyo Harvest)等区域再开发和公共性项目经验,有效地推动了东京在创新创业领域的发展。

三、借鉴"新世代东京",动员本地精英人才,深度参与城市治理与发展

总的来看,"新世代东京计划"在一定程度上对长三角各大城市打造国际超大型城市治理体系具有良好的借鉴作用。其核心思想聚焦"以市民为中心的共同治理",关键成功因素在于充分动员东京本地的精英贤达人士,并通过创设良好的多方交流机制,充分发挥他们对城市发展的热情和专业能力。

长三角作为中国乃至全球的人才高地,有一批在各个专业领域具备精深能力,在商业运作和管理方面具备长期经验,并兼具国际视野与本土关怀的精英人才。如何让他们将自己擅长的领域与区域发展诉求相结合,值得深度探究与思考。

我们也希望上海、杭州、苏州、南京、无锡、宁波等一系列城市,可以借鉴"新世代东京计划"的经验,打造植根本地、展望全球的本土计划,通过切实发挥本地企业、学者、专家的群体智慧,推动城市的国际化发展。

Enhance Megacity Co-governance Capability

—Lessons from the NexTokyo Project

A.T. Kearney

According to the result of Kearney's 2019 Global Cities Index (GCI), among the 130 global cities on the 2019 GCI ranking, 6 cities were from the Yangtze River Delta region. They are Shanghai, Nanjing, Hangzhou, Suzhou, Wuxi, and Ningbo, making the Yangtze River Delta city cluster one of the top global city clusters in terms of the number of cities making the list. Shanghai has remained top 20 in the 2019 GCI ranking. Nanjing, Hangzhou and Suzhou debuted on the list in 2015 and ranked between 85th and 100th currently. Ningbo and Wuxi made the list last year for the first time and currently ranked 116th and 124th respectively. This was also the first time in the past decade for a city cluster with more than 5 cities making the list at the same time since the launch of the GCI report in 2008, which reflected the overall influence and competitiveness of the Yangtze River Delta city cluster.

Besides economic development and business activity, increasing attention to human capital also drives the progress on GCI ranking of the Yangtze River Delta city cluster in recent years, which is a core driver of their remarkable performance. Looking forward, Kearney thinks that the Yangtze River Delta region still needs to focus on human capital and be citizen-centric not only on the broader human capital perspective, but more importantly, on the granular level of personal well-being improvement.

Citizen-centric goes beyond livable and comfortable environment, and efficient and convenient public services. It's more important to involve

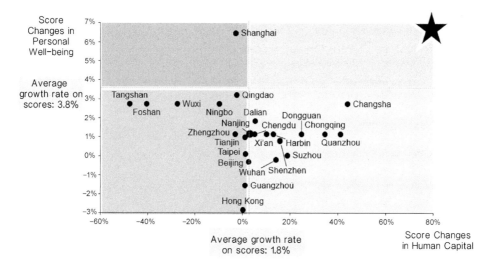

**Figure 1   Score Gains of Chinese Cities on Human Capital and
Personal Well-being (2015–2019)**

Note: Data of Changsha, Ningbo, Wuxi, Foshan, Yantai and Tangshan was from 2018–2019, as they
    embarked on the list in 2018
Source: Kearney 2019 Global Cities Index Report

citizens in regional development.

Given governmental requirements of high-quality city development and
modernized governance system and capabilities mentioned in recent years,
we think that major cities in the Yangtze River Delta region, including
Shanghai, should focus on seeking a leading and demonstrative role in the
"modernization of international megacity governance", which cannot
succeed without proactive engagement of local talents.

We're going to share something about this topic based on a series of
work of ours in Tokyo.

I. Experience of Tokyo: A hybrid approach for city co-governance

Global megacity governance practices show that how to collaborate
between government, enterprises and citizens, along with top-down planning
and bottom-up civil engagement is the key to megacity governance. Major
Chinese cities have begun to adopt these practices but are still limited in the
depth and width.

Several world-class megacities like New York, London, and Tokyo have set us good examples in this area.

We will use Tokyo as an example to interpret best practices of international megacity governance and highlight initiatives of the NexTokyo Project that facilitate city governance. NexTokyo was proposed in 2014 by Tak Umezawa, Chairman of Kearney Japan, along with which, the NexTokyo Social Elite Organization was founded. The aim of NexTokyo is to help the city leverage the opportunity of Olympic Games Tokyo 2020 to drive a second economic boom and build the most charming metropolis in the world.

The Social Elite Organization consists of 12 experts from all trades and walks, including architecture, urban planning, design, art, sports, media, and law. They design visions for the future of the city based on views and insights from the expert panel and put forward proposals on future development of Tokyo to people at all levels from central and local governments, real estate developers and industries.

NexTokyo Project has achieved good results at all levels since it was launched 5 years ago, drawing extensive social attention from media and politicians and sparking a series of key discussions about the future of Tokyo. Multiple initiatives led by the Project have been legislated by Tokyo metropolitan government, including international talent attraction, night-time economy management, and B&B (bed and breakfast) management. NexTokyo has also planned and sponsored implementation of several projects, including redevelopment of key areas, operation of innovation and entrepreneurship communities, and introduction of international educational institutions. All of these are driving the city development of Tokyo.

Ⅱ. Key success factors of the NexTokyo Project

The key to the success of NexTokyo lies in the mechanism to fully mobilize, protect and encourage the passion and vision of local elites for city development of Tokyo. For Shanghai, and the Yangtze River Delta region,

NexTokyo Project provides the following implications.

1. Bottom-up dialogue mechanism and interdisciplinary input of ideas to address future city development with compound knowledge

The NexTokyo Project adopts a novel approach to city development, especially on decision-making and construction. In decision making about city development, besides top-down decisions of the central and local leadership, opinions from the folk should also be considered and a smooth path to report these opinions to the higher authorities should be ensured. In city construction, special attention needs to be paid to approaches to renovation and conversion to maximize the reuse of existing assets.

NexTokyo Project focuses on attracting local experts and provides great room for local opinion leaders to play. The 12-person panel consists of experts from consulting firms and the business community, entrepreneurs from high-tech companies and start-ups, and senior lawyers promoting multiple public legislation, designer and artist from the University of Tokyo, publisher from Time Out Tokyo, Dean of the Department of Architecture at Harvard University, well-known urban planning experts, and former top Olympic athletes. Involvement of experts from multiple disciplines in the NexTokyo Project avoids knowledge monopoly and builds consensus among multiple parties through interdisciplinary and diversified expert inputs to explore key issues of city development.

2. Promote policy-making and local legislation to facilitate implementation of urban planning initiatives

There're always various laws and regulations impeding the progress of NexTokyo Project. To overcome existing regulatory obstacles, the Project team leverages national strategic special region program to seek regulation relaxation in specific regions or push for legal reform across the country.

The Project has established close communication and exchange mechanisms with governments at all levels of Tokyo and even the central government of Japan. It has submitted several proposals to the government's task group of the council of national strategic special region program and the regulatory reform promotion office. These proposals include relaxing work visa requirements for innovative talents, eliminating restrictions on night-time operations in the entertainment industry, setting up special zones for B&B, and opening public spaces in the city. Most of these proposals have received legal support and entered the implementation phase. In particular, the proposals of "relaxing visa requirements for innovative talents" and "eliminating restrictions on night-time operations" have been approved by the government and involved the NexTokyo Project team deeply in the execution.

In details, for example, the innovative talent policy involves the relaxation of visa requirements for senior talents and design graduates. The NexTokyo Project team proposed to include key talents in creative areas like design and arts to the "senior talent credit system" and set specific indicators for additional point granting. This policy was formally incorporated as a government policy in June 2017.

3. Initiate and involve in regional redevelopment and public projects as a "super project manager"

The NexTokyo Project team has also made achievements in the implementation of regional redevelopment and public projects, here are two examples.

The first was Tokyo Design Lab established by the Royal College of Art and the Institute of Industrial Science of the University of Tokyo in collaboration. In this partnership, the Academy of Arts dispatches faculty and researchers to Tokyo. They will leverage scientific and design technologies of both sides to turn people's vision of the future city into reality step by step in the form of projects.

This international partnership cannot be fulfilled without the efforts of three members of the NexTokyo Project. They also provided all-round support for the strategic conception to this partnership through strategic advancement conference of the Cabinet Office. The design lab will also serve as a leading international design center and is dedicated to enhancing international influence with mutual support from Japanese industries.

The second example was Tokyo Startup Park, which is still in progress.

The NexTokyo Project team is trying to communicate with global renowned business incubator CIC, with an attempt to establish its Tokyo branch.

Among the options for building a startup park in partnership with CIC, an initiative called "Adventure Cafe Tokyo" is currently undergoing a preliminary trial. Regular innovative community events are held every Thursday night in Toranomon Hills Cafe. This is an attempt of Tokyo to build more intensive innovation communities, with the hope that communities created through the Adventure Cafe Tokyo can lay foundation for the opening of the Tokyo Innovation Center.

Other regional practices for Tokyo proposed by NexTokyo are also being considered at the government level, including renovation plan for the Tsukiji fish market after relocation, and proposals on community demolition and rebuilding and regional transportation transformation for the Tokyo 2020 Olympic Games.

However, such programs are not unique to the NexTokyo Project. In fact, such models of city development initiated by elite citizens, backed by government, and in profound collaboration between public groups and businesses are common in Tokyo.

Mr. Kusuki, one of the 12 experts, had initiated and promoted several similar efforts in the past, such as redevelopment of the well-known Shibuya "Cat Street" and "Tokyo Harvest", and other public projects, which boosted Tokyo's development in innovation and entrepreneurship.

III. Learn from the NexTokyo Project and mobilize local elites to involve in city governance and development

To sum up, the NexTokyo Project provides significant implications for major cities in the Yangtze River Delta region to build international megacity governance system. Its core concept focuses on "citizen-centric and shared governance". The key success factor is to fully mobilize local elites of Tokyo and create a sound multi-party communication system to make the most of their passion and expertise in city development.

As a national and even global leader of talent pools, the Yangtze River Delta region has a group of elites with profound expertise in all areas, long-term experience in business operations and management, and both international vision and local footprints. How to match their expertise with local development requirements is worth deep exploration and reflection.

We also hope that Shanghai, Hangzhou, Suzhou, Nanjing, Wuxi, Ningbo and many other cities can learn from the NexTokyo Project, creating a development plan rooted locally with an international vision, and promoting international development of cities by exerting the collective wisdom of local enterprises, scholars and experts.

东京都市圈与日本城市群建设的特点以及对长三角一体化的经验借鉴

野村综研

日本以东京为核心的都市圈发展历时较长,城市间合作模式较为成熟,经济规模巨大,国际影响力较强。除以东京为核心的都市圈外,日本政府目前也在积极推进包含东京都市圈在内的日本三大都市圈的联动发展,构建超级大都市带(Super Mega-region)以提升城市群整体的国际竞争力。日本在都市圈和城市群的建设中有相当多的成熟模式,同时也存在值得关注的经验教训,在长三角一体化的过程中可以进行扬弃式的经验借鉴,结合我国区域一体化发展的现实与目标,可以更加高效高质量地推动长三角一体化的发展进程。

一、关于都市圈与城市群

以东京为中心的城市共同体存在不同区域范围的内涵。其一是东京都,是日本的一级行政单位之一,下辖中心城区的 23 区和 23 区外的市町村(郊区),总面积约 2 106 平方公里,人口约 1 250 万人。其二是东京圈,包含东京都及围绕在东京都外部的埼玉县、神奈川县、千叶县三县①,总面积约 13 373 平方公里,人口约 3 613 万人。其三是首都圈,包含整个东京圈以及山梨县、群马县、栃木县和茨城县,总面积 36 494 平方公里,人口约 4 383 万人。其四是广域首都圈,范围包括首都圈的一都七县以及静冈县、长野县、新潟县和福岛县,总面积 84 602 平方公里,人口约 5 400 万人。

上海市总面积约 6 340 平方公里,介于东京都与东京圈的范围大小之间;而上海市中心城区面积为 664 平方公里,与东京都核心部位 23 区的面积 627 平方公里相当。另一方面,长三角区域总面积约为 35.8 万平方公里,远远大于以东京为核心

---

① 县为日本一级行政单位,与东京都为同一行政级别。

的圈层中最大的广域首都圈的面积。值得关注的是,推进长三角区域一体化的工作中,长三角地区城市所形成的城市共同体是"城市群"的关系,而日本的首都圈、广域首都圈则更偏向能级较低的"都市圈"。地区内城市协同发展、推进一体化的过程中,需要根据物理条件的限制选择合理化的一体化方式。长三角地区范围广阔,从上海到南京的距离为 300 公里,从上海到台州的距离为 375 公里,从上海到合肥的距离为 477 公里,在整个长三角超过 30 万平方公里的空间范围的基础上,建立具备一体化城市机能的都市圈不但成本巨大、风险不可控,同时也没有明确的收益目标。从建立具备一体化城市机能都市圈的角度出发,最具可行性的范围是一日通勤较为可行的距离范围,即 60—80 公里的范围,对上海而言,该范围即为包含苏州吴江、嘉兴嘉善的区域。在这个小范围的区域中,可以率先建立共同的城市机能、互通的轨道交通,探索以大城市为核心的都市圈的建设方法与建设方向。

二、关于上海都市圈的建设

日前,国家发展改革委员会批复同意《长三角生态绿色一体化发展示范区总体方案》,拟通过在上海青浦、江苏吴江、浙江嘉善三地的面积约 2 300 平方公里的范围内建立长三角生态绿色一体化发展示范区,打造生态友好型一体化发展样本,其中示范区先行启动区为 660 平方公里。可以窥见,发展示范区的理念在生态建设工作中已被重视和实践运用,事实上发展示范区的理念同样可以被运用到城市功能一体化建设工作中来。以上海为中心,在 60—80 公里范围内建立实质上的上海大都市圈,在实践上具备可操作性,可以应用许多国际上著名都市圈在建设过程中的成熟经验,结合我国区域一体化建设的实际条件与发展目标,探索真正符合地区发展诉求和客观发展规律的都市圈建设模式,从而在整个长三角地区乃至更广域的范围内进行推广和复制。

日本国土交通省都市局到目前为止已经制定了六次"首都圈建设计划"以及两次"广域首都圈计划",其覆盖范围和内涵都经历了多次转变。从总体目标来看,"首都圈计划"还是希望将东京"一极集中"的地域结构改变为"多心多核"的结构,并实现区域内的"对流"。为此,除了在东京都内建设多个副都心,也在东京周边大力发展"业务核都市"。但由于东京都巨大的虹吸效应,规划的 22 个核都市中,仅有横滨、千叶、埼玉等少数发展相对较好,其余地区则不及预期。在一都七县的范围内,不同地区在都市圈内承担了不同的角色。东京都最核心的 23 区主要为总部经济、金融中心和商业中心;东京都区部外的郊区(多摩地区)主要为高科技产业、研发中心和精密制造。东京都外的三县中,千叶县主要为商务、文化、居住、港航枢纽和工业,埼玉县主要为政府机构、居住以及机械工业、物流、旅游业,神奈川县主要为港口、机械、电子信息产业与居住。更外围的四县中,群马县主要为自然资源、水电供应以及林业和畜牧业基地,茨城县主要为科研、空港交通,山梨县主要为旅游、环保等。

尽管日本国土交通省在平衡区域发展方面做出了巨大努力,甚至一度引发东京都的中心活力是否会被周边地区削弱的争议,但最终东京都仍然拥有更高的吸引力,尤其是地价回落之后,原先向外疏解的人口、城市功能、产业中都有很大部分开始回流,仅有部分土地密集或土地要素敏感型产业与功能外迁较为成功。反过来东京都自身通过完善配套设施、提升精细化管理,一定程度上缓解了交通堵塞、环境污染、生活质量下降等大都市病,提升了对回流人口与产业的承载能力,使得向外疏解的压力不再像过去那样急迫。

以上海为核心建立都市圈的过程中,上海应明确自身定位。从上海现实发展阶段和近期发展目标来看,上海现有的产业结构与东京都人均生产总值2万美元时基本一致,从国际城市发展经验来看,或许尚无主动大规模减少制造业比重的必要。上海的大都市圈建设,中心与郊区、上海与周边城市的协同发展需要符合市场经济规律,例如对土地不敏感的产业与功能即便基于一时政策导向外迁,也往往会基于集聚效应回流。因此在产业分工上,需要平衡大都市圈中核心城市与周边城市的"虹吸效应"与"分流效应"。同时,周边城市发展需要充分发展"个性",只有差异化错位发展,才能形成和核心城市的对流,避免此消彼长的无效竞争。

三、关于长三角城市群的建设

从短期来看,长三角地区整体的一体化工作,比起建立一体化城市机能,更重要的是建立具备强经济联系的广域经济圈。在经济圈的视角下,长三角一体化应着重关注产业机能的联系,上海作为核心城市,需要兼顾作为地区引领极和国际大都市发展的需求与区域共同发展的需求,对重点产业类别和产业机能进行区分,进行合理的产业与功能分工。

近年来,日本也出现了超越都市圈范围的城市间联动的概念。由日本中央政府国土交通省提出的超级大都市带旨在通过构建日本三大都市圈(以东京为核心的首都圈、以名古屋为核心的中部圈,以及以大阪为核心的关西圈)的联动,形成新的城市群或大城市带,在这个全新的城市间合作的层级促进各个地区在居住就业、经济沟通和城市机能等方面的协作。日本政府此举意在促进各有特色的三大都市圈一体化发展,打造巨大经济圈,使得原先都市圈的协同效果得到广域性的扩大,而实现这个目标的背景是日本三大都市圈的发展时间较长,目前形态都已经较为成熟,具备了进一步发展都市圈间协同一体化的条件。

超级大都市带的建设过程中,交通的进一步便利化是极为重要的内涵。日本中央新干线磁悬浮的建设将进一步促进日本三大都市圈的沟通与连接,从东京到名古屋的时间将缩短至40分钟,而从东京到大阪的时间将最快缩短至67分钟。交通的便利化对于人与产业的交流与发展具有深远的影响。一方面,中央新干线将增加人与人之间的交流机会,扩大交流时间,为孕育新的创新创造机遇。新线路的开通将解放时间与空间的束缚,为生活方式、工作方式、商业方式都提供更多可能性。另一方面,中央新干线的开通将从实质上促进三大都市圈的一体化,提升国际竞争力,吸引海外投资与人才。此外,新线路与原先具备的旧有线路如东海新干线等将构成有机结合的交通网络,通过多重性、替代性来降低灾害风险,构建具备生态与防灾韧性的城市群。在超级大都市带的建设中,除三大都市圈之外,作为地方经济核心的城市带沿线小都市圈也将发挥自身的特色与地处亚洲的优势,更多地走上世界舞台,成为地方经济发展的增长极。

立足上海和长三角地区,通过日本都市圈与超都市圈层级区域一体化发展经历得出可以借鉴的经验是,先促进都市圈层级的一体化区域成熟化发展,在各个区域具备了各自发展特性和内生力之后,再进一步寻求超越都市圈的一体化融合。结合中国与长三角地区实际的发展诉求,一种可能的发展路径是在近期内,重点推进以上海为核心的先行大都市圈以及以长三角其他地区城市为核心的都市圈的稳步一体化发展,同时,推进长三角地区整体范围的广域经济圈的发展,这个过程中需要上海更多地发挥国际大都市的牵引作用,促进整个长三角城市群的经济发展动力;在长期,寻求合适的机会点,在经历了充分发展、具备成熟条件的各个长三角内都市圈的基础上,通过交通等重要方面的突破性建设,创造都市圈的联动,构建在单纯经济协作之上的长三角城市群或大都市带,实现真正意义上的长三角一体化目标。

Characteristics of the Greater Tokyo Area and Japan Megalopolis

—Lessons to be Learned by the Yangtze River Delta

Nomura Research Institute

The Greater Tokyo Area, the largest regional economy in Japan which enjoys a long history and strong international influence, has developed a mature cooperation scheme among cities. Including the Greater Tokyo Area, the Japanese central government is also propelling a closer connection and cooperation among the three largest metropolitan areas (Greater Tokyo, Chukyo, and Keihanshin) along the Pacific coast, under the vision of Super Mega-region. Practices have been proved useful and lessons have been learned in the development of these metropolitan areas and megalopolis in Japan. Thus learning from and studying into the previous experience of Japan may shed a light on the discussion of the integration of the Yangtze River Delta. By combining local experience with an international perspective, the regional development goal of Yangtze River Delta may be achieved in a more efficient way.

I. Metropolitan areas and megalopolis

The terms of area surrounding Tokyo need to be defined first so as to better understand the comparability between the Yangtze River Delta and Tokyo region. Tokyo Metropolis, the Japanese prefecture① is a collective

---

① Prefecture is the first administrative level of division, equivalent to province in China.

entity of multiple smaller municipalities, including 23 special wards, 26 cities, 1 district, and 4 subprefectures, with a size of 2,106 km². The Tokyo Metropolitan Area, including Tokyo Metropolis and the three adjacent prefectures, Saitama, Kanagawa, and Chiba, covers an area of 13,373 km² with a population of 36 million. The Greater Tokyo Area (also referred to as the Capital Region) includes Tokyo Metropolis and the prefectures of Kanagawa, Chiba, Saitama, Ibaraki, Tochigi, Gunma and Yamanashi, with a total population of 44 million, covering an area of approximately 36,494 km². The Greater Kanto Area includes the Greater Tokyo Area and the prefecture of Shizuoka, Nagano, Niigata, and Fukushima, covering 84,602 km² with a population of 54 million (around 40% of the total population in Japan).

Shanghai covers an area of 6,340 km², falling in between the size of Tokyo metropolitan area and the Greater Tokyo Area. The central area of Shanghai is around 664 km², comparable to the central area of Tokyo (the 23 special wards, sizing 627 km²). On the other hand, the Yangtze River Delta, covering an area of over 358,000 km², is far larger than the Greater Kanto Area (84,602 km²). It needs to be clarified that the cities in Yangtze River Delta aim to form a megalopolis rather than a metropolitan area such as the Greater Tokyo Area or the Greater Kanto Area. Integration and cooperation among cities would need to take into consideration the physical restriction of distance. The distance between Shanghai and Nanjing is approximately 300 kilometers. Taizhou is 375 kilometers away from Shanghai, Hefei 477 kilometers. It would be too costly and risky to form one and only metropolitan area with highly integrated urban functions within the Yangtze River Delta, where little benefit could be expected. The most feasible range of a metropolitan area with highly integrated urban functions would be the distance of daily commute, in other words, within a radius of 60-80 kilometers. If Shanghai is the center of the range, the metropolitan area would include Wujiang District of Suzhou and Jiashan County of Jiaxing. In such scope, it would be more viable to explore indigenous practices of integrating urban functions, for example urban rail transit.

II. Development of Shanghai Metropolitan Area

National Development and Reform Commission issued *the Overall Plan for the Demonstration Area in the Yangtze River Delta on Ecologically Friendly Development* in 2019. The 2,300 km² demonstration area — Shanghai's Qingpu district, Suzhou's Wujiang district in Jiangsu province and Jiaxing's Jiashan county in Zhejiang province — sits in the middle of the delta, among which 660 km² is set as the pilot zone. As the concept of demonstration zone has been accepted and put into practice in strengthening environmental protection and promoting eco-friendly growth, it is also applicable to the integration of urban functions in the development of Shanghai metropolitan area on the radius of 60 – 80 kilometers, where practices of other renowned metropolitan areas could be adopted and referred to. In combining international experience with local condition and goal, a model could be explored based on regional development requirements. Such model could later be replicated and promoted to other areas in the Yangtze River Delta or even larger areas.

Through the history of developing metropolitan areas in Japan, Ministry of Land, Infrastructure, Transport and Tourism (MLIT) has issued six Development Plans of Capital Region and two Development Plans of Greater Kanto Area. The general goal of Development Plans of Capital Region is to ease the condition of over-concentration in Tokyo and to develop the region in a multipolar way, thus to propel convecting within the region. To achieve the goal, subcenters are designated in Tokyo Metropolis and regional core cities around Tokyo. However, due to the strong siphonic effect of Tokyo, only three (Yokohama, City of Chiba, and City of Saitama are all prefectural capitals) of the 22 designated core cities have met the original expectation while the others are not. Cities in the Greater Tokyo Area have different roles and functions. The 23 special wards in Tokyo have attracted headquarters, serving as the financial center and the commercial center, while high-tech industries, manufacturing R&D centers and precision manufacturing plants site in the suburban area of Tokyo. Of the three adjacent prefectures, Chiba Prefecture highlights its business, industry, residence, culture and port logistics; Saitama Prefecture serves for regional administrations, residence, mechanical industry, logistics and tourism; Kanagawa Prefecture shows strengths in port logistics, mechanical industry, electrical industry and residence. Of the remote four prefectures of the Greater Tokyo Area, Gunma Prefecture is rich in natural resources, renewable energy resources, and farms; Ibaraki Prefecture excels in scientific research and airport; Yamanashi Prefecture's key industries are tourism and environmental protection industry.

Although Ministry of Land, Infrastructure, Transport and Tourism has been committed to balancing among cities in the region even to the state that heated discussion was once aroused if Tokyo Metropolis would be impaired, Tokyo still enjoys the higher attractivity than its surrounding area. Especially when the asset price fell after the bursting of the Japanese asset price bubble, those who had moved outside Tokyo and those urban functions and industries which had once dispersed, started to flow back. Only those land-intensive ones remained. Meanwhile, Tokyo Metropolis has eased its urban disease, reduced servere traffic congestion, environmental pollution and raised living quality through a set of measures, including enhancing public facilities and improving urban management. Thus it became possible for Tokyo to accommodate more population and industry than it used to be. Tackling the issue of Tokyo concentration became less urgent.

In the process of developing Shanghai metropolitan area, it is of top priority for Shangai to define its function and status. Judging from Shanghai's development state and its goal, Shanghai has a similar industrial structure, comparing to Tokyo at the stage of 20,000 USD GDP per capita. So far, there is no urgency in dispersing manufacturing industry. The development of Shanghai metropolitan area would need to take into consideration the balance between urban and suburban areas, the cooperation among Shanghai and its neighboring cities and to follow the laws of the market economy. For example, industries or urban functions that are less land-intensive would be more likely to flow back once the political force reduced. Hence in terms of cooperation and division of industries, the siphonic effect and spill-out effect need to be balanced among the major cities and their neighboring cities. Meanwhile, cities ought to set discrepant goals and develop own strengths to promote convect and communication within the region, especially with the megacities, to reduce invalid competition, otherwise the regional economy would wax and wane in an unstable way.

III. The Development of the Yangtze River Delta

In the short term, as the approach of the overall integration of the Yangtze River Delta region, it is more practical to establish a wide-area economic cluster with strong economic relations than to integrate urban functions. The integration of the Yangtze River Delta should be focused on the connection of industrial functions on the merit of the whole regional economy. As the leading city, Shanghai should take into account both the needs of self being the oncoming international metropolis and the needs of regional overall development. The industries and functions need to be prioritized so that a reasonable division of industries and functions among the cities could be determined.

In recent years, the concept of inter-metropolis linkage beyond the scope of the metropolitan area has also emerged in Japan. The Super Mega-region proposed by the Ministry of Land, Infrastructure, Transport and Tourism of the Central Government of Japan aims to build a active connection among the three major metropolitan areas in Japan (the Greater Tokyo Area with Tokyo as its core, the Chukyo Area with Nagoya as its core, and the Kansai Area with Osaka as its core), envisioning a larger megalopolis or metropolitan interlocking region. Actions will be taken to promote cooperation in various respects in terms of residential employment, economic intercourse, urban functions, and etc. The intention of the Japanese government is to integrate the three major metropolitan areas as a huge economic belt, so that the synergy effect of the original metropolitan areas could be expanded to a larger scope. The background of these policies is that the three major metropolitan areas in Japan have been through a rather long period of development with remarkable achievements, which makes it possible to propel the integration among the metropolitan areas.

Facilitating transportation is a huge milestone for the construction of Super Mega-region. The construction of the Chuo Shinkansen maglev will strengthen the connection among the three major metropolitan areas in Japan and provide the people around the whole Super Mega-region with much convenience in terms of transportation and communication. It will take only 40 minutes from Tokyo to Nagoya and 67 minutes from Tokyo to Osaka by Chuo Shinkansen maglev. The facilitation of transportation would profoundly impact the communication of people and development of industry. On the one hand, the Chuo Shinkansen maglev will increase the opportunities for people to communicate with each other more frequently so as to make it more possible to breed innovation. The new line will relieve the restrictions of time and space, and provide more alternatives to life, business, and commerce. On the other hand, the Chuo Shinkansen maglev will substantially promote the integration of the three metropolitan areas, enhance international competitiveness, and attract overseas investment and talents. What's more, the new line along with the existing lines such as the Tokai Shinkansen will form an organically combined transportation network, and help to reduce disaster damage through multiple alternatives of transportation. In addition to the three metropolitan areas, the small metropolitan areas along the metropolitan belt as the core of the local economy will also give full play to their strong points with aim of boosting local economy and expand their international presence.

From the perspective of development of Shanghai and the Yangtze River Delta region, the experience of regional integration of the Japanese megalopolis can be drawn as that a practical and effective approach is to initially promote the economic development of each metropolitan area. Further integrative measures are to be planned when the metropolitan areas have developed their own strengths and endogenous growth. Combining the needs of both China and the Yangtze River Delta, one possible approach in the near future is to first ensure the steady development of the leading metropolitan area with Shanghai as its core, as well as the other smaller metropolitan areas in the Yangtze River Delta. Meanwhile, actions could be taken to promote the cooperation and relations in the Yangtze River Delta region as a wide-area economic cluster as mentioned before. In this process, Shanghai needs to shoulder the responsibility as an international portal so as to support the economic development of the entire Yangtze River Delta. In the long term, appropriate timing of further integrative development are to be determined when the metropolitan areas within the Yangtze River Delta have undergone sufficient development and been in mature conditions, where groundbreaking infrastructure projects and policies could take place to enhance regional convect. Hence, the integration of the Yangtze River Delta region as a closely-related megapolis would be achieved.

从世界级湾区一体化协同机制看长三角一体化合作的优化方向

普华永道

2018 年 11 月,习近平总书记在首届进博会上宣布,支持长江三角洲区域一体化发展并上升为国家战略。这块以不到全国 1/26 的国土面积、1/6 的人口创造了近 1/4 的经济总量、1/3 的进出口总额、2/3 的外商直接投资和 1/3 对外投资的战略要地,从此承载起非同寻常的国家使命。

从 1982 年提出"以上海为中心建立长三角经济圈"的探索开始,至 2019 年正式发布《长江三角洲区域一体化发展规划纲要》,长三角一体化进程已经过近 40 年的砥砺前行。"道阻且长,行则将至。"长三角一体化的发展与合作机制的构建,需立足国内,同时吸收国际成功湾区经验,实现中西荟萃,走出独具特色的新路。

一、从国内湾区/城市群发展看长三角区域一体化特点

1. 长三角是国内经济体量最大的城市群,但头部城市首位度低,核心城市引领作用不显著

单从经济体量来看,长三角在国内主要城市群中具备优势,但对比粤港澳和京津冀,长三角头部城市的首位度最低,尤其具备引领作用的上海的首位度大大低于北京和深圳。相较于粤港澳、京津冀的由核心城市驱动引领的发展模式,长三角地区的发展模式则更显"均质化"。

表 1　全国三大主要城市群/湾区基本情况

	长三角	粤港澳	京津冀
陆地面积(万平方公里)	21.2	5.6	21.5
占全国比重(%)	2.2	0.6	2.3
常住人口(亿人)	1.52	0.69	1.10

	长三角	粤港澳	京津冀
占全国比重(%)	10.9	5.0	7.9
GDP(2018/万亿元)	21.0	10.9	8.5
占全国比重(%)	23.4	10.8	9.5

资料来源:券商研报;公开资料整理

表2 全国三大主要城市群/湾区头部城市首位度对比

	2018年GDP(万亿元)	占城市群/湾区比重(%)
长三角	21.0	100
上海	3.27	15.6
苏州	1.86	8.8
杭州	1.35	6.4
南京	1.27	6.1
粤港澳	10.9	100
深圳	2.42	22.3
香港	2.40	22.1
广州	2.29	21.0
佛山	0.99	9.1
京津冀	8.5	100
北京	3.03	35.7
天津	1.88	22.1
唐山	0.70	8.2
石家庄	0.56	6.6

资料来源:公开资料整理;各省市统计公报

2. 相较于粤港澳和京津冀,长三角城市间的分工不明确,呈现竞争同质化

长三角地区产业的"均质化"发展,间接导致了区域内城市间的激烈竞争与同质化。

粤港澳地区已明确香港、澳门、深圳和广州的发展定位,其中深圳聚焦发展通信设备制造和电子信息产业,广州则聚焦发展新能源和新材料产业等。京津冀也确立了北京发挥首都功能,聚焦现代服务业和科技创新,而天津和河北梯度承接北京产业外溢,由此三地形成产业协作分工的模式。

表 3   粤港澳大湾区核心城市产业发展定位

主要城市	产业发展定位
香港	金融服务业、旅游业、贸易物流
澳门	博彩业、旅游业、建筑业、地产业
深圳	通信设备制造、电子信息
广州	新能源、新材料、海洋产业

资料来源：《粤港澳大湾区发展规划纲要》；券商研报

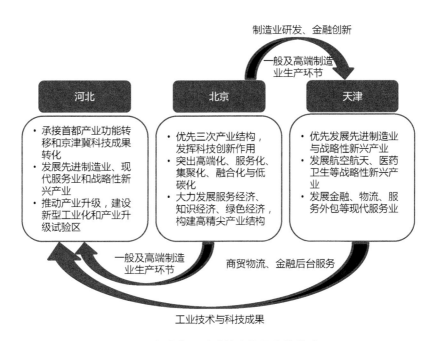

图 1   京津冀三地功能定位及合作模式

资料来源：公开资料整理；券商研报

相比于分工明确的粤港澳和京津冀，长三角区域产业同质化相对严重，区域内城市普遍聚焦在装备制造、电子信息设备、汽车及汽车零件、新材料等产业上，造成产业发展趋同。在头部城市的产业定位上，如上海与苏州的制造业、上海与杭州的金融业，都有进一步优化竞争合作格局的空间。

表 4   长三角地区部分城市主导产业方向

主要城市	主导产业方向
上海	金融业、批发和零售业、电子信息、汽车制造业、成套设备制造业等
苏州	电子信息、电气设备、钢铁、通用设备、化工、纺织、电子商务等
杭州	金融业、信息、传输软件和信息技术服务业、电子商务、文创产业、旅游业等
南京	金融业、文化产业、旅游业、信息技术、智能电网、节能环保、高端装备制造、新能源等

主要城市	主导产业方向
无锡	纺织服装、精密机械及汽车配套零部件、电子信息及家电业、冶金、精细化工及生物医药等
常州	装备制造业、新能源、辅变电设备、电子、化工、纺织业等
宁波	纺织服装业、日用家电业、输变电设备制造业、机械工业、汽车配套产业、石化工业、铁工业、电力工业、造纸工业等
嘉兴	纺织业、化工、化纤业、服装业、电气机械和器材制造业等
合肥	汽车及零部件、装备制造、家用电器、食品及农副产品加工、平板显示及电子信息、光伏

资料来源：公开资料整理

3. 区域经济一体化有其内在的发展逻辑和规律

一体化合作不是单纯的区域均衡发展，如把上海相对落后的产能转移到落后地区；也非简单的优势共享，如把经济发达地区的优质资源（医疗、社保、教育、科技等）共享给周边地区。探索长三角一体化合作机制，还需从全球领先湾区/城市群的发展中寻找经验和模式的借鉴。

二、从全球领先湾区发展经验看长三角一体化优化方向

（一）东京湾区

1. 基本概况

东京湾区是世界最大湾区之一[①]，由"一都三县"构成，分别是东京都[②]、埼玉县、千叶县和神奈川县。湾区面积 1.34 万平方公里（占全国 3.5%），人口规模 4 000 多万人（占全国约 1/3），经济总量接近全国一半，城市化率超过 90%。

2. 发展借鉴

日本中央政府主导湾区发展规划，推动形成以东京为主导的"雁形模式"城市分工体系。[③] 日本的东京湾区/都市圈的规划始于 20 世纪 50 年代，先后经历了 1958 年、1968 年、1976 年、1986 年、1999 年五个轮次。从第三次规划开始，日本国土厅下属的大都市圈整备局成为规划的核心负责机构，日本中央政府成为推动湾区一体化规划的主体。通过五轮发展规划，建立起了以东京为核心，以便捷的交通为互联的湾区一体化发展格局。

[①] 广义的东京都市圈又称"首都圈"，是在"一都三县"的基础上加入茨城、栃木、群马及山梨等四县（即"一都七县"），总面积达 3.69 万平方公里（占全国 9.8%）。

[②] 东京都主要由东京都区部（东京 23 区）和多摩地方（市部、西多摩郡等）等组成。

[③] 雁形模式指处于"雁首"地位的城市具备经济和科学技术等方面的核心地位，通过资金和技术供应、市场吸收及产业转移等，带动周边地区的经济发展。

表 5　东京湾区/都市圈五轮发展规划

规划时间	核心内容	主要规划机构
1958 年《第一次首都圈基本规划》	限制东京的无序蔓延,提出外围地区建立工业卫星城市的构想	首都圈整备委员会
1968 年《第二次首都圈基本规划》	提出构建多核地域结构,完善卫星城市功能,将城市中心职能有选择性地向卫星城分散	首都圈整备委员会
1976 年《第三次首都圈基本规划》	提出"多核多圈域"空间概念,建立除东京都以外多中心城市构想,形成都市群	大都市圈整备局(国土厅下属单位)
1986 年《第四次首都圈基本规划》	强化东京中心城市的国际竞争力,包括国际金融职能和高层次中枢管理功能	大都市圈整备局(国土厅下属单位)
1999 年《第五次首都圈基本规划》	提出"分散型网络结构",构建以据点城市为中心的网络型区域结构	大都市圈整备局(国土厅下属单位)

资料来源:券商研报

表 6　东京湾区核心城市首位度

	2018 年 GDP(万亿美元)	占城市群/湾区比重(%)
东京湾区	1.86	100
东京都	1.06	57
神奈川县	0.34	18
埼玉县	0.23	13
千叶县	0.22	12

注:2018 年三县数据缺失,以 2014 年度比例匡算
资料来源:日本统计年鉴 2019;公开资料整理。

同时,为加速规划目标的落地(如引导工业、教育和部分商务功能设施向周边地区转移),日本中央政府还采取了一系列财政金融政策加以配套。如:

• 财政转移支付(将中央税收的一部分转移给企业迁入地所属的地方政府);

• 搬迁企业的所得税减免;

• 新开发地区的政府发行地方债并由中央财政贴息;

• 中央政府通过政策性银行向市场主体定向发放产业转移专项贷款;

• 近郊整治地带、城市开发区内的新兴工业园开发还可享受法定的特别税制优惠。

日本中央政府的产业政策引导了东京湾区区域间、城市间的差异化发展,东京湾区内逐渐形成了以东京为"雁首"的"雁形模式"城市分工体系。

表 7　东京湾区/都市圈各区域发展定位

地区	发展定位
东京都(中心区)	功能定位:行政中心、金融中心、文化中心、科教中心 产业定位:金融业、商务服务业、批发零售业、科技研发

地区	发展定位
东京都 （多摩区域）	功能定位:接受中心区大学、研发机构和高新产业的转移 产业定位:高科技产业、科技研发
千叶县	功能定位:国际空港、港湾;工业集聚地 产业定位:化工制造、电气机械、钢铁制造、贸易物流
埼玉县	功能定位:承接东京部分首都职能 产业定位:批发零售、房地产
神奈川县	功能定位:工业集聚地、国际港湾 产业定位:电气机械、运输机械、化工制造

资料来源:券商研报

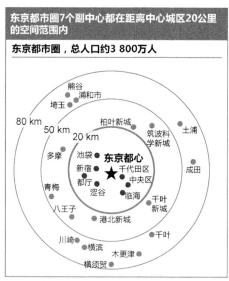

图 2　以东京为核心的圈层式城市分布

资料来源:公开资料整理

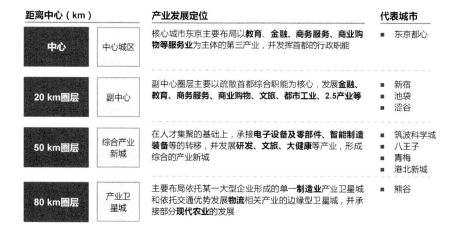

图 3　以东京为核心的产业梯度分工格局

(二) 纽约湾区

1. 基本概况

纽约湾区分布于美国东北部大西洋沿岸平原,由纽约州、康涅狄格州、新泽西州的共 31 个县联合组成,形成了以纽约为核心,以波士顿、费城、巴尔的摩、华盛顿等一系列大城市为中心的城市群。陆地面积 2.15 万平方公里,常住人口约 2 340 万人,城市化水平达 90% 以上,是美国人口密度最高的地区。

2. 发展借鉴

(1) 通过四轮规划和四轮产业升级,确立起以纽约为核心领导的湾区城市群合作发展模式

1921 年,纽约区域规划委员会(简称 RPA)成立。从成立起至今,该委员会先后主导了四轮纽约湾区的统一规划:

• 1929 年发布《纽约及其周边地区的区域规划》,核心是"再中心化"。规划制定了建立开放空间、缓解交通拥堵、集中与疏散和建设卫星城等 10 项政策。

• 1968 年开始第二次规划,核心是"再集中"。规划提出将就业集中于卫星城、恢复区域公共交通体系和建立新的城市中心等。

• 1996 年发布《危机挑战区域发展》,核心是"重建经济、公平和环境"。主要规划提升了城市各方面的宜居环境。

• 2017 年发布《共同区域建设》,核心是"区域转型"。通过复兴城市中心区、增加公共基础设施建设等,满足以人为本的发展需求。

同时,纽约湾区也经过了四次产业升级,都市型产业加速向纽约集聚,而高技术制造业和重工业则梯度分布在纽约城市周边。最终形成了纽约州以金融业为集聚地、新泽西州以高技术和服务业为特色、康涅狄格州以重工业为主导的区域城市产业分工体系。

• 转口贸易阶段(19 世纪初至 19 世纪 60 年代):依托纽约港优势,转口贸易快速发展并占据主导地位,劳动和资本密集型轻工制造业逐渐兴起。

• 制造业鼎盛阶段(19 世纪 60 年代至 20 世纪 40 年代):地理区位优势及工业革命等内外因素共同驱动,湾区制造业快速发展,成为美国重要的制造业中心。

• 后工业化阶段(20 世纪 40 年代至 20 世纪 70 年代):随着美国工业化进程的完成和信息技术的强大刺激,湾区开始步入后工业化阶段,第三产业兴起。

• 知识经济主导阶段(20 世纪 70 年代至今):经济危机导致传统制造业加速衰落,政策导向转向服务业和高技术产业,形成以知识经济为主导的产业格局。

表 8　纽约湾区核心城市首位度

	2018 年 GDP(万亿美元)	占城市群/湾区比重(%)
纽约湾区	2.40	100
纽约	0.90	38
华盛顿	0.46	19
费城	0.43	18
波士顿	0.40	17
巴尔的摩	0.20	8

资料来源:公开资料整理

表 9　纽约湾区差异化布局的三大产业集聚区

	主导产业	代表企业
纽约州	金融业、传媒业、电子无线通信	摩根大通、摩根士丹利、哥伦比亚广播公司、时代华纳、IBM 等
新泽西州	制药业、专业技术服务业、通信产业	默克、华纳兰伯特、霍尼韦尔、强生、惠氏、普天寿等
康涅狄格州	军事工业、设备制造、生物医药	通用动力、联合技术、施乐、特雷克斯、辉瑞等

(2)区域内城市共建非营利性投资开发机构,推动区域一体化发展

纽约湾区不同城市间、不同州之间行政关系复杂。为推动区域交通建设,纽约与新泽西州于 1921 年成立纽约与新泽西港务局(简称 PANYNJ),该港务局是非政府的法人机构,但拥有很高的权力,它不仅仅管港口、海港,还管空港、地铁、地下隧道,总之均有管辖。

纽约与新泽西港务局是一个非营利性机构,通过发债募资来投资建设交通基础设施,并收取过路、过桥费,以及基础设施的房租、装卸费、码头的使用费。因为其不以营利为目的,故收费相对也较低,间接为纽约湾区的发展提供了更好的营商环境,促进了经济的繁荣。

三、长三角一体化合作机制建议

东京湾区和纽约湾区的一体化发展都具备一个共同特征,即都发挥了核心城市的带动作用。不管是在都市圈范围之内的核心城区和周边地区之间,还是在城市群范围之内的核心都市圈和其他城市之间,经济向核心地区的集聚是经济规律使然,并且高度集聚的核心区发展能够对外围产生更强的带动作用。同时,核心区和外围区产生更为明确的分工,可以提高资源配置的效率。

结合长三角区域自身的特点,本文提出以下几条长三角一体化合作机制建议:

（一）宏观层面

第一，进一步提升上海在长三角区域中的首位度。发挥上海作为国际经济中心、国际金融中心、国际航运中心、国际贸易中心和科技创新中心的优势，与杭州、苏州、南京、宁波、合肥等区域性中心城市共同构建"雁形模式"城市分工体系。发挥上海在长三角一体化中的"雁首"作用。

第二，设立国家层面的长三角一体化建设领导小组，并设立领导小组办公室，成立相应的政府机构，确保有足够的领导力和权威性，将长三角作为一个整体，对长三角一体化建设发展进行全局性的指导、组织、推动、协调和管理。

（二）具体层面

第一，建立长三角重大产业项目布局协调机制。通过谋划"重大项目打分体系"标准，从地方产业承载力、产业匹配度、区域产业分工等维度，对长三角内适合落位该大项目的城市进行优先级排名，判断重大项目最佳、最优的落位区域，避免不同地方之间因恶性招商竞争所带来的资源浪费。

第二，建立产业特别合作区，并通过股权合作方式成立区域开发平台公司进行合作区开发，促进各城市互补共赢。该开发平台公司可由长三角各城市共同出资成立，并以企业化运作和管理方式参与到产业特别合作区的开发建设运营中，各城市按照出资比例、资源让渡情况（如产业特别合作区所在地的城市提供用地、产业配套和环保指标等）实现税收、GDP 指标等方面的共享。

Improving the Coordination of the Yangtze River Delta: Recommendations Based on a Deep Dive into Institutionalized Governance and Economic Cooperation in World-class Bay Areas

PwC

The integrated development of the Yangtze River Delta (YRD) has been elevated to a national strategy, as announced by President Xi Jinping at the opening ceremony of the first China International Import Expo in Shanghai in November 2018.

The YRD covers less than one-twenty-sixth of the country's land area and is home to 16 percent of the country's total population. As vanguard of China's fast-forward opening-up, the region boasts its strategic significance in China's economy by contributing nearly one-quarter of the country's total economic output and being responsible for one-third of total imports and exports, two-third of received foreign direct investment and one-third of outbound investment. Now in line with the national strategy, the YRD is set to put forward its mission-driven transformation into a world-class city cluster.

The past 4 decades have witnessed China's step-by-step efforts to explore and promote integrated development in the region. From the establishment of the Shanghai Economic Zone in 1982, which facilitated coordination in economic development among several cities in Zhejiang province, Jiangsu province and Shanghai, to the comprehensive blueprint pioneering future mega-urban governance as stated in *the Outline of the Integrated Regional Development of the Yangtze River Delta* issued by the Chinese government in

December 2019, the idea of the YRD integration has steadily evolved and embraced both opportunities and challenges that China and the YRD are facing. As the Chinese saying goes, the road is long while the way is approaching. To create a developing and cooperation mechanism that can best fit the YRD, we can, for one thing, seek to fully understand our local conditions and vision, and, for another, take the best of good practice that has taken place in well-developed bay areas and city clusters, both in China and abroad.

Ⅰ. Characteristics of the YRD integration in comparison to bay areas/mega-urban regions in China

1. As China's largest city-cluster-economy, the YRD demonstrates relatively low primacy effect of its Tier 1 cities and Shanghai as its core city

The Yangtze River Delta is the largest economy among all the major city clusters in China. When we take a look at the economic performance of its major cities such as Shanghai, Suzhou, Hangzhou and Nanjing, however, the primacy effect of such cities on the whole region is relatively insignificant as compared to leading cities in the Great Bay Area (GBA, Guangdong-Hong Kong-Macao) or in Jing-Jin-Ji (Beijing-Tianjin-Hebei). Further to this, Shanghai is playing a far less predominant role as compared to Shenzhen in the GBA or Beijing in Jing-Jin-Ji. Unlike the sharp gap in magnitude between core city and the rest of the region in GBA or Jing-Jin-Ji, which outlines the significant domination of Shenzhen and Beijing in driving the economic development of the whole mega-urban region, cities in YRD demonstrate more balanced or homogenized development that brings with less significant difference in magnitude and in scale.

Table 1　General Information of the Three Major City Clusters/Bay Areas in China:
　　　　YRD, GBA and Jing-Jin-Ji

	YRD	GBA	Jing-Jin-Ji
Area in 10,000 square kilometer	21.2	5.6	21.5
Proportion in the whole country (%)	2.2	0.6	2.3
Population (in million)	152	69	110

	YRD	GBA	Jing‐Jin‐Ji
Proportion in the whole country（%）	10.9	5.0	7.9
GDP（2018/trillion yuan）	21.0	10.9	8.5
Proportion in the whole country（%）	23.4	10.8	9.5

Source：Equity Research Report；Compilation of public information

Table 2　Primacy of the Tier-one Cities in the YRD，GBA and Jing‐Jin‐Ji in Comparison

	GDP（2018）in trillion yuan	Proportion in the Mega-urban Area
YRD	21.0	100
Shanghai	3.27	15.6
Suzhou	1.86	8.8
Hangzhou	1.35	6.4
Nanjing	1.27	6.1
GBA	10.9	100
Shenzhen	2.42	22.3
Hong Kong	2.40	22.1
Guangzhou	2.29	21.0
Foshan	0.99	9.1
Jing-Jin-Ji	8.5	100
Beijing	3.03	35.7
Tianjin	1.88	22.1
Tangshan	0.70	8.2
Shijiazhuang	0.56	6.6

Source：Compilation of public information；Statistical report of provinces and cities

2. Unlike the case of GBA and Jing-Jin-Ji, cities in YRD lack differentiated industry blueprint and coordinating division of labor, resulting in intense competition within the region

The homogeneous industrial development in the YRD region has indirectly led to fierce competition and lack of differentiation among cities in the region.

The Guangdong-Hong Kong-Macao region has clearly defined strategic positioning of Hong Kong, Macao, Shenzhen and Guangzhou. For instance, Shenzhen focuses on communication equipment manufacturing and electronic information industries, while Guangzhou focuses on new energy and new materials industries.

Beijing-Tianjin-Hebei has also developed its regional division of labor with differentiated industry development goals, according to which Beijing should function as the capital city and focus on modern services industry and tech innovation, while Tianjin and Hebei should undertake the industries transferred from Beijing.

Table 3　Industry Positioning of Core Cities in the Great Bay Area

City	Industry Positioning
Hong Kong	Financial Services, Tourism, Trade Logistics
Macao	Gaming, Tourism, Construction, Real Estate
Shenzhen	Communication Equipment Manufacturing, ICT
Guangzhou	New Energy, New Materials, Marine

Source：Outline Development Plan for the Guangdong-Hong Kong-Macao Greater Bay Area, Equity Research Report

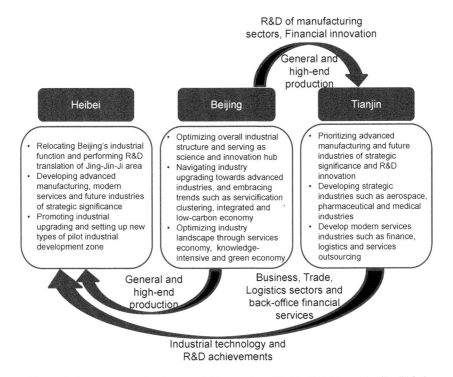

Figure 1　Sub-region Functions and Cooperation Model of Beijing-Tianjin-Hebei

Source：Equity Research Report；Compilation of public information

While GBA and Jing-Jin-Ji feature explicitly integrated division of labor between cities, industry positioning in the YRD is more fragmentated at the city level and cities in YRD turn out to share similar industry focus, such as equipment manufacturing, electronic information equipment manufacturing, automobiles and auto parts manufacturing, and new materials. As a result, the industry landscape in the sub-regions are more or less similar to each other. This also applies to the leading cities in the cluster. For instance, Shanghai and Suzhou share focus on electronics and equipment manufacturing, while Shanghai and Hangzhou are both developing financial services. There is for sure room for a more rational, cooperative strategy in regional division of labor.

Table 4　Leading Industries Positioning of Some Cities in the Yangtze River Delta

Major City	Industry Positioning
Shanghai	Financial industry, wholesale and retail industry, electronic information, automobile manufacturing, complete equipment manufacturing, etc.
Suzhou	Electronic information, electrical equipment, steel, general equipment, chemicals, textiles, e-commerce, etc.
Hangzhou	Financial industry, information, transmission software and information technology services, e-commerce, cultural and creative industries, tourism, etc.
Nanjing	Financial industry, cultural industry, tourism, information technology, smart grid, energy saving and environmental protection, high-end equipment manufacturing, new energy, etc.
Wuxi	Textile and clothing, precision machinery and auto parts, electronic information and home appliance industry, metallurgy, fine chemicals and biomedicine, etc.
Changzhou	Equipment manufacturing industry, new energy, auxiliary transformer equipment, electronics, chemical industry, textile industry, etc.
Ningbo	Textile and clothing industry, household appliances industry, power transmission equipment manufacturing industry, machinery industry, automobile supporting industry, petrochemical industry, iron industry, power industry, paper industry, etc.
Jiaxing	Textile industry, chemical industry, chemical fiber industry, clothing industry, electrical machinery and equipment manufacturing, etc.
Hefei	Automotive and parts, equipment manufacturing, household appliances, food and agricultural and sideline products processing, flat panel display and electronic information, photovoltaic

Source: Compilation of public information

3. Regional economic integration has its logic and trends

Integration and cooperation is not about balancing regional development, eg. by relocating relatively undeveloped production capacity from Shanghai to less developed areas; or simply sharing advantages and spreading high-quality resources (medical, social security, education, science and technology, etc.) from more developed areas to their neighboring regions. On our way to create an integrated cooperation mechanism for the YRD, it is worth a detour to learn from the world's leading bay areas/mega-urban regions and to understand other experience and mechanism.

II. Recommendations for improving the coordination of YRD based on good practices of world-class bay areas in institutionalized governance and economic cooperation

(I) Tokyo Bay Area

1. Overview

Tokyo Bay Area is one of the largest bay areas in the world, which is composed of one metropolis and three prefectures, namely, Tokyo, Saitama, Chiba and Kanagawa. The Bay Area covers an area of 13, 400 square kilometers (3.5% of the country' total), has a population of more than 40 million (about one-third of the country), and its economy is close to half of the country's total, with an urbanization rate of more than 90%.

2. Highlights

Japan's central government takes the lead in planning for the bay area development and facilitates the industry coordination between subregions which features a flying geese model, where Tokyo plays the leading role.

The planning of the Tokyo Bay Area/Metropolitan area in Japan began in the 1950s and has gone through five rounds of planning (in 1958, 1968, 1976, 1986, and 1999). Starting from the third planning, the Metropolitan Area Development Bureau under the Japan National Land Agency has become the core responsible agency of the regional planning, and the Japanese central government plays the dominant role in promoting the integrated planning of the Bay Area. As a result, the Tokyo Bay Area is transformed into an interconnective, intergrated region with Tokyo in its core and highly developed transport network spreading around.

Table 5　Five-round Development Plan of Tokyo Bay Area/Metropolitan Area

Time	Main Purpose	Planning Agency
The First City Planning Act, 1958	• to constrain the rapid urban expansion of Tokyo • to establish an industrial satellite city in the outer area	Bureau of Urban Development Tokyo Metropolitan Government

Time	Main Purpose	Planning Agency
The Second City Planning Act, 1968	• to build a multi-core regional structure • to improve the functions of satellite cities • to selectively decentralize the functions of city centers and transfer them to the satellite cities	Bureau of Urban Development Tokyo Metropolitan Government
The Third City Planning Act, 1976	• to promote a regional spatial structure with "multi-centers and multi-circles" • to conceptualize a city network that has more than one central city • to form a metropolitan cluster	Metropolitan Development Commission(MDC)(Department of Land Resources)
The Fourth City Planning Act, 1986	• to strengthen the international competitiveness of Tokyo as center city, by enhancing its international financial function and high-level central management function	MDC
The Fifth City Planning Act, 1999	• to build a "decentralized network structure" • to build a regional network structure with cities in the center	MDC

Source: Compilation of public information

Table 6　Ranking of Tokyo Bay Area Core Cities

	GDP, 2018/trillion USD	Proportion of city group/Bay Area（%）
Tokyo Bay Area	1.86	100
Tokyo	1.06	57
Kanagawa	0.34	18
Saitama	0.23	13
Chiba	0.22	12

Note: Missing the three counties data in 2018, calculation is base on the 2014 data instead
Source: Japan Statistical Yearbook 2019; Compilation of public information

At the same time, in order to accelerate the implementation of planning goals (such as guiding the relocation of industries, education and commercial facilities to surrounding areas), the Japanese central government had adopted a series of fiscal and financial policies to support it. Such as:

• Fiscal transfer payment (transfer a part of central tax revenue to local government of the place where the company relocates);

• Income tax exemption for relocated enterprises;

• Government in newly developed areas is able to issue local bonds and receive discount from the central government;

• The central government issued special loans for the relocation of industry to market entities through institutional banks;

• The development of emerging industrial parks in the suburban areas and urban development zones can also enjoy the preferential tax policies.

The industrial policies of the central government have guided the differentiated development between different regions and cities in the Tokyo Bay area, and gradually shaped a "flying geese model" urban division system with Tokyo as the "leading goose".

Tabel 7   Development Positioning of Tokyo Bay Area/Metropolitan Area

Area	Development Positioning
Tokyo (Central)	Function: Administrative center, Financial center, Cultural center, Science and education center Industry: Financial industry, Business service industry, Wholesale and retail industry, Scientific and technological R&D
Tokyo (Tama Area)	Function: accept the relocation of universities, R&D institutions and high-tech industries in the central area Industry: High tech industry, Scientific and technological R&D
Chiba	Function: International Airport and harbor; industrial gathering place Industry: chemical manufacturing, electrical machinery, steel manufacturing, trade logistics
Saitama	Function: Undertake partial capital functions of Tokyo Industry: Wholesale and retail, real estate
Kanagawa	Function: Industrial agglomeration and international harbor Industry: electrical machinery, transportation machinery, chemical manufacturing

Source: Equity Research Report

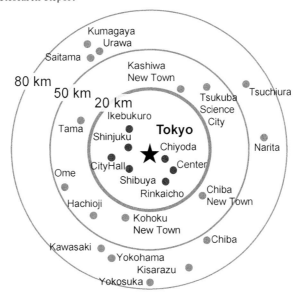

Figure 2   Circle City Distribution with Tokyo at the Core

Source: Compilation of public information

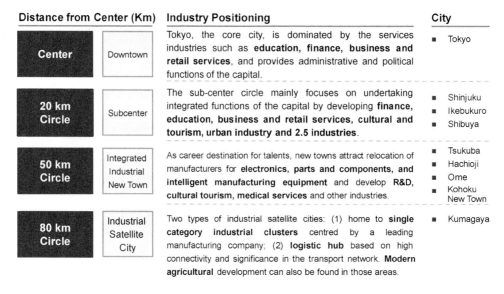

Distance from Center (Km)		Industry Positioning	City
Center	Downtown	Tokyo, the core city, is dominated by the services industries such as **education, finance, business and retail services**, and provides administrative and political functions of the capital.	■ Tokyo
20 km Circle	Subcenter	The sub-center circle mainly focuses on undertaking integrated functions of the capital by developing **finance, education, business and retail services, cultural and tourism, urban industry and 2.5 industries**.	■ Shinjuku ■ Ikebukuro ■ Shibuya
50 km Circle	Integrated Industrial New Town	As career destination for talents, new towns attract relocation of manufacturers for **electronics, parts and components, and intelligent manufacturing equipment** and develop R&D, **cultural tourism, medical services** and other industries.	■ Tsukuba ■ Hachioji ■ Ome ■ Kohoku New Town
80 km Circle	Industrial Satellite City	Two types of industrial satellite cities: (1) home to **single category industrial clusters** centred by a leading manufacturing company; (2) **logistic hub** based on high connectivity and significance in the transport network. **Modern agricultural** development can also be found in those areas.	■ Kumagaya

Figure 3　Industrial Gradient Division Pattern with Tokyo at the Core

(Ⅱ) New York Bay Area

1. Overview

The New York Bay Area is distributed along the Atlantic coast in the northeast of the United States, and is composed of 31 counties from New York, Connecticut and New Jersey, forming a cluster of cities such as Boston, Philadelphia, Baltimore and Washington and with New York as its core. With a land area of 21,481 square kilometers and a resident population of about 23.4 million, the urbanization level is more than 90%, and is the most densely populated area in the United States.

2. Highlights

(1) Through four rounds of planning and four rounds of industrial transformation, the Bay Area establish a cooperative development model for the urban cluster that features the predominance of the New York City

In 1921, the New York Regional Planning Association (RPA) was established. Since then, the committee has led four rounds of unified planning for the New York Bay Area:

• Regional Plan of New York and its environs was released in 1929, it proposed "recentralization". The plan formulated ten policies including establishing open spaces, alleviating congestion, concentration and evacuation of traffic, and building satellite cities.

• The second regional plan started in 1968, proposing "refocusing". The plan called for concentrating employment in satellite cities, restoring regional public transportation systems, and establishing new urban centers, etc.

• A Region at Risk was released in 1996, arguing the economy, equity and the environment rebuilding. The third plan improved the region's quality of life in many aspects

• The Common Area Construction was released in 2017, proposing "regional transformation". People-oriented development are satisfied by revitalizing urban central areas and expanding public infrastructure construction, etc.

At the same time, the New York Bay Area has undergone four industrial transformations. Urban industries are accelerating their concentration in New York City, while high-tech manufacturing and heavy industries are distributed around New York City. As a result, New York State has become a financial hub, New Jersey boasts its tech companies and service industries, and Connecticut has a focus on heavy industry.

• Re-export trade stage (early 19th century – 1860s): Relying on the advantages of the New York Port, the re-export trade developed rapidly and occupied a dominant position, which led to the gradual rise of labor and capital-intensive light industry manufacturing.

• The heyday of manufacturing stage (1860s–1940s): Driven by internal and external factors such as geographical advantages and the industrial revolution, the Bay Area manufacturing industry is booming and has become an important manufacturing center in the United States.

• Post-industrialization stage (1940s – 1970s): With the completion of the US industrialization process and the strong stimulation of information technology, the Bay Area began to enter the post-industrialization stage, with the rise of the tertiary industry.

• Knowledge-based economy stage (1970s–present): The financial crisis has led to the decline of traditional manufacturing industries, and government policy led efforts to the development of service industries and high-tech industries, shaping a knowledge-based economy industry pattern.

Table 8   Ranking of New York Bay Area Core Cities

Area	GDP in 2018(trillion US dollars)	Proportion in the city cluster/Bay Area（%）
New York Bay Area	2.40	100
New York	0.90	38
Washington DC	0.46	19
Philadelphia	0.43	18
Boston	0.40	17
Baltimore	0.20	8

Source：Public information

Table 9   New York Bay Area Regional Differentiation of Three Industries Area

Area	Leading Industry	Market Player
New York State	Financial industry, media industry, wireless communication	JP Morgan, Morgan Stanley, CBS, Time Warner, IBM, etc.
New Jersey State	Pharmaceutical industry, professional technical service industry, communication industry	Merck, Warner Lambert, Honeywell, Johnson & Johnson, Wyeth, Potevio, etc.
Connecticut State	Military industry, equipment manufacturing, biomedicine	General Dynamics, United Technologies, Xerox, Terex, Pfizer, etc.

（2）Non-profit investment and development institutions are jointly established by cities in the region to promote regional integrated development

The governance structure between different cities and states in the New York Bay Area is complex. In order to promote the construction of regional transportation, New York and New Jersey established the Port Authority of New York and New Jersey (PANYNJ) in 1921. With its supreme authority, it not only manages the port and sea port, but also manages air tunnel, subway and underground tunnel.

The Port Authority of New York and New Jersey is a non-profit organization that invests in the construction of transportation infrastructure by issuing bonds to raise funds. It also collects tolls and bridge tolls, as well as infrastructure rent, loading and unloading fees, and terminal usage fees. Because it is not for profit, its fees are relatively low, which indirectly provides a better doing business environment for the development of the New

York Bay Area and prosperity of economy.

Ⅲ. Recommendations for the integration and cooperation mechanism of the Yangtze River Delta

The integrated development of the Tokyo Bay Area and the New York Bay Area demonstrate one thing in common, that is, the core city plays a dominant role in the city cluster. Economic theories also echo the phenomenon of economic agglomeration in the core area. The agglomeration reflects in both the core urban area and surrounds within the metropolitan area, and the metropolitan area and other cities within the urban cluster. Besides, the development of core areas has a stronger driving effect on the periphery. At the same time, a clearer division of labor in the core area and the peripheral areas can improve the efficiency of resource allocation.

Based on the characteristics of the Yangtze River Delta region, this article recommends the following suggestions for the Yangtze River Delta integration and cooperation mechanism.

(Ⅰ) At the strategic level

First, further enhancing Shanghai's leading role in the Yangtze River Delta. Leveraging the advantage of Shanghai as an international economic center, international financial center, international shipping center, international trade center, and global sci-tech and innovation center, and working with Hangzhou, Suzhou, Nanjing, Ningbo, Hefei and other regional central cities to build a "flying geese model" urban division of labor system. Shanghai plays the role of "leading goose" in the integration of Yangtze River Delta.

Second, initiating the national Yangtze River Delta leading group, and establishing leading group office, a related government institute, to ensure influential leadership and authority. The leading group will provide integrated guidance, organization, promotion, coordination and management to the construction and development of Yangtze River Delta region.

(Ⅱ) At the implementation level

First, establishing cooperation mechanism for the distribution of major industrial projects in the Yangtze River Delta region. Through the planning of "major project scoring system" which includes the factors of local industrial carrying capacity, industry matching, and regional industrial division of labor, government officials will rank cities suitable for large projects in the Yangtze River Delta region and determine the best and the vital projects landing area, to avoid waste of resources caused by vicious investment competition between different cities.

Second, establishing exclusive industrial cooperation zones, and setting up regional developing platform-based company by equity cooperation model to develop cooperation zones, resulting in complementation and win-win. The platform-based company could be fund raised and operated in an enterprise-oriented manner by the cities in the Yangtze Delta River region. Each city shares the tax revenue and GDP indicators according to the proportion of capital contribution and resource transfer (such as the land providing by the cities in exclusive industrial cooperation zone, supporting industry and environmental protection indicators, etc.).

Synergistic Innovation in the Yangtze River Delta City Cluster

长三角城市群协同创新

深化一体化进程，打造具有区域经济韧性的全球城市群

波士顿咨询

一、全球不确定性背景下长三角一体化的战略使命

城市群已经成为国际主导的区域经济形态，全球经济体的竞争未来将成为城市群的竞争。2015年，全球前15大城市群用约12%的全球人口贡献了全球约30%的GDP。同时，全球约50%的GDP来自仅占约19%人口的300个大都市圈。从GDP总量和城市群人口来看，全球已经形成北美五大湖、美国波士华、英国中南部、欧洲西北部、中国长三角、日本太平洋沿岸等主要城市群，这些城市群的GDP总量都超过2万亿美元，人口都超过3 500万人。我国在国家"十三五"规划纲要里提出要在全国打造19个国家级城市群，其中长三角、京津冀、粤港澳大湾区将成为前三大。

图1　全球经济体的竞争未来将成为城市群的竞争

然而，在格局转变的大背景下，全球的不确定性持续提升，对城市群发展提出了新的挑战。从2006年起，BCG（波士顿咨询公司）的全球不确定性指数进入快速上升通道，一系列如2008年金融危机和2011年欧债危机的"黑天鹅"事件爆发，几

大方面值得重点关注：

（1）中美贸易摩擦持续发酵，虽然 2019 年 10 月双方取得了实质性的第一阶段磋商成果，但贸易摩擦尚未正式结束。

（2）全球经济增长持续放缓，发达国家经济疲软，我国 2019 年的 GDP 增速也开始以"保 6"为目标。

（3）国际金融风险不断累积，2008 年以来各发达经济体的宽松货币政策使得全球债务已经高达 232 亿美元。[①]

（4）全球政治不确定性也在提升，美国总统特朗普推行的"美国优先"政策和英国脱欧都对世界经济格局和全球治理体系造成一系列不确定性。

（5）新技术在争议中前行，人工智能、5G、基因工程等技术的法规限制和伦理道德问题尚未根本解决，存在巨大的潜在风险。

为应对不确定性，我国正在做出多层次的准备，对区域一体化提出了新的要求。策略方向层面，通过"去杠杆""供给侧改革""防范化解重大风险"构建多层次的防范体系；具体政策层面，在更强调城市群作用的同时，提出了对内生活力与质量的新要求，例如长三角一体化要引领全国高质量发展，粤港澳大湾区的城市群建设要保持港澳长期繁荣稳定。长三角作为中国范围最广、经济体量最大的城市群，在新时期的区域一体化中，应主动承担应对不确定性的新要求。

二、长三角一体化的现状与当前问题

近二十多年来，国家对长三角发展的重视程度显著上升。首先，战略要求不断提升，从 20 世纪 90 年代的"培育经济发展增长点"逐步升级为 2019 年提出的"引领全国经济高质量发展"；其次，覆盖城市不断扩容，从 1997 年的 15 座城市增加至 2019 年确定的 41 座；同时，协调内容不断深化调整，从最初的强调"与长江流域城市间的扬长避短、优势互补"深化至"提升在世界经济格局中的能级和水平"以及"长三角区域内的协调发展"。

放眼未来，长三角的一体化建设下阶段在提升区域经济体量的同时，更需增强区域经济韧性，从而打造根据区域竞争力的全球城市群。在关注快速增长、基础设施互联互通、均衡发展的基础上，应重点聚焦提升核心创新竞争力、扩大战略纵深以及强化抗风险能力。

但是，长三角在应对新时期的经济环境下，在技术创新、产业空间、协同机制三方面体现出韧性不足的短板。

---

① 资料来源：BCG 亨德森智库

1. 技术创新动能有限

长三角虽然有一定的科创基础,但整体科创生态体系存在一定缺失,科技转化能力不足。整体来看,长三角的科创产业基础良好。一方面科教资源丰富,拥有上海张江和安徽合肥 2 个综合性国家科学中心,囊括全国约 1/4 的"双一流"高校、国家重点实验室以及国家工程研究中心,并且上海、南京、杭州、合肥 4 座城市的研发强度都已超过 3%,远高于全国平均水平。另一方面,科创产业紧密融合,行业龙头多,集成电路产业规模占全国约 1/2,软件信息服务产业规模占全国约 1/3。但是,相比深圳,长三角的科技转化能力稍逊,科创生态体系有待完善。人才留存上,区域内重点高校的本地就业率存在较大差距,复旦大学和上海交通大学的留沪率约为 75%,深圳大学则高达约 88%,同时每年有约 25% 的中山大学毕业生从广州去深圳工作,且这一比例正逐渐攀升;科创成就上,每万人发明专利的拥有量,上海与杭州都只有深圳的 50% 左右;创新氛围上,深圳同样在排名上领先上海和杭州。所以,长三角下阶段需要切实利用好科创本底,通过构建创新生态体系,实现科技转化引领。

2. 产业空间纵深不足

长三角区域内局部产业复制现象明显,中小城市尚未成为坚实的产业节点。当前各地政府单独制定产业政策,存在盲目性,缺乏有效配合。在细分产业选择上,各地争相追逐智能装备、信息科技、生物医药等高频产业,存在产业重叠、资源争夺的现象;在产业目标的制定上,各地政府各自为政,脱离市场实际,在区域内形成了以新能源汽车为代表的产能过剩问题(2018 年长三角的产能达到约 238 万辆,占全国约 30%,销量达到约 53 万辆,占全国约 50%)。长三角的产业空间纵深不足突出体现在部分中小城市产业跟风发展,缺乏主线。区域内中小城市分工不明晰,整体抗风险能力较弱。同样以新能源汽车为例,仅浙江省就有 7 个相关特色小镇,在近两年产能过剩的背景下,当地企业受冲击较大,拖欠薪资、供应商贷款、裁员、新品延迟发布等问题频出。因此,长三角应厘清区域内的产业错位分工,避免重复竞争;同时要注重发挥中小城市产业节点的支撑作用。

3. 协同机制瓶颈

长三角现有的协同机制以事件导向为主,缺少统一牵头机构和长期规划,亟需多方参与、动态反馈的长效协同机制。目前,"一事一议"的上位政策或会谈是长三角内协同机制的载体,并且不同事宜归口不同牵头机构。同时,区域内目前的协同机制对产业外部带动性和人才跨区域流动的考虑较少,一些机制仅是"名义协同"。例如上海-南通的大数据产业合作,目标是推动南通形成完善的大数据产业链,但最终入驻企业以技术含量不高的数据基础设施服务商为主,对南通的大数据研发带动作用比较有限。所以面向未来,长三角应设立多方参与、动态反馈的长效区域经济协同机制,注重区域提升与人才流动。

三、长三角一体化未来的发展建议

基于前述三方面问题,长三角下一步强化区域经济韧性,可借鉴国际经验,重点把握三大方向:第一,协同创新生态。组建跨区域产学研协同组织,并且创新搭建创新产业的全流程服务平台。第二,产业分工纵深。首先统筹制定全域产业的产异化布局,然后建立常态化的产业沟通协调机制,引导节点城市融入区域分工。第三,协同体制机制,在统筹的基础上重点消除要素流通壁垒。

1. 协同创新生态上,长三角可以借鉴美国波士华城市群的经验,以组建跨区域产学研协同组织和垂直产业的创新服务平台为抓手,打造区域一体化的创新生态

美国波士华城市群北起波士顿、南至华盛顿,是美国人口密度最高的地区、美国最大商业贸易中心、国际金融中心和创新中心,制造业产值占全国的30%。波士华城市群产业梯级布局合理,各地区优势差异明显。纽约为主核,作为全美金融与商贸中心,为地区提供发达的商业与生产服务业支持;波士顿集聚院校、高科技、医疗等优势资源,成为全美电子、生物和宇航等创新产业中心;华盛顿依托政治中心地位,吸引全球政策金融机构,并在周边巴尔的摩发展国防工业,应对政府采购与发展需求。

波士华城市群拥有世界领先的生物技术产业,麻省生物技术委员会(MassBio)是该地区生物技术企业成员的贸易联合机构,汇集了区域内生物医药企业、商务服务企业、基金/孵化器、大学/科研机构、医疗机构和政府机构共921家会员单位。它从加速药物审批、企业税收减免、联合采购、教育培训等多方面为地区内生物技术产业服务。同时,波士华城市群拥有一系列垂直产业全流程创新平台,涵盖人才促进、资金对接、行业交流、技术服务和大数据共享等关键环节,政府和市场各自主导与自身特点契合的平台。总结波士华城市群的经验,对长三角有两点启示:第一,要确保行业组织的引领地位,以政产学研多方参与的协同创新组织作为创新生态营造的核心;第二,要强调功能平台的赋能作用,政企多方搭建专业精准的功能平台,通过聚集和调配产业要素来赋能各细分产业环节。

2. 产业分工纵深上,长三角可以借鉴日本城市群的经验,统筹制定全域产业差异化布局,重点打造具有产业韧性的中小节点城市

日本城市群中最具代表性的是首都圈城市群,它以东京都为核心,包括神奈川、千叶、埼玉、茨城、栃木、群马、山梨共7个县,总面积仅占日本国土面积的9.8%,但经济体量与整个俄罗斯相当。

日本首都圈城市群的发展由战略引领,各层级政府形成"多核协调"的发展共识,并且通过政府、企业和市场之间公开持续的联席会议机制改进产业政策,同时,注重发挥如日本开发构想研究所(UED)等智库的保障衔接作用。因此实现了城市产业功能的差异化分工,打造出一批围绕东京都的产业节点城市。以东京都周边的川崎市和宇都宫市为例,川崎市被定位成产业创新节点,日本技术先进首都圈地区(TAMA)为其注入资源,帮助其从老旧工业区转型成创新转化中心,如今其科技服务人口占比日本第一;宇都宫市则是核心制造节点,是广域首都圈内政府划定唯一的"高度技术集聚区",聚焦机器人、电气、精密机械龙头企业的先进研发制造。

日本城市群的经验对长三角来说,有三点值得借鉴:首先要统筹制定全域产业差异化布局,其次要建立常态化的产业沟通协调机制,第三是注重节点城市融入区域分工。

3. 协同体制机制上,欧洲里尔城市群的经验对长三角很有借鉴意义,建议从顶层设计入手建立长效一体化协同机制

里尔城市群横跨法国、比利时两国,是由法国里尔、比利时科特赖克等区域组成的跨境城市群,其早期发展在行政壁垒破除、公共服务一体化发展等领域树立了城市群发展的典范。

2008年,里尔政府联合城市群内14个跨境发展机构,成立欧洲地区跨国合作组织(Lille-Kortrijk-Tournai Eurometropolis),三方市长组成领导小组,签署支持城市群合作举措在区域落地的法案。在协会内设置大都市局,一改传统"中央、行政省、行政市"的管控模式,形成"欧盟、跨境合作区、都市区、邻里社区"的城市群创新协同机制,由大都市局对市议会直接监管,监控城市群协同政策与举措的落地效果。同时,通过开设一年一度的社区长官和市长大会,对协会的工作和政策落地成果进行监管。里尔城市群现已成为欧洲历史最长、面积最大、发展最好的跨境合作区之一。

为消除区域内资本、人才流动停滞的问题,里尔政府通过欧洲里尔(Euralille)复兴计划,联合法国、比利时约150个社区,在产业复兴、就业引导、住房市场升级和城市可持续发展管理等领域统一计划,大大提升了部分落后地区的公共服务水平,从根本上推动人才与资本等关键生产要素的区域流动,助推区域经济协同发展。

对长三角来说,建议优先统筹协调机构机制,建立统一的牵头机构;此外,在各细分领域快速有序地消除要素流通壁垒,通过数据协同、财税共享、政策创新等方式,从根本上解决要素流通的障碍。

四、总结

长三角一体化是分层次、多步走的。除了强化连通性,协调重大项目,实现包含路网协调、轨交联系、环境治理和区域基建的基础设施一体化外,更重要的是面向区域经济韧性的建设才是真正的深水区,需要更深度的一体化,以及更广泛、更坚决的各方行动,包括:促进与保障要素在区域内部流通与积累实现要素流通一体化(物流、人流/商流、资金流、信息流)、打造有韧性的区域产业经济体实现产业协同一体化(统筹规划、引领创新、产业生态),以及为区域协调乃至进一步融合提供保障的机制体制一体化(组织架构、法规政策、管理机制)。

Deepening the Integration Process and Building a Global City Cluster with Regional Economic Resilience

Boston Consulting Group

Ⅰ. Yangtze River Delta integration: Charting a course amidst global uncertainty

The city cluster has become the mainstay of regional economies worldwide. In future, individual city clusters will become the front line of competition between economies. In 2015, the world's 15 largest city clusters, home to approximately 12% of the world's population, generated 30% of global GDP. In contrast, about half of global GDP was generated by 300 large metropolitan circles, which are home to only 19% of the world's population. By GDP and population, globally the largest city clusters are the Great Lakes, BosWash, Central and Southern England, Northwest Europe, the Yangtze River Delta, and the Taiheiyō Belt. The GDP of these megalopolises all exceed USD 2 trillion, and they all have a population of over 35 million. In the outline of the 13th Five Year Plan, the central government pledged to create 19 country-level city clusters, of which the Yangtze River Delta (YRD), Beijing-Tianjin-Hebei, and Greater Bay Area (GBA) Region would be the three largest.

However, city cluster development now faces new challenges due to ongoing change and global uncertainty. Beginning in 2006, BCG's Global Uncertainty Index began to climb in the face of a chain of "black swan"

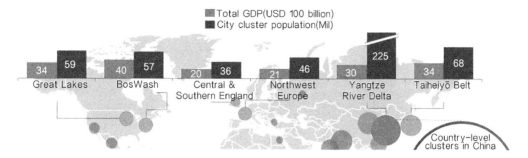

■ Total GDP(USD 100 billion)
■ City cluster population(Mil)

| 34 | 59 | 40 | 57 | 20 | 36 | 21 | 46 | 30 | 225 | 34 | 68 |

Great Lakes   BosWash   Central &
Southern England   Northwest
Europe   Yangtze
River Delta   Taiheiyō Belt

Country-level
clusters in China

Figure 1   Clusters will Become Key to Competition between Economies

incidents including the 2008 financial crisis and the 2011 Eurozone debt crisis. There are several areas which bear continued attention:

(1) The continuing China-US trade war. Although concrete gains were made in October 2019 with the reaching of an initial trade agreement, the trade war is not yet over.

(2) Continued slowdown of the global economy. Developed countries are seeing sluggish growth, while China set 6% as its minimum target for GDP growth for the year for the first time.

(3) Continuous buildup of risk in the international financial system. Since 2008, loose monetary policies instituted by developed economies have inflated global debt to a colossal USD 23.2 billion.①

(4) Global political uncertainty is climbing. US President Trump's populist "America First" policy and Brexit have sent ripples of uncertainty coursing through the global economic landscape and governance system.

(5) Controversial new technologies are mushrooming. Legal and ethical frameworks for AI, 5G, and genetic engineering are not yet in place, leaving immense potential risks unresolved.

In the face of these uncertainties, China has recently made preparations at multiple levels, and has stipulated new demands regarding regional integration. In terms of policy direction, the government has adopted a package of protective measures including deleveraging, supply-side reform, and fending off of major risks. At the individual policy level, the

---

① Source: BCG Henderson Institute.

government has emphasized the importance not just of city clusters but also domestic vitality and quality. For example, the YRD integration should drive high quality development nationwide, and city cluster development in the GBA Region should ensure the longer-term prosperity and stability of Hong Kong and Macao. As the largest city cluster by land area and economy in China, the YRD should produce solutions to respond to uncertainty as part of regional integration.

II. YRD integration so far and current issues

For more than two decades, the central government has increasingly focused on developing the YRD region. Firstly, the YRD has played an increasingly important role in strategy, developing gradually from the "fostering of economic growth points" in the 1990s to last year's "driving national high-quality growth". Secondly, the YRD has continually expanded to cover ever more cities, from 15 in 1997 to the 41 cities last year. Over the same period, the scope of reform has continually deepened, from the prior emphasis on "playing to the strengths of each YRD city and complementarity in development" to "increasing the clout and status of these cities in the world economy" and "synergistic development within the YRD".

Looking ahead, the next stage of integration of the YRD region will focus more on improving the agility of the economy while enhancing regional economic growth to create a global city cluster that is regionally competitive. In addition to spurring economic growth, infrastructure connectivity and balanced development, the government should focus on core innovative competitiveness, expand its strategic depth, and beef up its ability to withstand risk.

However, the response of the YRD to the new economic landscape demonstrates insufficient agility in three areas: technological innovation, industrial layout, and collaboration mechanisms.

1. Limited impact of technological innovation

There is some innovation in science and technology (IST) in the region already, but the overarching ecosystem lacks long-term sustainability, and commercial application of research findings is weak. Overall, there is a firm foundation for future growth in the technological innovation industry in the YRD. The region does have ample scientific research resources, with Shanghai's Zhangjiang and Anhui's Hefei comprehensive national science centers, accounting for one quarter of China's "Double First Class" universities, National Key Laboratories and National Engineering Research Centers. Furthermore, R&D intensity in Shanghai, Nanjing, Hangzhou and Hefei is over 3%, far above the national average. Science and technology are closely integrated, with many leading players: over 50% of China's integrated circuit industry, and over one-third of China's software information services industry, are in the YRD region. However, bringing research to market in the YRD lags behind Shenzhen, so there is a need for a more complete IST ecosystem. In terms of talent retention, there are large disparities within the YRD concerning employment of graduates from national key universities. Approximately 75% of graduates from Fudan University and Jiaotong University stay on in Shanghai after graduation; 88% of Shenzhen University graduates stay in the city, compared with Sun Yat-Sen University graduates, of whom 25% leave Guangzhou for jobs in Shenzhen every year. Moreover, this last figure is climbing. The total number of patents per 10,000 people in Shanghai and Hangzhou is just half of that in Shenzhen, which also ranks ahead of Shanghai and Hangzhou in ratings for its innovation-friendly atmosphere. Therefore, the next step for the YRD region is to fully tap its technology and innovation potential and build an innovation ecosystem that will allow it to drive commercial application of research findings.

2. Industry layout lacks strategic depth

There is a pronounced issue with multiple companies in the same industry in parts of the YRD region, and small and medium-sized cities have yet to fully integrate into the value chain. Currently, local governments formulate policy individually without a clear view of the bigger picture or effective collaboration. In terms of segmentation, smart equipment, along with IT and biomedicine are the new high frequency must-haves for each locality, with local governments competing to attract these industries. Distribution is therefore irrational, and localities are fighting over resources. Local governments set industry development goals without reference either to the broader context or to actual market demand, leading to overcapacity as exemplified by that in new energy vehicles (in 2018, new energy vehicle production capacity in the YRD was 2.38 million units, or 30% of the national total, with 530,000 units sold, accounting for 50% of sales nationwide). The lack of strategic depth in the industry layout of the YRD is particularly evident in the faddish development of industries, without due consideration to suitability, in some small and medium-sized cities. There is no clear industry segmentation between these small and medium-sized cities, and their overall risk resilience is weak. Looking again at new energy vehicles, there are 7 feature towns in Zhejiang Province alone where local companies have been severely impacted by overcapacity over the last two years. These companies have suffered from a host of issues, including delayed or unpaid wages, loans to suppliers, layoffs, and delayed product launches. Therefore, the YRD needs to take a serious look at industrial mismatch to avoid repeated competition; furthermore, small and medium-sized cities need to be fully integrated into the industry ecosystem.

3. Synergy mechanisms have hit a bottleneck

YRD coordination mechanisms work on a case-by-case basis; there is no single responsible organization or long-term plan in place. There is an urgent need for a long-term working mechanism with multi-party engagement and real-time feedback. Currently, coordination in the YRD region takes the form of case-specific policies or conferences held at the next level up of government. Another issue is that different kinds of problems are managed under the purview of different organizations. Such coordination mechanisms do not fully factor in the driving forces acting on industries or cross-regional talent flows; some of these mechanisms deliver little meaningful value. For instance, the aim of Shanghai's big data sharing initiative with Nantong was to help Nantong build a big data industry chain, but in the end, mainly data infrastructure providers moved to the industrial park, which had only a modest effect on big data R&D in Nantong. Looking ahead, the YRD should build a coordination mechanism that allows multi-party engagement and real-time feedback. The mechanism should focus on development at the regional level, and talent flows.

III. Development suggestions for YRD integration

To address the three issues detailed above, the YRD should strengthen agility of the regional economy. International experience offers lessons, the most important of which are the following.

1. Collaboration on an innovative ecosystem. Form a cross-regional organization with input from enterprises, academia and research institutions, and create an all-in-one service platform for innovative industries

The YRD can reference the experience of the BosWash Corridor, with the core focus being on setting up a cross-regional organization with input from enterprises, academia and research institutions, and establishing an innovation service platform for verticals. The BosWash Corridor runs from Boston in the north to Washington in the south and is the most densely populated region in the US. The corridor is the country's largest commercial trade center, international financial center and innovation center, and its manufacturing sector provides 30% of the US' output. The BosWash industrial layout is rationally tiered, with each locality playing to its strengths. New York is the core of the corridor: it is the financial and trade center of the US, providing developed commerce and production/service support to the entire country. Boston is home to many universities, high-tech companies, and medical institutions, which have allowed it to become the US center for innovative industries like electronics, biological and aerospace. Washington leverages its status as the country's political center to attract policy-making and financial institutions from around the globe and has developed the national defense industry in nearby Baltimore in response to government procurement and development needs.

BosWash has the world's leading biotechnology industry. Massachusetts Biotechnology Council (MassBio) is an organization representing the region's biotechnology firms, and its 921 members include biopharma companies, business services companies, funds/incubators, universities/science & research institutions, medical institutions and government entities. MassBio helps biotechnology firms across the BosWash Corridor with a range of areas including expediting drug approvals, corporate tax exemptions and reductions, joint purchasing, and education & training. BosWash also has several comprehensive innovation platforms for verticals, supporting key areas including talent recruitment, funding sources, industry exchanges, tech services, and big data sharing. Both government and the private sector can select the platform that best plays to their strengths. The experience of the BosWash Corridor offers two lessons for the YRD: firstly, the leading role of industry organizations must remain, while innovation coordination organizations in which government, industry, academia and research institutions all engage function as the core of an innovation ecosystem. Secondly, the empowering role of functional platforms should be emphasized, with multi-party engagement from government and businesses to build professional, accurate platforms that empower every segment by clustering and deploying industry essentials.

2. Strategic depth in industrial division of labor. First of all, formulate an industrial blueprint for the whole YRD region, tailored to the needs of each industry. Then, establish a regular mechanism for communication and coordination between businesses, and encourage cities along the value chain to structure their industrial layout to match regional demand

The YRD can tap the Japanese experience with regard to city clusters, namely industry segmentation and ensuring that small and medium-sized cities participate in the value chain and develop their own resilient industries. The most iconic of Japan's city clusters is the Greater Tokyo Region, which includes Kanagawa, Chiba, Saitama, Ibaraki, Tochigi, Gunma, and Yamanashi prefectures. The metropolis covers 9.8% of Japan's total territory, but its economy is the size of Russia's.

The Greater Tokyo Region cluster is the result of a strategic decision; multiple levels of government reached a consensus on its development, and public and ongoing joint conferences were held with input from government, businesses and the market to inform industrial policy decision-making. At the same time, the Japanese government was careful to involve think tanks like the UED to ensure continuity. The government was thus able to achieve industry differentiation and integrate cities around Tokyo into the industry value chain. Taking the example of Kawasaki and Utsunomiya near Tokyo, Kawasaki was earmarked for industry innovation, and received resources from TAMA, helping it to transform from an outdated industrial region into an innovation base. Today, Kawasaki has the largest services sector workforce of any Japanese city. Utsunomiya on the other hand is the sole government-designated "high-tech cluster" in the metropolitan area, an advanced manufacturing and R&D base with leaders in robotics, electrics, and precision machinery.

The Japanese experience offers three points for YRD: firstly, formulate an industry-differentiated, whole-of-region approach; secondly, form a long-term communication and coordination mechanism for businesses; and thirdly, node cities must be integrated into the regional value chain.

3. Leverage institutions and flesh out the blueprint by focusing on removing barriers to circulation of vital goods

The Lille cluster in France has many lessons for the YRD; we suggest building a unified, long-term integration synergy mechanism from the top down.

The Lille-Kortrijk city cluster straddles the border between France and Belgium, and when first inaugurated, the cluster was a model study in elimination of administrative barriers and development of integrated public services.

In 2008, the Lille government, together with 14 cross-border development organizations in the cluster, established the transborder Lille-Kortrijk-Tournai Eurometropolis, headed by three mayors, and signed a law allowing the implementation of cluster measures within the region. The region is governed by a special bureau, in a departure from the traditional governance pyramid of central government, Departement, and municipality, towards a new four-tier collaboration hierarchy with the European Union, cross-border cooperation region, metropolis and then resident community. The bureau directly regulates the municipal parliament, monitoring the implementation of policy and measures within the city cluster. At the same time, the work and policy implementation of the association are subject to scrutiny via annual district governor and mayoral town hall sessions. The Lille cluster is now one of the most long-lasting, largest, and most successful cross-border clusters ever seen in Europe.

In order to energize the movement of capital and talent within the area, the Lille government passed the Master Plan for Euralille, involving 150 communities across France and Belgium. The Plan offered a unified blueprint that spanned industrial rejuvenation, attracting jobs, housing market upgrade and sustainable urban development management. The implementation of the Plan led to a tremendous improvement in public services in a backward region, and had a fundamental impact in terms of driving movement of core factors of production like talent and capital within the region, in turn driving synergistic economic development.

With regard to the YRD, the takeaways are to firstly prioritize the setting up of coordinating institutions and a single leading organization; and secondly, to swiftly remove barriers to the movement of economic elements by leveraging data synergy, sharing of financial data, and policy innovation.

IV. Conclusion

The YRD integration should take place at multiple levels and be implemented gradually. In addition to enhancing connectivity by coordinating and integrating large-scale programs such as road network development, rail transport linkups, environmental governance and regional infrastructure, more importantly, the key focus for reform should be developing a more agile regional economy. Deeper integration is needed, and all parties need to implement this across a wider scope and more decisively. This includes: pushing the movement and accumulation of key elements within the region, leading to integration (flows of goods, people/commerce, capital, information), and thereby forging an agile regional economy with integrated industry (overall planning, encouragement of innovation, and creation of an industry ecosystem) as well as integrated institutions (organization structure, regulations and policies, governance structures) for regional coordination and even further integration.

区域协同的深化更新：以长三角为例

麦肯锡咨询

    区域协同发展的新时代下，物流贸易、信息技术、政策干预等多方因素均在一定程度上推动了一体化进程。然而纵观全球城市群演进历程，作为影响人口流动、基础设施建设、政策机制的决定性因素，产业发展才是区域协同的第一驱动力。因此，本文将聚焦"产业链"视角，剖析中国区域发展态势。

    随着国际地缘政治紧张局势的不断升级，过去 50 年的全球分工和价值链体系正在加速变化，产业链的"重塑"将对中国区域经济发展路径与模式产生深远的影响。我们认为，通过深入研究长三角的宏观发展趋势，厘清未来区域协同发展路径，将为中国政府、企业的战略方针提供新的视角与启示。

一、响应"协同"新时代：全球供需变革对中国区域发展的影响

    受地缘政治波动的影响，全球经贸格局正在发生巨变：国际贸易增量明显放缓，2010—2017 年间年均增速从 5% 下跌至 1%；对外贸易依存度持续走低，过去十年内下滑幅度超过 6%。[①] 全球价值链体系正在从"全球分工"走向"区域化布局"，呈现出一个半径更小的经贸格局。

    全球大势下，中国区域供需格局加速转变：作为全球 33% 的制造产业所在地，国际经贸格局的变化推动了中国从"外向型"向"内生型"经济转型。在内需市场快速崛起及国内供应链建设进一步完善的双重作用下（图 1），中国产业链"本土化"布局进程加速：约 63% 的中国制造业（产值占比）对进出口贸易的依赖度正在下滑；全国整体外贸依存度 2007—2017 年间从 15.5% 下降至 8.3%，跌幅达 50% 以上。

---

    ①   资料来源于麦肯锡全球研究院。

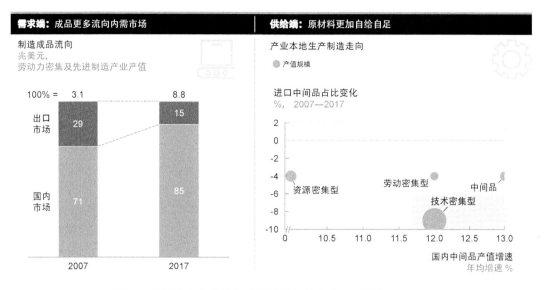

需求端：成品更多流向内需市场

制造成品流向
兆美元，
劳动力密集及先进制造产业产值

100% = 3.1   8.8

出口市场 29   15

国内市场 71   85

2007   2017

供给端：原材料更加自给自足

产业本地生产制造走向

● 产值规模

进口中间品占比变化
%，2007—2017

资源密集型   劳动密集型   中间品
技术密集型

国内中间品产值增速
年均增速 %

图1　供需的本土化是推动中国外贸依存度下跌的主要原因

资料来源：麦肯锡全球研究院

"本土化"趋势下，中国传统地域经济面临重构，供应链在区域内的延伸与布局将成为联通城市，促进人才、资金等资源要素流通的"主动脉"，构建起一个基于产业价值链分工的区域一体化格局。

麦肯锡认为，中国区域发展正处于转型的"十字路口"。在产业链的带动下，区域发展模式正从各自为政、割裂发展的"单城逻辑"向多城分工、区域联通的"城市群逻辑"全面过渡。通过深入剖析不同区域的产业格局与发展路径，我们希望能厘清一体化实践中存在的机遇、挑战与核心成功要素，为政府、企业参与下一阶段的区域布局提供启示。

二、把握"协同"新走向：政策催化下的长三角区域再平衡发展

目前，以上海为中心，长三角已形成南、北翼两大发展格局：由江苏、安徽各城市为主体的北翼（图2）聚焦大国重器，侧重于解决国家在战略性行业"卡脖子"的技术难题；以上海为核心，围绕先进制造产业链条形成了从西到东、"原材料—成品制造—出口"的产业梯队格局。而由浙江各城市为主体的南翼（图3）则以民营经济为特色，侧重于通过民间力量推动纺织、化纤等轻工业为主的加工制造经济；相比北翼区域一体化初显的态势，南翼由于产业工艺简单、环节单一，未形成区域内分工的需求，导致城市间缺少互动、相对割裂及独立。

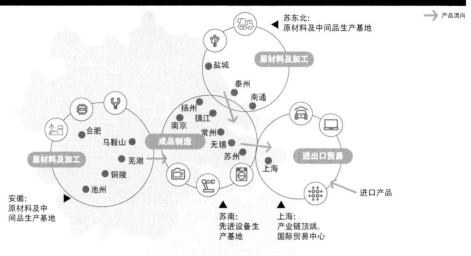

图2 长三角北翼城市产业分工协同明显,已形成一体化联动的格局

资料来源:公开资料整理;麦肯锡分析

南翼城市产业分布与产品流向

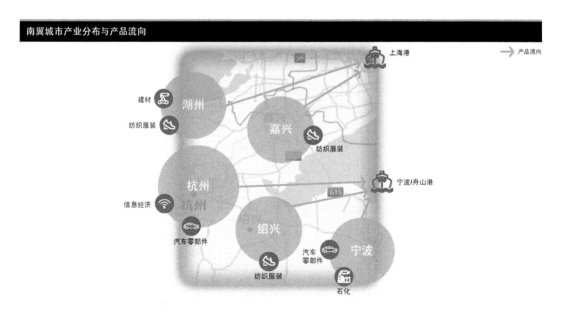

图3 长三角南翼产业"链条短、环节少",城市间缺少互动,割裂发展

资料来源:公开资料整理;麦肯锡分析

　　未来,预计南北动能不一,产城格局进一步分化:着眼北翼,在国家促进制造业升级的大方针下,苏锡常、南京等传统制造高地将进一步强化,尤其在电子信息、汽车制造、生物医药等高技术含量领域迎来跨越式发展机遇。相比之下,合肥、苏东北等地区虽然当前发展较为滞后,仍然以资源密集和低端制造业为主,但得益于土地、人口红利,有潜力承接来自发达地区的产业溢出与供应链延伸布局,以此加强与苏锡常等北翼发达城市的联动,形成强有力的"一体化"经济发展动能。着眼南翼,虽然杭州等城市在互联网、文创等高端三产的推动下,一跃成为全国经济转型的良好样板,但整体来看,绍兴、温州等诸多南翼城市赖以生存的传统轻工制造业近年来面临巨大挑战。受人工成本上涨、海外市场疲软等负面因素影响,全省超过49%的制造业近3年来呈负增长态势,①其中以纺织、化工等"出口型"产业最为明显。虽然南翼各地政府过去几年积极推动产业创新转型,但均各自为政、单打独斗,未能形成合力。在南翼整体土地、人口、资源、行政资源偏少的劣势下,转型尚未形成发展动能。

往前走,长三角一体化发展面临两大核心问题:一是加速北翼传统制造高地的先进产业向欠发达区域延伸,促进区域整体平衡发展;二是打破南翼割裂局面,强化与上海、北翼各城市之间的协同,通过资源要素的流通与共享,为南翼制造业注入转型所需的新动能。

一系列高能级国家政策落地,或将打破掣肘:随着长三角一体化上升为国家级发展战略,近年来政府围绕产业创新升级、民生疏导、交通互联互通等多个维度正在筹备或已经落地了一系列高能级干预措施与政策机制(例如推动新兴产业落地的"G60科创走廊"、助力安徽加速科技创新的"合肥国家科学中心"、深化杭州辐射带动效应的"杭州湾大湾区"),旨在规避传统"行政化"区域掣肘,通过统一规划与管理,打破三省一市间的行政壁垒,促进关键要素(人才、科教、技术、资金等)的流通与共享。

G60科创走廊:以高速公路作为连接轴,打造区域协同发展实践样本

G60科创走廊以高速公路为主线,串联长三角三省一市九地市(区),覆盖了7.6万平方公里面积、近5 000万人口,以及长三角25%的GDP。

作为融合了九地市创新资源和产业优势的集合体,G60科创走廊旨在通过三大举措,促进长三角区域协同格局由东向西、由北向南沿走廊梯次拓展:(1)产业链分工一体化布局,G60科创走廊已形成7大先进制造产业集群、集聚了845家龙头企业、吸引了1 467亿元总投资额,包括海尔智谷、国能新能源汽车等大批百亿元级项目;(2)制度和资源一体化配置,G60科创走廊已实现九地交互投资2 280亿元,12万台(套)科学仪器共享互通,以打破行政壁垒、促进科创要素高效对接;(3)基础设施一体化联通,随着沪苏湖高铁开工建设,G60科创走廊已实现2小时同城效应,同时推进30个事项"一网通办",促进生产、生活、生态深度融合。

---

① 资料来源于2015—2017浙江省统计年鉴。

随着 2019 年 6 月新签署一批总投资高达 2 192 亿元的 86 个区域一体化合作项目,G60 科创走廊将持续推动区域内创新要素流通,成为长三角一体化发展、南北翼高质量协同的主要载体。

在国家政策的助力下,部分城市将实现跨越式发展:以麦肯锡预测为例,苏锡常等传统先进制造引擎将持续推动长三角实体经济发展,而在 G60 科创走廊、国家科学中心等高能级政策手段的催化下,合肥、杭州等城市圈的产业结构或将迎来颠覆性变化,成为未来长三角高新制造产业的新动能。

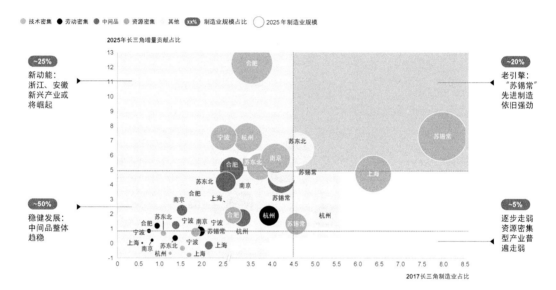

图 4　在国家政策推动下,传统制造业高地得到强化,新机遇或将出现
资料来源:麦肯锡全球研究院;中国统计年鉴;世界银行;麦肯锡分析

总的来看,长三角当前存在一定的不平衡以及供需错配,而在国家政策推动下的"再平衡"将成为捕捉区域发展红利、占据突破性先机的关键。

三、制胜"协同"新做法:通过自身"变革"应对时代"变迁"

从城市管理者的角度来看,未来产城发展必从"一极独大"的单城市配置走向"多极并驱"的城市群平衡,积极打破行政壁垒、融入区域分工协同、拥抱一体化发展,是占据新时代发展高地的关键。

第一,经济与产业发展从"分化割裂"到"分工明确":过去各城市主导产业割裂,存在恶性竞争、资源低效的同构现象;未来需要深化区域内产业结构战略整合,明确优势互补、互利共生的城市间分工与协作,构建一体化的产业链梯度布局。

第二,城市建设与政策创新从"点状集聚核心"到"网状疏导共享":过去资源集中于单体核心城市,大城市虹吸效应显著,周边城镇人才空心化,城市功能断层;未来需要强化区域资源统一配置、创新要素流通共享,通过建设大型基础设施(如珠江大桥)、出台协同创新政策(如 G60 科创走廊)、构建利益共享机制,发挥大城市造血辐射效应,向后进地区疏导资源要素、形成合力,提升整体区域繁荣度。

对企业管理者而言,把握区域变革需从等待机遇到来的"红利追逐者"走向前瞻宏观趋势的"先机创造者",转换思路、从被动接受变革到积极影响变革,是打造新时代价值高地的关键。

第一,业务布局思路从"存量逻辑"到"增量逻辑":过去基于既有业务需求、扫描区域投资布局机遇的做法仅能带来有限的短期增量提升;未来需要着眼整体区域格局变化,搜寻"价值洼地",提前卡位关键节点形成控制力,锁定长期增长空间。

第二,能力建设路径从"延伸价值链"到"拓展生态圈":过去依附主业进行业务能力的逐步拓展难以独当一面、形成特色优势;未来需要前瞻行业大生态趋势,以积极合作共建与孵化共享的方式,建立"多面护城河"。

第三,行业参与方式从"接受规则"到"影响规则":过去被动接受政策与监管框架限制,从既定规则中寻找点状红利的心态难以在价值链的再重构中形成突破;在区域一体化中,行业规则面临重构,领先企业应当发挥龙头优势,主动出击,参与制定新的行业标准,影响政策趋势,占据独特先机。

Deepening and Renewing Coordinated Regional Development: Taking the Yangtze River Delta as an Example

McKinsey & Company

In a new era of coordinated regional development, logistics, information technology (IT), and policy intervention are some of the factors that have promoted integration. A survey of the evolution of city clusters around the world nonetheless revealed that industrial development, the determinant of population flows, infrastructure building, and policy mechanisms, is the key driver of regional coordination. This article analyzes China's regional development landscape from the perspective of "industry chains".

As international geopolitical tensions continue to escalate, the global specializations and value chains developed over the last five decades have changed rapidly. A "reconstruction" of industry chains will have a profound impact on China's regional economic growth path and model. We believe that by conducting an in-depth study of the macro growth trend of the Yangtze River Delta (YRD), we will be able to identify the future path of coordinated regional development and provide new insights that will be useful for the strategic policies of the Chinese government and enterprises.

I. Responding to a new era of "coordinated development": The impact of global supply and demand changes on China's regional development

Geopolitical fluctuations have led to dramatic changes in the global economic landscape: International trade has grown at a significantly slower pace, with the annual growth rate between 2010 and 2017 falling from 5% to 1%. Dependence on external trade has continued to decline, with the magnitude of this decline at more than 6% over the last decade.[①] The global value chain is shifting from "global specialization" to a "regionalized structure", resulting in smaller economic and trade landscapes.

Global trends have accelerated changes in China's regional supply and demand landscape: As the home to 33% of the global manufacturing sector, changes in the international economic and trade landscapes have spurred the transformation of China's "export-oriented" economy to one of "domestic consumption". The rapid rise of the domestic market along with further improvements in the construction of domestic supply chains (Figure 1) have promoted the localization of China's industry chain. The dependence on trade is calling in approximately 63% of China's manufacturing sector (share of output value), and nationwide dependence on external trade between fell from 15.5% to 8.3% between 2007 and 2017, a decline of more than 50%.

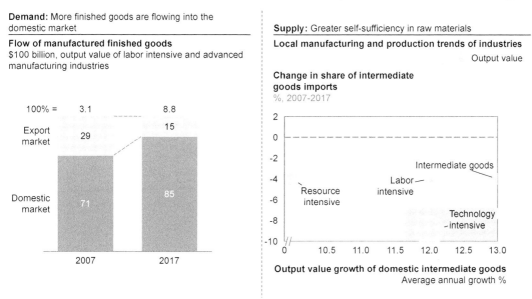

Figure 1　Supply-demand localization is the reason for the decline in foreign trade dependence

Source: McKinsey Global Institute

---

① Source: McKinsey Global Institute.

The trend of localization will require a reconstruction of China's traditional regional economy. The extension of supply chains into different regions and their layouts will become the main conduits linking cities, promoting the circulation of talent, capital, and other resources. This will create an integrated regional landscape based on industry value chain specialization.

McKinsey believes that China's regional growth stands at a crossroads. Driven by industry chains, regional growth models are in the process of transiting from the fragmented development of a single city to "city clusters", where different cities with their own specializations are connected in a regional cluster. Through an in-depth analysis of the industrial landscapes and development paths of different regions, we hope to identify the opportunities, challenges, and core success factors of integration so as to inspire governments and enterprises to take part in the next phase of regional structuring.

II. Grasp new trends in coordinated development: Policy promotes a regional rebalancing of growth regional integrated development

Current conditions reveal that two major development patterns, one in the north and one in the south, have formed in the Shanghai-centered YRD: The northern region, dominated by cities in Jiangsu and Anhui (Figure 2), is focused on industries that constitute the "Pillars of a Great Power". The priority in this region is to resolve the technical difficulties that result from bottlenecks for strategic industries. With Shanghai at its core, an industrial echelon centered on the advanced manufacturing industry chain comprising "raw materials-finished goods manufacturing-export" has been formed running from west to east. The southern region, dominated by cities in Zhejiang (Figure 3), features a strong private sector economy. Its priority is to leverage the private sector to drive the processing economy based primarily on light industries such as textiles and chemical fibers. In contrast to the north, where we can see the first signs of integration, intra-regional specialization is as yet unnecessary in the south because its industries have relatively simple processes and segments. This has, in turn, led to a lack of inter-city interaction, fragmentation, and independence.

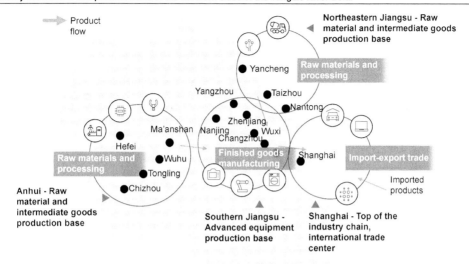

Figure 2   Significant synergies from industrial specialization in the northern cities of the Yangtze River Delta has led to an integrated linkage

Source：Data search；McKinsey

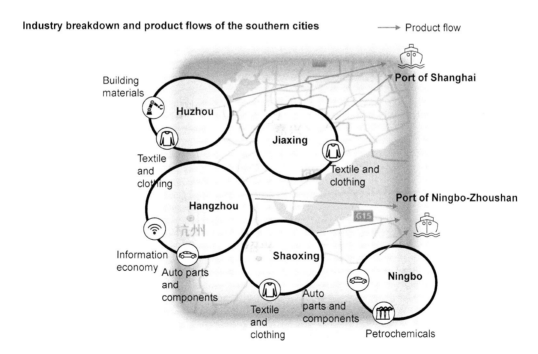

Figure 3   Industries in the southern Yangtze River Delta have short industry chains and fewer segments, inter-city interaction is lacking, and growth is disjointed

Source：Data search；McKinsey

As the northern and southern drivers differ, industry-city patterns will further diverge in the future: Benefitting from the State's promotion of an upgrade in manufacturing, traditional manufacturing bases such as Suzhou-Wuxi-Changzhou and Nanjing will grow even stronger. In particular, sectors involving advanced technology, such as information technology, auto manufacturing, and biomedical, will see opportunities for exponential growth. In contrast, resource-intensive and low-end manufacturing will continue to dominate in Hefei and northeastern Jiangsu, which are now lagging behind in terms of development. Nonetheless, thanks to advantages in land and population, these regions have the potential to benefit from industrial spillover and supply chain extensions from developed regions. This will enhance their links with developed cities in the north, such as Suzhou, Wuxi, and Changzhou, and form a driver for integrated economic development. Although Hangzhou and other cities in the south are beneficiaries of the Internet, cultural and creative sectors, and other high-end tertiary industries, on the whole, the traditional light manufacturing industries of many of the southern cities, such as Shaoxing and Wenzhou, have faced enormous challenges in recent years. Rising labor costs, weak overseas markets, and other difficulties have resulted in negative growth trends for more than 49% of the province's manufacturing sector in the last three years[①]. This is particularly apparent in the textiles, chemical, and other export-oriented industries. Although the governments of the southern regions have actively promoted industry innovation and transformation, each city has continued to go at it alone, rather than forming coalitions. Given the overall disadvantages of the south in terms of land, population, natural resources, and administrative resources, transformation has yet to form a driver of growth.

Going forward, two major core challenges confront integrated development in the YRD: First, the region must accelerate the extension of advanced industries in the north toward less developed regions to promote the balanced development throughout the region. Second, the region must

---

① Source: Zhejiang Statistical Yearbook, 2015—2017.

eradicate the fragmented landscape of the south, enhance the coordination between Shanghai and the cities of the north, and inject new drivers required for transformation into the south's manufacturing industry by circulating and sharing resources.

The implementation of a series of high-level national policies may overcome constraints: With the integration of the YRD having been elevated to a national level development strategy, in recent years, the government has prepared and begun implementing a series of high-level intervention measures and policy mechanisms centered on industrial innovation and upgrade, standards of living, transport interconnectivity, and many other areas (such as the "G60 Science and Innovation Corridor" which promotes the implementation of emerging industries, helping Anhui accelerate the "Hefei National Science Center", and deepening the influence of Hangzhou on the "Hangzhou Greater Bay Area"). These efforts seek to work around traditional "administrative" regional constraints, overcome the administrative barriers between Zhejiang, Jiangsu, Anhui, and Shanghai, and promote the circulation and sharing of key factors of production (talent, science and education, technology, and capital).

G60 Science and Innovation Corridor: Creating a practical example of coordinated regional development with expressways as the connecting axes

With expressways as the key axes, the G60 Science and Innovation Corridor links the three provinces, Shanghai, and nine cities (districts) of the YRD, encompassing 76,000 km² and close to 50 million people and accounting for 25% of the YRD's GDP.

By integrating the innovation resources and industrial strengths of nine cities, G60 aims to promote coordinated development in the YRD from east to west and from north to south along the corridor by adopting three major measures: (1) Integration of industry chain specializations. G60 has created seven major advanced manufacturing industry clusters, bringing together 845 leading enterprises and attracting total investments worth 146.7 billion RMB. It includes Haier Intelligent Valley, National New Energy Vehicle, and many other 10 billion RMB grade projects. (2) Integration of policies and resources. G60 has realized cross-city investments among the nine cities worth 228 billion RMB and the sharing and exchange of 120,000 scientific devices to overcome administrative barriers and promote the effective connection of key science and innovation factors. (3) Integrated infrastructure connectivity. With the commencement of the construction of the Shanghai-Suzhou-Huzhou high-speed rail, the G60 corridor has already merged cities within a 2-hour radius. It is also advancing the "One Netcom Office" solution for the convenient online handling of 30 items to promote the deep integration of production, daily life, and the ecosystem.

In June of this year, 86 regional integrated partnership projects worth 219.2 billion RMB will be signed. The G60 Science and Innovation Corridor will continue to promote the intra-regional circulation of key innovation factors and will become a key vehicle of integrated development as well as high-quality north-south coordinated development in the YRD.

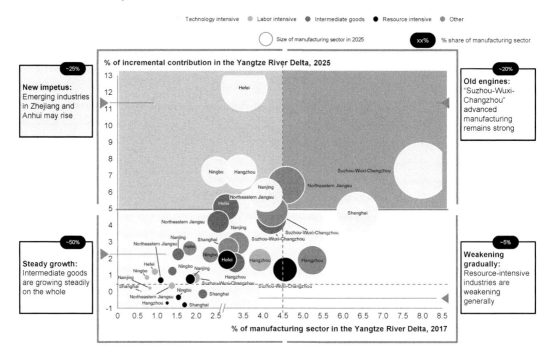

Figure 4 National policies will see traditional manufacturing strengthen further, and new opportunities may emerge

Source: McKinsey Global Institute; China Statistical Yearbook; World Bank; McKinsey

National policy measures will help some cities achieve exponential growth: McKinsey forecasts that the traditional advanced manufacturing engines of Suzhou, Wuxi, and Changzhou will continue to drive real economic growth in the YRD. Meanwhile, the G60 Science and Innovation Corridor, National Science Center, and other high-level policy measures may cause a disruptive change in the industry mix of Hefei, Hangzhou, and other urban areas, becoming new drivers for the YRD's advanced manufacturing industry.

On the whole, the YRD is currently experiencing certain imbalances and supply-demand mismatches. "Rebalancing" driven by national policies will become the key to capturing regional growth dividends and seizing breakthrough opportunities in the market.

III. New methods of successful coordinated development: Responding to changing times through self-transformation

From the perspective of urban governors, future industry-city development must shift from a configuration based on a single city with a "dominant driver" to a balanced "multi-driver" urban cluster. Actively breaking down administrative barriers, integrating coordinated regional specializations, and embracing integrated growth are key to raising development to new heights.

• Economic and industry growth-from "differentiated fragmentation" to "distinct specializations": In the past, the dominant industry of each city caused industrial fragmentation, giving rise to both vicious competition and resource inefficiency. In the future, strategic integration of the industry mix within a region must be intensified, and measures for inter-city specialization and coordination that will result in complementary and mutual advantages must be clarified so as to construct an integrated and gradated industry chain layout.

• Urban construction and policy innovation-from "dotted core clusters" to "network-channeled sharing": In the past, resources were concentrated in a single core city, and the talent in neighboring cities was siphoned off by large cities, causing dislocations in urban functions. In the future, the uniform allocation of regional resources should be enhanced, and key innovation elements circulated and shared. Through the building of major infrastructure (such as the Pearl River Bridge), the introduction of coordinated innovation policies (such as G60), and the establishment of benefit-sharing mechanisms, large cities can play a supporting role and channel resources to and create synergies with less developed regions. This will lift the prosperity of the entire region.

From the perspective of corporate managers, grasping regional change must entail shifting from being a "dividend chaser" who waits for opportunities to a "first mover" who looks ahead to macro trends. A change in approach, from passively accepting change to actively influencing change is key to creating a value high ground in the new era.

• Business layout approach-from "existing logic" to "incremental logic": In the past, practices based on existing business requirements and the exploration of opportunities presented by regional investment patterns could only bring about limited short-term incremental upgrades. In the future, focusing on changes in overall regional landscapes and looking for "value depressions" are required. Enterprises should seize critical nodes in advance to create control points and lock in long-term growth potential.

• The route to capacity building-from "extending the value chain" to "expanding the ecosphere": Expanding capacity simply by leveraging the core business, as in the past, is no longer feasible and is unlikely to result in special advantages. In the future, looking ahead to the general ecosystem trends of the industry is required along with a "multi-faceted economic moat" built by way of active cooperation and sharing.

• Methods of industry participation-from "accepting rules" to "influencing rules": Passive acceptance of policy and regulatory framework restrictions, as well as the mentality to seek points of advantage amid existing rules, will not result in break throughs in value chain reconstruction. In regional integration, industry rules must be reconstructed. Leading

enterprises should fully leverage their leadership advantages and take the
initiative to particulate in formulating new industry standards. This will
allow them to influence policy trends and seize unique first-mover
advantages.

优化生态，协同发展

——秉持一体化视角推进长三角创新产业合作

德勤

"科创＋产业"是深入实施创新驱动发展战略的关键所在。2019年12月1日印发的《长江三角洲区域一体化发展规划纲要》提出，要促进创新链与产业链深度融合，加强协同创新产业体系建设，到2025年时基本形成区域协同创新体系，把长三角建设成为全国重要创新策源地。面对大好政策背景，以及全球聚焦创新发展、中国创新生态系统焕发出勃勃生机这一时代趋势，通过深化科创与产业协调发展，合力打造长三角科技创新共同体，是长三角地区面临的历史性机遇。为此，需要对长三角城市的创新生态、既有产业基础以及创新产业发展趋势进行客观评估，推进沪苏浙皖创新生态优化，规划政策协同，助力长三角一体化更高质量发展。

一、创新生态：长三角主要城市的创新环境与潜力

创新生态反映一个地方的创新环境与发展潜力，是推进创新产业发展的基础性条件。2019年，德勤对中国主要城市的创新生态进行了评估，发现长三角城市的创新生态在全国处于领先水平。评价体系包括创新机构、创新资源、创新环境三个指标（参见表1），被评估的长三角城市包括上海、苏州、杭州、南京、合肥等。德勤发现，在全国19个城市中，上海以排名第2、杭州排名第4的成绩，与北京、深圳、广州位列全国第一梯队；南京（第6）、苏州（第9）为第二梯队；合肥（第16）为第三梯队。

具体到各项指标，长三角城市的情况是：第一，创新机构方面，上海与北京、深圳一起，在高新技术企业数量方面稳居全国前列。在独角兽企业方面，北京、上海、深圳、杭州拥有162家，占据全国80%。第二，创新资源方面，上海排名全国第2，杭州排名全国第4。北京、上海、深圳、杭州四个城市占据中国人工智能人才比重超过55%。上海创新资本充裕，全国排名第2；创新技术强大，全国排名第3。在众创空

表 1　创新生态评价体系指标

	一级指标	二级指标	指标含义
创新生态评价体系	创新机构	创新企业	城市拥有的高新技术企业数量,中国互联网百强企业数量以及独角兽企业数量
		高校数量	城市拥有的普通高等学校数量
		科研机构	城市拥有的国家重点实验室数量
	创新资源	创新人才	人工智能人才数量占全国总人数的比例
		创新资本	创投资本投入量
		创新技术	城市专利申请量
		众创空间	城市拥有的国家备案众创空间数量
	创新环境	创新战略	政府创新政策数量
		创新基础	城市智能化基础设施建设情况、城市经济竞争力、城市可持续发展力等
		创新氛围	城市"互联网＋"氛围
		创新成本	创业者面临的基本创新成本,包括工资水平与写字楼租金

资料来源:德勤研究

间数量方面,上海与北京全国最多,占全国总数的近两成。第三,创新环境是长三角城市的"短板"。在总体排名中,上海继深圳、广州、北京之后排第 4 位,而苏州、杭州、南京、合肥则分列全国 19 个城市中的第 8、第 9、第 14、第 17 位。在这方面,深圳市的创新氛围、广州市的政策力度、北京市的创新基础设施都值得长三角城市借鉴。

　　总体来说,长三角区域虽有不足,但综合创新水平高于其他地区,特别是杭州异军突起,能与北上广深并驾齐驱,表现十分亮眼。杭州的特点在于人工智能人才

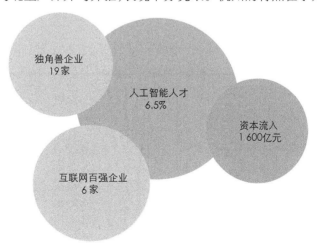

图 1　杭州的创新情况

资料来源:德勤研究

集聚明显,创新资本大量涌入。如杭州的人工智能人才占据中国总体人才数量的6.5%,2018年全年涌入资本量超过1 600亿元,2019年第一季度独角兽企业数量超越深圳。

二、创新产业:长三角创新发展的着力方向

未来长三角城市应该在哪些产业聚智发力?德勤认为有如下选择:人工智能、无人驾驶和智能制造等。从全国范围来看,长三角城市在这些方面都具备一定的优势。

1. 人工智能

全球人工智能市场将在未来几年经历现象级的增长。据Gartner预测,2025年世界人工智能市场规模将超过5万亿美元。中国是世界上应用人工智能技术最积极的国家之一,人工智能已成为影响中国经济发展的重要力量。2018年,中国人工智能投融资总规模达1 311亿元,融资事件597笔。截至2018年,中国人工智能领域融资总额占全球融资总额的60%。

基于广阔的市场空间,中国的人工智能企业不断涌现。目前,长三角与京津冀、珠三角一起,是人工智能企业最密集的地区。上海、杭州与北京、深圳一起,是聚集人工智能企业数量最多的城市,均超过了90家,处于第一梯队。为了最大限度地聚集优势,发挥合力,各种人工智能企业联盟纷纷成立,如2018年7月启动了面向沪苏浙皖的长三角人工智能产业联盟,2019年5月长三角G60科创走廊人工智能产业联盟在上海市松江区成立,2019年10月长三角产业互联网联盟在上海宝山揭牌成立。

人工智能的发展与核心基础技术的突破密切相关,长三角地区的丰富高校资源为此提供了充分支持。如上海借助复旦大学、同济大学、上海交通大学等优质高校资源,人工智能技术力量在全国位居前列。杭州的院校数量、院校实验室或企业实验室的数量仍然与北京、上海和深圳有一定差距,但可以依靠阿里巴巴这一巨头开展人工智能研究。南京的南京大学、合肥的中国科技大学等知名高校也都是长三角推动人工智能产业发展的重要智力来源。

2. 无人驾驶

无人驾驶是人工智能等技术在汽车领域深度应用的产物。据前瞻产业研究院的估计,全球无人驾驶将在2020年形成千亿美元市场。中国近年来在智能驾驶领域强劲增长,据中国汽车工程学会发布的《节能与新能源汽车技术路线图》,2020年中国智能驾驶汽车将达到1 500万辆。在研发端,中国的无人驾驶整体上与世界先

进水平还有一定差距,但在商用端,中国在全球范围内率先将无人驾驶清洁车、无人驾驶电动卡车、无人驾驶快递车投入使用。

长三角是无人驾驶企业研发投入的重心。根据德勤的统计,在全国各城市无人驾驶初创企业研发中心数量上,上海次于北京,居全国第二位,苏州居第四位。因为参与无人驾驶行业的许多企业希望将企业的创新核心部门安排在汽车产业、互联网产业的集聚处,以便更好地参与市场合作,因此上海等地受到开展无人驾驶技术创新活动企业的广泛青睐。

高校是无人驾驶领域的重要创新主体,为企业提供了前瞻性的技术指导和充足的人才资源,甚至许多无人驾驶初创企业本身就是由学生团队或实验室孵化形成的。长三角城市的大学生积极参加代表我国无人驾驶最高水平、规模最大的赛事——"中国智能车未来挑战赛",并取得了优秀成绩。另外,长三角城市还积极为无人驾驶企业划定智能驾驶测试区域与颁布测试牌照。目前,这样做的城市共有18 个,长三角城市就占了 5 席,分别为德清、杭州、常州、无锡、苏州。

3. 智能制造

智能制造是信息技术、智能技术与装备制造技术的深度融合与集成。中国政府 2015 年发布的《中国制造 2025》明确将智能制造作为主攻方向。通过加强顶层设计,开展试点示范、标准体系建设、培育系统解决方案供应商等方式,智能制造的发展取得明显成效,进入高速成长期。2013 年德勤曾调研全国 200 家制造型企业,结果显示中国企业智能制造处在初级阶段,且利润微薄。经过 6 年的快速发展,智能制造产品和服务的盈利能力显著提升。

兼具雄厚的技术与制造基础的长三角,在智能制造领域频频发力。从 2016 年起,江苏省人民政府就与工信部一起共同主办世界智能大会,迄今已举办了四届。浙江则推出产业互联网小镇、智能制造示范基地并成立了中国智能制造研究院。2019 年 7 月,上海市正式发布《上海市智能制造行动计划(2019—2021 年)》,提出推广应用智能制造新模式,实施上海智能制造"十百千"工程(培育 10 家 10 亿元规模的智能制造系统解决方案供应商、100 家智能制造示范工厂和推动 1 000 家规模以上制造企业实施智能化转型),推进长三角智能制造"百千万"工程(建设 100 家国家级智能制造工厂、1 000 家"三省一市"互认级智能制造工厂和推动 1 万家规模以上企业智能化转型),推动 5G 通信、人工智能、大数据及工业互联网等新兴技术和制造业深度融合,打造"一核(以临港为核心)一带(浦东、闵行、嘉定、宝山、松江等近郊产业带)"智能制造产业集群。

根据长三角智能制造协同创新发展联盟 2019 年 10 月发布的《2019 长三角智能制造发展白皮书》,长三角智能制造示范、试点项目数量,智能制造产业园区总量,以及从事高新技术企业科研活动人员的数量,均位于全国前列。通过智能制造引领产业升级,正在成为长三角高质量发展的重点方向。

三、创新未来:一体化引领创新产业协同发展

凭借良好的产业与技术基础,长三角各城市的创新产业百舸争流,发展势头良好。德勤认为,未来长三角创新产业发展应该根据《长江三角洲区域一体化发展规划纲要》要求,走"科创+产业"道路,在如下方面着重发力,协同施策,助力长三角实现"一极(全国发展强劲活跃增长极)三区(全国高质量发展样板区、率先基本实现现代化引领区和区域一体化发展示范区)一高地(新时代改革开放新高地)"这一战略目标。

第一,有针对性地补齐短板,特别是降低上海的创新成本。如前文分析,与国内其他城市相比,创新环境是长三角城市的"短板"。德勤通过进一步研究发现,其中创新氛围(城市"互联网+"氛围)、创新成本(工资水平与写字楼租金)两项指标尤其落后。德勤认为,随着《长江三角洲区域一体化发展规划纲要》大力强调科技创新以及相关政策的落实,长三角的整体创新氛围有望得到提升,但相关城市特别是像上海这样的一线城市在如何降低创新成本方面仍将面临艰巨挑战。该规划纲要提出,上海要提升科技创新策源能力,降低创新成本成为当务之急。德勤建议:进一步落实对创新企业或企业研发中心在用地、房租方面的优惠与补贴政策,加大人才公寓的建设力度与覆盖面,根据不同人才层次给予相应的购房和租房补贴等。

第二,建立全要素的创新资源交流与共享平台,加快推进建设长三角科技创新共同体。长三角城市创新生态各有优劣,要全部把"短板"补齐既不可能,也无必要,那样只会浪费资源,并对长三角一体化协调发展造成损害。因此,优化长三角创新生态今后主要是发挥"合力""合体"的作用。例如,上海拥有众多的科研机构、人才、众创空间与充分的金融资源等,而其他城市则在创新产业基础、政策支持等方面有自己的优势。建议以目前运行的长三角科技资源共享服务平台为基础,以重大科技基础设施和仪器共享为起点,尝试实现仪器与设施共享,信息、人才、资金、专利流动,打造全要素的创新资源共享与服务平台,加快建设科技创新共同体。

第三,依托各地优势及其龙头企业,打造一批世界级的创新产业集群。在长期的发展过程中,长三角的不同地方、不同城市已形成各自的优势。例如,在智能制造方面,上海在汽车、船舶、航空航天领域智能发展较快,江苏在电子信息、生物科技领域走得较前,浙江依托互联网在轻工纺织、电子信息领域有较强优势,安徽在家电、有色金属等领域上领先。今后,长三角各城市应针对现在各自产业优势以及

今后长三角产业协同发展方向,找准自己在长三角创新圈、产业链中的位置,做大优势,回避劣势,以错位竞争的形式实现最大限度的合作与共赢。建议通过长三角合作机制在各新兴产业分别确定一些龙头企业,鼓励其整合上下游企业和科研机构资源,依托其形成覆盖整个长三角甚至全中国的产业链与创新生态圈,打造世界级的创新产业集群。

第四,制定"长三角创新产业地图",加强沪苏浙皖的创新产业规划对接。目前,长三角城市在规范创新产业方面已显示出"各有侧重"的可喜迹象。例如,根据沪、杭两地发布的政策文件,上海旨在对标全球先进,杭州则对标全国领先;上海重在提供创新资源(金融、技术),杭州重在创新应用。但是,在具体的产业规划方面,两地仍有不少重合之处,产业协同仍有很大的改进空间。如上海强调发展智能驾驶、智能机器人、智能硬件、智能软件、人工智能芯片和智能传感器产业等,而杭州则强调智能机器人、智能网联汽车、智能传感器、智能芯片等,两者之间的重合度仍然比较高。为了摸清长三角创新产业分布及各自优势,建议委托相关机构制定"长三角创新产业地图",在此基础上推进各地创新产业规划对接。

Optimizing the Ecosystem for Coordinated Development

—Promoting the Integrated Cooperation of Innovation Stakeholders in the Yangtze River Delta

Deloitte

"Science + Industry" is the formula for successful implementation of innovation-driven development strategy. On 1 December 2019, *the Outline of the Integrated Regional Development of the Yangtze River Delta* (*the Outline*) proposed that an integrated system for regional innovation would be in place in the region by 2025, and be built into a cradle of innovation in China by deepening the integration of innovation and industry chains, as well as strengthening the development of a system for collaborative innovation.

With favorable policy support from government and promising trends elsewhere—a focus on the development of innovation across the world and the vitality of China's innovation ecosystem—the Yangtze River Delta has a historic opportunity to develop by deepening coordinated efforts in science, technology and industry, and building a community of scientific and technological innovation with the joint efforts of all participants.

Accordingly, there is a need for objective evaluation of the innovation ecosystem, existing industrial base and future development trends in innovation across every city in the Yangtze River Delta. This is the only way to optimize the innovation ecosystem in Shanghai and the provinces of Jiangsu, Zhejiang and Anhui, coordinate planning and policy support, and raise the level of integrated development across the region.

I. Innovation ecosystem: The innovation environment & potential of major cities in the Yangtze River Delta

An innovation ecosystem is fundamental to promoting the development of innovative industries, as it reflects the local innovation environment and development potential of a city. In 2019, Deloitte evaluated the innovation ecosystems of major cities in China and found that the leading regional innovation ecosystem was in the Yangtze River Delta. The evaluation used three indicators—institutions, resources and environment (Table 1). Shanghai, Suzhou, Hangzhou, Nanjing and Hefei were the Yangtze River Delta cities evaluated. Shanghai ranked 2nd among 19 cities in China and Hangzhou ranked 4th, both joining the list of 1st-tier cities alongside Beijing, Shenzhen and Guangzhou. Nanjing (6th) and Suzhou (9th) were listed as second-tier cities and Hefei (16th) as a third-tier city.

Table 1　Innovation Ecosystem Evaluation Indicators

Level-1	Level-2	Definition
Institutions	Enterprises	Number of high-tech, China Top 100 internet and unicorn enterprises in a city
	Higher Education Institutions	Number of higher education institutions
	Scientific Research Institutions	Number of key state laboratories
Innovation Resources	Talent	The proportion of AI talent in a city vs. the total amount of AI talent in China
	Innovation Capital	Capital invested in innovation
	Innovation Technology	Number of patent applications
	Space	State-filed mass innovation space
Innovation Environment	Strategies	The number of government policies on innovation
	Basis	Intelligent infrastructure construction, economic competitiveness and sustainable development power
	Climate	Urban "Internet +" innovation climate
	Cost	Cost of innovation for entrepreneurs, including salary and office rents

Source: Deloitte

The detailed evaluation results for cities in the Yangtze River Delta saw

Shanghai listed as a top city (alongside Beijing and Shenzhen) in number of high-tech enterprises. There were 162 unicorns across Beijing, Shanghai, Shenzhen and Hangzhou, accounting for 80 percent of the total in China. Shanghai ranked 2nd and Hangzhou 4th in innovation resources. Beijing, Shanghai, Shenzhen and Hangzhou together were found to have more than 55 percent of the AI talents in China. Shanghai has abundant innovation capital, ranking 2nd in China, and also ranked 3rd in innovation technology. In mass innovation, Shanghai and Beijing again ranked as the top two cities in China, accounting for nearly 20 percent of the total.

Environment is the relatively weaker aspect of innovation in Yangtze River Delta cities. Shanghai ranked 4th in overall innovation power after Shenzhen, Guangzhou and Beijing, with the other four cities in the Yangtze River Delta—Suzhou, Hangzhou, Nanjing and Hefei—ranking 8th, 9th, 14th and 17th out of the 19 cities evaluated. The innovation climate of Shenzhen, policy support in Guangzhou and infrastructure in Beijing are all good examples for Yangtze River Delta cities.

Generally, the Yangtze River Delta performed better than other regions in comprehensive innovation power, despite shortcomings in other aspects. Hangzhou in particular, an emerging innovation city with as much potential as Beijing, Shanghai and Guangzhou, has performed remarkably in

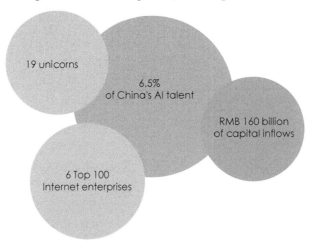

Figure 1　Innovation in Hangzhou

Source: Deloitte

innovation, with a strong pool of AI talent and massive inrush of capital. Hangzhou's AI talent accounts for 6.5 percent of China's total, and in 2018 more than RMB 160 billion flowed into the city. In the first quarter of 2019, Hangzhou's unicorn enterprise population surpassed that of Shenzhen.

II. Innovative industry: Innovation development in the Yangtze River Delta

What innovation-based industries should cities in the Yangtze River Delta focus on? We believe they should look at AI, unmanned driving and Intelligent manufacturing. From a national perspective, cities in the Delta have relative advantages in these fields.

1. AI

The global AI market is expected to experience phenomenal growth in coming years. Gartner predicts the global AI market will exceed USD 5 trillion by 2025. China is one of the most active countries in applying AI technology, and AI has become an important force with a massive influence on economic development. In 2018, China's AI investment or financing reached RMB 131.1 billion, with 597 individual transactions. In 2018, AI financing in China accounted for 60 percent of the global total.

AI enterprises are emerging in China's vast market space. The Yangtze River Delta, Beijing-Tianjin-Hebei Region and Pearl River Delta are AI hubs with the highest concentrations of related enterprises in China. Shanghai and Hangzhou, alongside Beijing and Shenzhen, are the 1st-tier cities with the most AI enterprises in China, together making up more than 90 of the total. Various AI enterprise alliances have been established in China to maximize their collective advantages and extend their joint efforts in AI. The Yangtze River Delta AI Industry Alliance between Shanghai and the provinces of Jiangsu, Zhejiang and Anhui was launched in July 2018, the Yangtze River Delta G60 Corridor AI Industry Alliance was established in Shanghai's Songjiang District in May 2019, and the Yangtze River Delta Industry Internet Alliance was inaugurated in Baoshan District, Shanghai in

October the same year.

AI cannot be developed without breakthroughs in core technology. Thanks to the Yangtze River Delta's rich higher education resources, the AI industry in its cities has received strong support. Shanghai leads in AI technology thanks to its excellent universities, including Fudan, Tongji and Shanghai Jiao Tong. Hangzhou has a relative lack of higher education institutions, labs attached to higher education institutions and enterprise labs compared to its peer cities (Beijing, Shanghai and Shenzhen). However, Hangzhou is still well-placed in AI research given it is home to Alibaba, China's AI giant, Nanjing University, the University of Science & Technology of China in Hefei, and other renowned higher education institutions. These are all important sources of intelligence for the promotion of AI in the Yangtze River Delta.

2. Unmanned driving

Unmanned driving is a product of the deep application of AI and other technologies in the automotive field. According to Qian Zhan Industry Research Institute, the global market for unmanned vehicles will be worth hundreds of billions of dollars by 2020. In recent years, China has experienced strong growth in intelligent driving. According to *the Technology Roadmap for Energy-saving and New Energy Vehicles* by the Society of Automotive Engineers of China (China-SAE), China will have 15 million intelligent vehicles by 2020. In R&D, there is still a gap between China and other advanced global players in unmanned driving technology. However, for commercial use, China was the first country to employee driverless cleaning vehicles, unmanned electric trucks and driverless delivery vehicles.

The Yangtze River Delta is a hotbed of R&D investment in unmanned vehicle enterprises. According to Deloitte statistics, Shanghai ranks 2nd behind Beijing in the number of R&D centers for unmanned vehicle start-ups, and Suzhou ranks 4th. Many players in the unmanned vehicle sector hope to set up core innovation departments based on automobile industry-internet sector convergence centers to enhance market cooperation. Shanghai and adjacent cities are favored by unmanned driving technology innovators.

Higher education institutions are important innovators in unmanned driving, providing enterprises with forward-looking technical guidance and plenty of talent. Many unmanned driving start-ups were incubated from student teams or laboratories at higher education institutions. College students from universities in the Yangtze River Delta participate in "Future Challenge", the highest level and largest unmanned driving technology competition in China, and have achieved excellent results. In addition, cities in the Yangtze River Delta have designated testing zones for intelligent driving and issued licenses for unmanned driving trials. Of the 18 cities in China that have conducted these trials, five are in the Yangtze River Delta (Deqing, Hangzhou, Changzhou, Wuxi, and Suzhou).

3. Intelligent manufacturing

Intelligent manufacturing is the deep fusion and integration of information, intelligent and equipment manufacturing technologies. *Made in China* 2025 issued by the Chinese government in 2015 specified that intelligent manufacturing will be its main area of focus. China's intelligent manufacturing sector can list several remarkable achievements and has entered an era of high-speed growth through efforts to strengthen top-level design, pilot demonstrations and standard system construction, as well as develop system solutions suppliers. According to a survey of 200 manufacturers across China by Deloitte in 2013, the intelligent manufacturing capacity of Chinese companies was still nascent and generated slim profits. Six years later, however, and manufacturers of intelligent products and intelligent services have developed rapidly, with substantial improvements in profitability.

The Yangtze River Delta, a region with technological power and strong manufacturing foundations, has strived to develop intelligent manufacturing. Every year since its first edition in 2016, the People's Government of Jiangsu has held the World Intelligence Congress with China's Ministry of Industry & Information Technology. Zhejiang Province has established its Industrial and Internet Town, Demonstration Base for Intelligent Manufacturing and China

Intelligent Manufacturing Research Institute. In July 2019, Shanghai's Municipal Government released the *Shanghai Intelligent Manufacturing Action Plan (2019—2021)*. This proposes to promote the application of new methods of intelligent manufacturing and implement the "10-100-1,000 Project" to nurture 10 intelligent manufacturing systems solution suppliers worth RMB 1 billion and 100 intelligent manufacturing demonstration factories, as well as promote the intelligent transformation of 1,000 manufacturing enterprises. Regionally, it proposes to build 100 state-level intelligent manufacturing factories, a further 1,000 intelligent manufacturing factories recognized across "three provinces and one city", and promote the intelligent transformation of 10,000 enterprises. Furthermore, to facilitate the deep integration of emerging technologies such as 5G, AI, big data and the industrial internet with manufacturing, it proposes to build the "One Core and One Belt" intelligent manufacturing cluster, which puts Lingang at the core of a suburban industrial belt covering Shanghai's Pudong, Minhang, Jiading, Baoshan and Songjiang districts.

According to *the White Paper on the Development of Intelligent Manufacturing in the Yangtze River Delta 2019* released by the Intelligent Manufacturing Collaborative Innovation & Development Alliance in the Yangtze River Delta, the region has China's largest numbers of intelligent manufacturing demonstration and pilot projects, intelligent manufacturing industrial parks, and personnel engaged in high-tech enterprise scientific research. Leading industrial upgrading through intelligent manufacturing has become the focus of Yangtze River Delta cities' efforts to improve quality.

Ⅲ. Future of innovation: Integrated development of innovative industries through collaborative effort

With sound industrial and technological foundations, innovative businesses in the cities of the Yangtze River Delta engage in healthy competition and have good development momentum. Deloitte believes the development of innovative industries in the region should follow the path of "science and innovation + industry" set out in *the Outline*. This includes a focus on collaboration in policy support to facilitate the Yangtze River Delta achieving its strategic aim of comprising "One Pole" (a dynamic growth center for national development), "Three Areas" (a national model layout for high-quality development, achieving modernization goals, and demonstrating integrated regional development) and "One Highland" (a paradigm of reform and opening up in a new era).

First, targeted efforts should be made to address Shanghai's weaknesses, especially to reduce the city's cost of innovation. As mentioned above, the innovation environment is relatively weak in Yangtze River Delta cities. According to our research, the region's cities lag behind in two particular indicators: innovation climate (urban "Internet +" innovation atmosphere) and cost (salaries and office rents). However, we believe the overall innovation climate in the Yangtze River Delta will improve, given scientific and technological innovation is a highlight of *the Outline* and the implementation of related policies.

Reducing the cost of innovation is still a daunting challenge for the Delta cities, however, especially 1st-tier ones like Shanghai. According to *the Outline*, it is imperative that Shanghai reduce its cost of innovation before improving its science and technology innovation capacity. Deloitte suggests Shanghai further implement preferential policies and subsidies for land use and rents for innovative enterprises and corporate R&D centers; invest more effort in constructing apartments for talent and widen the availability thereof; and provide housing and rent subsidies to different levels of talent.

Second, a comprehensive platform for exchanging and sharing innovation resources should be established, and more effort should be made to accelerate the construction of a science and technology innovation community in the Yangtze River Delta. Each city in the region has its advantages and disadvantages in innovation ecosystem. It is not possible or necessary to make up for all their shortcomings, as this would waste resources and hinder integrated and coordinated development. Therefore, efforts to optimize its innovation ecosystem should focus on how to develop "joint efforts" and "an integrated community". Shanghai has a surfeit of scientific research institutions, talent, mass innovation spaces and financial resources, and other cities in the Delta have distinct advantages in innovative industry foundations and policy support. Collectively, they should seek to share resources and promote the flow of information, talent, funding and patents based on existing science and technology resources and shared services platforms, starting with major science and technology infrastructures and instruments, to build a comprehensive platform for sharing innovation resources and services and accelerate the construction of a science and technology innovation community.

Third, build world-class innovative industry clusters based on local advantages and leading enterprises. Many parts of the Yangtze River Delta have accumulated advantages during their lengthy development. In intelligent manufacturing, Shanghai has developed rapidly in autos, shipbuilding and aerospace; Jiangsu Province has advanced electronic information and biotechnology sectors; Zhejiang Province has strong advantages in light industry, textiles and internet-based electronic information; and Anhui Province has taken the lead in home appliances and non-ferrous metals.

In the coming years, each city in the Yangtze River Delta should pinpoint its position in the innovation ecosystem and industrial chain of the Yangtze River Delta based on its extant advantages and coordinated development of industries in the region. This can maximize the results of cooperation and achieve mutually beneficial results by leveraging each city's advantages and avoiding disadvantages. Leading enterprises in each emerging industry should be identified through the cooperation mechanism, and they should be encouraged to integrate the resources of upstream and downstream enterprises and scientific research institutions. This would create an industry chain and innovation ecosystem covering the whole Yangtze River Delta and even the whole of China, leading to the creation of a world-class cluster of industrial innovation.

Finally, a map of innovation industries in the Yangtze River Delta should be drawn up to strengthen planning and collaboration efforts across Shanghai and the provinces of Jiangsu, Zhejiang and Anhui. The region's cities have shown encouraging signs of each having a different focus in the regulation of innovative industries. For example, according to policy documents issued by the local governments of Shanghai and Hangzhou, Shanghai targets regulation at benchmarking innovative industries against international leaders, whereas Hangzhou targets domestic leaders as a benchmark. Shanghai focuses on finance and technology innovation resources and Hangzhou emphasizes innovative applications. However, there are still overlaps between the two cities' industrial plans, and much room for better coordination. The overlap between Shanghai and Hangzhou in AI is one example. Both cities emphasize intelligent driving, intelligent robots, chips and sensors, with Shanghai additionally focusing on AI hardware and software. We suggest authorities and institutions draw a map of innovative industries in the Yangtze River Delta to establish their distribution and advantages, thereby facilitating region-wide planning and collaboration.

从长三角产业协同新动向
看未来着力点

戴德梁行

2018 年首届进博会上,长三角一体化上升到国家战略,2019 年迎来了长三角一体化的大年,就在 2019 年 12 月 1 日,中共中央、国务院印发《长江三角洲区域一体化发展规划纲要》,对这个话题的关注度又进入到了一个新高度,各方都从自己的角度出发,提供了很多有益的洞察。戴德梁行也从自己服务中国城市发展和产业发展 26 年的经验出发,以"产业协同"作为出发点,深度关注这个话题。2019 年 5 月,戴德梁行与上海社会科学院联合推出了《长三角一体化产业协同发展》白皮书。

一、产业转出

转出长三角的产业主要有两类,一类是被动迁出的类型,主要是一些"三高一低"产业,表现为高投入、高能耗、高污染、低效益,如纺织、压铸件、化工、印染等。这类行业基本搬离原产地之后,多数离开长三角去了中国内地或者东南亚。另外一类是一些需要规模化用地的高端产业门类,比如电子信息、汽车零配件等,这类产业多数是从长三角的核心城市迁往长三角的次级城市,比如常熟、盐城等地(图1)。

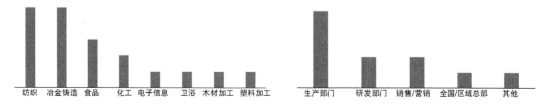

图 1 谁在搬离长三角

资料来源:戴德梁行分析

从长三角普遍的产业转出情况来看,主要的转出环节在整体上以价值链低端的生产功能为主。但一个不容忽视的现象是,在华东地区部分三线城市,存在总部、研发、销售等功能迁出去往上海、南京等一线城市回流的压力。

我们接触过的某高端外资汽车整车企业,原本把生产和研发都放在汽车产业链集聚度较高的三线城市,但是后来受制于当地科研能力薄弱、开放度欠缺、外国高管的配套跟不上等问题,研发可能要迁回上海。留不住外资企业高管、科研人才等方面是长三角三四线城市面临的痛点。

二、产业转入

目前长三角区域重点迁入的门类,主要集中在装备制造、电子信息、汽车等技术密集型产业。得益于长三角巨大的消费市场,高端食品、快消品等产业也是这几年重点进入长三角的行业领域(图2)。

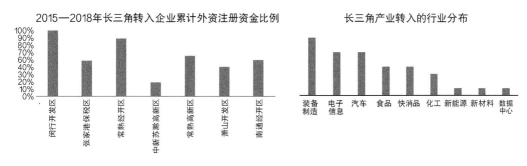

图2 谁在涌入长三角

资料来源:戴德梁行分析

我们选取长三角的一些标杆性开发区,从过去几年招商的情况来看,外资仍然是流入长三角最集中的类型,上海及经济发展较为成熟的苏南地区仍是外资企业发展的主战场。我们这个数据截至2019年第一季度,从外资来源来看,美国、德国、中国香港和日本是占据前几位的。预计中美贸易摩擦对这些数据还是会有一些影响。

三、产业流动影响要素

通过我们与各开发区的问卷调查和访谈,我们发现吸引企业进入长三角的影响因子,主要是对长三角圈层的区位交通、产业集聚的普遍认同。区位交通是吸引企业转入的首要因素。京沪和沪宁高速沿线的苏南地带,是最初承接上海产业转入的主要区域。随着高速公路网络、跨江跨海大桥和高铁的建设,南通、盐城等地已逐步加入承接上海产业转入的前沿阵地。对于这些城市来说,比上海、杭州等核心城市较低的企业成本、给予企业的政策优惠、用工保障等,是吸引产业转入的重要因素(图3)。

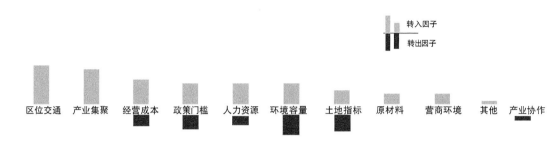

图3　长三角产业转移的影响因子

资料来源:戴德梁行分析

从转出因素来看,目前长三角城市群的环境容量收紧,环保安监多实行"一票否决制",环保问题成为长三角企业迁出最普遍的原因。土地指标紧缺、投资强度门槛提高、政府明确招商产业导向等因素,进一步加速部分企业外迁,寻求更适宜的发展环境。此外,部分行业随着上下游企业的迁出,迫于行业协同的需要,跟随供应链迁出原产地。最后,成本及招人问题,也是长三角企业迁出的重要影响因子。

四、上海产业区域协同

毋庸置疑,上海是整个长三角的龙头城市,在长三角一体化产业协同过程中,上海表现出自身的一些现象。上海的产业流动呈现出有意思的几个特点,一个特点是上海的外迁产业分化出两种截然不同的转移方式。一种是一些行业龙头企业具备空间布局能力、自主创新实力,但上海没有足够的土地整合生产研发,同时其他城市发出邀请,从而企业选择迁出上海。另一种是"三高一低"产业项目被淘汰,这类转出不可逆转。

另一个不容忽视的特点是,国际优质产业要素在加速向上海集聚,总部经济对上海青睐有加,持续加码。从国际产业分工与转移来看,以特斯拉、西门子医疗等为代表的企业落地上海,上海与全球的高端制造网络联系更加紧密。同时,高新制造业研发中心对上海的青睐度提升,2018年新增外资研发中心15家,成为上海嵌入全球创新网络的重要接口,2018年上海新增跨国公司地区总部45家,新增亚太区总部18家,上海已成为跨国公司全球网络的重要节点和增长点。内资科技企业如腾讯在上海设立华东总部;房地产总部抢滩上海,以闽系、浙系、西南等地的房地产企业如中骏、阳光城、东原等为代表,扎堆落户虹桥等枢纽商务区;同时以中国中铁、中邮集团旗下的中邮科技等国企、央企为代表,设立华东区域总部或迁址到上海。虹桥地区成为整个长三角一体化发展的一个门户高地和样板。

五、长三角城市群产业投资环境指数

从产业投资环境指数这一综合指标的评价结果来看,上海在长三角的领头羊地位稳固。南京、苏州、杭州位列第二梯队。第三梯队的代表为无锡、宁波、南通等江浙城市。这些城市近年发展势头迅猛,其中长江以北的南通等城市经济增长亮眼,大有反超之势(图4)。

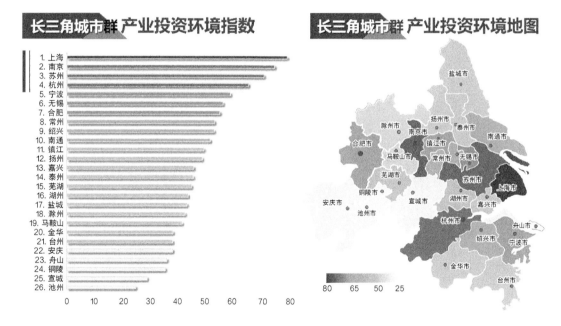

图4　长三角城市群产业投资环境指数及地图

资料来源:戴德梁行分析

六、挑战与建议

目前长三角一体化面临的挑战,主要还是来自地区壁垒。长三角一体化上升为国家战略,中共中央、国务院印发《长江长三角洲区域一体化发展规划纲要》,长三角区域合作办公室成立之后,对于打破地域藩篱,我们多了一些期待。我们主要从协助政府产业发展和招商的角度,提出以下四条建议。

(1)长三角跨区域政策普惠性弱,政策一致性亟待跨省协调。

（2）长三角缺乏统一的市场体系，需统一标准，提高合作效率。

（3）公共服务的区域一体化断裂，需打通跨区服务平台关卡。

（4）对标国际最高标准，建设一体化信用体系。

我们对于长三角一体化产业协同中的区域产业流动，持有几个核心观点：第一，环境因素是产业迁出的普遍因素；第二，影响产业迁进的三大要素是区位交通、产业集聚和人才优势；第三，地区产业发展动力不平衡，核心城市群优势明显。

对于长三角产业协同的优化发展，我们提以下三个着力点：第一，协同便捷城际交通网；第二，共建国际科创中心；第三，构建世界级产业集群。

New Trends and Future Plans for Synergistic Industrial Development in the Yangtze River Delta

Cushman & Wakefield

At the first China International Import Expo in 2018, the integrated development of the Yangtze River Delta (YRD) region was promoted to a national strategy. In 2019, the YRD's integration has been a hot topic. *The Outline of the Integrated Regional Development of the Yangtze River Delta* was jointly issued by the Communist Party of China Central Committee and the State Council on December 1, 2019, pushing the topic to a new level of importance. Experts in related fields discussed the theme in detail from different aspects and shared their valuable insights. Cushman & Wakefield, with 26 years of experience in serving China's urban development and industrial development, also paid close attention to this topic in the context of synergistic industrial development. In May 2019, Cushman & Wakefield, together with the Shanghai Academy of Social Sciences, released a joint white paper on Synergistic Industrial Development in the Yangtze River Delta.

Ⅰ. Industry transfers out of the YRD region

Basically, there are two types of industrial transfer. The first is passive migration, mainly encompassing high-input, high-energy-consumption, heavy-pollution and low-efficiency industries, such as textile, die-casting, chemical, printing and dyeing. Most of these industries have moved out of the YRD region to non-coastal or Southeast Asian areas. A second type includes high-end industries that require large-scale space or facilities, such as electronics and information technology, and auto parts. Most of these industries have transferred from the core cities of the YRD region to second tier cities such as Changshu and Yancheng (Figure 1).

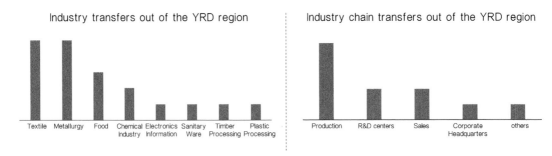

Figure 1   Industry transfers out of the YRD region

Source: Cushman & Wakefield

In general, most industries that have transferred out are at the low-end of the value chain, primarily with production functions. One notable phenomenon is with corporate headquarters, R&D centers and sales functions moving out of Tier-3 cities in East China and relocating to core cities such as Shanghai and Nanjing, creating back-flow pressure to these cities.

One example is with a high-end foreign automotive enterprise which previously located its production and R&D facilities in Tier-3 cities with a high automotive supply chain presence. However, weaker scientific research capacity, lack of market openness and insufficient supporting facilities for foreign executives may it may return its R&D center to Shanghai. An inability to attract and retain foreign enterprise executives and research talent remains a pain point for Tier-3 and 4 cities.

II. Industry transfers into the YRD region

At present, the key categories of industries transferring into the YRD region are concentrated in technology-intensive fields such as equipment manufacturing, information technology and automotive. High-end food products and FMCG sectors have also been key entrants into the YRD region in recent years, attracted by the huge consumer market (Figure 2).

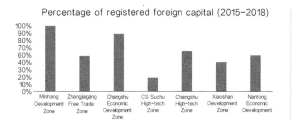 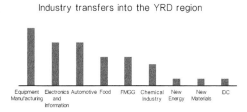

Figure 2   Industry transfers into the YRD region

Source: Cushman & Wakefield

We selected some benchmark development zones for the YRD. In terms of investment inflows in the past few years, foreign capital remains robust. As of Q1 2019, the U.S., Germany, Hong Kong SAR and Japan are the top sources of international investment. It is expected that the US-China trade dispute will have some impact on these Exhibits.

III. Factors affecting industrial flow

According to a survey and interviews carried out by Cushman & Wakefield, recognition of the YRD region's transportation network locational advantages and industrial clusters are the main drivers attracting enterprises to enter this market, and the transport network is the primary factor. The Southern Jiangsu area along the Beijing-Shanghai Express Railway and HuNing Expressway is the key area for the initial transfer of industries from Shanghai. With the construction of the expressway network, the sea-crossing bridge and the high-speed railway, cities including Nantong and Yancheng have now joined the vanguard in undertaking the transfer of industry from Shanghai. These cities' lower enterprise costs, preferential policies and secure workforces, when compared with core cities such as Shanghai and Hangzhou, are important factors to attract industry transfers (Figure 3).

Given the tightening of environmental capacity and the "one-vote veto system" implemented in environmental safety supervision in the YRD, environmental issues have become the most common reason for those

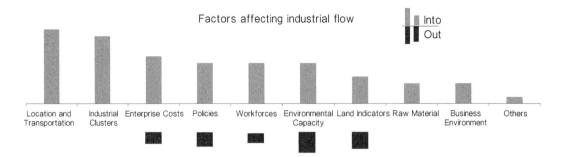

Figure 3　Factors affecting industrial flow

Source: Cushman & Wakefield

industries moving out. Factors such as the shortage of land indicators, the raised threshold of investment intensity, and the government's clear guidance on industry investment orientation have further accelerated the relocation of some enterprises who are seeking a more favorable development environment. What's more, with the migration of upstream and downstream enterprises, some industries are forced to follow the supply chain as it moves from its origin. Finally, costs and recruitment issues are also important factors affecting the relocation of enterprises in the YRD region.

Ⅳ. Coordinated development of regional industry in Shanghai

Shanghai is undoubtedly the leading city in the process of synergistic industrial development in the YRD region. There are several interesting characteristics of the industrial flow in Shanghai.

Firstly, industry transferring out of Shanghai has diverged into two distinct modes. One comprises leading enterprises in specific industries, which have spatial layout abilities and independent innovation strengths. Shanghai offers insufficient land to integrate production and R&D facilities, while other cities can offer opportunities to these enterprises. And the other is the elimination of the high-input, high-energy-consumption, heavy-pollution and low-efficiency industries, and this kind of transfer is irreversible.

Secondly, growing numbers of international high-quality industrial elements are entering Shanghai at an accelerating pace, and the headquarters economy is growing. From the perspective of the international industrial division and industry transfer, companies such as Tesla, Siemens Healthineers have entered the Shanghai market and extended their connections with the global high-end manufacturing network.

In the meantime, as a preferred destination for advanced manufacturing R&D centers, 15 new international R&D centers were established in Shanghai in 2018, representing an important interface with the global innovation network.

Also in 2018, 45 new multinational regional headquarters and 18 new APAC headquarters were set up in Shanghai, with the city playing an increasingly important role in the global network for MNCs.

Domestic technology companies including Tencent have set up their East China headquarters in Shanghai, as have real estate companies from Fujian, Zhejiang and southwest cities. For example SCE Group, Yango and Dowell Real Estate have established their HQs in hub business district such as Hongqiao submarket.

State-owned enterprises including China Railway, China Post, and the Postal Science Research and Planning Institute have also set up or moved their East China regional headquarters to Shanghai. The Hongqiao hub has become a gateway and model for the integrated development of the whole YRD region.

V. YRD agglomeration industrial investment environment index

In terms of the assessment of the comprehensive index of the industrial investment environment, Shanghai is the leading city in the YRD region. Nanjing, Suzhou and Hangzhou are ranked in the second tier, while Wuxi, Ningbo, Nantong and other cities in Jiangsu and Zhejiang Provinces are in the third tier. In recent years the cities in the third tier, especially Nantong, have been growing rapidly and have a bright economic growth potential and a strong likelihood of catching up with the first and second tier cities (Figure 4).

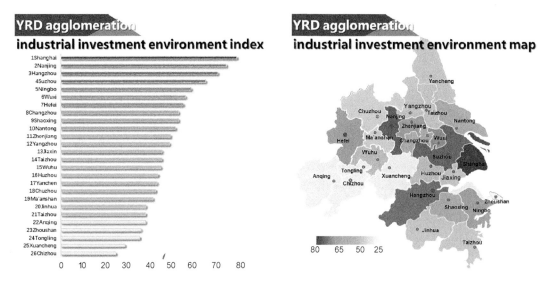

Figure 4　YRD agglomeration industrial investment environment index and map

Source: Cushman & Wakefield

Ⅵ. Challenges and suggestions

Until now challenges to the YRD's integration have mainly stemmed from region-level obstacles. The YRD integrated development has now been raised to the level of a national strategy, and an outline has been jointly issued by the Communist Party of China Central Committee and the State Council. After the establishment of the Regional Cooperation Office of the Yangtze River Delta, the region-level barriers are expected to be overcome. From the point of view of assisting the industrial development and investment environment we suggest four key points:

(1) Consistency of cross-regional inclusive policy in the YRD region needs to be coordinated urgently.

(2) The unification of city market systems and effectiveness of cooperation needs to be strengthened.

(3) Barriers from the cross-district service platform should be overcome.

(4) An integrated credit system needs to be built to the highest

international standards.

We would like to share several views on the synergistic industrial development in the Yangtze River Delta. First, environmental-related factors are the common drivers of industrial transfer. Second, the three factors affecting the industrial migration are transport locational advantages, industrial agglomeration and workforce/talent advantages. Third, momentum of regional industrial development is unbalanced, with the core city clusters having obvious advantages.

For the optimization and development of the YRD's industry coordination, we propose the following three focal points. First, to coordinate and facilitate intercity transportation networks. Second, to jointly build international science and innovation centers. Third, to develop a world-class industrial cluster.

Future Industrial Opportunities in the Yangtze River Delta

长三角未来产业机遇

长三角一体化
——超级产业集群正当时

罗兰贝格管理咨询

改革开放四十年来,通过大力招商引资和合理运用产业园发展模式,长三角区域已经发展成为我国最具经济活力、创新力和对外吸引力的区域之一。长三角的价值与影响力早已不再局限于所在地区,而是直接拉动了长江经济带和沿海经济带的联动发展,更是在中国改革开放和经济发展模式创新中起着带头示范与引领的作用。

随着中国科技产业的迅猛发展,以及中国企业在管理实践上的推陈出新,中国本土经济的创新力已逐步趋近于国际发达国家的水平。中国企业完成资本积累后,为巩固自身的竞争优势、提高利润率水平,存在着技术升级和产业升级的切实迫切需求。另一方面,虽然长三角地区富集中国最优秀的科研实力和最为绵密的产业生态,但是这类资源的分布并不均衡。

这就对长三角地区的经济治理模式提出了更高的要求,即如何才能够进一步优化本地区资源要素,特别是提升技术的流动性,通过合理配置,让科技与产业之间发生有效互动,最终实现高质量的经济发展?

长三角一体化并非为了一体化而一体化,而是随着经济发展的实际情况来实现众望所归的制度创新。我们认为,超级产业集群战略将是实现这一目标的重要路径。

一、超级产业集群

受供应链有效经济半径的影响,产业发展往往在地理范畴呈现聚集的特征。长三角地区的产业集群在发展上主要经历了两个时代,分别是伴随着改革开放而逐渐形成的以汽车、机械制造、精密加工、电子电器、轻工小商品为主的传统产业集群,以及随着高科技与信息技术产业发展而形成的医药、微电子、大飞机、互联网和人工智能等尖端技术产业集群。前者以产业为主,以市场需求拉动技术的商业化应用,而后者则更多地体现出技术创新对新市场领域的开拓与推动。

然而,随着技术在跨行业应用上的拓展,以及数字经济向各行业的快速渗透,各个产业集群孤立发展的模式不再适用,需要进行跨区域、跨产业集群的资源配置。实现这种发展的根本动力在于,以人才为载体的技术创新需要得到资本和商业模式的支持,需要在多个产业生态得以实现商业化应用。例如,发端于上海航空科研的碳纤维技术可以快速应用在浙江的汽车产业;生命科学的科研机构基于上海大光源等重大科学工程的研究成果,可以迅速转化到南京的医药企业和癌症治疗方案的研究中;基于合肥的声音信息人工智能技术可以有效运用于水下信号分析,进而转化为我们对长三角地区生态资源的保护和开发技术。

超级产业集群就是这样一种资源配置的组织构架,它不是长三角不同产业集群间松散的联盟,而是以技术产业化为主轴,通过长三角地区统一的衡量标准、组织构架、联合项目等手段,让跨三省一市产业集群中的教育、科研、企业、资本、初创企业、商会等要素进行有效沟通、增强它们之间的互信,从而让任意集群中的要素在进入其他集群时,都能迅速融入并且产生黏性。它可以表现为科研与产业资源所组成的跨地区产业集群,也可以表现为多个同时具有科研与产业资源的产业集群所组成的联合体。

作为多个产业集群之间的协调性制度构架,超级产业集群并不是一个新物种,它在欧洲有着近二十年的发展,并根据不同产业的特征,演化出三种模式:龙头企业协调型、联盟协调型,以及超国家协调型。这三种模式互为补充,为技术产业化和产业生态化提供基础,也为长三角的超级产业集群构建提供思路。

龙头企业协调型是较早的一种做法。典型案例是伴随着空客(Airbus)的诞生,而孕育而生的航空超级产业集群。它以空客具体的航空、航天器机型为龙头,拉动各国已有航空产业链上下游产业集群的协同发展。这种以空客为核心的协调能力,为整个产业生态带来溢出效应,增强企业之间合作的信任基础。例如汉堡的内饰生产商可以较为容易地与图卢兹的通用航空公司展开研发,并且找到彼此共同的验证手段与机构,进而获得欧洲航空安全监管方的适航许可。

另一种,则是以欧洲健康中轴线(Health Axis Europe)为代表的联盟协调型超级产业集群。它是欧洲大陆在生命健康领域技术最尖端的比利时鲁汶、德国海德堡、荷兰马斯特里赫特,以及丹麦的哥本哈根四大生命科技产业集群所组成的战略联盟,增强产业集群各要素间的信任基础,从而帮助这些产业集群研发成果实现跨地区转化,并为跨国投资人拓展科技网络。

与此同时，超国家协调型产业集群亦不可或缺，欧盟建立创新与科技研究所（European Institute of Innovation and Technology），它围绕 8 大产业在欧洲建立超级产业集群，为产业合作提供公共资源、消弭地区性发展差异。它的基础在于欧盟一体化发展时所展开的教育和科研一体化项目，即欧盟境内的联合硕士项目——Erasmus Mundus，以及以高科技战略为核心的研发共同体项目——地平线 2020（Horizon 2020），为产业的人才流动奠定基础。

与欧洲老牌工业国不同，长三角的产业集群虽然有产业上的集群形态，但大多数产业集群缺少科研要素。虽然许多地区试图引入优质科研资源，例如苏州引入中国科学院纳米研究所从而大大促进了当地的微电子产业发展，但是我们的科技发展和传统产业之间的互动较弱，这在一定程度上制约了新兴产业进一步发展所必要的整体工业实力。

因此，我们在打造长三角超级产业集群的时候，一方面要加强各产业集群自身的内功修炼，另一方面要实现有效的跨区资源配置。

二、长三角的三步走

对比欧洲的经验，超级产业集群的基础在于三个方面：一是各地对于产业集群概念的认知趋近；二是各产业集群的发展水平相当；三是欧盟和成员国政府将产业集群或超级产业集群作为科技政策的重要抓手。而长三角在这三个层面的基础均不完备，因此，我们认为长三角可因地制宜，考虑三步走战略：(1)建标杆、塑共识；(2)补要素、建构架；(3)创龙头、树品牌，采取自上而下和自下而上相结合的方法，充分调动各要素的积极性。

首先，建标杆。长三角需要建立产业集群的评价体系，从而为各地产业集群之间打造一个对话的平台。它不是以某行业的 GDP 为衡量标准，而是以某一支配性技术为线索，对大学、研究所、初创企业、中小企业、龙头企业、孵化机构的完备性和技术先进性为指标。因此，一个城市可有多个产业集群，例如，南京可以同时拥有以扬子石化和南京工业大学为核心的化工产业集群、以中航工业南京机电科技和南京航空航天大学为核心的航空产业集群，等等。对这些产业集群的各个要素维度进行打分，以便了解彼此发展的阶段。

长三角地区可以根据产业的技术等级，发起尖端技术产业集群战略，作为高科技战略的产业化落地方案。由长三角一体化办公室根据上述指标建立一套评价体系，以此度量长三角各地的产业集群，并围绕生命健康、移动出行、智能制造、信息科技等主要产业发展方向，通过"申报—评选"的方式，从中选出优质产业集群进行扶持,以此作为发展标杆,增强业界对产业集群建立共识,并为长三角地区进一步的科技政策联动打下基础。至于申报单位,不同产业集群可以组成联合申报体,但是核心在于,申报主体需要同时具备从科研到市场转化的各个要素。

其次,塑共识。需要建立长三角地区经济地图与创新地图,从而增强这一地区相关资源的可视化。以德国为例,在国家层面,德国建立工业4.0信息地图,将全德与工业4.0相关的企业、研究所、大学、检测机构、示范性工厂等信息均做成地图形式,并辅以案例资料。在城市发展层面,柏林建立城市经济地图,涵盖经济行为体、行会组织、研究机构以及楼宇的能效与有效光伏面积等经济信息。

长三角地区通过数十年的一体化发展,在基础建设、信息流通、人员流动、产业基础、制度构架等方面都已打下坚实基础。下一步的目标在于,如何能够在当前多个产业集群之间建立纽带,从而实现深层次的要素流动,促进市场经济活力,促进企业创新行为。虽然企业和高校对不同城市的核心资源有一定的了解,地方政府负责专利工作的部门也花大力气试图推动专利成果转化,但是目前的城市外宣还集中在政务活动的推广,距集群要素资源的市场化宣传和资源的有效使用尚有一定发展空间。

第三,补要素。针对要素不充分的产业集群,提供有针对性的扶持政策,从而帮助其快速补差。德国在20世纪90年代意识到自己在生命科技产业发展上与英美的差距之后,从1995年至今,先后实行了旨在集群组织能力建设的BioRegio政策、以科研人员职业发展和初创型企业扶持为目标的BioFuture政策、以支持初创企业和大学共同发起项目为核心的BioChance政策,以及系统性发展产业集群的尖端产业集群政策(Cutting Edge Cluster)和锁定增强国际化合作能力的政策。

德国的这套循序渐进的政策是根据自己的发展经验逐渐摸索出来的。长三角地区不同产业集群之间的差异很大,因此,也无须和德国模式一一对应。例如上海、南京、杭州、合肥四地的高等教育与科研资源富集,而昆山则是外企集聚,嘉兴、宁波多为民营中小企业。有些地市可以根据自己情况选择补差,有些地市可以根据自己产业的技术特征和其他地市的资源展开合作,组成跨地区的产业集群,同样实现科技对接产业的功能。

第四,建构架。帮助产业集群建立一套有效的决策与管理构架,从而提高产业集群能力水平。欧洲的产业集群在组织构架上一般分为两层,即议事层和执行层。议事层由集群内核心参与者构成,包括政府、研究机构和企业,它们一是对产业集群的发展方向等重大事项做出决议,二是调动自身所在机构的资源,为产业集群发展做出贡献。在执行层,往往采取矩阵式的管理构架,一方面有联合研发、职业教育、初创孵化、市场推广几个功能模块,另一方面根据本产业集群特色制定具体的技术商业化方向。

对于长三角超级产业集群来说,当前各地均建设大量国家级开发区或地区性产业园。然而,相关园区的管理以基础设施、税收减免、土地优惠、物业设施为主,在集群相关要素能力和黏性上的能力均有所不足。若超级产业集群采取相似的组织管理构架,可以大大降低彼此的沟通成本,提高合作效率。

第五,创龙头。发起跨长三角的旗舰型科研项目,从而为技术外溢的市场化起到龙头作用。以空客为例,发起 A380 项目后,欧洲多个产业集群积极"招商"。以航空内饰产业为核心的汉堡地区为了竞标 A380 客舱大部段的组装项目,不仅建立航空应用性研究中心,作为碳纤维航空辅材加工技术的公共研发平台,还建立汉堡航空训练中心,为在读的学生和在职的工程师提供职业教育培训,让他们的知识结构从铝合金加工转向碳纤维。

长三角地区有许多共同的课题有待展开超级产业集群合作。通过项目促进产业界和科研界的互动,避免大学的研发停留在实验室里。例如围绕跨界水系治理可以展开研发龙头项目,针对传感器等智能设备一方面展开科学研究,一方面拉动与此相关的设备制造和人工智能初创企业发展,并共同实现生态可持续。而航空产业更是可以围绕南京、上海的科研资源和无锡、宁波的产业资源建立期间项目,同时拉动邻省江西的通航产业资源。

第六,树品牌。打造科研国际化品牌,从而提高该地区与国际科研以及产业界的融入程度。目前,科技部、中科院以及相关大学都在探索科研国际化的道路,希望通过中国对科研的投资,以大科学工程、产业腹地以及创新生态与资本为杠杆,进一步增强我国科研产业与国际接轨。目前,合肥、上海、南京、苏州等地均设有大科学装置,但是它们的国际推广程度依然较低,鲜有国际科研课题组进驻展开研究。

因此,长三角超级产业集群可以打造科研品牌,结合各尖端科技与新经济领域特征,一方面通过参加海外高科技展会的方式推广国际知名度,另一方面可以就相关课题发起国际研究项目。与此同时,帮助相关高校积极参与欧盟地平线 2020 战略项目,并与欧盟创新与科技研究所旗下超级产业集群和欧洲一流科技产业集群建立沟通机制,进一步提高国际融入程度。

三、互动是互信的关键

在工业园时代,地方政府的核心工作是招商引资。虽然政府在经济发展上付出了艰辛的努力,但是毕竟优质资源有限,招商的边际效益越来越低。更有甚者,往往造成地区之间,甚至同一城市的不同板块之间的恶性竞争,并阻碍长三角一体化。

因此,我们所提出的超级产业集群,其核心在于两个层面:其一,通过提高各地市对产业集群发展理念的共识,修炼内功,提升政府在科技产业发展中的行政管理能力,提高产业界和学术界之间的互动意识与互动能力;其二,通过相似的管理构架以及旗舰型项目的带动作用,让超级产业集群间的各要素充分发生互动,从而建立互信关系,真正提高要素的流动性和经济与社会价值。

受产业发展时代性因素的影响,中国的经济发展越来越呈现出明显的区域特征,并在此基础上呈现出区域经济一体化的趋势。我们希望,通过长三角一体化的实践与管理迭代,发展出具有全国推广力的制度模式创新,让中国的科研与产业紧密结合,真正实现经济的高质量发展。

The Integration of the Yangtze River Delta

—Super Cluster Rises on Time

Roland Berger

Over the past 40 years of China's Reform and Opening-up, the Yangtze River Delta has been developing into one of the most economically vibrant, innovative and attractive regions in China by stepping up efforts to attract investment and applying industrial park development model. The value and influence of the Yangtze River Delta is no longer confined to the local region, but directly drive the joint development of the Yangtze River Economic Belt and the Coastal Economic Belt. Besides, the Yangtze River Delta plays a leading role in China's Reform and Opening-up and the economic development models' innovation.

With the rapid development of China's technology industry and the Chinese enterprises' innovation in management practices, China has been catching up with the developed countries in the world in terms of the economic innovation. Chinese enterprises have urgent needs for the technological and industrial upgrade to consolidate their own competitive advantages and improve profitability after their completion of capital accumulation. Although the Yangtze River Delta is rich in China's best scientific research resources and the densest industrial ecology, the distribution of such resources is uneven.

This puts forward higher requirements for the economic governance model of the Yangtze River Delta, i.e. how to further optimize the resources of the region, especially to improve the mobility of technology, and to make effective interaction between science and technology and the industry through reasonable allocation so as to ultimately achieve high-quality economic development?

The integration of the Yangtze River Delta is not for the sake of integration, but for the institutional innovation that is widely expected along with the actual situation of economic development. It is believed that Super Cluster strategy will be an important way to achieve this goal.

Ⅰ. Super Cluster

Affected by the effective economic radius of the supply chain, the development of the industry often presents a characteristic of geographical aggregation. The cluster development in the Yangtze River Delta has mainly experienced two stages, namely the traditional cluster stage and cutting-edge technology cluster stage. The former, mainly composed of automotive, machinery manufacturing, precision processing, electronic and electrical, light industrial commodity, etc. and gradually formed along with the Reform and Opening-up, is dominated by the industries and drives the commercial application of technology based on market demand; while the latter, mainly composed of pharma, microelectronics, large aircraft, Internet, artificial intelligence, etc., and formed along with the development of high-tech and information technology industries, reflects the development and promotion of new market segments based on technological innovation.

However, with the technological expansion in cross-industry applications and the rapid penetration of the digital economy into various industries, the mode of isolated development of each cluster is no longer applicable, thus cross-region and cross-cluster resource allocation is required. The fundamental driving force for achieving such development is that talent-based technological innovation can be commercialized in multiple industrial ecologies with the support of capital and business models. For example, carbon fiber technology originated from the aviation scientific research in Shanghai can be quickly applied to the automotive industry in Zhejiang Province; the research results of major scientific projects such as SSRF

(Shanghai Synchrotron Radiation Facility) conducted by life science research institutions can be quickly adapted to pharmaceutical companies and cancer treatment research programs in Nanjing; voice information AI technology in Hefei can be effectively used for underwater signal analysis and then transformed into the protection and development technology for ecological resources in the Yangtze River Delta.

Super Cluster is such an organizational structure of resource allocation. It is not a loose alliance among different clusters in the Yangtze River Delta, but a cluster with a focus on technology industrialization, which promotes effective communication and enhances mutual trust among education, scientific research, enterprises, capital, start-ups and chambers of commerce in the Yangtze River Delta by means of unified measurement, organizational structure, joint projects, etc.; as a result, the exchange of key elements among clusters becomes fast and the "stickiness" between each other can be developed. It can demonstrate as a cross-region cluster composed of scientific research and industrial resources, or a combination of multiple clusters with both.

As a coordinated institutional framework among multiple clusters, Super Cluster is not a brand-new topic, but has developed in Europe for nearly two decades and has evolved into three models according to the characteristics of different industries, namely Leading Enterprise Coordination, Alliance Coordination and Supranational Coordination. These three models are complementary to each other, laying the foundation for technology industrialization and industrial ecology and providing ideas for the construction of Super Cluster in the Yangtze River Delta.

Leading Enterprise Coordination is an earlier practice. A typical case is the aviation Super Cluster formed with the birth of Airbus. Taking the specific aviation and spacecraft models of Airbus as the leader, it promotes the coordinated development of upstream and downstream clusters in existing aviation industry chains in various countries. The Airbus-centric coordination capability brings spillover effects to the entire industrial ecology and strengthens the trust for cooperation among enterprises. For example,

Hamburg's interior manufacturers can easily carry out R&D with General Aviation of Toulouse, and find common verification methods and institutions to obtain airworthiness permits from European aviation safety regulators.

Another type of Super Cluster is Alliance Coordination represented by Health Axis Europe. It is a strategic alliance of the four major cutting-edge life science and technology clusters in Europe, including Leuven in Belgium, Heidelberg in Germany, Maastricht in Netherlands and Copenhagen in Denmark. It strengthens the foundation of trust among clusters, and therefore promotes the cross-region transformation of clusters' R&D results and the expansion of the technology network for multinational investors.

Meanwhile, Supranational Coordination Super Cluster is also indispensable. The European Union established the European Institute of Innovation and Technology, which built Super Cluster centered on eight major industries in Europe to provide public resources for industrial cooperation and eliminate regional development differences. It is based on the integrated project of education and scientific research carried out during the integrated development of the European Union, i.e. Erasmus Mundus, a joint master's program within the European Union, and Horizon 2020, an R&D community project centered on high-tech strategies, so as to lay the foundation for the industry's talent exchange.

Unlike the old industrial countries in Europe, most of the clusters in the Yangtze River Delta lack the elements of scientific research despite of the form. Although many regions have tried to introduce high-quality scientific research resources, such as the introduction of SINANO (Suzhou Institute of Nano-Tech and Nano-Bionics, Chinese Academy of Sciences) in Suzhou, to greatly promote the development of the local microelectronics industry, the interaction between technological development and traditional industries remains weak, which suppresses the development of overall industrial capability required for the further development of emerging industries, to some extent.

Therefore, when building Super Cluster in the Yangtze River Delta, we need to strengthen the capability of each cluster and to achieve effective cross-region resource allocation as well.

II. Three-step strategy for the Yangtze River Delta

Compared with European experience, the foundation of Super Cluster lies in three aspects. Firstly, the perception of the concept of clusters is getting more similar in different regions. Secondly, the development level of each cluster is equivalent. Thirdly, the European Union and member states regard the cluster or Super Cluster as an important starting point for science and technology policies. However, the Yangtze River Delta has incomplete foundations in all of these three aspects. Therefore, we believe that a three-step strategy based on local conditions can be considered for the Yangtze River Delta, i.e. (1) building a benchmark system and shaping consensus, (2) supplementing key elements and setting up frameworks, (3) creating leadership and establishing brands. A combination of top-down and bottom-up methods can be adopted to fully mobilize the initiative of each element.

Firstly, establishing a benchmark system. An evaluation system for clusters needs to be established in the Yangtze River Delta so as to create a platform for communication among clusters in various regions. It does not take the GDP of a certain industry as a measurement, but uses certain dominant technology as a clue and takes completeness and technological advancement of universities, research institutes, start-ups, SMEs, leading enterprises and incubation institutions as indicators. Therefore, there might be multiple clusters. For example, Nanjing has both chemical cluster with Sinopec Yangzi Petrochemical Company and Nanjing Tech University as the core, and aviation cluster with NEIAS Commercial Aircraft Company Limited, AVIC and Nanjing University of Aeronautics and Astronautics as the core. Each element of these clusters is scored to understand each other's development stage.

Based on the technology level of the industry, a cutting-edge technology cluster strategy can be launched as an industrialization implementation plan for high-tech strategies. The Yangtze River Delta integration office establishes a set of evaluation systems based on the above indicators to evaluate clusters in the region. Besides, with a focus on the development direction of major industries such as life and health, mobility, intelligent manufacturing and information technology, high-quality clusters are selected and supported as a benchmark through application and evaluation procedures in order to enhance consensus on clusters and lay the foundation for further scientific and technological policy coordination in the Yangtze River Delta. The reporting entity can be a joint reporting entity composed of different clusters, but the key point is that it needs to have all the key elements from scientific research to marketization.

Secondly, shaping consensus. Both economic map and innovation map of the Yangtze River Delta need to be established to enhance the visualization of related resources in the region. Taking Gemany as an example, it has established an Industry 4.0 information map at the national level, of which all information related with Industry 4.0 covering companies, research institutes, universities, testing institutions and exemplary factories in Germany has been made into a map format with supplementary case materials. At the level of city development, Berlin has established a city economic map that covers economic information including economic entities, organizations, research institutions, and energy efficiency and effective photovoltaic area of buildings.

Through decades of integrated development, the Yangtze River Delta has laid a solid foundation in infrastructure construction, information exchange, personnel mobility, industrial foundation and institutional framework. The next goal is to establish a bond among multiple current clusters so as to achieve an in-depth element exchange and promote the vitality of the market economy and corporate innovation. Although enterprises and universities have a certain understanding of the core resources of different cities and the in-charge departments of local governments have made great efforts to promote patent transformation, the currentpublicity of the city focuses on the promotion of government affairs, and there is still room for the development in market-based publicity and effective use of element resources.

Thirdly, supplementing key elements. Targeted supporting policies should be provided for clusters with insufficient elements to help them quickly make up for shortfalls. Having realized the gap between the UK and the US in the development of the life science and technology industry in the 1990s, Germany has, since 1995, implemented the BioRegio policy for building organization capacity of clusters, the BioFuture policy for the career development of scientific researchers and the support for start-ups, the BioChance policy for supporting co-sponsored projects by start-ups and universities, the Cutting Edge Cluster policy for systematic development of clusters, and the policy for strengthening the ability of international cooperation.

The step-by-step policies in Germany were gradually explored based on their own development experience. There are great differences among different clusters in the Yangtze River Delta, so it is unnecessary to exactly correspond with the German model. For example, Shanghai, Nanjing, Hangzhou and Hefei are rich in higher education and scientific research resources, Kunshan has an agglomeration of foreign companies, and Jiaxing and Ningbo have agglomerations of private SMEs. Some can choose to make up the gap according to their own conditions, and others can cooperate with other cities according to their technical characteristics of their own industries to form cross-region clusters and realize the linkage between technology and industry.

Fourthly, setting up frameworks. A set of effective decision-making and management framework should be established to improve the capabilities of clusters. European clusters are generally divided into two sides in terms of organizational structure, i.e. the deliberative layer and the executive layer. The deliberative layer is composed of core participants within clusters, including the government, research institutions and enterprises, who makes decision on major topics such as the development direction of clusters, and mobilizes their own institutional resources to contribute to the cluster development. At the executive layer, a matrix management structure is often adopted. On the one hand, there are several functional modules, including joint R&D, vocational education, start-up incubation and marketing. On the other hand, specific technology commercialization directions are formulated based on the characteristics of the clusters.

For the Yangtze River Delta Super Cluster, a large number of national-level development zones or regional industrial parks are currently being constructed in various places. However, the management of the relevant parks is mainly limited to infrastructure, tax relief, land concessions and property facilities, and the capacities of both cluster elements and stickiness are insufficient. If Super Cluster adopts a similar organization management structure, it can greatly reduce the cost of mutual communication and improve cooperation efficiency.

Fifthly, creating leadership. Flagship scientific research projects across the Yangtze River Delta should be launched to play a leading role in the marketization of technology spillover. Take Airbus as an example, several European clusters have actively "attracted investment" after the launch of the A380 project. In order to bid for the assembly of large sections of the A380 cabin, Hamburg, centered on aviation interior industry, has not only established an aviation application research center as a public R&D platform for carbon fiber aviation auxiliary materials processing technology, but also established an aviation training center, providing vocational education and training for students and working engineers to shift their knowledge structure from aluminum alloy processing to carbon fiber.

There are many common topics in the Yangtze River Delta for the cooperation of Super Cluster. The interaction between the industry and scientific research can be promoted through projects to prevent research results from being confined in the laboratory. For example, a leading R&D project can be launched on the treatment of cross-region water systems. Scientific research can be carried out on smart devices such as sensors, and the development of related equipment manufacturing and artificial intelligence start-ups can be promoted to jointly achieve ecological sustainability. Furthermore, the aviation industry can launch flagship projects based on the scientific research resources of Nanjing and Shanghai and the industrial resources of Wuxi and Ningbo, and drive the aviation industry resources of Jiangxi province as well.

Sixthly, establishing brands. International brands for scientific research should be established to advance the integration of the region with international scientific research and industries. At present, the Ministry of Science and Technology, the Chinese Academy of Sciences and relevant universities are exploring the paths of internationalization of scientific research, hoping that China's scientific research industry will be further in line with international standards through the investment in scientific research and the leverage of large scientific engineering, industrial hinterland, innovation ecology and capital. Currently, there are large-scale scientific facilities in Hefei, Shanghai, Nanjing, Suzhou, etc., but the international promotion is still not ideal, and few international scientific research groups have settled in to carry out projects.

Therefore, by combining the characteristics of various cutting-edge technologies and the new economy, a scientific research brand can be created. The Yangtze River Delta Super Cluster can increase international popularity by participating in overseas high-tech exhibitions and initiate international research projects on related topics. In the meantime, it can help relevant universities actively participate in the EU Horizon 2020 strategic projects and establish a communication mechanism with Super Cluster under the EU Industry and Technology Research Institute and the first-class European science and technology clusters to further promote international integration.

III. Interaction is the key to mutual trust

In the era of Industrial Park, the major work of local governments is to attract investment. Although the government has made arduous efforts in economic development, the marginal benefits of investment is getting lower and lower due to the limitation of high-quality resources. What's more, it often causes vicious competition among regions and even among different sectors of the same city, and thus hinders the integration of the Yangtze River Delta.

Therefore, the core of our proposed Super Cluster lies in two aspects. One is to improve the government's administrative management ability in the development of science and technology industry as well as the awareness and ability of interaction between the industry and the academia by promoting the consensus of each city on the cluster's development concept and strengthening the capability. The other is to make key elements of Super Cluster fully interact with each other, establish a mutual trust relationship and improve the element exchange as well as economic and social values through similar management structure and the leading role of flagship projects.

Affected by the epochal factors of industrial development, China's economic development is showing more and more obvious regional characteristics and thus presents a trend of regional economic integration. We hope that through the practice and management iteration of the integration of the Yangtze River Delta, an institutional model innovation with the power to be promoted nationally can be developed to promote a close integration of China's scientific research and industry, and truly achieve high-quality economic development.

新使命，新征程

——战略性新兴产业和长三角一体化

仲量联行

自 2018 年 11 月，长三角区域一体化发展正式上升为国家战略。2019 年 12 月 1 日，中共中央、国务院印发《长江三角洲区域一体化发展规划纲要》，这标志着长三角一体化发展进入全面实施的新阶段。在高质量发展的要求下，长三角需要更好地参与新一轮全球合作与竞争，打造成为中国发展强劲、活跃的增长极和科技创新的领头羊。

本文主要聚焦战略性新兴产业在长三角区域的发展这个视角，并结合仲量联行多年来在产业研究和协助跨国企业选址的行业领域给出一些观察和建议。

众所周知，中国经济发展进入了新常态，加快培育新动能是推动经济转型升级的重要途径。新动能从哪里来？战略性新兴产业将成为新的增长引擎：发展战略性新兴产业，既可以对当前调整产业结构起到重要支撑作用，更可以激发经济增长的内生动力，引领未来经济社会可持续地稳健发展。战略性新兴产业也是未来中长期内中国宏观经济政策的战略选择。

相比传统制造业、固定资产投资等，战略性新兴产业对经济增长的边际拉动作用将显著增强。而重点突破"卡脖子"技术及创新成果的转移转化，将会进一步提升中国经济在全球价值链中的位势。

习近平总书记在 2019 年 11 月进博会开幕前在上海考察时特别强调，要强化科技创新策源功能，努力实现科学新发现、技术新发明、产业新方向、发展新理念从无到有的跨越，形成一批基础研究和应用基础研究的原创性成果，突破一批"卡脖子"的关键核心技术。

我们注意到战略性新兴产业的发展已经形成良好的发展态势。在过去的一年中，虽然整体经济增速面临下行压力，但战略性新兴产业表现相对亮眼，近期的季度同比增加值增速显著高于同期 GDP 增长。当然，战略性新兴产业在发展中也出现了一些短板需要克服。

就战略性新兴产业的地理布局来看,毫无疑问长三角城市群具备极好的发展基础。从图1中可以看出,长三角R&D研发经费投入在近年来显著提升,在增速方面,R&D经费支出增速普遍高于GDP增速。在绝对值方面,2018年,长三角地区的R&D经费支出总额约为5 900亿元,总数接近德国的72%左右。我们再来看几个数字,长三角地区总体R&D相比GDP的投入强度约为2.8%,高于全国平均水平(2.2%)。2019年12月1日公布的《长江三角洲区域一体化发展规划纲要》中也提到,研发投入强度到2025年将达到3%以上。

图1 三省一市的R&D经费支出

注:由于各个城市2018年数据的可得性,我们使用三省一市数据;

由于对比需要仅标明长三角城市群中的15大城市

资料来源:国家及各地区统计局,CEIC

发展战略性新兴产业的另一个基础是区域经济,从我国三大主要城市群的经济整体发展水平来看,长三角城市群区域经济发展的均衡性情况最为良好。经济的外溢效应相比虹吸效应对于协同发展战略性新兴产业相对更加有利。图2非常清楚地显示出,在长三角城市群中第一大城市相比其他城市GDP的相对值更为接近。

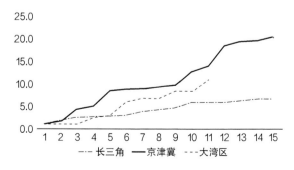

图2 城市群中第一大城市GDP相比第N大城市GDP倍数分布图

当然其他的要素对于发展战略性新兴产业同样重要,包括营商环境、开放程度、金融支持、人才基数、交通连通性等等。毋庸置疑,长三角拥有非常扎实的基础和历史传承下的基因。

与粤港澳大湾区及京津冀城市群这两个中国区域经济一体化的热点城市群相比,长三角城市群在综合联动效应方面具备良好的条件。在这里,引入"城市空间及经济引力模型"(GDP×人口×消费/通行时间)做一个比较直观的分析(图3)。

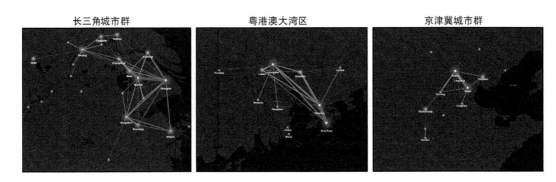

图 3　三大城市群城市空间及经济引力模型

注:长三角的展示区域为部分区域
资料来源:国家及各地区统计局;CEIC

从图3中可以发现:长三角区域的经济发展在空间上呈现出"树状"的结构特征,具体表现为以上海为核心,依托成熟发达的交通运输网络,以及技术和产业的扩散效应,带动周边包括苏州、杭州、宁波、南京等多个经济基础同样非常强的核心城市的经济发展,再逐步向周边三四线城市进行辐射。

与之相比,大湾区内部的经济特点是,以香港、深圳和广州为首的核心城市在经济体量、人口、与相邻城市的连接便利性上显著超过周边的二三线城市。而在京津冀城市群中,北京和天津的首位效应更加突出。当然,随着正在快速推进中的基础设施互联互通建设和多渠道融合创新的加深,城市间的经济联动效应有望显著提升。

在未来战略性新兴产业进一步演进的道路上,这三大城市群都将立足自身禀赋优势向国际一流的创新中心发展。良好的综合联动效应将助力并加速长三角城市群的发展。

战略性新兴产业与传统产业的驱动模式存在显著的不同。传统行业的发展偏向于产业链整合的模式,其生产要素主要是土地、原材料、人工等;战略性新兴产业是创新链和产业链深度融合的模式,其生产要素更依赖于研发、数据、资本及人才。产业链整合发展模式通常是由主导企业通过调整、优化相关企业关系使其协同行动,提高产业链运作效能,提升企业竞争优势的过程。而战略性新兴产业的发展更偏向于创新链赋能发展模式,即推动以企业为主体的产业技术创新体系建设,围绕产业重大应用和关键技术突破,形成从创意的产生到商业化生产销售整个过程的链状结构。

驱动方式以及生产要素的变化也对城市管理方式提出新的要求,长三角一体化的顶层设计体现在通过深化体制机制改革,释放市场创新红利,引导创新要素在区域间自然流动,构建区域创新共同体,重点突破"卡脖子"技术及创新成果转移转化,不断提升在全球价值链的位势,为高质量发展注入强劲动能。

在未来的长三角城市群内,中心城市将不会只是虹吸资源和人口的"黑洞",而将和周边地区形成"对流",生产要素将得到更好的配置,效率会提升,区域整体竞争力将健康成长。

在"长三角一体化高质量发展"的规划框架下,我们希望在具体落地层面,通过对相关战略性新兴产业企业在房地产策略领域的理解来给出一些观点和建议。在布局战略性新兴产业的物业载体上,有两个方面是重中之重,缺一不可。首先,土地、物业的规划需要考虑到战略性新兴产业的生态体系,第二就是所在行业内人的需求。具体来说,仅仅是一个以传统工业驱动的制造或研发物业载体空间设计远不能满足行业的发展,比如更多针对赋予创造性的小型及初创类的孵化器空间、金融类(如针对战略性新兴产业的私募等)办公的空间预留都需要加入考量的因素;同时,考量企业需求的重要性有时候要超过供应方面的设计。如何针对性地引入领头羊的"主力企业",以及该企业在某个细分领域中如何具备国际竞争力的技术或潜在技术可能会成为核心问题(图4)。

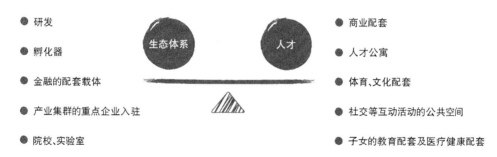

图4 战略性新兴产业对于物业市场的需求

当然,越来越多的规划已经开始关注到图4模型中左边的生态体系,而对于模型右边,即战略性新兴产业的从业人员需求的理解还有可以深入的空间。"安居乐业"是我们经常说的一个词,但哪些是战略性新兴产业从业人员最关注的需求?在进行土地、物业规划时是否需要给予足够的支持?我们注意到,很多战略性新兴产业企业的选址是在距离市中心相对较远的产业园区,但企业的从业人员,不仅仅是核心人才,期望在园区内有良好的商业、体育、文化以及有更多互动空间的配套,高品质的人才公寓以及足够良好的、可以让他们子女就学的配套等都影响着区域的吸引力。而这些源源不断的人才正是战略性新兴产业保持持续活力和国际竞争力的动能。

值得一提的是,不断提升的大数据分析提供给我们更多有力的工具,通过对企业、人才画像的理解进一步支持未能满足的需求,这将有助于在微观层面更好地为战略性新兴产业添砖加瓦。

在具体的微观企业物业选址需求方面,我们做了一些研究。我们在2019年10月针对33家战略性新兴产业企业进行了问卷调查,其中包括人工智能、集成电路、5G及相关企业。我们注意到战略性新兴产业在办公楼及产业园区都存在选址需求,它们在选址过程中的首要考量因素有所不同。比如在城市较为核心的CBD选址中,考量最多的除了租金成本以外,就是交通的便利性及楼宇的形象,两者对于吸引人才和与客户的会面都有非常显著的影响。而在距离市中心相对较远的产业园区的选址关注点中,产业集群、优惠的税收政策以及交房标准(尤其是对研发的物业要求)成为前三大考虑因素(图5、图6)。

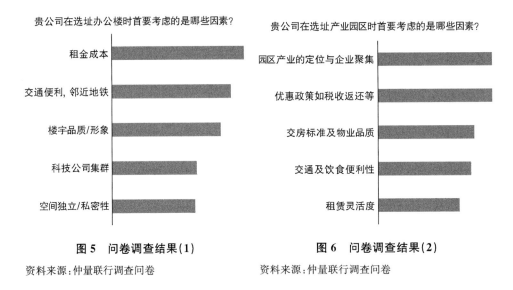

贵公司在选址办公楼时首要考虑的是哪些因素?

租金成本
交通便利,邻近地铁
楼宇品质/形象
科技公司集群
空间独立/私密性

贵公司在选址产业园区时首要考虑的是哪些因素?

园区产业的定位与企业聚集
优惠政策如税收返还等
交房标准及物业品质
交通及饮食便利性
租赁灵活度

图5　问卷调查结果(1)

资料来源:仲量联行调查问卷

图6　问卷调查结果(2)

资料来源:仲量联行调查问卷

调查发现,很多战略性新兴产业企业都在经历着快速的发展。在研究样本中,2018年企业人员扩张超过10%的占到了85%,这与传统行业的增长产生了鲜明的反差。因此,战略性新兴产业对于办公、研发空间的需求也就产生了明显的不同。在一般情况下,传统的园区或办公楼往往无法每年为企业预留相邻的扩张面积以等待其未来的使用面积增加,这就给企业在落实房地产策略上带来了一定的难度(图7、图8)。

贵公司在全国范围内过去一年的人员增速?

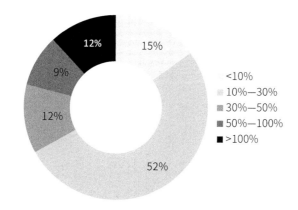

图 7 问卷调查结果(3)

资料来源:仲量联行调查问卷

贵公司在联合办公空间的使用比例?

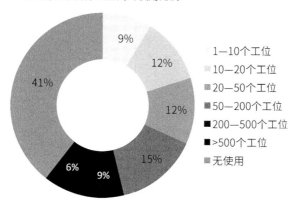

图 8 问卷调查结果(4)

资料来源:仲量联行调查问卷

同时,我们也注意到越来越多的战略性新兴产业企业更加重视它们的 CRE(企业不动产)部门。一方面,这类企业也像其他企业一样正在利用"未来办公"的理念通过空间的设计来提升员工的体验,并持续地提升效率和创新能力,另一方面,战略性新兴产业企业也正在利用联合办公等空间来增强其房地产策略的灵活性。调研发现,有 59%的该类企业正在使用联合办公空间。

2019 年 11 月,国家发展改革委正式公布了《长三角生态绿色一体化发展示范区总体方案》,建设长三角生态绿色一体化发展示范区,是实施长三角一体化发展战略的先手棋和突破口。要打造这一示范区,从仲量联行的角度观察,有几点建议:第一,政策细则落地。对有意愿扎根一体化示范区发展的企业,区域发展的要素流动、招商引资、规划管理等创新制度细则需尽快落地;第二,市场主体参与。建立包括企业、高校、研究院等更多社会主体参与的专家智库委员会,为示范区产业导入和发展模式建言献策;第三,城市管理创新。积极探索"大城区管理"创新模式,为生态友好型的空间发展规划及跨区域一体化管理服务机制构建提供支撑。

New Vision, New Journey

—The Integration of Strategic Emerging Industries in the Yangtze River Delta

Jones Lang LaSalle

The integrated regional development of the Yangtze River Delta officially became a national strategy in November 2018. On December 1st 2019, the central government released *the Outline of the Integrated Regional Development of the Yangtze River Delta*, which marked a new stage in the implementation of this plan. The Yangtze River Delta needs to better participate in a new round of global cooperation and competition in line with the requirements for achieving high-quality development, to become a strong and active growth point and a leader in technological innovation for China.

Since entering Chinese mainland market with the opening of its Shanghai office back in 1994, JLL has always been committed to leading the way with cutting-edge ideas and innovative reform in the development of industrial and commercial real estate in China. We have actively participated in the development, transformation and upgrade of a variety of industries in cities located in the Yangtze River Delta. In terms of attracting investment, the company has assisted hundreds of multinational companies in finding and securing investment locations in China, especially in the Yangtze River Delta region. This has covered industries such as advanced manufacturing, automotive and electronics, financial services, technology and Internet, consumer goods and retail. JLL has become an important partner across all levels for investment promotion departments and industrial parks in the region. In this article, we will focus on the development of strategic emerging industries in the Yangtze River Delta region and share some observations and suggestions based on our industry research and experience in assisting multinational companies in selecting locations over the years.

As we all know, a new norm has emerged in China's economic development. Accelerating the cultivation of new driving forces is an important way to promote economic transformation and upgrade, but where do these new drivers come from? Strategic emerging industries will become a new engine for growth. The development of strategic emerging industries can not only play an important role in supporting current adjustments to the industrial structure, but also stimulate internal drivers of economic growth and lead the sustainable and stable development of the economy and society in the future. Strategic emerging industries are also a key choice for China's macroeconomic policies in the medium to long term.

Compared with traditional manufacturing and fixed asset investment, strategic emerging industries will have a stronger pulling effect on marginal economic growth. The focus on the transfer and transformation of technological breakthroughs and innovation will further enhance China's position in the global value chain.

During his visit in Shanghai in November 2019 prior to China International Import Expo, President Xi Jinping emphasized the need to improve the function of scientific and technological innovation policy sources. He explained that we must strive to achieve new scientific discoveries, technologies, industry direction, and ideas for development, as well as create a new wave of original results in basic and applied basic research, and make breathroughs in a number of core technologies.

We have noticed that strategic emerging industries have formed a positive development trend. Although overall economic growth has faced pressure from slow-down in the past year, strategic emerging industries performed relatively well, and their year-on-year quarterly growth rate in recent times is significantly higher than GDP growth in the same period. Of course, there are also some shortcomings that need to be overcome in the development of strategic emerging industries.

Judging from the geographical layout of strategic emerging industries, there is no doubt that the Yangtze River Delta urban cluster has an excellent foundation for development. It can be seen from Figure 1 that R&D investment in the Yangtze River Delta has increased significantly in recent years. In terms of growth rate, R&D expenditures are generally growing faster than GDP. In terms of absolute value, in 2018, the total R&D expenditure in the Yangtze River Delta region was about RMB 590 billion, close to 72% that of Germany. Taking a closer look at some specific Exhibits, overall R&D investment intensity in the Yangtze River Delta compared to GDP is about 2.8%, which is higher than the national average (2.2%). The *Outline of the Integrated Regional Development of the Yangtze River Delta*, published on December 1st 2019, also mentioned that by 2025 the ratio of the region's R&D spending to its GDP should top 3%.

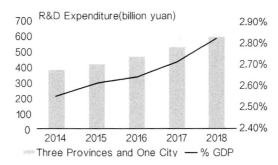

Figure 1   R&D Expenditure in Three Provinces and One City

Note: Due to the data availability of various cities in 2018, we used data from three provinces and one city; For comparison, only the data of 15 major cities in the Yangtze River Delta city group is displayed

Source: National and Reglonal Bureau of Statistics of China, CEIC

Another base for the development of strategic emerging industries is the economic foundation of the region. Looking at the overall economic development level of the three major urban clusters in China, the balance of economic development in the Yangtze River Delta is the most favourable. Compared with an economic siphoning effect, an economic spillover effect is more beneficial for the coordinated development of strategic emerging industries. Figure 2 clearly shows that the relative value of GDP of the largest city over the other cities within the Yangtze River Delta urban cluster is closer than that of China's other two major urban clusters.

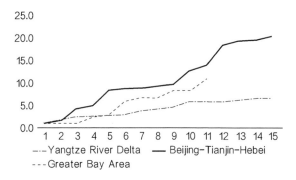

Figure 2　Distribution of GDP of the Largest City in the Cluster as a Multiple Compared to GDP of Other Cities

Of course, other factors are also important for the development of strategic emerging industries, such as business environment, openness, financial support, talent base, and transportation connectivity. There is no doubt that the Yangtze River Delta has a very solid foundation and historic background.

Compared with the other two city cluster hotspots, the Guangdong-Hong Kong-Macao Greater Bay Area and the Beijing-Tianjin-Hebei city cluster, the Yangtze River Delta city cluster is in a good position for generating a comprehensive linkage effect. Here, we would like to introduce the Urban Space and Economic Gravity Model (GDP × Population × Consumption/Travel Time) for a more intuitive analysis (Figure 3).

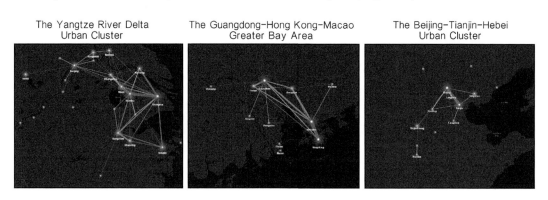

Figure 3　Urban Space and Economic Gravity Models of the Three Major City Clusters

Note: The area displayed for the Yangtze River Delta is only partial
Source: National and Regional Bureau of Statistics of China, CEIC

From Figure 3, we can see that the economic development of the

Yangtze River Delta region presents a tree-like structure. This structure features Shanghai as the trunk, relying on a mature and developed transportation network, and the diffusion effect of technology and industry to promote the economic development of surrounding cities including Suzhou, Hangzhou, Ningbo, Nanjing and other similarly strong economic bases, and then gradually radiating further to surrounding third-and fourth-tier cities.

In comparison, the economic characteristics of the Greater Bay Area feature core cities such as Hong Kong, Shenzhen, and Guangzhou significantly surpassing the surrounding second- and third-tier cities in terms of economic volume, population, and connectivity with neighboring cities. In the Beijing-Tianjin-Hebei city cluster, Beijing and Tianjin's distant leader effect is even more pronounced. Of course, with the rapid advancement of infrastructure interconnection and multi-channel integrated innovation, economic linkage between cities is expected to significantly increase.

On the road toward the evolution of strategic emerging industries, these three future city clusters will all develop based on their own unique advantages and turn into world-class innovation centers. Strong comprehensive linkage will assist and accelerate the development of the Yangtze River Delta city cluster.

The drivers of strategic emerging industries and traditional industries differ significantly. The development of traditional industries is inclined toward industrial chain integration. Its production factors are mainly land, raw materials and labor. Strategic emerging industries follow a model based on deep integration of the innovation and industrial chains. Its production factors are more dependent on research and development, data, capital, and talent. The integrated development model of the industrial chain is usually a process in which the leading companies coordinate and act together by adjusting and optimizing related enterprise relationships to improve the operating efficiency of the industrial chain and enhance the competitive advantage of the enterprise. The development of strategic emerging industries is more oriented towards a model of developing the innovation chain. It promotes the construction of industrial technology innovation systems with enterprises as the core. It also creates a complete chain from the creation of ideas to commercial production and sales, based on major industrial applications and key technological breakthroughs.

Changes in types of drivers and production factors also create new requirements for urban management methods. The ultimate design of the Yangtze River Delta integration is to continuously improve its position in the global value chain, and inject strong momentum for high-quality development. This can be done by deepening the reform of institutional mechanisms, releasing market innovation dividends, guiding the natural flow of innovation elements between regions, and building a regional innovation community, as well as focusing on the transfer and transformation of key technological breakthroughs and achievements in innovation.

In the future, the core cities in the Yangtze River Delta city cluster will not just be "black holes" which suck in resources and population, but will form a convection effect with the surrounding areas. Production factors will be better conExhibitd, efficiency will be improved, and overall regional competitiveness will grow healthier.

With the theme of "Integration of the Yangtze River Delta for High-quality Development", we hope to share our views and suggestions based on our understanding of strategic emerging industries as it relates to real estate from the executive level. In selecting real estate assets for these industries, there are two points of paramount importance. The first is that any land and property planning needs to consider the strategic emerging industry ecosystem. The second is accounting for the needs of those actually in these emerging industries, since a manufacturing or R&D property designed for traditional industry may far from meet the development needs of an emerging industry. When designing office space, elements such as incubators for small creative companies and start-ups as well as extra office space for financial industries need to be taken into account. Sometimes, considering the needs of a company is more important than the design, and the key issues may become how to incorporate a leading company and its international competitive edge in technology or potential technology(Figure 4).

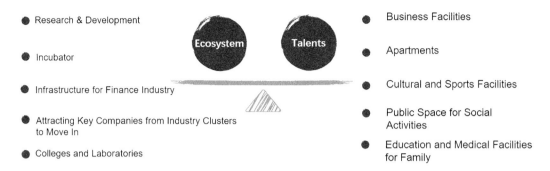

Research & Development

Incubator

Infrastructure for Finance Industry

Attracting Key Companies from Industry Clusters to Move In

Colleges and Laboratories

Business Facilities

Apartments

Cultural and Sports Facilities

Public Space for Social Activities

Education and Medical Facilities for Family

Figure 4 Strategic Emerging Industries' Demand for Property Markets

Of course, more and more planning has begun to focus on the ecosystem as shown on the left side of the model in Figure 4, but there is still room for further understanding of the needs of employees in strategic emerging industries as shown on the right side of the model. "Live and work in comfort" is a phrase we often use, but what are the key requirements for creating a comfortable life for employees in strategic emerging industries? Do we need to provide more support during land and property planning? We see that many strategic emerging companies are located in industrial parks that are relatively far from the city center. The employees of these companies expect to have good access to shopping facilities, social spaces for sports and cultural activities, high-quality apartments, and schools for their children, and all these facilities will make the area more attractive. The continuous supply of talent is the driving force for maintaining the vitality and international competitiveness of strategic emerging industries.

It is worth mentioning that the continuous improvement of big data analysis provides us with a further range of useful tools. Better understanding the portraits regarding companies and talents is expected to further support unmet needs, which will contribute to the development of emerging industries at the micro level.

We have carried out some research on the specific property location needs of micro enterprises. In October 2019, we conducted a questionnaire survey of 33 companies from strategic emerging industries, including artificial intelligence, integrated circuits and 5G. We noticed the demands that strategic emerging industries have in the selection of office buildings and industrial parks, and the differences in their primary considerations in the selection process. For example, when choosing a location in the CBD of the city, in addition to the cost of rent, the convenience of transportation and the image of the building are the most heavily-considered aspects. Both of these have a significant impact on attracting talents and customers. When choosing industrial parks that are relatively far from the city center, industry clusters, preferential tax policies, and delivery standards (especially for R&D properties) become the top three considerations (Figure 5, Figure 6).

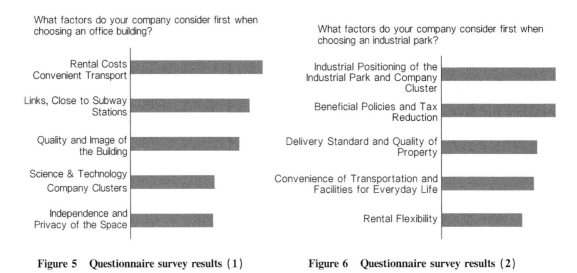

Figure 5 Questionnaire survey results (1)

Source: JLL Survey

Figure 6 Questionnaire survey results (2)

Source: JLL Survey

Through this survey, we also found that many companies from strategic emerging industries are undergoing rapid development. In our research sample, 85% of the companies experienced staff expansion of over 10% last year, which is in distinct contrast with the growth of traditional industries. Therefore, the demand for office and R&D space in strategic emerging industries has also changed significantly. Under normal circumstances, traditional industrial parks or office buildings are unable to reserve adjacent expansion areas for companies each year in anticipation of their future growth, which creates certain difficulties in terms of enterprises' real estate strategies (Figure 7, Figure 8).

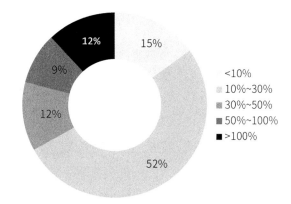

What is the rate of increase of your company's staff nationwide in the past year?

12%
15%
9%
12%
52%

<10%
10%~30%
30%~50%
50%~100%
>100%

Figure 7   Questionnaire survey results（3）

Source：JLL Survey

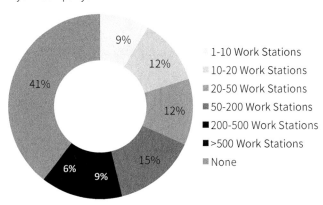

What is the percentage of co-working space in your company?

9%
12%
41%
12%
15%
6%
9%

1-10 Work Stations
10-20 Work Stations
20-50 Work Stations
50-200 Work Stations
200-500 Work Stations
>500 Work Stations
None

Figure 8   Questionnaire survey results（4）

Source：JLL Survey

At the same time, we have also noticed that more and more strategic emerging industry companies attach increasing importance to their CRE (Corporate Real Estate) department. On the one hand, these companies are using the future office concept to redesign space to enhance employee experience and continue to improve efficiency and innovation. On the other hand, strategic emerging industry companies are also using co-working spaces to enhance the flexibility of their real estate strategies. Our research found that 59% of businesses are using co-working space.

Recently, the National Development and Reform Commission formally announced the *Overall Plan for the Demonstration Area in the Yangtze River Delta on Ecologically Friendly Development*. The construction of this demonstration area in the Yangtze River Delta is the first move in implementing the integrated development strategy of the Yangtze River Delta. Based on our observations, we offer the following suggestions for the construction of this demonstration area.

First, availability of an implementation policy. For enterprises that are willing to devote themselves to the development of integrated demonstration zones, implementation policy details such as how to share the influencing factors for regional development, investment promotion, and planning management need to be shared as soon as possible.

Second, market participation. Establish an expert think tank committee that includes more social entities including enterprises, universities and research institutes, providing suggestions on the introduction of industries and a development model for the demonstration zone.

Lastly, urban management innovation. Actively explore "big city management" innovation models, to provide support for ecologically-friendly planning of spatial development and the construction of integrated cross-regional service management mechanisms.

如何发挥上海在长三角一体化上的引领作用

高风咨询

随着新兴科技的发展,中国各个地区的企业都面临着新的发展机会。2018 年 11 月,中共中央将长三角一体化发展上升为国家战略,随后,上海市、江苏省、浙江省及安徽省相继响应顶层设计,联手落实方案。此前,三省一市在各个领域都有不同的发展和竞争,我们也观察到在同质化竞争中的资源浪费。我们相信,深层次的一体化将进一步推进长三角的发展。我们总结了一些企业在上海遇到的问题,提出了上海在长三角一体化中应当承担的责任,总结归纳为以下三点。

一、牵头数据管理一体化

据悉,尽管目前长三角内多地均已成立各市数据管理中心,但各地对于数据的采集、开放、调取标准不一。在长三角跨省运营的企业在需要应用大数据时,它们发现各地采集数据标准不一,较难使用,并且,它们要向不同地方政府的大数据中心重复提交数据需求申请书。从政府处调取数据的程序本来就复杂,反复申请提取、等待审批给企业的研究与项目落地造成困难,耗时耗力。

在此,高风咨询公司建议,为了更好地助力这些需要公共数据的企业的发展,上海应牵头实现长三角数据管理一体化,组织三省一市实现长三角地区数据跨区域治理,建立长三角数据管理中心,确立开放数据标准化、精细化的管理。

近三年来,上海在第三方测评的地方政府数据开放排名中位列全国第一,在数据开放的管理制度上相比其他城市有了更加先进的探索。2019 年 9 月,《上海市公共数据开放暂行办法》已于上海市政府常务会议审议通过,该办法于国内首次提出了数据分级分类开放模式,并在持续推进数据安全、促进数据多元化、建立数据共享平台等方面做出了进一步的推进措施。

我们建议上海在试点数据开放的同时，归纳总结经验，为其他地方政府提供更多可复制、可推广的经验借鉴。我们还建议上海市政府在开放本市数据、打造共享数据平台之际，牵头区域内其他地方政府确立各项数据管理标准，整合长三角地区数据管理制度，统一数据收集及数据安全标准，着重数据平台打造并细化数据开放标准。第一，数据收集须明确数据来源，确保开放数据质量，才能更好地服务企业与社会民众。第二，上海市政府应积极建立公共数据安全管理办法，防止公共数据被盗取及非法利用，为长三角其他地方政府提供数据开放工作的经验借鉴。第三，在打造长三角大数据平台的过程中，上海市政府应明确平台数据输入标准，明确平台管理制度，保证数据来源均已审核并有隐私保护，明确各个政府调取、输入、修改权限，打造可靠的平台服务大众。第四，在数据开放方面，上海市应牵头其他地方政府，关注新兴发展产业的需求，对身处长三角地区的战略性新兴产业企业，如现代制造业、新能源汽车等将为长三角地区带来经济大发展的行业企业考虑数据优先开放。同时，上海应联合其他三省，统一数据使用申请所需材料及材料提交窗口、审核步骤，保证一地审核，多地使用，加快数据开放、使用速度。如此便可以简化关键企业数据申请步骤与时长，并在确保数据安全的同时，助力长三角企业发展。

二、物流资源一体化

随着长三角地区交通基础设施项目的建设，沿海、沿江交通大通道的发展，长三角地区越发联系紧密，逐步打破地理约束。但对于身处长三角地区的企业来说，它们往往有合作伙伴或者产业上下游伙伴于长三角各地布局，一个产品从零部件、模块部件生产、组装，到最后成品需要经历多个流程，往往需要横跨多个地区。在需要将物资运到产业链其他地方时，仍需花费高昂的运输成本。

对于长三角区域企业来说，在物流资源仍未最优化的情况下，这依旧是发展产业一体化的一大阻力。所以这些企业关心长三角各地如何持续优化物流资源，继续降低它们的运输费用，让它们有更少的地域限制，可以着力优化长三角地区的资源分配，让产业上下游之间、产业与产业之间的合作减少阻力。

新兴科技的进步带来了新的缩减成本的机会，随着智能驾驶技术的发展与应用，智能驾驶商用化将进一步为区域内的合作减少阻力。据高风咨询此前的分析，驾驶员人工成本占物流总成本的19%。2019年4月11日，长三角G60科创走廊智能驾驶产业联盟正式揭牌成立，来自九城（区）的智能驾驶企业、科研院所、金融机构等80多家单位共同协作，让无人驾驶技术的商用化离我们越来越近。菜鸟、美团、京东等物流公司纷纷发力物流"无人化",在降低货物移动方面进行了无人驾驶的探索。更多的汽车制造商也将发力无人驾驶技术。

上海早在 2018 年 3 月便发放全国首批智能网联汽车道路测试号牌,并于嘉定区开放了 5.6 公里的道路用于道路测试。直至 2019 年 9 月,上海智能网联车开放测试道路已达 53.6 公里,覆盖 1 580 个测试场景。嘉定区良好的测试环境为企业技术的优化提供了大力支持。

然而,园区内的模拟环境还是无法与真实的道路环境相比。无人驾驶的路测需要以大量数据,包括以复杂的交通环境与人流湍急的城市路口为基础不断优化算法,才能提升车辆在定位、感知、控制、决策的性能并持续优化行车安全。但即使作为中国智能驾驶技术的排头兵,上海的路测开放程度对标美国加州的道路开放仍需要很多政策突破。美国加州早在 2018 年 11 月就颁发了无人驾驶测试牌照,允许谷歌旗下公司 Waymo 的无人驾驶汽车在"没有驾驶员接管"的情况下在加州的公开道路上进行路测实验。相较于美国加州,上海与长三角区域内的无人驾驶企业面临着中国更加严格的路测法则。中国在无人驾驶汽车领域的政策法规仍需完善,需要政策突破。

上海作为"国内自动驾驶第一城",有责任推进长三角区域无人驾驶政策突破,积极推动指定跨省跨城高速公路对无人驾驶车辆的开放,推进发行"没有驾驶员接管"的路测牌照的步骤,赶超美国。在技术成熟的情况下,逐步开放上海与长三角其他省份的省级道路无人驾驶权限。另外,上海应牵头研究长三角地区主要交通枢纽与附近用地间的产业链关系,通过对每个站点的分析,打造长三角区域内的"跨城联网",让长三角地区更加紧密联系,赋能长三角区域的发展。

三、试点新思路,加速产业升级

随着科技的进步,各个产业也在逐渐变化。随着新兴科技比如区块链、云计算、大数据、5G、IoT 等技术的发展与创新,我们的很多客户都来咨询它们将会有什么样切身的影响,这样的新科技将有什么应用场景,企业将如何从中获益。

这些问题对于传统企业来说十分典型,在科技快速发展的时代,怎样才能打造一个快速研发、快速普及的闭环,让技术突破更快地实现落地,是一个十分值得研究的问题。我们建议上海作为国际科创中心,要持续发展上海的区域优势,在鼓励科技企业在上海设立研发中心的同时,与其他三省联合开展技术攻关,在实现技术突破的同时不忘将技术创新成果进行试点与风险评估。对有广泛商用价值的项目进行经验总结,并对长三角地区其他企业进行持续的科普能力建设。这样才能让科技突破成果迅速商用化,持续赋能企业。

在我们持续关注的新兴金融科技领域,区块链技术突破已有了新的商用机会。比如,对于跨国企业来说,区块链技术的应用可以解决跨国企业跨境资金池合规难等问题。以往,跨国企业在开展跨境资金池业务时,需要向银行、外汇管理部等相关部门提交报表,证明其资金来源、资金流出及资金往来等用途。这对于企业与政府审核方面来说均耗时耗力。而如今,区块链技术突破可以将监管的过程简化,相关合规部门可以实时查询企业跨境资金池业务的动向,确保操作规范。

这样的技术如果能快速商用,将使得跨国企业大幅缩减合规报表的制作成本,让它们在国内的资金进一步松绑,为企业带来切身的便利。但这项便商举措也正如其他便民的新兴技术一样,需要政府政策层面的大力支持开展试点,在金融风险得到控制的情况下,才能加快普及,惠及这些跨国企业。所以,我们建议上海在临港地区基于此类新兴科技的应用进行快速试点迭代、风险测算,持续深化企业科普建设,才能让成功的新兴科技应用在长三角区域并得到大力推广。

四、总结

作为长三角一体化的核心城市,上海应当明确自身定位,从制定标准、推进政策到试点先行,积极利用并共享上海既有的资源,持续进行创新项目的突破,以此为长三角一体化的高质量发展持续发力。

How Shanghai Municipality Can Play a Leading Role in Integration of the Yangtze River Delta

Gao Feng Advisory Company

Applications of disruptive technologies are growing in numbers and this means new innovative business opportunities for corporations all over the country. In November 2018, the Central Government formally declared its intent to make the Yangtze River Delta region the driving force for economic development of the entire nation. Subsequently, Shanghai Municipality, Jiangsu Province, Zhejiang Province, and Anhui Province quickly responded to the central-level initiative and formulated joint development plans. Earlier these four regions had their own separate developmental goals and sometimes even competed vigorously with each other, leading to a waste of replicated resources. Thus, a closer integration across these regions is expected to facilitate the development of the Yangtze River Delta. We have summarized the challenges faced by some companies in these regions, and put forward our recommendations for Shanghai's role in the integration of the Yangtze River Delta as follows.

I. Integration of data management

Currently, different cities in the Yangtze River Delta have established their respective data management centers and their standards for data collection, data accessibility, and data retrieval vary. When companies across the region try to use the data, they run into different data collection standards and the process of consolidation of data costs considerable amount of time, money and effort. What makes the problem even worse is they need to repeatedly apply for data access to different local governments, leading to complicated, and repeated application processes and time-consuming repetitive works.

Therefore, Gao Feng Advisory Company suggests Shanghai take the lead in integrating data management in the Yangtze River Delta. As such, Shanghai shall then be able to better assist companies that are in need of public data. Shanghai should organize cross-Yangtze River Delta data governance, and establish an integrated data management center. This will allow standardized and refined management of open data.

In the past three years, Shanghai has ranked first among Chinese local governments in terms of providing access to data because of its pioneering efforts in exploring data openness. In September 2019, Shanghai issued the Interim Measures of Shanghai Municipality on Opening up Public Data, the country's first local government regulation on public data accessibility. The approach focuses on unifying standards of data disclosure, data sharing and data security, which will likely guide the opening and utilization of public data in Shanghai to a new stage.

While spearheading opening up of data accessibility, Shanghai government should draw lessons from the past and provide other local governments more replicable and expandable insights. Moreover, Shanghai Municipality, while establishing the shared data platform, should also take the lead and encourage integration of data management systems across the region and unify data collection, management, opening, and security standards.

First, the collected data must have a clear source of origin. This ensures data quality and makes the data more useful for businesses and the public. Second, Shanghai Municipal Government should periodically inspect its public data security system to prevent data theft and illegal use and share its insights with others in the region. Third, while establishing a cross-Yangtze River Delta big data platform, Shanghai Municipal Government should outline data input and modification standards, ensuring availability of audited and protected data.

Moreover, Shanghai should also lead other governments to focus on addressing the needs of emerging industries. It may consider opening up data first to enterprises in strategically relevant industries in the Yangtze River Delta, such as smart manufacturing and new energy vehicles, which are likely to provide strong boost to the economy. One-time submission should be sufficient for companies to use data in multiple places, accelerate the opening up of data, ease the application process, ensure data security to help companies residing in the Yangtze River Delta.

II. Integration of logistics resources

With the ongoing transport projects along the coast and along the Yangtze River, the Yangtze River Delta region is becoming ever more connected, breaking geographical constraints. However, companies here often have business partners, including upstream and downstream supply chain partners located in other regions of the Yangtze River Delta. Typically, a product usually needs to go through multiple stages, from components production to assembly, before reaching the final product. The production sites often span across multiple regions. When materials need to be transported to other parts of the value chain, high transportation costs are still required to be incurred.

For companies in the Yangtze River Delta region, high transportation costs remain a major obstacle to the shift towards industry integration. As such, these companies are concerned about optimization of logistics resources, minimizing geographical restrictions so that they can focus on optimizing resource allocation and facilitate industry collaborations.

Advances in emerging technologies have brought new opportunities to reduce transportation costs. Development and application of intelligent driving technology will help facilitate regional cooperation. According to a previous analysis by Gao Feng Advisory Company, current driver costs take up around 19% of total costs in logistics. On April 11, 2019, the Intelligent Driving Industry Alliance of the G60 Science and Innovation Corridor in the Yangtze River Delta was officially established. More than 80 participants including intelligent driving companies, scientific research institutes, and financial institutions from the nine cities (regions) partnered to make commercialization of autonomous driving a reality. With logistics companies such as Cainiao, Meituan and JD. com carrying out testing of pilotless vehicles and more OEMs investing in driverless technology, realization of driverless goods movement is becoming more promising than ever.

As early as March 2018, Shanghai issued the country's first batch of plates for intelligent and connected cars for testing and opened up 5.6 kilometers in the Jiading District for road testing. As of September 2019, Shanghai has opened up over 53.6 kilometers, covering 1,580 test scenarios. Jiading's road test environment has strongly supported autonomous vehicles companies in the process of technology optimization.

However, the simulated environment in the geo-fenced zones is not comparable to real road environment. Road testing of pilotless vehicles needs to be based on a large amount of data to continuously optimize driving algorithms. Without testing in complex traffic environments and fast-moving urban intersections, vehicle performance in position tracking, perception, control and decision-making cannot be optimized. However, even as the leader in China's intelligent driving technology, Shanghai still requires a lot of policy breakthroughs for opening up roads for road testing compared to California, the United States. As early as November 2018, California had already issued driverless testing licenses, allowing Google's Waymo's self-driving cars to test on open roads. Compared to companies in California, companies in Shanghai and other regions in the Yangtze River Delta still face more stringent road-testing laws. China's policy in the field of driverless cars still needs to be improved, and currently there is no policy breakthrough.

As the leader in China's autonomous driving technology, Shanghai should further liberalize its pilotless driving policy and expand the coverage of designated inter-provincial and inter-city highways for pilotless vehicles, and issue driverless testing licenses to speed up road testing so that companies can catch up with the United States. As the technology matures, Shanghai Municipal Government and other provinces in the Yangtze River Delta shall gradually open up roads for testing driverless cars. Moreover, Shanghai should lead in studying the relationship between industrial chains and major transportation hubs in the region. Through analysis of each site, it can go ahead and design cross-city interconnection webs in the Yangtze River Delta region to make it more closely connected which shall spur development.

III. Piloting new ideas and accelerating industrial upgrade

The current pace of technological development is leading to profound changes in various industries. With the development and innovation of emerging technologies such as blockchain, cloud computing, big data, 5G, IoT and other technologies, many of our clients have asked us about how these technologies could materially impact their businesses, what are the application scenarios of such new technologies, and how could their companies benefit.

These questions are very typical for traditional companies. In the era of rapid developments in science and technology, how to create a close loop encompassing rapid research, development and commercialization, so that technological breakthroughs can be implemented more quickly is a question worthy studying. We recommend that while being the international science and technology innovation center, Shanghai continues to leverage its geographical advantages. It should continue to nurture its technological capabilities, encourage companies to set up R&D centers in Shanghai, and carry out research jointly with the other three provinces to achieve technological breakthroughs, pilot commercialization, while controlling for risks. This way, the breakthroughs in technology can be quickly commercialized and pushed to the market to empower businesses and consumers.

In the emerging fintech field that's currently under the spotlight, technological breakthroughs in blockchain have resulted in emergence of new opportunities and applications. For example, the application of blockchain technology can ease management of cross-border flows of money for multinational companies. In the past, companies had to submit relevant financial statements to banks and foreign exchange management departments to prove their sources of funds and the reasons for the remittances and exchanges. This is time-consuming and labor-intensive for both corporates and governments. However, nowadays, the breakthroughs in blockchain technology can simplify the supervision process. Relevant compliance departments can monitor companies' cross-border capital flows in real-time to ensure regulatory procedures are followed.

If such a technology can be quickly applied and used for real transactions, it can enable multinational companies to significantly reduce the cost of preparing compliance statements and free up their domestic funds, bringing them immediate benefits. However, similar to other emerging technologies that will bring convenience to the public, the application still requires regulatory support to be tested in pilot programs. Only when financial risks are found to be controllable, the application rollout can be accelerated. Therefore, we recommend Shanghai set up pilot programs for rapid iterations and risk assessments for application of such emerging technologies in the Lingang area, and continue to educate businesses about these applications, so once the pilots have been completed, the applications can quickly roll out in the Yangtze River Delta region.

IV. Conclusion

As the core of the Yangtze River Delta region, Shanghai should clearly define its positioning, from setting standards, advancing policies, to piloting new ideas. Additionally, Shanghai should actively share its existing resources with others in the region and continue to make breakthroughs in innovative projects. This will enable continuous and high-quality development of the Yangtze River Delta region.

Enterprise Development in the Context of the Yangtze River Delta Integration

长三角一体化背景下的企业发展

机遇与期待
——论长三角一体化进程中的跨国企业发展

美中贸易全国委员会

长三角地区是中国经济最重要、最开放、最创新的区域之一。第一届进博会期间，长三角一体化发展正式上升为国家战略。2019 年 12 月，《长江三角洲区域一体化发展规划纲要》公布，充分体现了长三角在全方位开放格局中的战略地位。为了解企业对长三角一体化政策的具体想法，美中贸易全国委员会专门对部分会员企业组织了非正式调研。结果显示，较多企业对参与长三角一体化发展很有兴趣，想要了解一体化对商业产生哪些影响。同时，一些企业也结合自身运营经验，对长三角一体化的发展提出了关切和期待。

一、长三角一体化为外资企业带来的机遇

企业发展与地区建设之间的关系十分密切。地区基础设施建设完备、市场规范是企业发展的稳固基础；而企业入驻后在该地的经营与投入，也会进一步促进当地经济发展。长三角一体化政策的提出会助力地区经济高质量发展，并为商业提供更多的参与机会。当前，区域内基础设施联通、港航一体化建设、专业服务等方面的发展，受到外资企业的支持。

1. 跨区域基础设施建设

建设区域内跨省高速和公路，为物流和交通减负，是长三角一体化基建的重点。例如，当前上海与江浙相连接的通道堵车成为新常态，交通压力已经较大。

2018 年，沪苏浙皖四省市共同签署了《长三角地区打通省际断头路合作框架协议》，第一批重点推进 17 个省际"断头路"项目。2019 年 10 月，长三角首条省际"断头路"——上海青浦盈淀路与江苏昆山新乐路打通，之后苏皖等交界地的"断头路"也在迅速建设中。这些省道的贯通往往能节省一半以上的跨省通行时间，大大降

低两地间的交流和运输成本。此外,在能源配套方面,交界地带的能源保障水平也稳步提升,浙沪天然气联络线一期工程建成投产。区域油气、电网等基础设施的建设将为企业带来便利,鼓励企业开展跨省业务。

2. 港航一体化

港航一体化对企业的区域内运输和联通而言具有重要意义。

当前,太仓港与洋山港之间的"太仓快航""沪太通"等物流模式已经起到了很好的示范作用。它们一方面大幅降低了物流成本、节约能源,缓解了上海陆路集疏运难题和长江中下游外贸需求的压力;另一方面迅速提升了太仓港的集装箱吞吐量。宁波舟山港与合肥地区的"海铁合作"也是双赢的典范,不仅发挥了宁波舟山港海铁联运的独特优势,而且合肥班列的开通也为周边地区的货运提供了新选择。长三角一体化将进一步推动跨省区域港口航道运输的合作。

3. 专业服务发展

随着长三角区域一体化在投融资方面取得进展,海外金融机构、律所及咨询机构也有望入驻,享受到区域一体化政策带来的利好。例如,中国银行未来五年将在长三角新增投入一万亿元信贷资源,已与长三角区域 24 家企业签署合作备忘录。三省一市纷纷提出加强金融创新合作,签署了《长三角科创板企业金融服务一体化合作协议》,助推科创板和注册制试点落地。

2019 年 5 月,长三角一体化保险创新研发中心在上海成立,包含安达保险在内的多家跨国金融企业不断向中国市场引进创新性保险产品,并在长三角医药业、高新制造业、互联网科技等领域获得了巨大成功。这说明金融行业的创新与长三角一体化建设已经形成了良性反馈机制。随着中国金融业对外开放的脚步不断加快,上海金融改革持续推进,长三角区域一体化将持续增强对跨国企业的吸引力。

二、外资企业对长三角一体化发展的关切与期待

随着未来地方配套政策逐步细化,长三角地区将结合各省市的比较优势,吸引更多的优质社会资源。同时外资企业也结合在长三角地区的实际运营需求,提出对于长三角区域内固废处理、知识产权保护、海关执法及产业转移等方面的具体关切与期待,值得政策制定部门纳入考量范畴。

1. 环境保护与固体废物处理

绿色发展是长三角一体化发展中的一大主题,外资企业关注环保问题,尤其是长三角地区固体废物(特别是危险废物)的处理情况和相关政策。

一些跨国企业提出,中国固废处理面临产能有限、收费高、固废处理服务质量

不一等问题。根据招商银行研究院出具的一份报告,中国每年新产生的固废中,仅危险废物量便超过1亿吨。全国2 000多家有资质的危险废物处理企业的产能仅有7 200万吨,其中的缺口高达近3 000万吨。根据2018年上海市固体废物污染环境防治信息公告,截至2018年底,上海市共有10家危险废物处置单位,处理能力捉襟见肘,市场供需矛盾突出。这导致市场上固废处理的单位价格迅速攀升,不少外资企业发现国内固体废物处理的渠道有限、价格高,处理质量也难以保证。2019年11月中旬,国务院批复了江苏响水天嘉宜化工有限公司"3·21"特别重大爆炸事故调查报告,认定这是一起由于公司长期违法贮存危险废物导致自燃进而引发爆炸的特别重大生产安全责任事故,更是将固废、危废处理问题的严峻性暴露出来。

考虑到上述情况,很多会员企业从三方面提出了可参考的解决方案。

首先,规范危废处理市场,规制危废处理质量。长三角各省市的管理监督部门要实行跨区域联合监管,共同消灭固废处理"黑市",严厉打击固废非法跨界转移、倾倒等违法犯罪活动,建设固废转移、回收基地。据新华网报道,由于长三角下游地区正规渠道的危废处理价格在每吨6 000至8 000元不等,而经营固废非法处置的"黑市"价位相对极低,每吨不过几百元。这中间巨大的利差,在某种程度上来说是长江流域固废跨省倾倒问题久治不绝的根本原因之一。因此,有关部门应关停资质欠缺的固废处理机构,并适时新设一些有资质的处理机构。

其次,优化固废处理资源配置,推动固废区域转移合作。由于单独省内有资质的固废处理企业的数量、能力有限,无法满足长三角区域一些经济重地的大量固废处理需求。在长江流域开展污染赔偿机制试点的同时应借鉴碳排放交易平台的经验,建立排污权跨省市场交易制度、统筹区域内的固废处理资源具有重大意义。经济发达或固废处理经验丰富地区可以向经济欠发达或经验缺乏的地区提供技术支持;需求较低的地区可以发展固废处理第三方产业,缓解固废处理需求较大地区的压力,打破固废处理的省市地域限制。这样的跨省合作能够解决区域内的供需错配问题,平衡各省之间的固废处理资源。

第三,加大对固废处理技术和提升产能的投入。通过一些具体的举措扩大危废处理服务范围。在我国固废处理总量中,目前焚烧和填埋占80%。过时的固废处理技术阻碍了固废处理产能提升,更环保的新技术出现之后因为价格问题而难以推广。所以我们希望长三角地区政府能够积极帮扶固废处理企业,倡导和推广固废处理新技术;在固废处理需求量大的地区加大技术投资、提升区域固废处理能效,降低企业通过正规渠道处理固废的成本;同时从政策上引导企业将生态理念深入到工业生产的链条前端,实现固废减量。

2. 跨省市知识产权保护

虽然中国在落实知识产权保护方面已经取得了不少进展,但根据 2019 年美中贸易全国委员会对会员企业的调查,仍有 91% 的受访企业或多或少对该问题存有关切。超过三分之一的受访企业表示,知识产权执法水平直接限制了它们的在华研发活动。

以执法属地管辖问题为例,当一些外资企业的注册地和侵权行为发生地不属于同一执法管辖区域时,由于两地执法部门缺乏信息合作渠道,维权过程会尤为艰难。

我们很欣慰地看到,目前在长三角区域一体化框架下,已有更多的合作机制落成。上海与浙江已经建立了跨区域线索通报、案件协查、联合办案等市场监管机制,尤其是在电商打假方面,国内首个网络市场监管领域跨区域协作联盟在杭州成立。另外,我们也关注到苏沪浙三家法院(嘉善县、吴江区、青浦区)建立了司法协作机制,提供跨区立案,深化跨域执行联动。

这种跨区域的行政及司法合作,不仅将更有助于我国对跨国企业知识产权的保护,也将吸引更多研发和科技创新投资。

3. 产业转移与政府支持

高端制造业是长三角地区显著的区域优势,也是长三角地区受到跨国企业运营、投资青睐的原因。但随着地方政策和市场行情的变动,许多外资企业为满足战略发展需要,考虑在长三角区域内重新布局以提升竞争力。

然而企业迁移是一项大工程,需要花费诸多精力在多属地的各部门之间辗转沟通。当涉及地方政府的税收分配竞争问题时,更是阻力重重。因此,美中贸易全国委员会会员企业希望在未来发展中,能妥善处理地方税收分配之间的竞争,从而优化地区营商环境,让企业可以基于市场发展做出合理选择。

长三角一体化发展应着眼全局,不囿于地方的利益。我们期待在未来,企业能在区域内享受平稳、顺畅的迁入迁出体验,获得更多跨区域的政策和协调方面的支持,例如企业登记、土地管理、投融资、财税等等。

4. 海关监管

长三角地区坐拥各大港口、自贸区及保税区,进出口量大,开放程度高。由于跨国企业进出口活动频繁,海关监管自然成为关注的重点。美中贸易全国委员会开展会员企业访谈期间,若干企业反映了在运营中遇到的长三角地区清关标准不一的问题,认为海关服务仍有优化的空间。

跨国企业也期望看到长三角地区出台海关便利、合作措施。目前,据报道,上海口岸与张家港口岸、安徽等地正在开展大通关物流数据、信息交换和查询工作。

长三角地区内的类似合作可以探索海关检查标准化、清关数据互认等内容,简化跨国企业进出口程序,促进自长三角进出的国际贸易。

三、结论

根据《长江三角洲区域一体化发展规划纲要》,到 2025 年,长三角地区将在科创产业、基础设施、生态环境和公共服务等领域基本实现一体化。受访企业认为这些总体发展目标非常积极,同时也希望有关部门能加强与企业的沟通,帮助企业切实解决问题。企业也期待能在未来继续助力长三角发展,并且建言献策,做出一份贡献。

Opportunities for MNCs in the Integrated Development of the Yangtze River Delta Region

US-China Business Council

The Yangtze River Delta (YRD) is one of the most significant, open and innovative regions of the Chinese economy. During the first China International Import Expo, the integrated development of the YRD region was elevated to a national strategy, and *the Outline of the Integrated Regional Development of the Yangtze River Delta* released this December further highlights the strategic importance of the YRD region in China's economic reform and opening.

The US-China Business Council(USCBC) informally interviewed select member companies to better understand businesses' views on policies in the YRD region. The feedback shows that many of our member companies look forward to participating in the YRD regional development and are interested in learning more about policies in the region and the potential impact on business. USCBC member companies have also raised some concerns and recommendations for the YRD regional integration from the standpoint of their respective operations.

I. Opportunities for MNCs on the YRD regional integration

Business is deeply intertwined with regional development. Established infrastructure and a well-regulated market provide a solid foundation for business development, while business investments and operations in turn contribute to local economic development. The proposed integration of the YRD region will help promote a higher quality of economic development and provide businesses with opportunities to participate in the integration. The region has been making progress in terms of infrastructural connectivity, port integration, services development, among many other areas, which is supported by the business community.

1. Infrastructure and connectivity

The proposed YRD regional development and integration plan has highlighted the need to improve inter-city highways and roads in the region. This would be welcome to address some concerns regarding improving logistics and flow of traffic. For example, congested traffic between Shanghai, Jiangsu, and Zhejiang can have an impact on the efficiency of transportation in the region.

In 2018, Shanghai, Jiangsu, Zhejiang, and Anhui jointly signed the YRD Regional Cooperation Agreement on Connecting Provincial "Dead-end Highways", with the first batch of projects focused on 17 inter-provincial "dead-end highways." Progress has already been made, for example, in October 2019, the first inter-provincial "dead-end highway" in the YRD region was connected between Shanghai and Jiangsu. The connection of these provincial highways can help reduce inter-provincial transit time, which greatly reduces costs of transportation. In addition, supporting energy infrastructure along provincial borders has also been steadily improving. For example, the first phase of Zhejiang-Shanghai natural gas pipeline was completed and put into operation. Interconnectivity within the YRD region will continue to bring convenience to businesses and encourage them to participate in inter-provincial operations in the region.

2. Ports integration

Improvement in ports integration in the YRD region has been greatly beneficial for intra-regional transportation and connectivity.

For example, the "Taicang Express" and "Shanghai-Taicang Connection" between Taicang Port and Yangshan Port (in Shanghai) has showcased benefits. The integration has sharply reduced logistical costs, saved energy, and alleviated pressure on Shanghai's land transportation network. The volume of containers handled by the Taicang Port has since expanded. Recent cooperation between Ningbo Zhoushan Port and Hefei is also an example of how cooperation improves efficiency connecting ocean freight with railway transportation.

3. Services development

Investment in the integration of the YRD region also provides opportunities for services firms, including foreign financial services, law firms, and consulting companies.

For example, Bank of China will invest an additional one trillion RMB in credit resources in the YRD region over the next five years, and has signed cooperation memoranda with 24 companies in the region. Shanghai, Zhejiang, Jiangsu and Anhui have all proposed to strengthen financial innovation cooperation.

Also, the Insurance R&D Center for the YRD Regional Integrated Development was set up this May in Shanghai led by multinational corporations, which have been continuously introducing innovative insurance products into the YRD region, providing new products to serve business in pharmaceuticals, high-end manufacturing, and new technologies. Innovation in the financial sector and development of the YRD region has formed a positive feedback cycle where the region is becoming increasingly appealing for MNCs with further reforms and opening-up measures of the financial sector in Shanghai and across China.

II. Concerns and recommendations by MNCs on the YRD regional integration

With more specific local implementation policies coming out in the near future, the region has the potential to better utilize the comparative advantages of various localities and delegate resources to promote high-quality development of the region. MNCs are in a good position to contribute. Policies in four areas have been emphasized by USCBC member companies for policy makers reference, including regarding waste disposal, IPR protection, customs enforcement, and industrial relocation.

1. Solid waste disposal and environmental protection

Green economic development has been one of the priorities of YRD regional integration. One of the focal points in regards to environmental protection for MNCs is solid waste disposal and related policies.

Some MNCs have observed limited supply, high prices, and varying quality of solid waste disposal services and hope to see improvement. According to a report led by the China Merchants Bank, it is reported that China produces over 100 million tons of hazardous waste every year, yet of the 2,000 companies qualified to provide hazardous waste disposal services only amounts to 72 million tons, leaving a gap of nearly 30 million tons. According to the information publicly released by the municipal government, Shanghai only had 10 qualified companies for hazardous waste disposal in 2018, showing a stark supply and demand imbalance. This has been driving up the market price for solid waste disposal. In November, the State Council approved a report on the unfortunate industrial explosion in Jiangsu in March 2019. The report concludes that the cause of the accident was due to illegally storing dangerous waste, which accentuating the necessity of proper solid waste (especially hazardous waste) disposal.

Three approaches to resolving the issue of solid waste disposal issues have been proposed by USCBC member companies.

First, policing quality of solid waste disposal services. As a starting point, policymakers can focus on the "black market" of solid waste disposal services. This would require concerted efforts of regulatory bodies and resources. It is reported by Xinhua that in the lower reaches of the Yangtze River, solid waste disposal through official channels costs around 6,000 - 8,000 RMB per ton whereas the price in the black market is only several hundred RMB per ton. Policymakers should focus on eliminating unqualified solid waste disposal services and look at adding more qualified capacity.

Second, optimizing resource distribution for solid waste disposal services. In cities like Shanghai where there is a gap between the supply and demand of qualified solid waste disposal services, more qualified waste disposal agencies should be encouraged to be established to help service demand. Cross-provincial cooperation should be encouraged for solid waste disposal services by drawing experience from current carbon trading system to better coordinate resources. Relatively developed areas could potentially provide technical support for relatively less developed areas on solid waste disposal, enabling greater flexibility regarding the sharing of waste disposal service resources. Cooperation and sharing of waste disposal services between provinces can help bridge the gap between supply and demand of solid waste disposal in the YRD region.

Third, investing in solid waste disposal technologies and capacity. A number of actions can be taken to improve access to qualified waste disposal services in the future. The government can support innovation and of solid waste disposal technologies. For localities in need of more solid waste disposal capacity, governments should coordinate to build capacity of qualified waste disposal companies. Governments can provide policy incentives for companies to reduce solid waste by incorporating environmental protection into upstream production processes.

2. Regional IPR enforcement

While there have been improvements in IPR enforcement in China and the YRD region, USCBC's 2019 member survey suggests that 91 percent of companies expressed they are still concerned or somewhat concerned over China's enforcement of IPR protections. Over one third of interviewed member companies reported that the level of IPR enforcement has limited their R&D activities in China. USCBC members hope that the YRD can continue to improve IPR protections and enforcement to encourage more companies to invest in R&D in the region.

One example of potential problems is jurisdictional enforcement of IPR. When the place of registration of an MNC is different from the place where the infringement happens, IPR protection is weakened when the regulators at two jurisdictions do not communicate to resolve the issue.

It is positive to see there is now more communication between YRD region. For example, Shanghai and Zhejiang have established stronger communication when it comes to IPR enforcement cases and information sharing. In ecommerce there has been improvement to address counterfeit sales with increased coordination between Shanghai, Zhejiang, and Jiangsu. Also, Jiangsu, Shanghai, and Zhejiang local courts have cooperated on regional case-filing.

Inter-agency cooperation across different jurisdictions in the region would help address MNCs' IPR concerns and help boost encourage more investment in R&D and technological innovation.

3. Industrial relocation

High-end manufacturing has been a significant comparative advantage of the YRD region, and the region as a whole is attractive for MNCs to set up operations and continue to invest. Given changing market circumstances or local policies, MNCs may redistribute their operations across provinces in the region to increase competitiveness and their footprint in the region as a whole.

Relocation of manufacturing facilities is a common practice which also requires close communication among various local governments, and sometimes involves competition among local governments in terms of tax revenues. This can create significant obstacles for companies. In order to improve the business environment in the region and allow companies to make decisions based on market situations, USCBC member companies hope issues regarding competition between localities regarding tax revenue may be addressed in future YRD regional integration plans.

The integrated development of the YRD region should progress beyond the scope of development at the local level, and we hope that cooperation between local jurisdictions will allow for a smoother experience for companies that may be relocating offices or operations. USCBC member companies hope to see more support and communication between jurisdictions when it comes to business registration, land use, taxation, and other areas which will help encourage investment in the whole YRD region.

4. Customs regulation

The YRD region enjoys a large volume of import and export through various ports, free trade zones, and bonded areas, and customs regulation is therefore a top interest for MNCs engaging frequently in import and export activities. Interviews with USCBC member companies has revealed that some of our members have experienced operational issues with different customs clearance standards in the YRD region, and recognize there may be room for improvement.

MNCs hope to see improved customs facilitation and cooperation within the YRD region. Recently, according to media reports, cooperation among ports has seen progress in Shanghai, Zhangjiagang (Suzhou, Jiangsu), and Anhui in terms of logistics data and information sharing. USCBC members hope that the YRD region can continue to standardize customs inspections and share recognition of customs declaration data, which would simplify import/export processes for MNCs and promote international trade in and out of the region.

III. Conclusion

According to the *Outline of the Integrated Regional Development of the Yangtze River Delta*, the region will reach the initial stage of integration by 2025, focusing on technology and innovation, infrastructure integration, environmental protection, and public services. Multinational corporations represented by USCBC find the overall development vision to be encouraging. We hope that local governments attach importance to communication and help streamline issues facing regional companies. Our members look forward to paying continuing contribution to the Yangtze River Delta Region, and we are glad to provide input and suggestions at any time.

对长三角地区高质量发展的
期待与建议

日本贸易振兴机构

一、中日关系现状及华东地区对日本经济的重要性

在中日关系中扮演着门户作用的上海乃至长三角地区,从很早就开始吸引日本企业的投资,而且其投资规模也在不断扩大。现在上海有大约 11 000 家日资企业,占整个中国日企数量的 32%,和北京相比更是有其 10 倍之多,甚至超过整个美国的日企数量(7 800 家)。而从近几年的投资来看,2017 年日企在整个华东地区,包括上海、江苏、浙江、安徽三省一市的实际投资额达到了 28 亿美元,占全国的 84%。在 2019 年 11 月举办的中国国际进口博览会上,日本企业参展数更是位列各国之首,达到了 371 家,并且成功举行了多场商务洽谈。华东地区对日本经济的重要性,通过这一系列的数字如实地反映出来。

从国家层面来看,2018 年是中日两国缔结和平友好条约的 40 周年,通过首脑互访,两国关系健康发展,并在此基础上为构建"中日新时代"达成了共识。2019 年 6 月,习近平主席参加在日本大阪召开的 G20 峰会之际,和安倍首相举行了会谈。两国领导人同意,本着化竞争为协调的精神,加强在第三方市场、科技创新、知识产权保护、食品及农产品等经贸投资、金融证券、医疗照护、节能环保、旅游观光等有发展潜力领域的合作。双方维护公正的自由贸易体制,确认为对方企业提供公平、非歧视、可预期的营商环境。而且更重要的是,安倍首相邀请习近平主席于 2020 年春天对日本进行国事访问,习主席也欣然接受。

另一方面,中日两国关系通过多边贸易体制正变得更加紧密。包括两国在内、亚太各国参加的自由贸易协定"区域全面经济伙伴关系(RCEP)"谈判也进入到最后阶段。在 2019 年 11 月召开的第 3 次 RCEP 首脑会议上,各成员达成共识,结束

了所有谈判并准备在 2020 年签署协议。

而中国通过于 2020 年 1 月起实施的《外商投资法》及《优化营商环境条例》等一系列措施，来加快推进世界各国的对华投资力度。这是扩大深化中日经济关系发展的大方向，也显示了中国吸引日本等各国外资的决心。

二、长三角地区营商环境的改善

随着各个方面的不断改进和完善，日本企业一方面对中国的关注度持续提高、投资也不断扩大，另一方面在实际运营中遇到各种各样的麻烦事也是事实。日本贸易振兴机构(JETRO)上海代表处会同上海商工俱乐部以及上海日本总领事馆，汇集了在沪日资企业遇到的各种问题和要求，形成了"完善营商环境的建议书"提交给上海市政府。另外，在华日企也会把华东地区日资企业遇到的问题编入白皮书并公布。我们希望长三角地区能利用自贸区等优势来解决这些问题，从而吸引更多日企投资。

1. 环境保护与经济成长并行

日本准备利用过去的许多环境公害防治经验，为建设"美丽中国"积极贡献力量。在《长江三角洲区域一体化发展规划纲要》中，虽然支持改善生态环境被提到了日程，但日企也指出了不少问题，特别是在制度的执行方面。

比如，有关部门对增设生产设备的审查时间应当缩短。即使不批准，也应该明示具体的法律依据、告知是和哪一条款冲突而造成的结果。而且环境管控应考虑到利用整个产业链来应对。政府在新的环境管控措施实施或者限制生产通知发布之时，应充分考虑企业对包括客户对应所需要的时间和费用，而且过度限制生产命令也应尽量减少。

2. 建立完整的工业体系

长三角经济带的特征之一是拥有完整的工业体系，其中注重安全的化学工业也承担着重要的一环。但是由于受到此前化学工厂事故等的影响，安全管控措施也被重新修改，使企业对化学品工厂的选址突然变得十分困难。比如，有的化学品厂家由于无法更新生产许可证，陷入无以为继的困局。对有的企业，危险化学品的既定保税通关却无法进行，造成关联费用的大幅上涨。政府为使负有供给责任的企业能顺利发展，应考虑到个例的特殊性。而且为了维持完整的工业体系，长三角三省一市应互相协助，在确保安全的同时，有必要探寻促进长三角化学工业的发展之策。

3. 加大贸易促进力度

海关一方面通过实施扩充电子通关等制度来缩短通关时间，但另一方面，同一商品通关时,不同的海关经办人归类为不同的 HS 编码的情况依然存在。或者本来无需提交的资料有时也被要求提交。作为世界最大贸易港的上海港和长三角的各个港口应通力合作,加快一体化发展步伐,使报关程序更加明确化、快速化、简洁化。

4. 强化金融中心功能

在金融领域,利用自贸区政策红利的改革成果不断涌现。而上海为构筑国际金融大都市的地位,更需持续改革创新。对外汇的管制造成了诸如区域外的融资受阻、汇款受限等结果。特别是在从人民币兑换外币时,各有关部门的指导意见因地区不同而异,希望长三角能搭建统一透明的制度运行平台。

5. 城市规划

伴随着城市发展和产业构造的快速变化,各大城市都出现了要求工厂搬迁,或由于生产许可证无法更新而不得不停止生产的事例。但另一方面,也应考虑该厂为当地经济提供了不可或缺的产品,对产业链作出了不菲的贡献。如果需要搬迁,除了在长三角区域提前预备生产候补地之外,同时也应留出因搬迁所需的一定的宽限期。

6. 创新合作

特别是在中国的技术能力不断提高的大背景下,日本企业和中国企业共同进行的创新活动更加引人注目。2019 年 4 月中日创新合作体制第一次会议在北京召开。双方围绕电动车、氢能源规格、监管协调、初创企业间的交流等有关事项交换了意见。

长三角在 AI、5G 等领域的研究开发中处于领先地位,也涌现出许多快速成长的独角兽。而且 2019 年,上海证券交易所又设立了科创板来推进中国的创新。上海是 JETRO 在全世界选定的开展创新活动的 12 个城市之一,我们上海代表处也在为许多日本大企业和创新型企业与中国企业的商业对接牵线搭桥。创新是两国新的合作领域,正不断扩大合作规模;而长三角作为引领日本企业来华投资的桥头堡,希望今后能发挥出更大的作用。

Expectations and Suggestions for High-quality Development in the Yangtze River Delta

Japan External Trade Organization

Ⅰ. Status of Sino-Japan relations and the importance of East China to the Japanese economy

Shanghai and the Yangtze River Delta region, which play a gateway role in Sino-Japan relations, have been attracting investment from Japanese companies for a long time, and their investment scale is also expanding. There are now approximately 11,000 Japanese companies in Shanghai, accounting for 32% of the total number of Japanese companies in China. Compared with Beijing, it is 10 times as many, and even exceeds the number of those in the United States (7,800). In terms of investment in recent years, the actual investment of Japanese companies in the entire East China region, including Shanghai, Jiangsu, Zhejiang, and Anhui provinces, reached $2.8 billion in 2017, accounting for 84% of the country. 371 Japanese companies participated the China International Import Expo held in November, ranking first in the number among all participating countries, and they held many fruitful business negotiations. The above statistics reflect the true importance of East China to the Japanese economy.

From a national perspective, last year marked the 40th anniversary of the signing of the Sino-Japan Treaty of Peace and Friendship. Through bilateral visits of government heads, the relations between the two countries have developed steadily, and on this basis, a consensus to initiate "a new era for China and Japan" has been reached. In June of this year, President Xi Jinping held talks with Prime Minister Abe while attending the G20 summit in Osaka, Japan. Leaders of the two countries agree that in the spirit of turning competition into coordination, there is potential for development and cooperation in third-party markets, technological innovation, intellectual property protection, food and agricultural products and other economic and trade investments, financial securities, medical care, energy conservation and environmental protection, and tourism. Both countries strive to maintain a fair free trade system to provide a fair, non-discriminatory and predictable business environment for the other country. And more importantly, Prime Minister Abe invited President Xi Jinping to pay a state visit to Japan in the spring of 2020, and President Xi accepted it.

On the other hand, Sino-Japan relations have become closer through the multilateral trading system. Negotiations on building the Regional Comprehensive Economic Partnership (RCEP) participated by the Asia-Pacific countries including the two countries have entered the final stage. A consensus was reached at the 3rd RCEP summit in November, and member states concluded all negotiations and were ready to sign an agreement in 2020.

And China has adopted a series of measures including the implementation of the *Foreign Investment Law* and the *Regulations on Optimizing the Business Environment* since January 2020, to accelerate and encourage countries around the world to invest in China. I think this is the general direction in expanding and deepening the economic relations between Japan and China, and it also shows China's determination to attract foreign investment from Japan and other countries.

II. Improving the business environment in the Yangtze River Delta

With the continuous improvement in various aspects, Japanese companies continue to increase their attention to China and expand their investment, but they also face different kinds of troubles in doing business in

China. Japan External Trade Organization (JETRO) Shanghai Office, together with the Shanghai Japanese Commerce & Industry Club and the Consulate-General of Japan in Shanghai, gathered various problems and demands encountered by Japanese enterprises in Shanghai, and submitted the "Proposal of Creating a Better Business Environment" to the Shanghai municipal government. In addition, the Japanese Chamber of Commerce and Industry in China also compiled and published a white paper listing the problems encountered by Japanese companies in East China. It is hoped that the Yangtze River Delta region can take advantage of the free trade zone and other advantages to solve these problems, thereby attracting more Japanese investment.

1. Environmental protection and economic growth go hand in hand

Japan is prepared to make active contributions to the "Beautiful China Initiative" with its past experiences in environmental pollution prevention. In the *Outline of the Integrated Regional Development of the Yangtze River Delta*, Japanese companies' support to improve the ecological environment has been on the agenda, whereas they also pointed out many problems, especially in policy implementation.

For example, departments concerned should shorten the time required to review the addition of production equipment. Even if they do not approve, they should clearly state the specific legal basis and inform them of the conflicting terms and conditions. And environmental control should respond by considering the entire industry. When the new environmental control measures are implemented or the production restriction notice is issued, the government should take into full account the response time and expenses required by the enterprises and their customers, and excessive production restriction orders should be minimized.

2. To establish a complete industrial system

The Economic Belt in Yangtze River Delta is characterized by a complete industrial system, in which the safety-oriented chemical industry also plays an important role. However, due to the impact of previous chemical factory accidents, safety management and control measures have also been re-modified, making it suddenly very difficult for companies to choose the location of chemical factories. For instance, some chemical manufacturers are caught in an unsustainable situation because they cannot renew their production licenses. Other companies cannot pass their established bonded customs clearance of hazardous chemicals, resulting in a substantial increase in associated costs. To ensure the smooth development of enterprises with supply responsibilities, the government should consider the specialities of individual cases. And in order to maintain a complete industrial system, Jiangsu, Zhejiang, Anhui as well as Shanghai should make concerted efforts to explore strategies to safely develop the chemical industry in the Yangtze River Delta.

3. To enhance trade promotions

The Customs has shortened the clearance time by implementing systems like electronic customs clearance on the one hand. But on the other hand, different customs officers may label different HS codes to the same commodity. Or, information that was not required to be submitted is sometimes required for customs clearance. The Port of Shanghai, the world's largest trading port, should work together with other ports in the Yangtze River Delta to accelerate the integrated development and make the customs declaration process more clear, rapid and simplified.

4. To strengthen the functions as a financial center

In the financial field, reform results that use the FTZ policy dividends continue to emerge. To build Shanghai as an international financial metropolis, continuous reforms and innovations are needed. Restrictions on foreign exchange have caused consequences such as blocked financing outside the region and restricted remittances. Especially when exchanging RMB from foreign currencies, the guidance of relevant departments varies from region to region. We hope that the Yangtze River Delta can build a unified and transparent operation platform.

5. City planning

With the accelerated development of the city and the rapid change of industrial structure, major cities have seen cases where factories have to be relocated or production has to be stopped because production licenses cannot be renewed. However, it should also be considered that these factories have provided indispensable products for the local economy and made a considerable contribution in the industrial chain. If relocation is required, in addition to preparing in the Yangtze River Delta region the candidate production land in advance, a certain grace period for relocation should also be set aside.

6. Innovation cooperation

The innovation activities jointly conducted by both Japanese and Chinese companies have become more noticeable, especially in the context of the continuous improvement of China's technological capacities. The first meeting of the Sino-Japan Innovation Cooperation System was held in Beijing this April. The two sides exchanged views on issues related to electric vehicles, hydrogen energy specifications, regulatory coordination, and exchanges between start-ups.

The Yangtze River Delta is in a leading position in research and development in the fields of AI and 5G, and many fast-growing unicorns have also emerged. And this year, the Shanghai Stock Exchange has set up a science and technology board to promote China's innovation. Shanghai is one of the 12 cities selected by JETRO to carry out innovation activities around the world. Our Shanghai Office also brings many Japanese large enterprises and innovative companies into contact with Chinese companies. As a new area of cooperation between the two countries, innovation continues to grow. The Yangtze River Delta, as a bridgehead that leads Japanese companies to invest in China, hopes to play a greater role in the future.

在华印度企业的商业环境

印度工业联合会

印度工业联合会(CII)与易唯思(Evalueserve)合作,于 2019 年年初对在华的印度企业进行了一项调查。调查结果显示,大多数印度企业有兴趣继续在华投资。这份调查报告——《在华印度企业的商业环境》,得到了 57 家在华印度企业的积极参与。

一、2019 年调查的一些重点内容

1. 在华的印度企业中有 72% 在上海投资。此外,江苏、浙江是华东地区热门的投资目的地。

2. 在过去十年,超过 50% 的被调查印度企业开始在中国运营。每年平均有 3 家公司在华成立。特别是在 2005 至 2009 年间,见证了最多数量的印度企业在华开展业务。

3. 受访企业遍布三大行业:制造业(40%),服务业(48%),制造及服务业(12%)。

4. 超过 50% 的企业在中国开展业务之初是以代表处的形式存在。当它们在中国站稳脚跟后,16% 的企业改变了实体性质,转为外商独资企业。

5. 30% 的受访企业 2018 年在中国获得的收入超过 1 亿元人民币。

6. 98% 的受访企业计划在华进行投资。

7. 约 70% 的受访企业相信在中国的运营将在未来 5 年内取得成功。

二、在华印度企业面临的一些主要挑战

1. 约 81% 的受访企业将高昂的劳动力成本列为主要的外部挑战。超过 60% 的

受访企业认为经济放缓、原材料成本增加是其他的外部挑战。

2. 约74%的受访企业将寻找和留住人才列为一项管理挑战,而44%的受访企业表示了解法规和监管是一项管理挑战。

3. 超过80%的受访企业指出,严格的规章制度与不清晰且不断变化的规章制度是企业的主要关注点,其次是获取所需的许可证和环保政策。

4. 约40%的受访企业强调,不清晰的新标准和复杂的认证程序是雇用外籍员工的主要挑战。

然而,约70%的受访企业相信它们在中国的运营将在未来5年内取得成功。超过80%的工业制造、IT和BPO、物流、消费品企业对它们在中国的成功运营持积极态度。

三、在华运营印度企业提出的反馈意见

1. 外资企业和国内企业之间劳动力不平等

印度公司遵守中国当地的社会保障政策。然而,许多中国本土企业选择按照最低工资标准为员工缴纳社保。这就造成了超过50%的成本差距。为了避免这种情况,2019年年初就有政策出台,称税务局将统一征收社会保险和所得税,以应对这种不公平的市场竞争。但是,该法规至今尚未实施。

2. 短期招聘的挑战

许多技术项目都是短期的,且分布在不同的城市。这就要求外国公司为临时的具体项目聘请专家。有时这些项目是一次性的,因此公司可能在此之后就不需要这些人力资源了。本土公司可以雇佣人力资源,并在项目结束或项目提前终止时立即解除关系。然而,这种情况不会发生在外国公司身上,因为它们被建议不可以这样做。

我们要求在针对因特定项目咨询而产生的聘用人员方面的问题出台明确的指导方针,这样一旦项目结束或终止,公司将不会存在其他的责任。需要强调的是,在解雇人员时,外国公司在任何情况下都需要支付遣散费。

3. 限制流动性

根据中国法律,印度IT企业要为所有来华的外国专家办理合法入境手续和工作许可。现行法律规定,在进入中国之前,他们必须选择在他们工作的城市办理工作许可。

然而,一些印度企业比如IT企业模式,需要这些海外专家前往客户所在的城市提供技术支持。在这种情况下,整个申请过程不得不重新开始,这不仅增加了公

司的成本,也耗费了时间。

这类工作许可的流程通常需要 2 至 3 个月才能完成,相比中国企业,这造成印度 IT 企业无法开拓新的商机或按时完成项目,尤其是短期项目。

例如,有一家印度公司在上海注册,而且长期要为其他省市的客户提供服务。那么在法律上,它就必须为员工办理其在客户所在城市的工作和居留许可。为此,这家公司要么在客户所在城市注册一家公司,要么获得当地的工作和居留许可,这样的话,客户必须与员工签署协议,并将他们显示在员工名册上。如果客户无法提供帮助的话,这就成了一项阻碍。

那么,印度公司要么放弃商业机会,要么通过繁琐的程序获得当地工作和居留许可,非常耗时。

4. 要求设立多个办事处

外国公司为了开展满足特定客户需求的小项目,需要在项目所在地的省份或城市设立多个分支机构或子公司。

对于规模较小的交易,设立分支机构或子公司显得尤其麻烦,因为这涉及大量的法律法规要求和管理,从而增加了运营成本。目前,在公司已经在同一省份其他城市设立分支机构或分公司的情况下,还是需要在所在城市设立分支机构或分公司,这样才能雇佣当地员工并办理工作签证。

例如,一家公司在江苏无锡有分公司,但这家公司雇佣的当地员工不能在苏州工作或办理苏州的工作签证,即使无锡和苏州都是在江苏省。

综上所述,以下内容可以作为在长三角地区推进印度公司进一步扩张的方法。

(1) 在本地和外国企业之间营造公平的竞争环境来解决社保问题。

(2) 增加短期招聘的透明度。

(3) 更大的流动性,并且允许在长三角注册的公司可以在多个地点开展业务,而无须在中国境内设立多个注册办事处或为短期工作人员重新申请从一个办事处到另一个办事处的居留工作许可证。

The Business Environment of Indian Companies in China

Confederation of Indian Industry

Confederation of Indian Industry undertook a survey of Indian companies in China in partnership with Evalueserve in early 2019. As per the survey most of the Indian companies have shown interest to continue to invest in China. The survey, "Business Climate for Indian Companies in China", drew responses from 57 Indian companies in China.

Ⅰ. Some of the key highlights of the 2019 survey

· 72% of the Indian companies in China have made investments in Shanghai. Jiangsu, Zhejiang are other popular destinations in the east China region.

· More than 50% of the companies started operations in China in the past 10 years, on an average 3 companies were established each year. In the last decade, the 2005—2009 saw the highest number of Indian companies starting their operations in China.

· Companies have presence across three broad industries: Manufacturing (40%), Services (48%) and Sourcing (12%).

· More than 50% companies set up a representative office at the time of starting their operations in China. After establishing their foothold, 16% changed their legal status to WOFE.

· 30% of the companies generated revenue of more than RMB 100 million in 2018.

· 98% plan to make some investment in China.

· 70% are confident that their operations will be successful in next 5 years.

II. Some of the key challenges the companies face in China

· About 81% companies listed High Labour cost and primary external challenge and more than 60% considered economic slowdown, increasing raw material costs as other challenges.

· About 74% respondents rated finding and retaining talent as a management challenge, while 44% highlighted understanding regulations as a management challenge.

· More than 80% companies rated stricter regulations and unclear changing regulations as main concerns followed by obtaining required licences and environmental policies.

· About 40% highlighted unclear new standards and complicated certification procedures as main challenges in hiring foreign employees.

However, 70% respondents are confident that their operations will be successful in the next 5 years. More than 80% Industrial Manufacturing, IT & BPO, Logistics, Consumer goods, are positive about their success.

III. Feedbacks received from Indian companies on their operations in China

1. Inequity of cost of labour between foreign and domestic companies

Indian companies comply with Chinese social security polices for employees. While many Chinese local companies choose to pay social security according to the minimum wage standard. This aspect creates a cost gap of over 50%. To avoid such a situation, there was a policy announcement in the beginning of the year, that the tax bureau will be unified in levying social security, and income tax to address this unfair market competition. However, this regulation has not been implemented till now.

2. Challenges in short term hiring

A number of technology projects are short term and are in different cities. This requires a foreign company to hire experts for the specific project at hand. At times these projects are one off, and hence the firm may not need these resources after that. Local firms are able to hire resources and release them immediately at the end of the project or in case the project is terminated earlier. However, this does not happen with foreign companies as they have been advised against doing so.

We request for clear guidelines around the hiring of resources for specific projects/consultants, such that there is no other obligation for the company once the project is ended or terminated. It is important to highlight that in the event of release of resources, foreign companies are expected to pay severance cost in all situations.

3. Restrictions in mobility

Indian IT companies handle legal entry formalities and work permits for all foreign experts who come to China in accordance to the local laws. Current laws stipulate that before entering China, visitors must select the city where they work to handle work permits.

However, some Indian business eg. IT businesses model needs these overseas experts could go to the city where the customers are located to provide technical support. In such cases the entire application process has to start afresh, thus this increases the cost for companies but also the time.

The process for such work permits usually take about 2 to 3 months to complete because of which Indian IT companies are unable to tap new opportunities or and execute a project on time, especially the short-term projects compared to Chinese companies.

For example, If an Indian company is registered in Shanghai and it has to service clients in other provinces/cities over a long period of time, legally it has to get work and resident permit for its employees in client's city. For this company has to either register a company at client's city or get local work and residence permits for which client has to sign agreement with employees and show them on their rolls. This can be a bottleneck if client does not help.

Thus, Indian companies either forego business opportunity or go through cumbersome process to get local work/resident permits which is time consuming.

4. Requirement to set up multiple offices

There is need for having multiple branch or subsidiary at each province or city where a foreign company would like setup even a small project for some specific client needs.

For smaller transactions it becomes too much of hassle to setup branch/subsidiary as it involves lots of statutory requirements and governance resulting in added cost of operation. Currently there is also a need of branch/subsidiary in cities where in companies already have a branch/subsidiary within the same province in some other city to hire locals as well as process Work Visas.

For example, if a company has a branch in Wuxi which is part of Jiangsu Province, a company cannot hire locals or process Work Visa for Suzhou which is in same province.

In conclusion the following could be considered as a way forward in the Yangtze River Delta Area to facilitate greater expansion by Indian companies.

· Addressing the social security issue by making it at a level playing field amongst local and foreign companies.

· Clarity in terms of short term hiring.

· Greater mobility and allowing a registered company in Yangtze River Delta to operate in multiple location without going through the tedious process of setting up multiple registered offices or re-applying for residents/work permits of people on short terms assignments from one office to other within China.

长三角一体化背景下的企业数字化转型与数字化人才战略

凯捷咨询

自 2018 年 11 月习近平主席在进博会开幕式上首次提到支持长江三角洲区域一体化发展并上升为国家战略以来,长三角一体化规划与落地的政策措施被加速推进。而上海作为长三角一体化发展的领头城市,必须抢抓长三角一体化机遇,推动区域数字化经济发展、数字化人才战略构建,以夯实区域数字化建设基础,为未来可持续发展助力。

基于凯捷中国对全球市场及中国本土经济、技术发展的洞察,在长江三角洲区域一体化发展的大背景下,凯捷深刻意识到实施企业数字化转型及构建数字化人才战略的必要性和重要性。

一、企业数字化转型势在必行

全球数字化浪潮奔腾而来,"数字化"三个字不再是停留在理论和技术层面的概念,已经切实体现在产业发展和个体生活的各个层面。从数字产业化到产业数字化的递进发展,直接改变了消费者的日常生活,也间接向企业"敲响警钟"——若想不被市场抛弃,数字化转型势在必行!因此,已经有越来越多的企业将"数字"视为核心资产、新资源和新财富。究其根源,数字化转型是产业的转型升级,是在新一轮市场竞争中抢占新的竞争制高点的有效助力。

企业必须进行数字化转型以便迅速应对日益分散化的客户需求,通过网络选择更广泛的供应商,获取更详细的客户洞见,推出更丰富、更复杂的产品线,更精准地联通消费者,满足他们的需求。数字化转型更为企业与消费者的每一次互动增加了价值。此外,数字化转型同样可赋能企业内部的运营管理,无论是提供更高效的协同管理、完善员工知识管理体系、提升组织运营效能等,都需要用数字化来助力推进。

这些数字化转型的变革在全球范围内正在进行。这就是"传统""陈旧"的企业在数字化浪潮中的命运:不转型则衰退!

长三角地区作为全国经济发展的样板示范区,是全国经济体量最大的城市群,仅用全国10%的人口,创造了近20%的GDP、25%的进出口总额和34%的货物吞吐量。长三角地区正乘着新型城镇化、区域一体化、数字经济等东风继续迈进。

在数字经济领域,长三角地区表现依旧出色。2018年全国数字经济达到31.3万亿元;其中长三角地区达到8.63万亿元,占全国数字经济总额的28%。数字经济已经成为长三角一体化的新动力,是长三角高质量发展的金名片。

新一轮长三角地区一体化发展,必须借助数字经济实现产业转型升级,培育出具有国际竞争力的产业集群和经济发展新动能。

二、企业数字化转型是一场巨量级战争

由上可见,企业数字化转型势在必行。就目前形势可见,随着互联网、大数据、物联网等数字化基础设施和能力的加速构建,各种企业都在创造巧妙、有效和颠覆性的技术利用方式。被数字化浪潮包围的当下,技术也逐步从"实验室"带到更广泛的"应用场景"。

同时数字化转型正在改变业务开展方式,在某些情况下,正在创造全新的业务类别。通过数字化转型,公司正在退一步,重新审视它们所做的一切,从内部系统到在线亲自与客户互动。它们提出了一些大问题,例如:"我们是否可以通过改进流程来改变决策流程,改变游戏规则的效率或通过更好的个性化来改善客户体验?""如何精准预测市场需求,控制供需平衡?"

在数字化转型这场"巨量级战争"中,无论是新技术的应用还是商业问题的解答,这并不是个别企业能够单独完成和解决的。可以预见,数字化转型并不仅仅是几家企业或某几个行业参与的一次变革运动,而是一场"巨量级战争"。

三、数字化人才战略,至关重要

在数字化转型"巨量级战争"中,企业面临着这些前所未有的新挑战;企业需要专业领先的咨询合作伙伴,去帮助它们迅速高效、精准无误地解决这些问题。可以预见,这场"巨量级战争"对人才的渴求也是"巨量级别"的。

与企业数字化转型相对应,数字化人才战略的构建也至关重要。这一点对推

动长三角一体化与高质量发展也是具有积极战略意义的。

长三角是我国经济发展最活跃、开放程度最高、创新能力最强的区域之一，在全国经济中具有举足轻重的地位。

2018年11月5日，习近平总书记在首届中国国际进口博览会开幕式讲话时指出，支持将长江三角洲区域一体化发展上升为国家战略。2019年5月13日，中共中央政治局会议审议通过《长江三角洲区域一体化发展规划纲要》，明确长三角通过一体化发展，使其成为全国经济发展强劲活跃的增长极，成为全国经济高质量发展的样板区，率先基本实现现代化的引领区和区域一体化发展的示范区，成为新时代改革开放的新高地。

而推动社会经济实现更高质量发展的最关键、最基础的因素就是人才，没有强大的人才队伍作后盾，推动高质量发展就是无源之水、无本之木。因此，人才是引领发展的战略资源，构建区域创新人才共同体成为践行长三角区域一体化国家战略的重要手段之一。人才一体化是实现长三角一体化发展的内在要求，是支撑长三角一体化的重要保障，也是检验长三角一体化的重要标准。

四、凯捷中国对人才的培养与管理的重视

对于提供数字化转型相关咨询服务的咨询公司而言，在帮助企业客户之前也必须理清这些问题——如何帮助企业客户与它们的消费者进行更加快速高效的沟通？如何从企业客户的角度出发，真正做到为其找到症结所在、定制数字化转型解决方案？传统的咨询形式和作业模式是否还能满足在数字化浪潮中求新求变求异的企业客户需求？传统的精英化咨询模式能否快速帮助客户企业迅速获得数字经济的红利？

这些都是每一家战略咨询公司需要思考并探讨的关键问题。

在全球科技二元化的时代背景下，凯捷中国作为一家拥有全球资源、欧洲血统的中国公司，判断 IT 咨询服务市场仍将持续增量，客户已清晰地认识到自身在数字化转型中的需求并持续加大投入，需求量和更新频次也在持续变化。聚焦国内，从政府机构到寻常百姓都已高度数字化，云经济普及，IT 咨询服务已成为如一日三餐般的必需品。

相较于传统的咨询模式，凯捷中国提出"2022 年，凯捷中国成为庶民化 IT 咨询服务的领导者"这一战略使命，并加大对人才战略的重视，正如凯捷集团的愿景"成长无极限"所诠释的那样，凯捷集团坚信人是技术、商业之本。

凯捷中国认定最合适的人才加最好的平台等于必然的成功。凯捷中国一步一

个脚印构建最优的良性竞争平台,供员工去创造、积累,协同客户和合作伙伴持续成长、持续成功。成功的凯捷无输家,失败的凯捷无赢家。

凯捷中国的数字化人才战略提出JTP青年人才计划。随着凯捷中国的团队与业务不断壮大和发展,2015年青年人才计划启动。凯捷协同专业的合作伙伴,高效推进青年人才计划,迄今为止,已为凯捷输送了数百名优秀员工。

凯捷青年人才计划不仅引入凯捷大学先进的培训课程和理念,还在昆山设立凯捷中国企业大学。通过所拥有的IT咨询服务行业最权威技术方案、最领先云服务和大数据能力,课程库中上万门线上线下课程,配合经验丰富的教学团队,和专业全面的认证能力,已成功培养了数千名优秀学生加入凯捷成为行业领先的IT咨询顾问,并协助高校教师在教学过程中向更适应时代需求的IT咨询顾问进行角色转换。

整个培训计划共经历三个阶段,首先凯捷会为参加青年人才计划的学生提供为期3周的通用培训,内容包括结构化思维、邮件礼仪、商业案例写作等通用的软硬技能,同时,还会安排诸如定向越野等活动。其次是专业技术培训,主要分为ERP、移动开发、测试和人力资源管理等方向。最后,在掌握专业技术之后,学生会进入真实的项目进行实操,在项目经理的管理下,在技术专家的指导下,参与技术开发、功能设计或方案撰写等工作。

五、结语

中国经济发展已呈现出新常态,同时也面临着国际形势发生重大变化,国内经济正处于转型升级关键期的新挑战。随着中国经济发展步入新常态,经济增长从要素投资驱动转向创新驱动。这意味着更高起点的改革开放,完善中国经济的空间布局,策应国家已有的"一带一路"、京津冀、长江经济带、粤港澳大湾区战略,都需要长三角地区加快一体化发展,以更好地发挥中国经济的引领作用。

而在长三角一体化和高质量发展过程中,企业数字化转型及相应的数字化人才战略都将为之助力,帮助企业及其所在区域积极策应、主动抓住时代机遇。

Digital Transformation and Digital Talent Strategy of Businesses Against the Background of the Yangtze River Delta Integration

Capgemini

Since Chinese President Xi Jinping proposed to support the integrated development of the Yangtze River Delta and elevate it to a national strategy for the first time at the opening ceremony of China International Import Expo in Nov. 2018, policies and measures for planning and implementing Yangtze River Delta integration have been accelerated. As a leading city in the integrated development of the Yangtze River Delta, Shanghai must seize the opportunity in Yangtze River Delta integration, promote the development of a regional digital economy and digital talent strategy, so as to consolidate the foundation of regional digital construction and contribute to future sustainable development.

Based on the insights of *Capgemini* China into global markets and local economic and technological development in China, against the background of Yangtze River Delta integration, *Capgemini* is well aware of the necessity and importance of implementing digital transformation and developing a digital talent strategy for businesses.

I. The digital transformation of businesses is imperative

The tide of global digitization is coming. Digitization is no longer a theoretical or technical concept, but has been embodied in all aspects of industry development and individual life. The progressive development from digital industrialization to industry digitization has directly changed the daily life of consumers and indirectly sounded the alarm for businesses: if businesses don't want to be abandoned by the market, digital transformation is imperative! As a result, more and more companies are treating digital asset as a core asset, new resource and new wealth. At bottom, digital transformation is industry transformation and upgrading, an effective way to seize a new competitive commanding height in the new round of market competition.

Companies must go through digital transformation to respond quickly to the increasingly fragmented customer needs, select a wider range of suppliers, obtain more detailed customer insights, launch richer and more complex product lines and reach consumers more accurately through the Internet, to satisfy their needs. Digital transformation adds value to every interaction between businesses and consumers. In addition, digital transformation also can enable operations management within companies. Digitalization is needed to provide more efficient collaborative management, improve the knowledge management system, enhance organizational operation efficiency.

Such changes brought by digital transformation are happening all over the world! Traditional old-fashioned companies' fate is set in the tide of digitalization: change or die!

As a national model and demonstration area for economic development, the Yangtze River Delta is the largest urban agglomeration with the largest economic volume in China. With only 10% of national population, it has created nearly 20% of national GDP, 25% of national import and export and 34% of national cargo throughput. The Yangtze River Delta is moving forward taking advantage of new urbanization, regional integration and digital economy.

In the digital economy, the Yangtze River Delta is still doing well. In 2018, China's digital economy reached 31.3 trillion RMB, in which the Yangtze River Delta contributed 8.63 trillion RMB, 28% of the national total. Digital economy has become a new driving force for the integration of the Yangtze River Delta and a golden card for the high-quality development of the Yangtze River Delta.

In the new round of integrated development, the Yangtze River Delta must realize industry transformation and upgrading, and create industry clusters and new drivers of economic development with international competitiveness with the help of the digital economy.

II. The digital transformation of businesses is a huge war

Thus, digital transformation is an imperative for businesses! As things stand now, with the accelerated construction of digital infrastructure and capabilities such as the Internet, big data and Internet of Things, all kinds of companies are creating smart, effective and revolutionary ways to use technology. Surrounded by the tide of digitization, technology is also gradually brought out of labs into a wider range of application scenarios.

Meanwhile, digital transformation is changing the way business is done. In some cases, entirely new categories of business are being created. Through digital transformation, companies are stepping back and reexamining what they do, from internal systems to online interaction with customers in person. They have raised some big questions. For example, can we change the decision process by improving business procedures, improve efficiency by changing the rules of the game or improve customer experience through better personalization? How to accurately predict market demand and keep supply and demand in balance?

In the huge war of digital transformation, whether it's the application of new technologies or solutions to business problems, it is not something that specific companies can accomplish or solve alone. It can be foreseen that digital transformation is not just a movement involving a few companies or a few industries, but a huge war.

III. A digital talent strategy is crucial

In the huge war of digital transformation, companies are facing these unprecedented new challenges. They need professional leading consulting partners to help them solve these problems quickly, efficiently and accurately. It can be predicted that the demand for talent in this huge war is also huge.

Corresponding to the digital transformation of businesses, the development of a digital talent strategy is also crucial. This is also of positive strategic significance to promoting the integration and high-quality development of the Yangtze River Delta.

The Yangtze River Delta is one of the regions with the most active economic development, the highest degree of openness and the strongest innovation ability in China. It is in a pivotal position in the national economy.

On Nov. 5, 2018, Chinese President Xi Jinping pointed out in his speech at the opening ceremony of the First China International Import Expo that China will support the integrated development of the Yangtze River Delta and elevate it to a national strategy. On May 13, 2019, the meeting of the Political Bureau of the CPC Central Committee passed *the Outline of the Integrated Regional Development of the Yangtze River Delta*. The document makes it clear that the Yangtze River Delta, through integrated development, will become a strong and dynamic growth pole for national economic development, a model for national high-quality economic development, a region leading in the basic realization of modernization and a demonstration area for regional integrated development, and a new highland for reform and opening up in the new era.

Talent is the most critical and most basic factor in achieving higher-quality social and economic development. Without the backing of a strong talent team, promoting high-quality development is like water without a source or a tree without roots. Therefore, talent is a strategic resource to lead in development. Building a regional innovative talent community has become one of the important means to implement the national strategy of regional integration in the Yangtze River Delta. Talent integration is an intrinsic requirement to realize the integrated development of the Yangtze

River Delta, an important guarantee to support the integration of the Yangtze River Delta, and an important criterion to judge the integration of the Yangtze River Delta.

IV. *Capgemini* China attaches importance to talent training and management

For consulting firms that provide consulting services concerning digital transformation, the following problems must be sorted out before helping corporate clients. How to help corporate clients communicate with their customers more quickly and efficiently? How to find the crux of their problems and customize digital transformation solutions from the perspective of corporate clients? Can traditional consulting forms and operation models still meet the needs of corporate clients who are seeking novelty, change and differentiation in the tide of digitalization? Can the traditional elitist consulting model help corporate clients benefit from the digital economy quickly?

These are all essential problems that every strategy consulting firm needs to think about and discuss.

In the era of global technology dualization, as a Chinese company of European origin with global resources, *Capgemini* China judges that the IT consulting service market will continue to grow. Clients are clearly aware of their own needs in digital transformation and are continuing to increase investment. The quantity demanded and update frequency are also constantly changing. In China, every aspect from government agencies to ordinary people's life is highly digitalized. The cloud economy is everywhere. IT consulting services have become a daily necessity like three meals a day.

In contrast to traditional consulting models, *Capgemini* China has put forward the strategic mission of becoming a leader in IT consulting services for general public in 2022 and increased emphasis on the talent strategy. The vision of *Capgemini* is infinite growth. *Capgemini* believes that the business value of technology comes from and through people. People matter, results count.

Capgemini China firmly believes that the most suitable talent plus the best platform equals inevitable success. *Capgemini* China builds an optimal healthy competition platform step by step for employees to create, accumulate, and work with clients and partners for sustainable growth and success. A successful *Capgemini* has no losers. A failed *Capgemini* has no winners.

As part of its digital talent strategy, *Capgemini* China put forward JTP. With the continuous growth and development of *Capgemini*'s team and business in China, JTP was launched in 2015. *Capgemini* works with professional partners to efficiently promote JTP. So far, JTP has provided *Capgemini* with hundreds of excellent employees.

Capgemini JTP not only introduces the advanced training courses and concepts of *Capgemini* University, but also has established *Capgemini* Business School in Kunshan. With the most authoritative technical solutions, the most advanced cloud services and big data capabilities in the IT consulting service industry, more than 10,000 online and offline courses in the course library, coupled with experienced teaching teams, professional comprehensive certification capabilities, *Capgemini* JTP has successfully trained thousands of outstanding students to join *Capgemini* as industry-leading IT consultants, while assisting university teachers to switch their role into IT consultants better adapted to the needs of the times in the teaching process.

Capgemini JTP consists of three stages. First, *Capgemini* provides students participating in JTP with 3 weeks of general training, covering general hard and soft skills such as structured thinking, email etiquette and business case writing, supplemented with activities such as orienteering. The second stage is professional skills training, mainly covering ERP, mobile development, testing and HR management. In the last stage, after mastering professional skills, students practice in real projects, participating in technical development, function design or proposal writing under the management of the project manager and the guidance of technical experts.

V. Conclusion

China's economic development has presented a new normal. At the same time, China is facing major changes in the international situation. The domestic economy is facing new challenges in the critical period of transformation and upgrading. As China's economic development enters a new normal, economic growth is shifting from being driven by factor investment to being driven by innovation. This means reform and opening up from a higher starting point, improving the spatial distribution of China's economy, and the Guangdong-Hong Kong-Macao Greater Bay Area strategy which supports China's Belt and Road, Beijing-Tianjin-Hebei Region and Yangtze River Economic Zone, all need the Yangtze River Delta to accelerate its integrated development, to better play its leading role in China's economy.

In the process of Yangtze River Delta integration and high-quality development, the digital transformation of businesses and the corresponding digital talent strategy will contribute to it, helping businesses and the region act actively and seize the opportunities in our era.

Higher-quality Integration in the Yangtze River Delta

长三角更高质量一体化

以自贸区联动为引领，推动长三角一体化更高质量发展

毕马威

一、自贸试验区从"成立"到"深化"，再走向"联动"

从 2013 年 9 月我国第一个自贸试验区在上海挂牌，到 2017 年唯一一个由陆域和海洋锚地组成的浙江自贸试验区设立，再到 2019 年 8 月江苏自贸试验区成立，长三角深化改革开放的战略部署打开了新局面。通过突出自贸试验区的引擎效应，全面开放，以及深度参与国际分工与全球竞争，长三角一体化从建设引领中国经济高质量发展的增长极，进一步发展为引领全国、辐射全球的世界级开放城市群。

长三角区域历来是我国改革开放的先行者，自贸试验区的内核外延也在此得到了深化与拓展。2018 年进博会上习近平主席宣布增设上海自贸试验区新片区，一年后临港新片区挂牌，"投资贸易便利化"向"投资贸易自由化"转变，实现了大跨度历史性升级，剑指"国际竞争力最强的自由贸易区"；浙江在全国首提建设"自贸试验区联动创新区"，探索更大程度发挥自贸试验区在制度创新、产业引领、贸易便利、综合监管等方面的辐射效应；江苏自贸试验区虽然成立时间短，但精准聚焦，回归初心，"着力打造开放型经济发展先行区、实体经济创新发展和产业转型升级示范区"，更多地为实体经济开放转型服务。

长三角区域的自贸试验区已经跨过了"成立"和"深化"两个里程碑，我们认为下一步的关键将在于"联动"。依靠沪浙苏三地自贸试验区在制度创新、机制探索方面的先天优势，主动突破限制区域协同发展的瓶颈，以自贸试验区的联动发展推动高端要素的跨区流动，放大制度创新的溢出效应，实现长三角区域一体化的更高质量发展。

二、自贸试验区联动,构建营商环境、产业协同、区域港口三个一体化

1. 以体制规范为基准,构建营商环境一体化

2018年我们讨论如何进一步优化上海营商环境,当时上海在全球排名是第46位,一年过去,这个排名提升了15位,站在了"三环边"。这个进步来自高位推动,上下协同,也来自100项改革政策,狠抓落实。2019年我们希望把这个话题更进一步,探讨如何利用三地自贸试验区在营商环境方面的有益探索,形成一套稳定的体制规范,以此为基准,带动整个长三角区域整体构建对标国际高水平的一体化营商环境。

从实践来看,此前上海、江苏、浙江、安徽四地联合签署了《长三角地区共同优化知识产权营商环境合作意向书》,三省一市将在提高知识产权审查质量和效率,引入惩罚性赔偿制度,显著提高违法成本等方面进行共同探索,通过知识产权保护和服务来加强优化营商环境。上海自贸试验区在知识产权方面进行了一些有益探索,包括成立专利、商标、版权"三合一"知识产权局,将原本分散在管委会、工商局的行政管理和执法体制机制统一在一个机构之下,有效解决了知识产权领域"条块分割、多头执法、执法力量分配不均"等问题,并促进执法标准统一,执法效能提升;建设国家知识产权运营公共服务平台国际运营(上海)试点平台,开展知识产权交易服务、海外布局及维权等业务。三省一市可以在该合作意向书的基础上,借鉴上海自贸试验区知识产权保护和服务的有效经验,建立知识产权统一行政管理和执法体制机制的工作方案,共同遵循严格、高标准的知识产权保护国际规则与标准,在区域内应用同样严苛的惩罚性赔偿制度,提高长三角区域整体知识产权保护和服务力度,避免跨区域知识产权纠纷和行政执法漏洞,增强对拥有自主创新能力企业和知识产权保护敏感的外资企业的吸引力。

知识产权是一个切入点,再进一步,我们建议长三角区域在开办企业、登记财产、获得信贷、跨境贸易、合同执行等方面都去达成一些一致性的合作意向,上海、浙江、江苏自贸试验区要做好领头羊角色,突出高标准规则引领,与国际上通行的、有效的做法进行对接,对于适合复制推广、经受住了压力测试的政策实践要尽快在整个长三角区域内推广应用。一个具体的尝试是,在上海也可以登记一家江苏的企业,并且这个登记手续不管在哪里都是5个步骤就能做完,按照同样的要求提交材料,相关部门也按照同样的标准去审核这些材料,最快2天内这项登记就可以完成了,这时候企业不管是在上海还是在江苏,都可以享受无差别化的登记标准流程。所以在营商环境这个话题下,我们希望下一步不仅要强调上海自贸试验区的

准入负面清单是不是缩减了,浙江自贸区"最多跑一次"是不是使得登记流程更简便了,把这些当作各个自贸区差异化的吸引力,而且要把重点转到体制规范的轨道上来,要求自贸区承担起引领重任,带动整体构建与高标准全球营商环境规则相衔接的国内规则和制度体系,开展优化地区营商环境的锦标赛,降低区域制度性交易成本,构建一体化的营商环境。

2. 以要素流通为驱动,构建产业协同一体化

基于一体化的营商环境,过去受制于行政管理体制的一些"断点"可以打通,整个区域的各类要素都可以高效流动和优化配置,给产业的合作创造了一个非常好的条件。

我们注意到,纽约湾区的产业结构是一个比较好的集群系统。核心城市纽约依托其独一无二的地理优势,对内背靠世界最大的消费市场和广阔腹地,对外是美国面向海外最主要的港口。再加上作为全美第一个也是范围最大的自贸区,高度自由的国际贸易规则、极具竞争力的关税政策和效率极高的政府服务与审批,使得纽约在工业时代就储备了雄厚的经济基础,后工业时代,其对日益衰退的第二产业进行改造,发展小型制造业和高科技产业,进一步发展形成了以金融为引领的外向型生产性服务业,带动各种实体经济的发展。湾区北部的波士顿依托哈佛大学、麻省理工学院、波士顿大学等诸多高校为整个纽约湾区发展提供了高素质的人力资源和高新科技;南部的费城是美国工业化最早的区域,持续在重工业、港口经济等产业领域发力。整个纽约湾区通过明确的分工协作和合理的功能定位,发挥了自贸区境内境外两个市场要素灵活流动的优势,区域内产业结构呈现多元化和互补性的格局。

对于长三角区域而言,产业类型、驱动主体和驱动方式上都已经有一些差异化的定位。以上海为中心节点,南翼途径杭州,与宁波、舟山等相连,主要由数量众多的小微企业和民营资本驱动,浙江自贸区围绕油气全产业链突出强化了自身特色;北翼途经苏州、南京,再和安徽的芜湖联结,一直延伸到合肥。除了一部分民营资本和外商投资之外,更多的是由国有资本驱动,主要产业包括电子信息、智能装备制造、新能源汽车等,江苏自贸试验区也一再强调着力打造实体经济创新发展和产业转型升级示范区,支持制造业创新发展。

基于此,借鉴纽约湾区经验,在空间格局上,上海要充分利用自贸试验区特别是临港新片区的门户效应,成为连接国际和区域要素资源的接口,着力发展以金融为引领的高端生产性服务业,以人才为支撑的创意产业,以业态创新为特征的新兴商业等,实现对区域整体产业活力的带动。浙江和江苏两地要基于自身特色强化和上海之间的产业分工与互动,例如浙江自贸区与上海期货交易所在油品贸易方面的"期现合作",江苏自贸区与上海自贸区在金融创新、金融开放方面的联动等。在协同生态上,长三角要利用资金、技术、创新人才等高端要素的强流动实现产业的动态匹配和双向迁移。以长三角自贸区优势制造业集成电路为例,当前上海企业的投资2/3来自境外,来自江苏和浙江的投资不到5%。长三角协同优势产业基金等一系列母基金的成立,将吸纳来自三省一市国企、民企和金融机构的投资,投向"硬科技""完善产业链""自主创新"等长三角产业协同关键领域,通过规模化的资本撬动,引导长三角资本要素打破行政区域限制,以市场化配置手段匹配区域企业的需求。

3. 以管理创新为切入,构建港口运营一体化

港口经济是长三角区域一个比较具有地域或地理位置特色的方面。长三角区域有16个港口,整个港口群分布密集、吞吐量大,其中包括上海港、宁波舟山港两个全国吞吐量最大的深水良港。随着江苏自贸试验区的设定,可以看到长三角区域的港口在自贸试验区这个创新区域概念下其实已经被联系起来,下一步是在自贸试验区提供的创新机制平台基础上,找到一些管理创新的切入口,更快、更有效地实现长三角港口群的运营一体化,未来也可以作为一个范本在全国其他港口群进行推广。

纽约港的管理机制是比较有突破性的,因为它们成立了一个在法律上独立于纽约和新泽西两州而存在的跨州机构——纽约与新泽西港务局。这个港务局保证了整个大纽约地区三个大港和若干个小港之间港务的无缝运作,没有再因为跨州而造成机构之间的争执。同时,这个港务局还是整个纽约港自贸区的管理机构,在关税政策、进出口程序、质量监控、企业准入审查等方面拥有被中央政府授权的自主权,与整个港务运营达成高度协调。

阿姆斯特丹港务局实行"港区合一,高度授权"的机制,管理机构的权威性非常强,阿姆斯特丹市政府下设经中央政府授权成立的港务管理专门机构——阿姆斯特丹港务局,负责管理和协调阿姆斯特丹港及内部自由贸易区的整体事务、投资建设必要的基础设施,并且有权审批项目立项,在自由贸易区与城市功能的相互促进,金融、保险、商贸、中介等第三产业发展上成效显著。而跨市港口的管理由港务局下属的中央航运管辖中心负责,并获得中央政府和当地市政的统一授权,各个港口设立港务长办公室,执行管辖中心规定,负责港口畅通、安全、发展。

在港口管理机制上,新加坡最值得借鉴的做法是建设和应用了一套先进的港口综合运营信息平台。不同于纽约和荷兰"政企合一"的港口管理运营机制,新加坡是"政企分开"的运营模式,由新加坡海事港务管理局和新加坡港务集团分管运营,自贸区的管理职能在海事港务局之下。整个港口综合运营系统是联系和协调

船东、货运、航线和港口的全球航运处理系统,下设有新加坡航运中心信息平台Portnet、贸易信息平台 TradeNet、一站式货运服务系统 CargoD2D、管理并简化中转运输的 ezShip 系统,以及提供 2—4 年航运报告信息平台 TRAVIS 等高科技信息平台。虽然是政企分开的独立机构,但基于综合信息平台也能对五个港区进行一体化管理,特别是实时反馈的数据对于港区资源的协调起到了极大的帮助。

长三角区域的港口一体化已经在进行一些探索,如上海、浙江以股权合作的方式共同推进了小洋山港区的综合开发,上港集团与江苏港口集团、中国远洋海运集团签署了战略合作备忘录促进两地港口协同发展,江苏港口集团与浙江海港集团达成了互相参股意向,安徽省港航集团在成立之初就与上海组合港管委会办公室、上港集团、浙江省海港集团等签署了战略合作协议。在一些具体的抓手举措上也有探索,例如浙江自贸区率先打破区域限制形成的系统化跨关区直供监管互认模式,已经与宁波、南京、上海等海关辖区形成深化合作,上海口岸办正在推进长三角单一窗口建设等,从信息共享、监管互认、执法互助等角度为长三角港口一体化提供基础土壤。但我们也看到,这些尝试都相对零散,在整个高层级的管理机构、协调机制等方面还没有实质性的突破。自贸试验区一方面与港口天然联系在一起,另一方面有着最适合进行机制创新的土壤,可以借着这个机遇推动长三角区域港口一体化和大港区经济的协同发展。

三、建议

基于上述思考和经验,我们希望能从大处着眼、小处着手,对于工作的开展提出一些具体的建议。

1. 建立稳定化、常态化的长三角区域沟通机制

这个对象包括政府,比如现在已经成立的长三角区域合作办公室;包括在长三角一体化区域中要发挥引领作用的自贸试验区,三地的自贸试验区要迅速建立一个沟通机制,落实营商环境这个基础的一体化,推动产业协同这个核心动力的一体化,探索港区运营这个重点领域的一体化;也包括智库机构、高校院所等社会力量,活跃于各个机构之间,为自贸试验区与长三角一体化的高度融合开拓更多的思路。

2. 借鉴自贸试验区成效评估经验,长三角区域一体化也要有一套特色体系

前两批自贸试验区取得的成效非常明显,一个很大的原因就是大家都在推动改革成效评估,从政策创新、实施效果、辐射带动等多个角度进行客观评价。随着《长三角生态绿色一体化发展示范区总体方案》等一系列方案的出台,工作进度、实施成效、改进反馈都需要有参考依据来推进,既带有国际惯例的高标准,又能体现

出区域发展特征的评估体系就急需建立起来,并能够据此进行实际评估和有效反馈。

3. 信息化合作是这个时代最有效的协同手段

长三角区域是我国数据基础设施建设最成熟的地区,同时在云计算、大数据、物联网、人工智能等数字技术方面拥有前沿的技术能力。在以自贸试验区为引领,促进区域协同的过程中,应加快数字资源的开放、共享利用,优化数字资源配置效率,深化重点领域智慧应用的区域联动。

Promoting Higher-quality Development in the Integration of the Yangtze River Delta Led by the Linkage of Free Trade Zones

KPMG

Ⅰ. From the "establishment" and "deepening" of the pilot free trade zones to "linkage"

China's first pilot free trade zone (FTZ) was established in Shanghai in September 2013; then, the Zhejiang Pilot Free Trade Zone, the only FTZ consisting of both land and marine anchorages, was established in 2017; and the Jiangsu Pilot Free Trade Zone was established in August 2019. The establishment of these FTZs marked a new milestone in the effort to deepen reform and opening-up in the Yangtze River Delta region. By highlighting the driving effect of these pilot free trade zones, fully opening-up, and deep participating in the international division of labour, and competing globally, the integration of the Yangtze River Delta is moving forward from building growth poles that steer the high-quality development of China's economy towards creating world-class city clusters that lead the country and serve as a beacon to the world.

The Yangtze River Delta region has always been a pioneer in China's reform and opening-up, and the core value of the region's pilot free trade zones has been enriched and expanded. At the 2018 China Expo, President Xi Jinping announced the establishment of a new area in the Shanghai Pilot

Free Trade Zone. A year later, the Lingang New Area was established. The Lingang New Area represents a historical transition from investment and trade facilitation towards investment and trade liberalisation, with the ultimate goal of positioning itself as the most competitive free trade zone in the world. Zhejiang was the first province in China to propose building an Innovation Linkage Zone in the Pilot Free Trade Zones, and was also the first to explore ways to make greater use of the radiation effects of a pilot free trade zone in terms of system innovation, industry leadership, trade facilitation, comprehensive supervision, and other areas. The Jiangsu Pilot Free Trade Zone has only been established for a short period of time, but it has stayed true to its original goal by focusing on "building an opening-up zone for economic development and a model demonstration zone for innovative development of the real economy and industrial transformation and upgrading". In this way, the Jiangsu Pilot FTZ aims to better serve the opening-up and transformation of the real economy.

The pilot free trade zones in the Yangtze River Delta region have already crossed the two milestones of "establishment" and "deepening". We believe that the next key step will be "linkage". The pilot free trade zones in the Shanghai-Zhejiang-Jiangsu region have certain inherent advantages in terms of system innovation and mechanism exploration. By relying on these advantages and proactively breaking through the bottlenecks that restrict regional coordinated development, we should be able to promote the cross-regional flow of high-end factors, facilitate the interactive development of the pilot free trade zones, boost the spillover effects of system innovation, and encourage the higher quality development of regional integration in the Yangtze River Delta.

II. Linking the pilot free trade zones to integrate the region's business environment, industrial synergies, and ports

1. Building an integrated business environment based on institutional norms

Last year, we talked about how to further optimise the doing-business environment in Shanghai. At that time, Shanghai was ranked 46th in the world in this regard. This year the city's ranking increased 15 places, almost reaching 30th. This progress was the result of high-level promotion and top-to-bottom coordination, as well as the introduction of 100 reform policies which are being implemented quite effectively. This year we hope to take this topic one step further by exploring how to use the progress that has been made in the business environment by the three regions' pilot free trade zones to produce a set of stable institutional norms. Based on these norms, we aim to encourage the Yangtze River Delta region as a whole to build an integrated business environment that meets international high-level standards.

Shanghai, Jiangsu, Zhejiang and Anhui have jointly signed the *Letter of Intent on Cooperating to Optimise the Business Environment for Intellectual Property Rights in the Yangtze River Delta Region*. The three provinces and Shanghai will jointly explore ways to improve the quality and efficiency of intellectual property rights (IPR) reviews, introduce a punitive compensation system, and significantly increase the cost of violations. In this way, the region aims to optimise the business environment by strengthening IPR protection and improving services. The pilot free trade zone in Shanghai has extensively explored IPR. As part of its efforts, the FTZ established a "three-in-one" IPR office for patents, trademarks and copyrights. Within this office, the Shanghai Pilot Free Trade Zone unified the administrative management and law enforcement system and mechanisms that were originally allocated to the management committee and the Industry and Commerce Bureau, thereby effectively solving the problems of "barriers between different departments and regions, multiple offices conducting enforcement, and uneven distribution of enforcement power" in respect of IPR. Through this office, the FTZ has been able to promote uniform law enforcement standards and improve the effectiveness of law enforcement. The FTZ has also established an International Operations (Shanghai) Pilot Platform for the National IPR Public Services Platform in order to carry out IPR transaction services, make overseas arrangements, secure rights, and

长三角一体化与高质量发展
Integration of the Yangtze River Delta for High-quality Development

perform other tasks. Based on their Letter of Intent on Cooperating, the three provinces and Shanghai can draw on the experience of the Shanghai Pilot Free Trade Zone in the area of IPR protection and services, develop a plan to build a unified IPR administration and enforcement mechanism, and jointly follow strict and high-standard international IPR protection rules and standards. The Yangtze River Delta region should implement a uniform punitive compensation system to improve the overall quality of IPR protection and services, avoid cross-regional IPR disputes, close administrative enforcement loopholes, and enhance the attractiveness of the region to enterprises with independent innovation capabilities and to foreign-funded enterprises that are sensitive to IPR protection.

These IPR initiatives represent a significant step forward for the region. We also recommend that the Yangtze River Delta region cooperate to achieve consistency in areas such as starting a business, property registration, obtaining credit, cross-border trade, contract execution, etc. In this regard, the pilot free trade zones in Shanghai, Zhejiang and Jiangsu should play a leading role. They should focus on high standard rules and align their rules with internationally accepted and effective practices. Policies and practices that are suitable for replication and that have withstood stress testing should be promoted and applied throughout the Yangtze River Delta region as soon as possible. For instance, a Jiangsu company may attempt to register in Shanghai. In such a case, it should be possible to complete the registration process in five steps wherever the company is; the required materials for submission should be the same; the same standards should be adopted by the relevant departments to review the materials; and it should be possible to complete the registration in 2 days. This would mean that enterprises could enjoy the same registration procedures regardless of whether they are in Shanghai or Jiangsu. So in terms of the business environment, we hope that the next step is not only to highlight whether the negative list for access to the Shanghai Pilot Free Trade Zone has been reduced, or whether the "one-stop application" measure in the Zhejiang Pilot Free Trade Zone has made the registration process easier, but also give the shift toward institutional norms as a priority. The free trade zones should take a leading role and drive the overall construction of domestic rules, systems and institutions that are in line with global business environment standards. They should strive to optimise the regional business environment, reduce institutional transaction costs in the region, and build an integrated business environment.

2. Factor circulation as a driving force, and enabling industrial coordination and integration

With the support of an integrated business environment, certain breakthrough points that were previously constrained by the administrative system can be overcome; various essential factors can flow efficiently and be optimised throughout the entire region; and conditions can be created that are favourable for industrial cooperation.

We noticed that the industrial structure of the New York Bay Area provides an example of a good cluster system. New York City, which is the area's core, has unique geographical advantages. Internally, it has access to the world's largest consumer market as well as vast hinterland. Externally, it is the United States' most important port for overseas shipping. New York is the nation's first and largest free trade area. It has implemented international free trade rules, highly competitive tariff policies, and efficient government services and approvals. New York laid a solid economic foundation during the industrial age and transformed its declining secondary industries into small manufacturing and high-tech industries during the post-industrial age. This ultimately led to the creation of an export-oriented productive service industry led by finance that drives the development of various real economies. Furthermore, Harvard University, MIT, Boston University and many other colleges are located north of the Bay Area. These institutions provide high-quality human resources and technologies that facilitate the development of the New York Bay Area. South of the Bay Area lies Philadelphia, which was the first region in the country to industrialise. Today it continues to promote heavy industry and its port economy, among other industries. Through a clear division of labour and reasonable positioning of functions, the entire New York Bay Area and its free trade zone enjoy advantages that arise from the flexible flow of factors in both domestic and overseas markets. In this way, the region boasts an industrial structure that is diversified and complementary.

Within the Yangtze River Delta region, there is already some differentiated positioning in terms of industry types, driving entities and driving methods. Taking Shanghai as the centre, the south wing of the region connects to Ningbo and Zhoushan via Hangzhou. The Zhejiang Pilot Free Trade Zone, which is in this wing, has strengthened its own advantages by focusing on the entire oil and gas industry chain. Its efforts in this sector are mainly driven by a large number of small and micro businesses and private capital. The north wing of the region passes through Suzhou and Nanjing, connects with Wuhu, and then goes all the way to Hefei in Anhui province. The Jiangsu Pilot Free Trade Zone is more driven by state-owned capital, in addition to some private capital and foreign investment. Its main industries are related to electronic information, intelligent equipment manufacturing, new energy vehicles, etc. The Jiangsu FTZ has also repeatedly emphasised its efforts to build a demonstration zone to facilitate the innovative development of the real economy and industrial transformation and upgrading. In this way, the FTZ aims to support the development of innovative manufacturing.

Using the New York Bay Area as an example, Shanghai should make full use of the portal effect of its pilot free trade zone — especially in the Lingang New Area — in terms of the spatial layout in order to become an interface for international and regional factor resources. In addition, Shanghai should focus on developing high-end productive service industries led by finance, creative industries supported by talented individuals, and other new sectors characterised by business innovation so as to improve the overall industrial vitality of the region. Based on their own characteristics, Zhejiang and Jiangsu have strengthened their industrial division and interaction with Shanghai. Examples include the Futures and Spot Commodity Cooperation between the Zhejiang Pilot Free Trade Zone and the Shanghai Futures Exchange for oil product transactions, and the linkage between the Zhejiang Pilot Free Trade Zone and the Shanghai Pilot Free Trade Zone in financial innovation and financial opening-up. Through this synergetic ecosystem, the region will enable the strong flow of high-end factors such as capital, technology and innovative talent in order to achieve dynamic matching and two-way migration of industries. For example, with respect to integrated circuits manufacturing, which is a leading industry in the Yangtze River Delta's free trade zones, foreign investment accounts for two-thirds of total investment in Shanghai enterprises in this sector, with less than 5 percent coming from Jiangsu and Zhejiang. With the establishment of a series of parent funds such as the Yangtze River Delta Synergy Advantage Industry Fund, funds from state-owned enterprises, private enterprises and financial institutions in the three provinces and Shanghai will invest in key areas to drive industrial collaboration in the Yangtze River Delta. These key areas include core technologies, perfect industrial chains, and indigenous innovation. By leveraging large-scale capital, capital factors in the Yangtze River Delta will be used to break administrative restrictions, and market-based allocation methods will be adopted to match regional enterprises with each other so that they can fulfil their needs.

3. Integrating port operations through management innovation

In the Yangtze River Delta, the port economy is full of regional and geographic characteristics. There are 16 ports in the Yangtze River Delta region. The entire port group is densely distributed and has a large throughput. The region's port group includes the Shanghai Port and Ningbo Zhoushan Port, which are the two most important deep-water ports in the country. As the dust settles following the construction of the Jiangsu Pilot Free Trade Zone, we can see that the ports in the Yangtze River Delta region have actually been linked under the innovative pilot free trade zone concept. The next step for the region is to identify entry points for management innovation based on the innovation mechanism platform provided by the pilot free trade zones in order to integrate the operations of the Yangtze River Delta port group in a faster and more effective manner. In the future, this approach can also be promoted as a model for other port groups in the country.

The New York Port's management mechanism is quite standard. It established a new interstate agency that is legally independent of New York and New Jersey called the Port Authority of New York and New Jersey. The Port Authority ensures the seamless operation of port affairs between the three large ports and several small ports within the Greater New York area. In addition, because it has interstate jurisdiction, no disputes arise between different agencies. At the same time, the Port Authority is also the management agency for the entire New York Port free trade zone. As authorised by the central government, the Port Authority has autonomy with respect to tariff policies, import and export procedures, quality control, and enterprise access reviews, and it has achieved a high degree of coordination with the entirety of the port's operations.

The Port Authority in Amsterdam has implemented an "integrated and highly authorised port" mechanism, and its management authority is very authoritative. The Port Authority of Amsterdam is a specialised port management agency that has been set up under the Amsterdam Municipal Government with authorisation from the central government. It is responsible for managing and coordinating the overall affairs of the Port of Amsterdam and the internal free trade zone and for investing in necessary infrastructure. It also has the authority to approve projects. It has achieved remarkable results in the mutual promotion of the free trade zone and urban functions, and the development of tertiary industries such as finance, insurance, commerce and trade, and intermediaries. With authorisation from the central government and local municipalities, the Central Shipping Management Centre under the Port Authority is responsible for the management of inter-city ports. Each port sets up a port director's office, which implements the rules of the Management Centre and is responsible for smooth traffic and the safety and development of the port.

The most valuable aspect of Singapore's port management has been its construction and application of an advanced integrated port operation information platform. Unlike New York and the Netherlands, which have adopted a "government-enterprise integration" port management mechanism, Singapore has adopted a "government-enterprise separation" operating model. The Singapore Maritime Port Authority and Singapore Port Group operate separately, and the free trade zone management functions are the responsibility of the Maritime Port Authority. The entire port's integrated operation system consists of a global shipping processing system that links and coordinates shipowners, freight, routes and ports. It controls high-tech information platforms such as Singapore's shipping centre information platform (Portnet); trade information platform (TradeNet); one-stop freight service system (CargoD2D); the ezShip system, which manages and simplifies transit transportation; and TRAVIS, a platform that provides 2 to 4 years of shipping report information. Any independent agency that is separate from the government and enterprises can conduct integrated management of the five ports using these comprehensive information platforms, especially by making use of real-time data feedback, which has greatly improved the coordination of port resources.

Port integration in the Yangtze River Delta region has already been explored to a certain extent. For example, Shanghai and Zhejiang have jointly promoted the comprehensive development of the Xiaoyangshan Port through equity cooperation; Shanghai Port Group has signed a strategic cooperation memorandum with Jiangsu Port Group and China Ocean Shipping Group to promote the coordinated development of the two ports; Jiangsu Port Group and Zhejiang Sea Port Group have reached an agreement regarding their equity participation intentions; and at the time of its establishment, Anhui Port and Shipping Group entered into strategic cooperation agreements with the Shanghai Port Management Committee Office, Shanghai Port Group, Zhejiang Port Group, and other parties. There are also explorations on specific projects. For example, the Zhejiang Pilot Free Trade Zone has alleviated regional restrictions in order to form a systematic cross-customs direct supply supervision and mutual recognition model. The Zhejiang FTZ is also cooperating more deeply with Ningbo, Nanjing, Shanghai and other customs jurisdictions. Furthermore, the

Shanghai Port Office is promoting the construction of a "single window method" in the Yangtze River Delta so as to provide a foundation for the integration of ports in the Yangtze River Delta from the perspective of information sharing, mutual recognition of supervision, and mutual assistance in law enforcement. However, we also see that these efforts have been relatively fragmented, and there have been no practical breakthroughs in terms of the entire high-level management organisation and coordination mechanism. The pilot free trade zones are naturally associated with the ports, and they have the best conditions for developing innovative mechanisms. Therefore, they should take this opportunity to promote the integration of the Yangtze River Delta's ports and drive the coordinated development of the economy in the Greater Port Area.

III. Recommendations

Based on the above considerations and experiences, we will focus on the big picture. We will start with concrete steps that can be taken and also put forward some detailed recommendations.

1. Establish a stable and regular communication mechanism in the Yangtze River Delta region

Efforts in this regard should involve governing bodies, such as the existing Yangtze River Delta Regional Cooperation Office, and also the pilot free trade zones, which will play a leading role in the integration of the Yangtze River Delta. The three pilot free trade zones should quickly establish a communication mechanism to achieve the basic integration of the business environment, promote the integration of industrial synergies, and explore the integration of the key areas of port operations. Social institutions such as think tanks, colleges and universities should also be involved, and exchanges and contacts should take place between the various institutions in order to generate more ideas for how to integrate the pilot free trade zones and the Yangtze River Delta.

2. Drawing on the experience from the assessment of the effectiveness of the pilot free trade zones, a unique system also adopted for the Yangtze River Delta Integration

The results achieved by the first two batches of pilot free trade zones have been quite obvious. One of the reasons for the clarity of these results is related to the objective assessment of the effectiveness of the reforms. These assessments are conducted from multiple angles such as policy innovation, implementation and radiation effects. With the promulgation of a series of programmes such as the Overall Plan for the Demonstration Area in the Yangtze River Delta on Ecology Friendly Development, references are needed in order to monitor the programmes' progress, implementation effectiveness and improvement feedback as they are carried out. An evaluation system that follows high international standards and reflects regional development characteristics should be set up. Such a system would be capable of conducting real assessments and providing effective feedback.

3. Information cooperation is the most effective way to achieve synergies in this era

The Yangtze River Delta region is the most mature region in the country in terms of data infrastructure construction. The region boasts cutting-edge technical capabilities in digital technologies such as cloud computing, big data, the Internet of Things, and artificial intelligence. In the process of promoting regional collaboration led by the pilot free trade zones, the opening and sharing of digital resources should be accelerated; digital resource allocation should be made more efficient; and the regional linkage of smart applications in key areas should be deepened.

长三角一体化发展趋势洞察

安永

长三角区域一体化发展上升为国家战略后,由国家发展改革委牵头,会同国家有关部委和上海市、江苏省、浙江省、安徽省拟定的《长江三角洲区域一体化发展规划纲要》已正式审议通过并印发,长三角将紧扣"一体化"和"高质量"两个关键,形成高质量发展的区域集群。长三角一体化经过多年的发展推进,其中城市群一体化发展已经从 1.0 版本上升到 2.0 版本的阶段,2.0 版本要求突破行政壁垒、在新型城市合作中带来新的发展增量,通过技术进步与创新的管理体制机制,形成比肩美国大西洋沿海城市群、日本太平洋沿岸城市群和英伦城市群的具有全球竞争力的世界级城市群。

要了解长三角一体化发展趋势,一定要看长三角的历史。初期,长三角发展是以外向型产业为发展动力。通过上海发挥对外合作、对内辐射单核枢纽作用,成为带动长三角发展的引擎。受上海的辐射带动,苏州和宁波优先通过"三来一补"形成产业的原始积累。而当时杭州、南京、合肥等区域,在产业和城市发展上与上海的互动还比较低。长三角初步形成了以上海为核心,进一步向内陆辐射的产业发展格局。但是长三角面临着城市等级差异分明、产业层次较低、外贸依存度较高、产业要素流动受限等挑战。

而今天,长三角城市群已经形成大中小城市齐头并进的发展格局,其中 2018 年万亿元 GDP 城市达到 6 个,占中国 17 个万亿元 GDP 城市的 35%,包括上海(32 679 亿元)、苏州(18 597 亿元)、杭州(13 500 亿元)、南京(12 820 亿元)、无锡(11 438 亿元)和宁波(10 745 亿元),常州和南通也紧随其后。而县级城市如昆山2018 年 GDP 达到3 875 亿元,甚至超过部分内陆省份。

如今长三角区域顺利完成产业迭代,传统劳动密集型制造产业已经向长江中上游及长三角周边区域转移,如苏州的笔记本代工企业已经转移至内陆城市重庆,而以苏锡常为代表的核心区域现今重点发展高附加值先进制造业,如生物医药、人工智能,而以杭州为代表重点形成互联网产业,南京正积极打造包括绿色智能汽车、电子信息为主的"4+4+1"产业。

但是,现今长三角发展也面临两个显著的问题。一是产业同质化竞争比较严重,主导产业和争夺方向大体相同,包括电子、石化、汽车、装备制造等基础产业,同时争夺新兴产业资源。如多个城市都提出发展集成电路产业,而城市内部也在争抢优质产业资源。我们曾经服务的一个集成电路企业倾向落户临近机场的某区,但是由于区域之间的争夺,最终落户在远离机场且跨江的另一个行政区,导致企业高管和研发人员每天上下班拥堵在跨江大桥上近一小时,很不方便,而且包括物流成本在内的企业各项成本也有所上升,极大浪费了政府资源。二是自主创新能力仍然薄弱,虽然通过产业迭代大力发展高附加值产业,但是"卡脖子"现象仍然存在,对标珠三角区域,其已经形成部分具有较强创新能力和国际竞争力的龙头企业,如大疆、华为等,但是长三角企业多处在战略性新兴产业的低端环节,原生性研发能力和生产性服务业发展较为薄弱。

面向"十四五"时期,国际和国内形势都发生着深刻的变化。放眼国际,发达国家贸易保护主义横行,中美关系走向战略僵持阶段,美国对中国的全面围堵和遏制将呈现长期化、常态化发展,未来经济全球化将面临巨大的不确定性和结构变化,倒逼中国产业价值链核心环节升级,提升关键产业基础能力和开拓新市场。中国将继续以开放为导向,以"一带一路"倡议为战略重心,通过密集的开放政策,塑造更加开放公平的营商环境;而且中国拥有巨大的市场和消费群体,高技术制造业和高端服务业"引进来"不可阻挡,将与本土融合催生出具有全球竞争力的解决方案。与此同时,新一轮科技革命和产业变革兴起,产业迭代融合加速,"十四五"时期将是以5G为主要标志的新技术突破期和应用期,人工智能、生物技术、智能物联技术和生态能源技术等带来的系列产业变革将对产业生态体系产生革命性影响,带来弯道超车机遇。

纵观国内,"十四五"时期经济下行压力将持续增大,预期我国货币政策保持稳健,在保持投资稳定的基础上坚持"房住不炒"不动摇,同时将以精准和积极的财政政策刺激内需市场和新兴产业发展。同时科技创新仍然是破解当前局面的核心,也是加快转变发展方式、转换增长动力的重要抓手,以创新驱动提高全要素生产率,促进产业结构调整和高质量发展。"十四五"时期人口形势将发生巨大变化,年轻劳动力将大幅减少,新型城镇化思路发生转变,大量中小城市将逐渐消亡,代之以城市群区域集约配置人口,提升资源利用效率。

着眼未来,长三角应以开放和创新为区域发展的新动力,发挥中国集中力量办大事的体制优势,优化资源配置,围绕五大核心城市群构建多层次开放创新合作传递体系。

上海应进一步深化开放,以开放促改革,以开放促创新,打造对内对外双向开放平台,积极利用两种资源、两种市场,积极参与国际创新标准、规则、制度的制定,为中国产业参与全球产业链协同和价值链融合,提供科技服务、商业咨询、金融、物流、国际法律仲裁等全方位专业服务,在这个过程中不断探索机制体制创新。同时按照国家部署积极打造全球科技创新中心,发挥上海在企业、大学、科研院所方面的优势及其在创新中的主体作用,建设成为原创新科技成果的发源地。充分释放辐射带动作用,提升整个区域科创新能力,如通过区域性引导基金的设立,培育高校、科研机构,实现前瞻性的基础研究和引领性技术成果的产业化。

长三角五大城市群则应依托自身优势,强化国际产业合作和科技成果转化,形成特色鲜明的现代产业集群高地,例如杭州都市圈建设世界级"互联网＋"科技创新高地;苏锡常都市圈建设世界级先进制造业产业创新中心;南京都市圈打造创新名城和产业创新高地;合肥都市圈建设综合性国家科学中心和产业创新中心等。每个都市圈通过核心城市在更高层面建立协调机制,向上游核心技术和下游现代服务业两端延伸,形成一批产业基础高级化、产业链现代化的高能级产业集群,构建差异化核心竞争力。

而长三角周边中小城市,应围绕长三角核心产业集群建设一批高端产业集群配套,形成门类更加齐全、产业更加高端、综合技术能力最强、跨区域构建的完整产业链条。通过完备的产业集群建设,有效降低创新成本,形成"创新—制造"闭环良性发展产业生态圈。

纵观未来发展,挑战前所未有,机遇也前所未有。对于安永而言,我们愿与在座的政府、协会组织和企业一道,共建高质量发展的长三角城市群。

Insights into the Development Trend of the Integration of the Yangtze River Delta

Ernst & Young

After the integrated regional development of the Yangtze River Delta region became the strategy at national level, *the Outline of the Integrated Regional Development of the Yangtze River Delta*, drafted by the National Development and Reform Commission, in conjunction with relevant national ministries and commissions, governments of Shanghai, Jiangsu, Zhejiang and Anhui has been formally reviewed, approved and issued. The Yangtze River Delta region will closely follow the two key elements, which are integration and high quality to form a regional cluster of high-quality development. The integration of the Yangtze River Delta region has been promoted through years of development, the integration of city cluster has upgraded from version 1.0 to version 2.0, the new version requires less administrative barriers and bringing developing opportunities among urban cooperation, through technological progress and innovative management systems and mechanisms, a brand new competitive world-class city cluster will be established, which is comparable to the other world-class city clusters, such as city clusters on London, Atlantic coast of the United States and the Pacific coast of Japan.

The history of the Yangtze River Delta must be deeply analyzed if to see the development trend of integration of the Yangtze River Delta region. In the early days, the development of the Yangtze River Delta was driven by export-oriented industries. Through Shanghai's role as a core hub for external cooperation, Shanghai has become the engine driving the development of the Yangtze River Delta region. Driven by the industrial radiation of Shanghai, Suzhou and Ningbo took the lead in forming the original accumulation of the industry through "the 'three-plus-one' trading-mix[①]" policy. At the time, Hangzhou, Nanjing, Hefei and other regions had relatively low interaction with Shanghai in terms of industry and urban development. The Yangtze River Delta region has initially formed an industrial development pattern with Shanghai as the core to further impact the inland, however, the Yangtze River Delta region is facing challenges such as significant differences in city hierarchy, relatively low industrial levels, high degree of dependence on foreign trade, and restrictions on the flows of industries' critical success factors.

Today, the city cluster in Yangtze River Delta region has formed a pattern of common development in all large, medium and small-scale cities. Among them, there were 6 cities with GDP exceed 1 trillion RMB in 2018, accounting for 35% of China's 17 cities with GDP exceed 1 trillion RMB, including Shanghai (3,267.9 billion RMB), Suzhou (1,859.7 billion RMB), Hangzhou (1,350 billion RMB), Nanjing (1,282 billion RMB), Wuxi (1,143.8 billion RMB) and Ningbo (1,074.5 billion RMB), Changzhou and Nantong are also close behind. And county-level cities such as Kunshan had a GDP of 387.5 billion RMB in 2018, even exceeding some inland provinces.

Now that the Yangtze River Delta region has successfully completed its industrial iteration, the traditional labor-intensive manufacturing industries are now transferring to the middle and upper reaches of the Yangtze River and the surrounding areas of the Yangtze River Delta region. For example, Suzhou's laptop OEM enterprises have transferred to the inland city of Chongqing; the core area represented by Suzhou, Wuxi and Changzhou is currently focusing on the development of high value-added advanced manufacturing industries, such as biomedicine and artificial intelligence; Hangzhou focuses on developing the internet related industry; Nanjing is actively building a " 4 + 4 + 1 " industry consisting mainly of intelligent vehicles and electronic information technology.

---

①   Custom manufacturing with materials, designs or samples supplied and compensation trade.

However, the developing perspective of the Yangtze River Delta region now also faces two significant problems. The first is the serious competition of industry homogeneity. The primary industries such as electronics, petrochemicals, automobiles, and equipment manufacturing related basic industry are broadly the same among cities within the Yangtze River Delta region, while the same issues also exist for developing the emerging industry as well. For example, many cities have proposed to develop the integrated circuit industry, and the cities are also vying for high-quality industrial resources. An integrated circuit company we once served tends to settle in a certain area near the airport. However, due to the competition between different districts and areas, the company finally settled on the other side of the river and also far away from the airport. As a result of this, it causes inconvenience for business executives and R&D staff of which they will have to commute through the cross-river bridge for nearly an hour every day, various costs of the company, including logistics costs, have also risen, which leads to the low utilization of government resources. Secondly, the capability for independent innovation is still relatively weak. Although it is vigorously developing high value-added industries through industrial iteration, the issues of bottleneck still exists. For the Pearl River Delta region, it has already formed some leading enterprises with strong innovation capabilities and international competitiveness, such as DJI and Huawei, but many companies in the Yangtze River Delta are at the lower end of strategic emerging industries, and still lacks of independent R&D capabilities, in addition to this, the productive services in the Yangtze River Delta region is also relatively weak.

In the duration of "14th Five-Year Plan", profound changes have taken place and would have impact on both domestic and international perspective. Looking around the world, protectionism is raising in developed countries, and the relationships between China and US are moving towards a strategic stalemate. In the long run, the US's comprehensive containment of China will come at a regular basis. In the future, the global economy will face huge uncertainty and structural changes, which will force and accelerate the process of upgrading the core area of China's industrial value chain and also improve the basic capabilities of the key industries, which means the new market can also be developed. China will continue to be open-oriented and take the Belt and Road Initiative as its strategic focus, and to build a better business environment with more fairness through intensive introduction of new open up policies. In addition, China has a huge market and consumer base, therefore the "bringing in" of high-tech manufacturing and high-end service-related industries is foreseeable and unstoppable, and it will integrate with the local industry to produce comprehensive solutions with global competitiveness. At the same time, a new round of scientific and technological advancements and industrial revolution is emerging, and the iterative integration of the industry is accelerating as well. The "14th Five-Year Plan" period will be the breakthrough and application period of new technologies based on 5G, a series of industrial changes brought by artificial intelligence, biotechnology, intelligent IoT technology and ecological energy technology will have a revolutionary impact on the industrial ecosystem and bring opportunities for overtaking.

Looking back at China, the downward pressure on the economy will continue to increase during the "14th Five-Year Plan" period. On the basis of maintaining investment stability and adhere to the principle of "housing is for living in, not for speculation", it is expected that China's monetary policy will remain stable, at the same time, the domestic market and emerging industries will be stimulated with precise and proactive fiscal policies. Meanwhile, scientific and technological innovation is still the key to the current situation, and it is also an important starting point for accelerating the transformation of both the development methods and the growth momentum, to improve the total factor productivity through innovation and creativity, and also to promote the process of industrial restructuring and high-quality development. During the "14th Five-Year Plan" period, the demographic structure will change significantly, such as the significant reduction on the young labor force, changes on the direction of urbanization, and a large number of small and medium scale cities will gradually disappear. Instead, the city clusters will intensively allocate populations to improve the efficiency of resource utilization.

Looking forward to the future, the Yangtze River Delta region should take openness and innovation as the new driving force for regional development, take the advantages of China's mechanism in resource optimization, and build a multi-level open and innovative cooperation system around its five core city clusters.

Shanghai should further deepen the progress of opening up, promote reform and innovation with opening up, create a multi-way open up platform at both internal and external perspective, and also to utilize both domestic and international markets and resources, actively participate in the formulation of international innovation standards, rules, and systems to help Chinese industries participate in integration of global industrial value chain. At the same time, provide comprehensive professional services such as technology, business advisory, finance, logistics and international legal arbitration, and also continuously explore mechanism innovation in the duration of progress. Meanwhile, to actively build a global science and technology innovation center in accordance with the national deployment, to make Shanghai become the birthplace of original scientific and technological achievements by making the full use of Shanghai's advantages in enterprises, universities, and research institutes, plus Shanghai's main role in innovation. Give fully play to Shanghai's leading role to enhance the innovation capability of the entire region. For example, to realize the industrialization of the forward-looking basic research and the leading technological achievements through the establishment of regional industrial funds, universities and research institutions.

The five major city clusters in the Yangtze River Delta should rely on their own strengths, strengthen international industrial cooperation and the transformation of scientific and technological achievements, and form distinctive highland for modern industrial cluster. For example, the Hangzhou metropolitan area can build a world-class "Internet +" highland of technology and innovation; Metropolitan area of Suzhou, Wuxi and

Changzhou to build the world-class advanced manufacturing industry innovation center; Nanjing metropolitan area to build the innovative city and the highland of industrial innovation; Hefei metropolitan area to build a comprehensive national science center and industrial innovation center. The coordination mechanism can be established through core cities in each metropolitan area, which can help the city clusters extend themselves to the ends of core technology at upstream and modern service industry at the downstream, and ultimately to form a batch of high-level industrial clusters with advanced industrial foundation and modern industrial chain, and also with differentiated core competition edge.

The small and medium-scale cities around the Yangtze River Delta region are recommended to develop the high-end industrial clusters which to support the core industries in the Yangtze River Delta region to form a complete high-end industrial value chain with more diverse categories, comprehensive technical capabilities and abilities to operate cross different regions. Through the construction of a complete industrial cluster, the cost of innovation can be effectively reduced, and ultimately to form the close-loop industrial ecosystem for innovation & manufacture.

Looking at the future perspective, there are unprecedented challenges and opportunities around us. EY has strong willingness to work with the governments, associations and companies present to together build a high-quality city cluster around the Yangtze River Delta region.

Part 2

2019 年上海国际智库高峰论坛实录

Record of the 2019 Shanghai International Think Tank Summit

Opening
Address

开幕致辞

陈　靖　Chen Jing
上海市人民政府秘书长
Secretary General of Shanghai Municipal People's Government

尊敬的各位领导、各位来宾,女士们、先生们、朋友们:

大家下午好!

非常高兴和大家相聚在美丽的浦江之畔,共同参加 2019 年上海国际智库高峰论坛。虽然初冬时节略显寒意,但我仍能感受到大家的热情。在此,我谨代表上海市人民政府,向本次论坛的举办表示热烈的祝贺!向各位领导、各位嘉宾和专家学者的到来,表示诚挚的欢迎和衷心感谢!

上海国际智库高峰论坛是探讨国内外合作与发展议题的高水平智库平台,近年来论坛水平不断提升、影响力不断扩大,为上海发展汇聚了大量宝贵的经验智慧。本届高峰论坛的主题是"长三角一体化与高质量发展",这一主题高度契合当前区域发展新形势,具有很强的现实意义,论坛内容和成果都值得期待。

长三角地区人口占全国的 17%,GDP 占全国的 23%,人均 GDP 达到 1.42 万美元,超过了世界银行的高收入经济体门槛,是我国最有条件率先实现现代化的区域之一。党中央、国务院高度重视长三角一体化发展,2016 年《长江三角洲城市群发展规划》出台,要求长三角地区建成具有全球影响力的世界级城市群。2018 年 11 月,习近平总书记在首届中国国际进口博览会开幕式主旨演讲时郑重宣布,支持长江三角洲区域一体化发展并上升为国家战略。2019 年 11 月,习近平总书记再次考察上海,强调要聚焦重点区域、重点领域、重大项目、重大平台,把一体化发展文章做好。12 月 1 日,党中央、国务院印发《长江三角洲区域一体化发展规划纲要》。这些充分表明,长三角一体化发展任重道远,潜力巨大,机会空前。

一年多来,长三角区域合作全面提速。三省一市按照党中央和国务院部署,不断深化改革、创新突破,积极探索区域合作的有效路径,各项工作取得显著成效。基础设施互联互通、公共服务便利共享、生态环境联防联控,长三角生态绿色一体化发展示范区、G60 科创走廊等一批合作载体逐步形成,呈现出合作多领域、多主体、多层次、全面深入推进的良好势头。

当前,长三角已经成为投资的热土,吸引和聚集了一大批国内外知名企业来长三角投资。今天上午,我有幸主持台商投资长三角项目签约仪式,今年以来,在已投 900 亿元人民币的基础上,今年又新增 454 亿元投资项目。据了解,台商在长三角的投资占在大陆投资的 1/3,销售收入占在大陆的 1/2。

上海土地面积不到全国的千分之一,人口不到全国的百分之二,贡献了近十分之一的财政收入,人均期望寿命 83 岁。今年以来,上海保持了利用外资的良好势头,1—10 月全市新设外资项目数、合同外资、实到外资实现"三升",分别同比增长 34.3%、15.1%、11.9%。总部经济加快集聚,1—10 月新增跨国公司总部 40 家,外资研发中心 452 家。我们将进一步营造国际化、便利化、法治化的一流营商环境,为企业发展提供更优的服务保障。借此机会,欢迎更多的企业来上海、长三角投资兴业。

女士们、先生们!加快推进长三角一体化发展,需要汇聚众智、多方协同,衷心希望大家畅所欲言、献计献策,提出宝贵的意见建议,为长三角一体化发展和上海发展贡献智慧和力量。

最后,预祝本次论坛取得圆满成功!祝愿各位嘉宾工作愉快、身体健康!

谢谢大家!

Your Excellencies, Distinguished Guests, Ladies and Gentlemen, Friends,

Good afternoon!

It is my pleasure to attend the 2019 Shanghai International Think Tank Summit and have the opportunities to meet with you at the side of the beautiful Huangpu River. Despite the slight chill of early winter, your incredible passion infects me nevertheless. On behalf of the Shanghai Municipal People's Government, I wish to offer my warm congratulations on the opening of this meeting! To all the government officers, guests, and experts of the academia, let me extend my hearty welcome and sincere thanks!

Shanghai International Think Tank Summit, as a high-level think tank summit for research and discussions on domestic and international cooperation and development, has enjoyed growing quality and influence in recent years, pooling valuable experience and wisdom for the development of Shanghai.

The theme of this year's summit, "Integration of the Yangtze River Delta for High-quality Development," is highly relevant. It dovetails with the new situation of current regional developments. Therefore, we eagerly expect to have your insights and comments.

Home to 17% of the country's population, the Yangtze River Delta region generates 23% of national GDP with GDP per capita reaching 14,200 dollars, exceeding the World Bank's threshold for high-income economies. As a result, the Yangtze River Delta has the most favorable conditions to be developed as one of the first modernized regions in China.

The CPC Central Committee and the State Council attach great importance to the integrated development of the Yangtze River Delta. In 2016, *the Development Plan for Yangtze River Delta Urban Agglomeration* was released, aiming to establish a world-class conurbation with global influence in the Yangtze River Delta.

In November 2018, the CPC General Secretary and President Xi Jinping announced at the opening ceremony of the First China International Import Expo that China would support integrated development of the Yangtze River Delta region and would upgrade it as a national strategy.

In November 2019, during his survey in Shanghai, General Secretary Xi Jinping pointed out that key regions, areas, significant projects, and major platforms should be focused on in order to boost the integrated development.

On December 1, The CPC Central Committee and the State Council issued *the Outline of the Integrated Regional Development of the Yangtze River Delta*.

All of the above fully demonstrates that the integrated development of the Yangtze River Delta remains a daunting task, yet it also bears unlimited potential and will bring an unprecedented opportunity.

Since last year, cooperation in the Yangtze River Delta region has been comprehensively accelerating. According to the arrangements of the CPC Central Committee and the State Council, the provinces of Jiangsu, Zhejiang, Anhui, and Shanghai Municipality have made notable achievements in the deepening of reform and in innovations and breakthroughs while vigorously exploring effective paths for regional cooperation.

A number of carriers for cooperation are gradually formed, such as infrastructure connectivity, facilitative sharing of public services, joint protection and control of the ecology and environment, the demonstration area in the Yangtze River Delta on ecologically friendly development, and the G60 Science and Innovation Corridor. This presents a good momentum of multi-level, multi-field, and multi-agent cooperation with an overall and profound promotion.

The Yangtze River Delta has now become an investment hot-spot, which attracts and assembles a large quantity of well-known enterprises at home and abroad to invest.

This morning, I was honored to host the signing ceremony for Taiwan-funded projects. So far this year, Taiwan enterprises had invested 90 billion RMB, and on that basis, more investment projects with a total investment of 45.4 billion RMB were inked at the ceremony. According to some statistics, investment by Taiwanese businessmen in the Yangtze River Delta takes up 1/3 of the investment in the mainland, and their sales revenue accounts for 1/2 of the total.

Shanghai, with less than 0.1% of the country's land and 2% of the population, contributes nearly 10% of China's fiscal revenue, and the average life expectancy of residents in Shanghai has reached 83 years.

This year, Shanghai maintained a good momentum of utilizing foreign capital. In the first ten months of 2019, the number of newly established foreign-funded projects, the amount of contractual and paid-in foreign capital in Shanghai continued to increase, respectively 34.3%, 15.1%, and 11.9% on a year-on-year basis.

The agglomeration of a headquarters economy had also been accelerated during the period, with 40 new headquarters of multinational corporation and 452 foreign-funded R&D centers introduced.

China will continue to foster a facilitated first-class business environment that is up to international standards and ruled by law, so as to provide better services and guarantee for the development of enterprises. Here I avail myself of this opportunity to welcome more enterprises to invest and prosper business in Shanghai and the Yangtze River Delta.

Ladies and Gentlemen, to quicken the integrated development of the Yangtze River Delta, it is necessary to pool your wisdom and to coordinate multiple parties.

We sincerely hope that all the participants will engage in free and open discussions and contribute your insights and ideas. Your advice and suggestion on our work will be most valuable and will make more contribution to the integrated development of the Yangtze River Delta and the development of Shanghai.

In conclusion, I wish the Summit a full success! I wish everyone good health and successful work!

Thank you!

Keynote
Address

主题演讲

张忠伟　Zhang Zhongwei

上海市人民政府发展和改革委员会副主任

长三角生态绿色一体化发展示范区执委会副主任

Deputy Director General of Shanghai Municipal Development
and Reform Commission

Deputy Director of the Executive Committee of the
Yangtze River Delta Ecologically Friendly Demonstration Area

今天非常高兴能和大家做一个长三角话题的交流。

长三角一体化是一个热词，是国家战略。国家战略会释放出长期持续的战略红利。前两天，国家正式公布了《长江三角洲区域一体化发展规划纲要》。明天上午国家发展改革委同三省一市会在北京专门召开一个新闻发布会，对"纲要"做进一步的解读。今天，借此机会，我向大家报告一下有关的情况。

长三角全称是长江三角洲，这个"洲"是指土里有水，长三角的东部区域大部分是由于长江冲击而成的。两千年前的一张地图显示，上海2/3的面积还在海里。随着长江泥沙的不断冲击，堆沙成陆，陆域面积不断向东扩，到1100年宋代，上海陆域面积基本形成。上海总面积为6 340平方公里，其中崇明岛占了1 200平方公里。到宋代，崇明岛还没有堆沙成陆，依旧是沙洲。到近代，也就是一百多年前，人们称上海为"小苏州"，因为当时的苏州人、南京人，在周末休闲的时候常到上海来。现在人们称上海为"魔都""大上海"。上海人周末度假休闲也常到千岛湖乃至更广阔的长三角去。

在长三角规划的编制过程中，我们经常会讨论到，如果一百年前上海"小苏州"的命运被确定了，那么我们怎么努力也不会成为现在的"大上海"。如果现在"大上海"的基因也是确定的，那么，我们不用做任何努力，也是会保持下去的。但是，经济社会发展规律告诉我们，不是这样。其实从整个长三角的演变看，这两千年来，上海有着长三角的地位，国际中心城市的地位。实际这跟从内河到外海、中国大陆与整个世界连接的地理变迁有关，与外贸的带动对接有关，与要素集聚也有关系。

世界银行在2009年基于很多专业团队的研究，发布了一个报告——《重塑世界经济地理》，这与长三角两千多年的变迁所发现的规律是一样的。如果区域能提高竞争力，那开出来的"药方"和途径到底是什么？我们可以怎么做？世界银行的专家告诉我们：第一，要关注经济密度，也就是要提高经济集聚度；第二，要缩短和经济中心城市的距离;第三,要降低区域之间的行政壁垒。总结起来就是 9 个字:提密度、缩距离、降分割。但这个"距离"不是实际的物理距离,指的是通勤时间。比如上海到苏州,这个距离没法改变,我们如果骑自行车,要大半天,开车一个半小时,高铁修通以后 20 分钟。这个"距离"指的是怎样用快速的交通、便捷的工具进一步缩短通勤时间。这些都为我们提供了非常好的智慧借鉴。

正因为如此,《长江三角洲区域一体化发展规划纲要》的前言中开宗明义,讲了这么几句话:推动长三角一体化发展,增强长三角地区创新能力和竞争能力,要提高经济集聚度、区域连接性、政策协同效率。这对引领宣传高质量发展、建设现代经济体系意义重大。开宗明义,长三角一体化推进的切入口,就是在提高经济承载能力、提升区域连接性和政策协同效率上下更大的功夫。

长三角太大了,刚才陈秘书长专门讲到,我们三省一市的经济总量占全国的23%,接近 1/4,这是什么体量? 2018 年京津冀的 GDP 总和是 8 万亿元,而长三角中江苏省的 GDP 就是 9 万亿元;粤港澳大湾区面积 5.6 万平方公里,GDP 10 万亿元,GDP 只比江苏省多一点点。这就是长三角的体量和在全国的能级。长三角已经形成了圈层结构,实际除了三省一市这个大范围的区域,还形成了"一核五圈"的结构,即上海是一个核心城市,上海周边也有一个都市圈。除此之外,杭州、南京、宁波、合肥,都形成了这个都市圈。这是什么含义? 经济功能是围绕经济中心城市的,GDP 过 1 万亿元以后,从吸收到慢慢地扩散,双向对流开始形成。长三角目前过 1万亿元 GDP 的城市有 6 个,2018 年宁波刚刚迈到这个门槛,上海遥遥领先。这几个城市里,毫无疑问,上海的经济效益是最好的。刚才陈秘书长也讲到了这一点,我们贡献了全国 1/10 的税收。上海的一般公共预算收入为 7 000 多亿元,第二位至第六位加起来比上海稍微多一点点。经济活动的功能是围绕着中心城市、经济中心城市为核心的都市圈慢慢展开的。

因为空间特别大,三省一市之间的差异还是比较明显的。比如说,到一个省域内部,江苏省有苏南苏北,安徽有皖南皖北,浙江有浙西浙东,区域内不平衡都存在,发展均质化程度也比较低。那么,能不能找出一个实体的空间来? 它是一个小的区域,可以探索三省一市在面上想做但做不了的事情。于是,长三角一体化示范区的战略构想便应运而生。它就是要做一些压力测试,在区域一体化发展中做三省一市面上做不了的事情。大家知道,这个区域选址是在以虹桥商务区为动力核,沿着G60、沪杭高速、G12 沪杭高速两个交叉口打开的扇面。这个选址是经过多方案比选的,研究团队从 2018 年 1 月研究到 9 月,做了 9 个月的反复论证。那么一体化示范区的独特特征是什么? 与雄安、粤港澳大湾区相比有什么不同?

核心有三个:第一,跨省域;第二,最江南;第三,超级都市圈。

首先,跨省域。它在沪苏浙两省一市的交界。

第二,最江南。这个地方的水、湖荡、古镇是世界级的料子。前段时间上海市规土局牵头编制空间规划,三家顶级团队——清华、东南、同济规划院,一致认为这个地方20%的水面率比荷兰兰斯塔德区域还好,那怎样保护这些生态基底?在有风景的地方,如何生长出创新经济?这是示范区非常有挑战的一个命题。

第三,超级都市圈。毫无疑问,这个地方依托的整个大区域是上海、苏州、嘉兴。这个区域面积总共2万平方公里,人口4000万人,GDP 6万亿元。6万亿元的GDP相当于1万亿美元,这和东京都目前的经济体量是相当的。所以这个地方潜力是巨大的。

从示范区的空间圈层来看,现在做空间规划安排了三个空间层次:中间的空间层次叫两区一县,范围差不多2400平方公里,就是青浦、吴江、嘉善。再往下走,有个先行启动区,因为这件事情要一步步做。该区由5个镇组成,660平方公里。但这个区域因为水系河网密布,仅仅在行政区域上勾勒出空间规划框架还不够。比如淀山湖60平方公里,2/3的面积在青浦,1/3的面积在苏州昆山市。但示范区没有把昆山市纳入这个范围,那在做空间规划生态专项、水治理专项时就要考虑。所以还有个协调区,把涉及淀山湖水系相关的昆山市的三个镇——淀山湖镇、锦溪、周庄总共200多平方公里容纳进来。另外嘉兴市秀洲区两个镇像大拇指一样嵌入了示范区,这个地方水系交错,也要放进来,这两个地方的面积为190平方公里。所以从整体的空间能加强协同的角度来看,它实际是2800平方公里左右,这样三个圈层就出现了:协调区2800平方公里,规划区2400平方公里,先行启动区660平方公里。

示范区的特殊使命是什么?国家的总体方案非常明确,有两个"率先",在不打破现有行政隶属的情况下,探索形成跨两省一市的一体化治理机制。这个难度是非常大的。大家知道,过往区域发展要做实,必须采取并购式的方法。把你那块区域化给我管理,这种方式已经有很多探索,各有千秋,有经验也有教训。示范区的独特探索在于不破行政隶属。

第一,率先将生态优势转化成为经济社会发展优势。这非常难。这个地方是"最江南"的区域,生态怎么样更好地加以保护,生态品质怎么样提升,生态容量怎么做起来?这是首要任务,但仅此还不够。这个地方并不是要搞成名山大川式的自然保护区,要有人的经济社会活动,而且可能比较频繁,是贯通区域的,那就要把这些优势转化为经济社会发展优势。也就是说,尝试走高质量发展的这条路子,要在"转得成"上做文章。

第二,率先探索区域项目协同走向区域一体化制度创新。区域项目协同要做,跨区域的交通一张网、跨流域生态治理都体现为项目。但仅仅有项目还不够,要有跨区域的制度创新,"从道德约束走向法律约束"。比如上下游环境的标准不一样。要形成一个统一的环保标准,有监测平台,有统一的执法标准,而且必须有法律约束力。这跟过往跨区域的协同是不一样的。同时,这个地方的战略目标里:一是"新标杆",生态优势转化的新标杆,二是"试验田",一体化制度创新试验田,三是"新高地",创新发展新高地,四是"人居品质的新典范",它把五个发展新理念都融入战略目标。

这些制度做多少,应该怎么做?目前近期建设聚焦的有几个方面。

第一,规划管理。过往跨省域的都有自己的空间规划,但这次首先是"一张蓝图管全域",两区一县2 000多平方公里要有一个统一的国土空间规划,要有一个规划实施平台;能全过程地监督、实施规划;要有一个示范区的建设导则,要体现出它的建设高标准来,且是"国际水准"。第二是生态,要探索"三统一制度":标准、监测、执法"三统一"。制度探索的同时,也要考虑高质量发展。怎样在有风景的地方让新经济成长起来,国际上有很多经验。比如,华为研发中心项目落户在青浦的金泽镇西城社区,沿着南面就是非常好的蓝色珠链,有连绵的水体。怎样提升生态品质,发展高质量的经济?同时,这个地方又是金泽古镇所在地,总体看,创新、绿色、人文怎么样融合在一起?这是示范区高质量发展方面要探索的路子。

一体化示范区要怎样监测它的进展程度?做一年,做两年,做三年,三年以后和现在有什么不一样?我们也开发了一个大数据的治理平台。最重要的是,一体化示范区经过一体化制度的探索要有结果,就是促进跨区域的要素流动,这是最关键的。企业的经济活动、人跨区域的经济活动这个量是增加的,所以我们至少会从四个方面对指标进行监测。比如,流动速度是高了还是低了,比如流量大了还是小了,比如流动成本怎么样,高速公路收费,省界之间的收费,移动的成本,要素移动的方向。最好的结果是双向对流,而不是单极化,双向对流才能实现共赢。

总结,一体化要带来红利。非常多的人在讨论,这个一体化示范区也是示范引领性的,到底会带来什么好处?至少有以下四个方面:第一,从区域发展角度来讲,"大就是美"。这是欧洲经验。会拓展战略纵深,战略格局。大也就是可以腾挪的空间大了。第二,会促进跨区域的要素流动,提升整体的竞争力。第三,扩大区域发展容量,增强区域吸引力。第四,跨区域的统筹规划、统筹重大项目,在一定程度上会避免无效投资。

由于时间关系,我就和大家交流那么多。谢谢大家!

It's my great pleasure that I am here today to present my report on the Yangtze River Delta.

As a hot phrase, "The integration of the Yangtze River Delta" is a national strategy, which will produce steady profits. The past two days witnessed the official announcement of *the Outline of the Integrated Regional Development of the Yangtze River Delta*. And tomorrow morning, the National Development and Reform Commission and the representatives from the Delta's three provinces and one city will hold a special press conference in Beijing to further interpret the outline. I would like to take the opportunity today to talk about it.

The YRD is short for "Yangtze River Delta". "Delta" refers to an area of land with several smaller rivers. Alluvial plains form most of its eastern part, thanks to the floods of the Yangtze, two-thirds of Shanghai is under the sea on a map of two thousand years ago. With the floods of sands from the Yangtze River, the land had been continuing to expand eastward until 1100AD in the Song Dynasty, by which Shanghai had formed. The current area of Shanghai covers 6,340 square kilometres, with 1,200 square kilometres occupied by the Chongming Island, which, in the Song Dynasty, had not yet been piled up and was just a sandbar. About a century ago, natives of Suzhou and Nanjing (chief cities of the Delta at that time) often came to Shanghai at weekends, and it was thus nicknamed "Little Suzhou". Nowadays, Shanghai is generally called "Demon City" or "Grand Shanghai" and its people likewise spend the weekends at places in the vicinity, for example, Qiandao Lake and other spots in the Delta.

When we were still hatching the Plans, we often discussed the fate of Shanghai. If it was predestined that Shanghai was "Little Suzhou" a hundred years ago, it could hardly become "Grand" no matter how hard we tried. And if it is Shanghai's fate to be "Grand", there is no need to make any effort since it will remain so. However, the patterns of economy and social development have denied that. If we look back on the evolution of the Yangtze River Delta for the past two thousand years, Shanghai has gained its status in the Delta and the world as an international metropolis owing to several factors, namely the geographical expansion from the rivers to the sea, the communication between China and the world, the stimulation of foreign trades, and the agglomeration of resources.

Based on researches conducted by many professional teams, the World Bank issued a report in 2009 — *Reshaping Economic Geography*. It echoes with the patterns revealed in the vicissitudes of the Delta in the past two thousand years. What should be the prescriptions and methods for increasing regional competitiveness and what could we do? According to the experts of the World Bank, we must first focus on economic density by intensifying the economic concentration. Second, we must reduce the disparity between economic centres and other regions. Third, we must lower administrative barriers between regions. To summarize, three keywords: density, distance and division. To increase density, shorten the distance and avoid division. But the "distance" here has nothing to do with spatial distance. It refers to the commute time. For example, from the spatial distance between Shanghai and Suzhou cannot be changed. Riding a bicycle will take half a day, automobile, one and a half hours, while high-speed rail, 20 minutes. Shortening the distance means further reducing commuting time with fast transportation and convenient tools.

Therefore, the preface *the Outline* lays its cards on the table first off: to facilitate the integrated development of the Yangtze River Delta as well as its innovation and competitiveness, the agglomeration of economy, the connection of regions and the efficiency of policy synergy are to be promoted. This is of great significance for the promotion of high-quality development and a modern economic system. The entry point for the integration is to work harder to reach these clear goals.

The Delta is too large. As Secretary General Chen just mentioned, the economic aggregate of the three provinces and one city accounts for 23% of the country, which is close to 1/4. What does this volume mean? In 2018, the total GDP of Beijing, Tianjin and Hebei Province was 8 trillion RMB, while the GDP of Jiangsu Province (one of the three provinces) alone was 9 trillion RMB; the Guangdong-Hong Kong-Macao Greater Bay Area covers an area of 56,000 square kilometres and the GDP is 10 trillion RMB, which is only a little more than that of Jiangsu. This is the volume of the Delta and its energy level in the country. The Delta has formed a circle. As a matter of fact, in addition to the basic structure of three provinces and one city, a "one core and five circles" structure has been formed. That is to say, Shanghai, as a core city, has a metropolitan circle in its vicinity. What's more, Hangzhou, Nanjing, Ningbo, and Hefei have their respective metropolitan circles as well. What does this mean? The economy functions in the core city. When the GDP exceeds 1 trillion RMB, there would appear bidirectional function, with the city spreading instead of integrating. There are currently 6 cities in the Delta with a GDP of 1 trillion RMB. Among them, Ningbo is the latest, which just met this threshold in 2018, while Shanghai is the leader far ahead, with the best economic benefits. Chen also mentioned this point just now. We have contributed 1/10 of the country's tax revenue. Shanghai's general public budget revenue is more than 700 billion RMB, which is a little less than the aggregate of the second to the sixth on the list. The function of economic activities is slowly expanding around the core city and its metropolitan circle.

Due to the vastness of the Delta, there still exist obvious differences between its three provinces and one city. The imbalance between regions within one single province, for example, southern Jiangsu and northern Jiangsu, southern Anhui and northern Anhui, western Zhejiang and eastern Zhejiang, still exists and the rate of growth ranges from place to place. So, is it possible to find a small place where one can explore what is currently impracticable in the three provinces and one city? Then came the strategic idea of the demonstration zone of the Yangtze River Delta integration. It aims to do some stress tests by finishing tasks that are beyond the reach of regional integration. As you know, this area is fan-shaped, with Hongqiao Business District as the core, and extending along the intersections of G60, Shanghai-Hangzhou Expressway and G12 Shanghai-Hangzhou Expressway. The location was selected through multiple scheme comparisons, which took the research team nine months to do so, from January to September in 2018. So what are the unique characteristics of this area? How is it different from Xiong'an and the Greater Bay Area?

The area is unique in three aspects: first, it is inter-provincial; second, it shows classic features of Jiangnan; third, it scatters over a super metropolitan area.

First, inter-provincial, it is located on the border of one municipality, Shanghai, and two provinces, Jiangsu and Zhejiang.

Second, classic features of Jiangnan. The water, lakes, and ancient towns are world-class resources. Not long ago, the Shanghai Municipal Bureau of Planning and Land Resources oversaw the preparation of its spatial design. Three top institutes from Tsinghua University, Southeast University and Tongji University have all agreed that the rate of water, which is 20%, is better than that of Randstad of the Netherlands. So how to protect these ecological bases? And how can an innovative economy grow in places with scenery? This is a very challenging proposition.

Third, the super metropolitan area. There is no doubt that this place relies on Shanghai, Suzhou, and Jiaxing. The total area is 20,000 square kilometres, with a population of 40 million and a GDP of 6 trillion RMB. 6 trillion RMB is nearly equivalent to 1 trillion USD, which is equivalent to the current economic volume of Tokyo. So the potential of this place is huge.

In terms of its concentric zones, three rings have been established. The middle ring, called the two-district-and-one-county (Qingpu, Wujiang, and Jiashan) zone (also called the planning zone), covers an area of about 2,400 square kilometres. It needs to be done step by step. Beyond this ring is a start-up area composed of 5 towns, with an area of 660 square kilometres. However, due to the dense network of river systems in this area, it is far from enough to outline these zones within the administrative framework. Take Dianshan Lake, which is 60 square kilometres, as an example, 2/3 of the lake is located in Qingpu District, while 1/3 is in Kunshan City, Suzhou Province. This makes it necessary to involve Kunshan regarding ecological planning and water management despite it being currently excluded from this area. As a result, there is also a coordination zone that includes three towns of more than 200 square kilometres. They are located in Kunshan and connected to Dianshan Lake, namely Dianshan Lake Town, Jinxi Town and Zhouzhuang Town. The two towns in Xiuzhou District of Jiaxing City, 190 square kilometres in area, are also embedded in the area due to their interlaced water systems. These make up three rings, the coordination zone, with an area of 2,800 square kilometres, the planning zone, 2,400 square kilometres, and the start-up zone, 660 square kilometres.

What is the mission of this area? The Plan makes it clear by proposing two "leads". Without confusing the existing administrative affiliation of a region, an integrated governance mechanism across two provinces and one city has to be explored. This is very difficult, for it is generally known that M&A, i.e. the management of another region, is inevitable for substantial regional development. There have been practices of various methods and each has its peculiar merits, with experience gained and lesson learned. The uniqueness of our exploration lies in the circumvention of the confusion of the administrative affiliation.

Take the first lead in transforming ecological advantages into economic and social development advantages. It's very difficult. As I have just mentioned, the place is characterized by classic features of Jiangnan. How to protect its ecology in a better way? How to improve its ecological quality? And how to have and expand the ecological capacity? This is the priority, but not enough. The place is not intended to become a nature reserve with famous mountains and rivers but one with people as well as economic and social activities, which may be frequent and widespread. Therefore, ecological advantages must be transformed into economic and social development advantages. In other words, high-quality development and successful transformation is the key.

Take the second lead in exploring the coordination of innovative regional projects. Regional projects need to be coordinated and relevant projects also include trans-regional transportation networks and cross-basin ecological governance. Having projects is not enough. Innovation in systems across different regions is highly needed. For example, the environmental standards for upstream area and downstream area are different. Thus a unified environmental protection standard is to be set up with a monitoring platform and uniform law enforcement standards, and it must be legally bound. This is different from previous cross-regional collaborations. In the meantime, the goals of this strategy include "a new benchmark", the new benchmark for the transformation of ecological advantages, "test fields", the integrated system innovation test fields, "a new highland", the new highland of innovation and development, and "the new paradigm for human habitation", the integration the five development concepts of "innovation, coordination, green, openness and sharing".

To what extent should these principles be applied and how to apply them? There are several foci of recent construction.

First, planning management. Every province used to have its spatial plan. But in this Plan, there is "one blueprint for the entire area", which means that there are a unified spatial plan and a platform of plan implementation in the two districts and one county, covering an area of more than 2,000 square kilometres. The implementation will be under supervision from the very beginning to the end. And there will be a construction guide that reflects the high international standards. Second, it is ecology. We are going to explore how to achieve the harmony of three aspects: standards, monitoring, and law enforcement. High-quality development is also worth considering. There is a lot of international experiences in how to make the new economy grow in places with the scenery. For example, the Huawei

R&D Center project, located in the Xicheng community in Jinze Town, Qingpu District, has a blue chain of a continuous body of water to the south. How to boost both the ecology and the economy? And how to combine innovation with ecology and humanity in this ancient Jinze Town? These are to be explored.

Then how to monitor its progress? One year, two years or three years, what's the difference between now and then? We have also developed a big data governance platform. Factor mobility across regions is the ideal result. This is critical. The economic activities of enterprises and people across regions should be increasing. We will thus monitor the index from at least four aspects. Take the factor mobility as an example, is the movement fast or slow? Are the flow of the factors increasing or decreasing? What about the cost, such as the tolls of the highway, tolls between provinces, the transportation? Where do the factors move? Bidirectional movement is the best, which leads to a win-win situation.

In conclusion, integration brings a bonus. A lot of people are wondering about the benefits brought by this demonstration area. There are benefits in terms of at least four aspects. First, from the perspective of regional development, vastness is beautiful, which is learned from European practice. As for strategies, we will go deeper and broader thanks to the ample space. Second, it will stimulate the factor mobility across regions and make the whole area more competitive. Third, the potential of regional development will be explored and the regions will be more attractive. Finally, cross-regional planning and coordination of major projects will, to a certain extent, avoid invalid investment.

How time flies! That's all for my presentation. Thank you for your attention.

Keynote Speech

主旨发言

打造具有区域经济韧性的全球城市群的关键是一体化

朱 晖

波士顿咨询公司全球合伙人兼董事总经理

我们谈长三角一体化,有两个前提。一个前提是,在全球经济发展的大格局下,越来越多的竞争不再是由单纯的、传统的国家经济形态构成,而越来越多地转移到以城市群落为主体的城市群之间的核心竞争。全球前五大城市群落,聚集了全球12%以上的人口和20%以上的GDP。全球排名前300的城市群,GDP超过全球一半,到2030年再看这个数据,全球60%以上的经济活动都将在这样的城市群发生。所以越来越多的经济发展方向、未来机遇,会出现在城市群。另一个前提,也是很重要的变化,就是随着过去几十年经济相对平稳的发展,全球经济、政治和区域格局,正在进入波动和不确定性越来越强的一个时代。这个时代下,如何应对未来越来越不确定的发展新趋势?这是我们下一步要重点加以关注的。

国家层面提出了去杠杆、供给侧改革,这是在大范围的风险层面上拥有更多未来发展的格局,在区域发展中对区域一体化、城市群的发展,就带来了更多的要求和挑战。

具体看,长三角这个概念在20世纪90年代被提出,国家相应也制定了很多相关的政策和制度。除了区域均衡发展、增强连通性、协同发展以外,2016—2019年,进一步提出整个区域或区域内城市群如何更好地在全球层面更多地参与全球竞争,并树立自身的核心竞争力。这也是未来城市群越来越多地需要面对的挑战和将要发展的机遇。背后的核心逻辑是,过去的城市或区域一体化发展,主要强调或要求区域产业协调布局和经济快速发展,以形成较好的经济产业互动和分布,推动区域均衡或更大的发展。经济增长是过去很多城市群或区域发展的重要要求。但未来,随着不确定性不断增加,尤其国际冲突增加,一个区域的韧性会成为将来区域一体化或深化的核心要素。其中三个要素很关键:一是内生性的,即自身创新、竞争力的构建,这是未来要塑造的核心能力;二是如何打开区域的空间和纵深层次,使整个区域的要素资源有更好的匹配,形成更强的韧性;三是在未来不确定的大背景下,不管是贸易冲突、经济体量的变化,还是科技带来的一系列对产业的冲击,如何使得区域之间形成更好的互联,提升抗风险能力。

回到长三角这个话题,我们到底做得怎么样?我们提到了创新、产业布局、未来协同机制的构建,有很多工作已经在做了,而且很多领域是领先的。但同样有很多地方还值得探讨和进一步提升。

先看整个技术的构成。长三角不仅经济体量大,而且有一个非常重要的要素,就是科研能力也很强大,长三角有两个综合性的国家科学中心,一个在上海,一个在合肥。同时,"双一流"高校、科研院所、学生数量都非常大。但是,整个长三角的创新氛围,包括创新转化实力有所欠缺。在很多重点攻克的领域中,上海的长三角周边地区,做得比较好的一般是输入型的创新,比如生物医药,大量的突破其实是在国外完成研发、申请专利以后,再到中国进行商业化生产。但在很多其他内生性的科技突破方面,还有很多空间。尤其创新的核心要素方面,比如人员流通、专利层面的保护、研发和实体经济的直接结合,还有大量工作要做。

第二是关于产业布局和产业协同。有一个有趣的现象,我们跟长三角的地方政府就产业规划进行探讨时,地方政府经常会问:隔壁的市现在在做什么?政府之间的交流、协调不太够。很多时候大家是站在自己的立场上进行未来整体的相关规划。这样很容易带来同一领域的重复性投资,大量政策或相同的资源投入到同样的产业上,会带来很大的浪费,也使得很多产业没有形成很好的组合、拉升。

最后,是协调机制问题。过去几年,长三角已经开始形成比较好的协同制度和要素。但现在主要还是一事一议,局限于某些专题层面的协调机制。整个区域层面的一体化制度还没有形成。我们把制度层面的创新和突破作为非常重要的方面,这个维度上,我们将来还有很多工作要做。

从国外看,有很多相应的案例或先进经验值得探讨。

在创新维度,美国波士顿有很多值得借鉴的地方,尤其是政策层面。比如波士华城市群的麻省生物技术委员会(MassBio),在生物领域的创新制度上做得很好,它建立了整体的协调机制,学校、科研院所、保险机构、生物制药公司、医院、政府都充分参与,通过协调机制,保证了创新的有效运作。它有一个很重要的委员会,建立了专门的政策协调机制,帮助政府提前预判产业和未来科技发展方向,不让现在的制度和规定成为创新的瓶颈。

在产业分工、布局层面,东京湾地区有很好的协调。大中小城市都形成了比较好的产业分工,其中非常值得借鉴的是,从整个战略层面上,它们有整体的"7+1"产业分工布局,有从东京都到周边县市的整体协调机制,由各个市的首脑参加,保证制度和政策的直接推行;同时又有专门的智库机构提供服务,保证未来片区内产业有较好布局和合理互动。

协调机制层面是未来最为难的一个部分,而海外有很好的经验。比如里尔城市群,不仅是跨省,还是跨国的,建立了比利时和法国城市群之间的整体协同。它在制度层面实行大创新,摆脱了过去传统的制度架构模型,形成了从欧盟、跨区域,再到城市、社区的四层合作运行机制。通过机制层面的革新变化,形成了有效、长效的决策和协调机制。这可能是更长远的情况下,未来长三角进一步深度一体化的时候需要达到的方向和目标。

总结来说,长三角一体化分为很多不同的层次和领域,过去我们在基础设施一体化层面上做了很多有效的工作,连通性上、道路互联和通勤能力上有了很好的基础,但在要素、产业协同、机制一体化层面,还有很多工作要做。尤其是有些层面,可能比较好推动,比如物流、商流,已经有很好的解决方案,但下一步在人流、资金、信息的流通方面,还有很多工作可以进一步突破和探索。

我们觉得长三角的一体化进程,一定会呈现一个递进的发展,不仅是空间层面上,更是制度和生态层面上的递进发展。

The Key to Build a Global City Cluster with Regional Economic Resilience is to Deepen the Integration Progress

Zhu hui

Managing Director and Partner of Boston Consulting Group

There are two premises when we talk about the integration of Yangtze River Delta (YRD): the first premise is that in the general pattern of global economic development, more and more competition is no longer made up of simple and traditional national economic forms, but more and more shifts to the core competition between city clusters. The world's largest five city clusters, home to approximately 12% of the world's population, generated over 20% of global GDP. Half of global GDP was generated by 300 leading city clusters, in a decade's time, over 60% of the global economic activities will take place in city clusters like these. Hence, more and more economic development direction and future opportunities will appear in city clusters. The other premise, also a very crucial change is that with the relatively smooth an steady economic development of the past few decades, the global economy, politics and regional patterns are entering an era of increasing volatility and uncertainty. How to deal with the growing uncertainty of the new development tendency in such an era? That's what we are going to focus on next.

At the national level, China has adopted deleveraging and supply-side reform, these measures will leave us more future development options in case of large scale risks. In the mean time, it has stipulated new demands and brought new challenges regarding regional integration and city cluster development at the regional level.

To be specific, the concept of YRD first came up in the 1990s, the central government has also tailored relevant policies and regulations. In addition to goals like balanced regional development, enhanced connectivity and coordinated development, from 2016 to 2019, it's further proposed that how can the whole region or city clusters within the region better participate in global competition at the global level and establish their own core competitiveness during the process. It is also both the development challenge and opportunity at the same time that city clusters need to deal with in the future. The core logic behind it is that in the past, the development of city or regional integration mainly emphasized or required the coordinated layout of regional industries and the rapid development of economy, so as to form a better interaction and distribution of economic industries and promote the balanced or greater development of the region. Economic growth was an important requirement for many city clusters or regional development in the past. But in the future, with increasing uncertainty, especially international conflicts, the resilience of a region will be a core element of future regional integration or deepening. There are three crucial elements. One is endogenous, namely the construction of self-innovation and competitiveness, which is the core competence to be shaped in the future. Second, how to expand the space and depth of the region, so as to better match the element resources of the whole region and thus to form stronger resilience. Third, how to form a better interconnection between regions and improve the ability to resist risks in the context of the uncertain future, whether it is trade conflicts, changes in economic volume, or a series of industrial impacts brought by science and technology.

Back to the Yangtze River Delta, how are we doing? We've mentioned innovation, industry layout, the construction of coordination mechanism in the future, a lot of work is already being done, and many areas are leading. But there is also much to explore and improve.

Let's have a look at the composition of the whole technology. The Yangtze River Delta not only has a large economy, but also has a very important factor, that is, a strong scientific research capacity. The Yangtze River Delta has two comprehensive national scientific centers, one in Shanghai and the other in Hefei. At the same time, the number of top universities, research institutes and students is very large. However, the whole Yangtze River Delta's innovation atmosphere, including the innovation transformation strength, still need to be improved. In many key fields, the areas around Shanghai in the Yangtze River Delta are generally good at imported innovation, take bio-medicine industry as an example, in fact, a lot of breakthroughs were first researched, developed and even patented in foreign countries, and then put into commercial production in China. But there is plenty of room for many other endogenous technological breakthroughs. In particular, much remains to be done on the core elements of innovation, such as human resource mobility, patent-level protection, and direct integration of research and development with the real economy.

The second is about industrial layout and coordination. We have noticed a very interesting phenomenon, when we talk to local governments in the Yangtze River Delta about industrial planning, they often ask, what's going on in the city next door? There is not enough communication and coordination between local governments. Most of the time they do the overall future planning only from their own position. This can easily lead to repetitive investment in the same field, a large number of policies or the same resources were invested in the same industry, which will lead to a lot of waste, and also lose the chance to construct a well combined and mutual promoting industrial layout.

Finally, the coordination mechanism. Over the past few years, the Yangtze River Delta has begun to form a better collaborative system and elements. But the current coordination mechanism is mainly in the form of case by case discussion, limited to some thematic level. The system of integration at the regional level is not yet in place. We see innovation and breakthroughs at the institutional level as very important, and we still have a lot of work to do in this dimension.

There are a lot of corresponding cases or advanced experience worth discussing if we look abroad.

In terms of innovation, we have much to learn from Boston, especially at the policy level. For example, MassBio, the Massachusetts Biotechnology Commission (MassBio) in the BosWash city cluster, has done a good job in the innovation system of the biological field. It has established an overall coordination mechanism, in which not only schools, scientific research institutes, insurance institutions, bio-pharmaceutical companies, hospitals and governments are fully involved, but also ensured the effective operation of innovation through the coordination mechanism. It has an important committee and has set up a special policy coordination mechanism to help the government predict the direction of industry and future science and technology development in advance, so as not to let the current systems and regulations become the bottleneck of innovation.

At the industry segmentation and layout level, we can reference Japan's Tokyo Bay Area's experience regarding coordination. In Tokyo Bay Area, large, medium and small cities have cultivated a relatively good industry segmentation, of which, the most worth learning thing is that at the overall strategic level, they have built an overall "7 + 1" industrial segmentation and a coordination system involving Tokyo and the surrounding counties. The heads of member cities, on behalf of their city to ensure the direct implementation of the system and policy. At the same time, there are specialized think tank organizations to provide services to ensure a better layout and reasonable interaction of industries in the area in the future.

The synergy mechanism will be the most difficult part in the future, there is also good experience overseas. Take Lille cluster as an example, is not only cross-provincial, but also cross-national, creating an overall synergy between the Belgian and French city clusters. It carries out great innovation at the institutional level, gets rid of the traditional institutional architecture model in the past, and forms a four-tier cooperative operation mechanism from the EU, across regions, to cities and communities. Through the innovation and change of mechanism, an effective and long-term decision-making and coordination mechanism has been formed. This may be the direction and goal that needs to be achieved in the future when the Yangtze River Delta is further integrated in the longer term.

To sum up, the integration of the YRD is divided into many different levels and fields. In the past, we have done a lot of effective work on the integration of infrastructure. We have a good foundation on connectivity, road connection and commuting capacity, but there is still much work to be done on the integration of elements, industry coordination and synergy mechanism. In particular, some aspects may be relatively easy to put forward, such as logistics and commercial flow have been taken care of, but for next step in the flow of people, capital, information, there are still a lot of work waiting us to further break through and explore.

We believe that the integration process of the Yangtze River Delta must be a progressive development, not only at the spatial level, but also at the institutional and ecological level.

构建长三角超级产业集群

许季刚

罗兰贝格高级合伙人、中国区副总裁

今天,我们准备从科技产业化、产业生态化的角度,来看如何推进长三角一体化和高质量发展。具体来说,包括如何提升发展质量、会碰到什么挑战、有些什么机制可以帮助或参考这样一些话题,从而形成一些我们自己有特色的创新的管理模式。

刚才提到的科技产业化、产业生态化问题,进一步具像化,就是在长三角一体化背景下,对经济治理模式提出了更高的要求。本地区的资源要素如何增强流动性?同时,如何进一步提升科技和产业之间的有效互动?

长三角一体化过程中,我们很多机制创新不是为了一体化而一体化,而是要根据实际情况,做一些定制化发展。结合过去与长三角区域内很多政府的沟通以及海外相关经验的积累,我们提出了一个观点:超级产业集群是长三角一体化过程中可以参考借鉴的非常重要的一种管理架构和模式。

首先介绍一下定义。超级产业集群并不是产业集群之间的一个松散联盟,而是更多强调资源配置的一种创新模式,需要以技术产业化为主轴,通过统一的衡量标准、统一的组织架构、统一的联合项目等方式,促进包括资本、科研、企业、教育、商会等多个相关方实现有效沟通,实现要素之间的有效流动和互相融合。它可以表现为科研、产业资源所组成的跨地区的产业集群,也可以表现为多个同时具有科研产业资源所组成的集群的联合体。

作为区域一体化产业的协调性机制制度,今天超级产业集群并不是一个新"物种",也不是完全意义上的一个畅想。过去二三十年时间里,尤其是以欧洲为代表的一些地区在推进科技产业化、产业生态化等方面已经有比较成熟的经验。这些经验体现出多种类型以及类型的互相叠加,也会给长三角一体化提供一些输入性的思路。

这是一个比较好的机制,但还是有比较多的前提条件,对比欧洲来看:一是各地对产业集群概念的认知要趋近;二是各产业集群发展水平要有相当的可比性;三是以欧盟和成员国政府为代表,它们把产业集群或超级产业集群作为科技发展的一个重要抓手,在政策方面,这也要实现某种意义上的突破。

结合这些分析,我们认为,如果长三角一体化过程中要参考一些欧洲的做法,应该因地制宜地"三步走"。

第一步,建标杆、塑共识。建标杆就是在区域经济发展过程中,包括长三角区域合作办公室等的工作中,可以围绕一些重点产业方向进行选择,并形成产业集群,树立地区的发展标杆。但这种标杆的打造,涉及如何选择的问题。我们认为长三角地区如果要进行产业集群的选择,首先要有个评价体系,因为涉及的地市比较多,也是为了各地产业集群之间有个比较一致的对话平台。所以它不是以行业、GDP 作为衡量标准,而是以某种支配性技术作为线索,以大学、研究机构、初创企业、中小企业、孵化机构等完备性和技术先进性作为指标,进行综合评价,进而进行选择。同时,塑共识也非常重要,20 世纪 90 年代德国政府确立了"绿色科技立国"的国策,每两年要求罗兰贝格帮助做产业经济地图,把全德和这个主题相关的企业、研究机构、大学、检测机构、示范性工厂做成地图形式,辅以案例参考,推进行业内部对话以及资源有效利用。这个工作,目前在绿色科技领域已经比较成熟,现在已经进入工业 4.0 等新的话题了。这种经济地图和创新地图的绘制,可以增强区域相关资源的可视化,推进相关发展。我们觉得这个部分,在共识里有些可以参考的点。

第二步,补要素、建架构。补要素是指针对要素不充分的产业集群,需要有针对性的扶持政策,并且针对产业集群建立合理的管理架构、决策机制。产业政策在各国都有很有效的利用,以德国为例,20 世纪 90 年代,德国发现它的生命科技领域跟美国以及英国产生了比较大的差异,它就在集群组织能力、初创企业扶持、联合项目发起等一系列领域,发布了很多专项政策,这些是值得学习的。同时,这还不会被其他国家政府指责。建架构也很重要,因为所有管理机制都需要有架构、组织执行。一般会分成两层:一层是议事层,一层是执行层。议事层往往是由政府、研究机构、企业共同组成,对产业集群的发展方向、重大事项做出一些决议,调动资源,为发展做贡献。执行层,一般就是通过联合研发、初创孵化、市场推广等一系列更偏向于实操层面的措施,在企业、商业环境下做很多工作,推进其相关发展。

第三步,创龙头、树品牌。最终要创造一些龙头和树立品牌。目前,整个长三角区域内很多大科学装置也是存在的,但国际性的研究课题、国际推广度方面,还是存在一些落差。这部分也有很多工作可以做,同时可以参考欧洲的地平线 2020

策略,做一些借鉴。

今天我们提出超级产业集群这样一个思路,也是希望供各位参考。核心是两个方面:一是要提高各地市对集群发展理念的共识,修炼内功,提升政府在科技产业发展中的行政管理能力,提高产业界和学术界的互动意识和能力;二是通过相似的管理架构以及旗舰型项目的带动作用,让超级产业集群之间的各要素充分地发挥互动,建立起互信关系,最终提高要素流动性和经济发展价值。希望我们的制度创新和实践,不仅帮助我们区域实现具体的高质量发展,也帮助中国经济找到高质量发展的方向,为此做出一些贡献。

Building Super Clusters in the Yangtze River Delta

Alex Xu

Global Senior Partner and Vice President of Roland Berger Greater China

Today we are going to look at how to promote the integration of the Yangtze River Delta and high-quality development from the perspective of technological industrialization and industrial ecology. Specifically, it includes how to improve the quality of development, what challenges will be encountered, and what mechanisms can help or reference. Such topics have formed some of our own unique and innovative management models.

The issue of the industrialization of science and technology and the ecologicalization of the industry just mentioned has become more concrete, which means that in the context of the integration of the Yangtze River Delta, higher requirements are imposed on the economic governance model. How can the region's resource elements enhance mobility? At the same time, how to further improve the effective interaction between technology and industry?

During the integration of the Yangtze River Delta, many of our mechanism innovations are not integrated for integration, but for some customized development based on actual conditions. Combining the past communication with many governments in the Yangtze River Delta region and the accumulation of relevant overseas experience, we have put forward a point of view: Super clusters are a very important management structure and model that can be used for reference in the process of Yangtze River Delta integration.

First let me introduce the definition. The super cluster is not a loose alliance between industrial clusters, but an innovation mode that emphasizes resource allocation more. It needs to take technology industrialization as the main axis, and adopt unified measurement standards and a unified organizational structure. And unified joint projects to promote effective communication between various parties including capital, scientific research, enterprises, education, and chambers of commerce, and to achieve effective flow and integration of factors. It can also be expressed as a cross-region industrial cluster composed of scientific research and industrial resources, or it can be expressed as a combination of multiple clusters composed of scientific research industrial resources.

As a coordinating mechanism system of regional integrated industries, today's super cluster is not a new species, nor is it a complete imagination, but in the past two or three decades, especially in some regions represented by Europe, which have mature experiences in the industrialization of science and technology and the ecologicalization of the industry. These experiences reflect multiple types and their superimposed past, and will also provide some input ideas for the integration of the Yangtze River Delta.

This is a relatively good mechanism, but there are still a lot of prerequisites. Compared with Europe: first, the awareness of the concept of industrial clusters in different regions should be closer; second, the development level of each industrial cluster must be comparable; the third is represented by the EU and member governments. They regard industrial clusters or super clusters as an important starting point for the development of science and technology. In terms of policy, they must also achieve a breakthrough in a certain sense.

Based on these analyses, we believe that if some European practices are to be referenced during the integration of the Yangtze River Delta, we should take "three steps" according to local conditions:

The first step is to establish a benchmark system and shape consensus. Establishing a benchmark system is the process of regional economic development, including the Yangtze River Delta Regional Cooperation Office, which can choose around some key industry directions and form industrial clusters to set regional development benchmarks. But the creation of this benchmark involves the question of how to choose. We think that if the Yangtze River Delta region is to be selected for industrial clusters, it must first have an evaluation system, because there are many cities involved, and it is also for a more consistent platform for dialogue between industrial clusters in various places. Therefore, it does not take the industry and GDP as the measurement standard, but a certain dominant technology as the clue, and uses the completeness and technological advancement of universities, research institutions, start-ups, small and medium-sized enterprises, and incubation institutions as indicators to conduct a comprehensive evaluation. Make your selection. At the same time, shaping consensus is also very important. In the 1990s, the German government established the national policy of green science and technology. Every two years, Roland Berger was asked to help make an industrial economic map, and to integrate companies, research institutes, and universities related to this topic in Germany. Testing institutions, and demonstration factories are made into maps, supplemented by case references, to promote internal industry dialogue and effective use of resources. This work is currently relatively mature in the field of green technology, and has now entered new topics such as Industry 4.0. The drawing of such economic maps and innovative maps can enhance the visualization of regional related resources and promote related development. We feel that there are some points in this consensus that can be referenced.

The second step is to supplement key elements and set up framework. Supplementing key elements refers to industrial clusters with insufficient elements, which require targeted support policies, and establish a reasonable management structure and decision-making mechanism for industrial clusters. Industrial policies have been used effectively in various countries. Take Germany as an example. In the 1990s, Germany discovered that it had a big gap between the United States and the United Kingdom in life sciences and technology industry. It launched a number of special policies in fields like cluster organization capabilities, startup support, and joint projects. At the same time, this will not be accused by other governments. Setting up framework is also very important, because all management mechanisms need to have a framework and organizational implementation. Generally, it is divided into two layers: one is the deliberative layer, and the other is the executive layer. The deliberations are often made up of the government, research institutions, and enterprises. They make decisions on the development direction and major issues of industrial clusters, mobilize resources, and contribute to development. The executive level is generally through a series of measures that are more practical, such as joint research and development, start-up incubation, and marketing.

The third step is to create leadership. The end is to create some leaders and build a brand. At present, many large scientific installations also exist in the entire Yangtze River Delta region, but there are still some gaps in international research topics and international promotion. There is also a lot of work to do in this part. At the same time, you can refer to the European Horizon 2020 strategy and make some reference.

Today we put forward such an idea of super clusters for your reference. The core idea of my speech today consists of two aspects. On one hand, it is necessary to improve the consensus on the concept of cluster development in various cities, cultivate internal skills, enhance the government's administrative management capabilities in the development of the science and technology industry, and increase the interaction and ability of the industrial and academic circles. On the other hand, through the similar management structure and the leading role of flagship projects, the elements of the super clusters can fully interact with each other, establish a relationship of mutual trust, and ultimately increase the mobility of elements and the value of economic development. It is hoped that our institutional innovation and practice will not only help to achieve specific regional high-quality development, but also help to find a high-quality development direction for national economy.

从一体化视角看长三角创新产业合作

刘明华

德勤华东主管合伙人、中国创新主管合伙人

今天探讨长三角一体化、高质量发展,可以说是在一个非常恰当的时间,讨论一个最热门的话题。为什么说时间很恰当? 因为在 2019 年 12 月 1 日《长江三角洲区域一体化发展规划纲要》(以下简称"《规划纲要》")出台了。这是一个非常宏大的议题,我从当中找了一个切入点来进一步探讨。这个切入点,就是在《规划纲要》中提出的,要促进创新链和产业链的融合,加强创新产业体系的建设,到 2025 年基本可以形成区域协同创新体系,把长三角建设成为全国最重要的创新的策源地。所以今天我们从"创新 + 产业"这个角度来进行探讨。

德勤在 2019 年发布了一份有关创新的报告,在创新领域,对全国主要 19 个城市做了一个评估。我们从三个大的维度进行评估:一是创新机构,二是创新资源,三是创新环境。整体评估下来,上海排名第二,杭州排名第四,南京排名第六,苏州第九,合肥第十六。长三角地区主要城市的排名还是非常亮丽的。

从这三个维度,我们具体来看:创新机构方面,长三角这些城市的成绩非常亮丽,独角兽方面,北上深、杭州一共有 162 家独角兽,占全国的 80%;创新资源方面,资源最重要的就是"人才 + 资金",所以这个集群里我们也有很大的优势;我想指出的是我们的一个短板——创新环境,它的整体排名有所下降。深圳市的创新氛围,广州市的创新政策力度和北京市的创新基础建设,这些方面都很值得长三角借鉴。

但整体来说,就整个创新评价而言,长三角的主要城市都有非常好的成绩,特别是杭州,可以说是一名新秀,2018 年全年涌入资本量超过 1 600 亿元,2019 年第一季度独角兽的数量超过深圳。

从长三角创新发展的着力方向来看,我们做了更细颗粒度的分析。有三个方面是长三角"创新 + 产业"可以加大力度的。

一是人工智能。人工智能的热度已经毋庸置疑,上海、杭州的人工智能公司数量排在全国前列。但数量多,不一定就意味着有非常大的力量,怎样形成联盟才是更重要的。这方面,整个长三角地区的城市已经意识到了,所以在2018年7月启动了面向沪苏浙皖的长三角人工智能产业联盟,到2019年10月长三角产业联盟、互联网联盟也已经成立。联盟的力量是非常重要的。

二是无人驾驶。无人驾驶研发中心,上海是仅次于北京的,在全国居第二。参与无人驾驶行业的许多企业,其实都希望将核心部门安排在汽车行业、互联网行业集聚的地方,更好地和产业相融合。另外,长三角地区城市还积极为无人驾驶企业规划智能驾驶测试区域,颁布测试牌照。目前,全国这样的城市有18座,长三角占了5席(德清、杭州、常州、无锡、苏州)。

三是智能制造。因为智能制造是信息技术、智能技术加上装备制造技术深度融合和集聚的一个新着力点。2013年德勤面向全国200家制造企业做过一个调研,当时的调研结果显示:中国智能制造还处在初级阶段,而且利润非常薄。经过六年的发展,我们智能制造产品和服务的盈利、能力已经得到了很大的提升。长三角地区有一个天然优势,就是制造业和技术、研发、高校的力量有非常大的集聚。根据长三角智能制造协同创新发展联盟2019年10月发布的白皮书,长三角智能制造示范、试点项目的数量,智能制造产业园区的总量以及从事这些行业的人数,都居于全国前列。通过智能制造引领产业升级,将成为长三角一体化高质量发展的重点方向。

谈了着力点之后,我接下来要跟大家分享的是未来我们应该怎样做,朝哪里去。《规划纲要》里提出走"科创+产业"的道路,从而实现"一极、三区、一高地"的愿景,德勤有以下四个方面的建议。

第一,有针对性地补齐短板。从创新报告里可以看到,我们的一个短板就是创新成本过高,特别是创新氛围、城市互联网、创新成本、工资水平以及楼宇的成本。所以《规划纲要》里也提出,上海要提升创新策源地的能力,降低创新成本是当务之急,要进一步降低企业和企业研发中心在用地、租房方面的成本,提高优惠补贴政策,加大人才补贴力度。这也是降低成本的一个方向。

第二,建立全要素的创新资源共享平台,加快推进建设长三角科创共同的一个平台。上海拥有众多科研机构、人才和众创空间、资金,长三角其他城市在产业基础、政策支持方面有各种优势。要求所有人都补齐短板是不现实的,成本也过高,所以我们要相互借力,有一个长三角科研资源共享的服务平台,可以实现设备、设施、信息、人才、专利的流动,打造全要素的创新共享服务平台,加快打造整个科创、科研和产业的共同体。

第三,依托各地优势,打造龙头企业,打造一批世界级的创新产业群。前文我们提到,长三角不同城市在产业群中已经形成了各自的优势。比如智能制造,上海在航空航天、汽车、船舶这些制造领域发展很快,江苏在电子信息、生物医药,以及浙江依托互联网、电子信息科技方面都有很多优势。所以我们建议,通过长三角合作机制,在各个新兴领域分别确定一批龙头企业,然后鼓励整合上下游,从科研到制造能力,形成产业集群。

第四,制定长三角创新地图,加强沪苏浙皖产业规划的对接,实现各有侧重,避免更多的重复投入和建设。产业规划方面,长三角各地还有一些重合,仍有提升空间。为了摸清长三角创新产业的分布和各自优势,建议委托相关机构制定一份完整的创新地图,在此基础上实现创新产业规划对接。

希望在《规划纲要》推出之后,我们能实现更强的长三角一体化高质量发展。

Promoting the Innovative Industry Cooperation in the Yangtze River Delta from the Perspective of Integration

Dora Liu

Managing Partner of Deloitte China Eastern Region and Leader of Deloitte China Innovation

Today, it's a good timing to discuss the hottest topic — the Yangtze River Delta's integrated and high-quality development. Why? Because the *Outline of the Integrated Regional Development of the Yangtze River Delta* was just issued on 1st December, 2019. This is a very big issue, and I'd like to explore further from the perspective of "innovation + industry". It is proposed in *the Outline* that an integrated system for regional innovation would be in place in the region by 2025, and be built into a cradle of innovation in China by deepening the integration of innovation and industry chains, as well as strengthening the development of a system for collaborative innovation, and the Yangtze River Delta will be built as the most important origin of innovation.

Deloitte has released an innovation report in 2019, which made an assessment of 19 major cities across China in the field of innovation from three dimensions, thus innovation institutions, innovation resources, and innovation environment. From the overall evaluation, Shanghai ranked 2nd among 19 cities in China and Hangzhou ranked 4th, Nanjing, 6th, Suzhou, 9th and Hefei, 16th. The leading regional innovation ecosystem was in the Yangtze River Delta.

Let's take a closer look at these three dimensions. In terms of innovation institutions, the Yangtze River Delta performs a leading role in China. In terms of unicorns, there are 162 unicorns in Beijing, Shanghai, Shenzhen and Hangzhou, accounting for 80% of the country. In terms of innovation resources, the most important thing is "talents + funds", so we also have a great advantage within this cluster. What I want to point out is one shortcoming — the overall ranking of innovation environment has declined. Shenzhen's innovation atmosphere, Guangzhou's innovation policy intensity and Beijing's innovation infrastructure are all worth referring to for the Yangtze River Delta.

Overall, in terms of the total innovation score, the major cities in the Yangtze River Delta have obtained very good results, especially Hangzhou, which can be said to be a rookie. In 2018, the inflow of capital exceeded 160 billion RMB. Unicorns outnumbered those of Shenzhen in the first quarter of 2019.

From the aspect of the Yangtze River Delta's innovation development, we also made a more detailed analysis. There are three aspects that can be strengthened in the "innovation + industry" of the Yangtze River Delta.

The first is artificial intelligence. There is no doubt that the artificial intelligence is very popular, and the number of artificial intelligence companies in Shanghai and Hangzhou ranks among the top in China. But the large number does not mean the great power. How to form an alliance is more important. In this regard, cities in the entire Yangtze River Delta region have been aware of it, so the Yangtze River Delta's artificial intelligence industry alliance was launched for Shanghai, Jiangsu, Zhejiang, and Anhui in July 2018. By October of this year, the Yangtze River Delta's Industry Alliance and Internet Alliance had also been established. The power of the alliance is very important.

The second is pilotless driving. The pilotless driving R&D center, Shanghai ranks the second in China, only after Beijing. Many companies participating in the industry of pilotless driving all hope to arrange their core departments in places where the automotive industry and the Internet industry are concentrated to better integrate with the industry. In addition, cities in the Yangtze River Delta also actively plan smart driving test areas and issue test licenses for companies of pilotless driving. At present, there are 18 such cities in the country, and five of them was in the Yangtze River Delta (Deqing, Hangzhou, Changzhou, Wuxi, and Suzhou).

The third is intelligent manufacturing. Intelligent manufacturing is the deep integration of information technology, intelligent technology and equipment manufacturing technology. In 2013, Deloitte conducted a survey of 200 manufacturing companies across the country. At that time, the results showed that China's intelligent manufacturing was still in early stage and the profit was very thin. After six years of development, the profitability and capabilities of our intelligent manufacturing products and services have greatly improved. One of the Yangtze River Delta's natural advantages is the large concentration of manufacturing, technology, research and development, and universities. According to the white paper released by the Yangtze River Delta Intelligent Manufacturing Collaborative Innovation Development Alliance in October 2019, the number of the Yangtze River Delta's intelligent manufacturing demonstrations and pilot projects, the total number of intelligent manufacturing industrial parks, and the number of staff engaged in these industries are among the top within China. Leading industrial upgrading through intelligent manufacturing will become the key point for the Yangtze River Delta's high-quality development.

After talking about the key points, I will share what to do and head for in the future. *The Outline* proposed "science + industry" for "one pole, three districts and one highland". Deloitte proposed the following four suggestions.

First, make up for the shortfalls in a targeted manner. From the innovation report, it can be noticed that one of our shortcomings is the high cost of innovation, especially the atmosphere of innovation, the urban Internet, the cost of innovation, the level of wages, and the cost of rent. Therefore, *the Outline* also proposes that Shanghai needs to improve the ability of science and technology innovation and reduce the cost. It is imperative to further reduce the cost of land and rent for enterprises and

R&D centers, increase preferential and talent subsidies.

Second, establish a comprehensive platform for sharing innovation resource and accelerate the construction of a common platform for science and technology innovation in the Yangtze River Delta. Shanghai has many scientific research institutions, talents, and creative space and funds. Other cities in the Yangtze River Delta have various advantages of industrial foundation and policy support. It is unrealistic for all cities to make up for the shortcomings, since the cost is too high. The service platform for sharing scientific research resources in the Yangtze River Delta can realize the circulation of equipments, facilities, information, talents, and patents, create a full-element innovation and shared service platform, and accelerate the entire science and technology research and industry community.

Third, make use of local advantages to build leading enterprises and world-class innovative industrial clusters. It was also mentioned earlier that different cities in the Yangtze River Delta have their own advantages in the industrial cluster. For example, in the field of intelligent manufacturing, Shanghai has developed rapidly in the aerospace, automotive, and marine manufacturing. Jiangsu has advantages in electronic information, biomedicine, and Zhejiang relies on the Internet and electronic information technology. Therefore, it's suggested that through the Yangtze River Delta's cooperation mechanism we should identify some leading enterprises in each emerging field, encourage the integration of upstream and downstream, and then form industrial clusters from scientific research to manufacturing capabilities.

Fourth, formulate the Yangtze River Delta's innovation map, strengthen the integration of Shanghai, Jiangsu, Zhejiang, and Anhui's industrial planning, achieve different priorities and avoid more repeated investment and construction. In terms of industrial planning, there is still some overlap and room for improvement. In order to find out the distribution of the Yangtze River Delta's innovation industries and their respective advantages, it is recommended to entrust relevant institutions to make a complete innovation map and form a docking of innovation industries on this basis.

It is hoped that after planning, we can achieve the Yangtze River Delta's high-quality development.

长三角一体化背景下的产业协同发展

黎庆文

戴德梁行华东区董事总经理

　　长三角一体化这个概念提出有十年了,以前叫"协同发展",随着习近平主席提出将长三角一体化发展上升为国家战略,它提速了。戴德梁行一直在跟踪长三角企业的流动特点,做了一些研究,2019年也针对长三角产业流动编制了一份白皮书,在这里我跟大家分享一下。

　　谁在搬离长三角?主要是纺织、冶金、食品三大门类。总结来看就是"三高一低"——高投入、高能耗、高污染、低效益。哪些产业环节在迁出?主要是生产部门、研发部门、营销部门三大环节。研发部门往往是从三线城市转移到一线城市。

　　谁在迁入、转入长三角?我们调研了7个比较典型的开发园区,发现外资占迁入产业的50%以上,迁入外资来源地主要是德国、美国、中国香港、日本。迁入行业主要是三大块:装备制造、电子信息、汽车。它们是扩张还是新建的企业?大部分是新设企业。

　　这些产业转移主要关注哪几个关键因素?转入的企业会关注几个因素:一是区位交通,二是产业聚集,三是经营成本,四是人才资源。迁出企业最关注的是环境容量、土地指标、政策门槛。非常有趣的是,迁入和迁出企业都认为人才资源是很重要的一个因素,因为迁入的往往都是高端企业、服务业企业,对高质量的人才要求非常高,所以长三角的人才资源是有优势的,但迁出企业往往都是劳动密集型企业,对熟练技工资源有要求,所以人才资源对于迁入迁出都有很大的影响。

　　以上海为例,上海迁出的产业包括两大部分。一部分是高端制造业。迁出的产业往往都有一种自主布局能力,也就是它们做得很大,产业链很广,包括资本的聚集、技术聚集,它们需要更大的土地空间实现扩张,所以搬离了上海。另外一部分是低端制造业,对此大家也理解。从转入上海的来看,最明显的就是总部经济,2018年,我们统计有78家总部经济企业落户上海,同时高端制造业包括特斯拉、西门子,也转到上海了。从国内来看,央企的地区总部也陆陆续续从各个地方迁到上海。很明显,福建系的开发商总部基本都在上海。

为了更全面和客观地评价长三角各个城市的产业发展竞争力,我们采用八大方面、48 个指标的评价体系来进行评价。

首先,产业投资环境指数。很明显,上海、南京、苏州是排在前列的,投资环境比较好的地方,都是和大都市板块圈有关系的。上海、苏州、杭州、南京有最好的投资环境。

其次,产业成长性。我们发现,合肥、徐州、南京表现不错,合肥的科研基础非常雄厚,所以产业成长性方面能够有突出表现。

第三,产业创新力指数仍然围绕几个大的都市圈。诸如上海、苏州、南京、杭州,科研的基础非常好,所以长三角城市的产业创新力排名是靠前的。

我们一直在协助这些产业在长三角的重构或转移。在这个过程中,我们也发现了一些可能需要改善之处。

比如政策一致性问题。我们建议,可以从产业链的角度,制定统一跨省的产业政策。针对缺乏统一市场体系的现象,应该设立跨省审批事项清单,实现证照资质互认。针对跨省公共服务便利性问题,要改善这个"断崖",我们认为可以探索社保、公积金互认,统一企业服务平台,建立一个跨地区的信用信息共用机制。

总结一下,环境是造成产业迁出的普遍因素;影响产业迁入的因素则是区位交通、产业聚集、人才优势、产业发展动力不平衡,核心城市群的优势明显。

我们提出几个建议:一是发展协同便捷的城际交通网。长三角高铁网络在中国是领先的,但不能完全解决城际交通问题,应该有一个更便捷的网络,比如购票系统,能不能一张卡走遍整个长三角? 十年前,我们研究过广州、佛山的同城化,广州和佛山已经有一个市政级别的交通网络,几块钱可以从广州到达佛山,非常便利。二是协同共建国际科创中心。建议吸引江苏、浙江、安徽的国家级科研机构来上海设立分支机构。三是构建世界级的产业集群。这是上海最核心的竞争力。

The Synergistic Industrial Development Against the Backdrop of Integration of the Yangtze River Delta

Kelvin Li

Managing Director for East China at Cushman & Wakefield

The concept of the "Integration of the Yangtze River Delta" has been introduced for ten years. It is previously called "coordinated development." As President Xi Jinping proposes that the integration of the Yangtze River Delta into a national strategy, it accelerates. Cushman & Wakefield has been tracking the characteristics of the flow of companies in the Yangtze River Delta, and has done some research. This year, we also make a white paper on the industry flow in the Yangtze River Delta. Here I will share with you.

Who is moving away from the Yangtze River Delta? Mainly three categories of textile, metallurgy and food. In summary, it is "three highs and one low", with high investment, high energy consumption, high pollution, and low efficiency. Which industrial links are moving out? There are three major links in the production department, R&D department and marketing department. R&D departments are often moved from third-tier cities to first-tier cities.

Who is moving in and out of the Yangtze River Delta? We have surveyed 7 typical development parks and found that foreign investment accounts for more than 50% of the industries moved in. The countries/regions of the source of foreign investment are mainly Germany, the United States, Hong Kong SAR and Japan. There are three major sectors in the relocation industry: equipment manufacturing, electronic information, and automobiles. Are these expansions or new businesses? Most are new businesses.

What are the key factors that these industrial transfers focus on? The transferred companies will pay attention to several major factors: first, location and transportation; second, industry clusters; third, operating costs; and fourth, human resources. Emigrated enterprises are most concerned about environmental capacity, land indicators, and policy thresholds. It's very interesting. Both the companies that move in and out think that human resources are a very important factor, because the companies that move in are often high-end companies and service companies, and they have very high requirements for high-quality talents. Resources have advantages. However, the relocated enterprises are often labor-intensive enterprises, which require skilled labor resources, so human resources have a great impact on relocation.

Taking Shanghai as an example, the industries that move out of are divided into two parts. One part is high-end manufacturing. The relocated industries often have an autonomous layout capability, that is, they have done a lot and the industrial chain is very wide, including the accumulation of capital and technology. They need more land space to achieve their expansion, so they move out of Shanghai. The other is low-end manufacturing, which everyone understands. From the perspective of transferring to Shanghai, the most obvious is the headquarters economy. In 2018, 78 headquarters economy companies settled in Shanghai, while high-end manufacturing industries, including Tesla and Siemens, also transferred to Shanghai. Domestically, the regional headquarters of central SOEs have gradually moved from various places to Shanghai. Obviously, the Fujian related headquarters of property developer are basically in Shanghai.

In order to better and comprehensively evaluate the industrial development competitiveness of each city in the Yangtze River Delta, we use an evaluation system with 48 indicators in eight aspects.

First, the industrial investment environment index is very important. Obviously, Shanghai, Nanjing, and Suzhou are in the forefront. The places with better investment environment, which are related to the metropolitan plate circle. Shanghai, Suzhou, Hangzhou and Nanjing have the best investment environment.

Second, industry growth cannot afford to be ignored. We found that Hefei, Xuzhou, and Nanjing perform well, and Hefei's scientific research foundation is very strong, so it has outstanding performance in terms of industry growth.

Third, there is also the industrial innovation index, which still surrounds several large metropolitan areas, including Shanghai, Suzhou, Nanjing, and Hangzhou. The scientific research foundation is very good, so the industrial innovation of the Yangtze River Delta cities is ranked high.

We have been assisting in the reconstruction or transfer of these industries in the Yangtze River Delta. In the process, we also discovered some areas that may need improvement.

For example, policy coherence should be considered. We suggest that a unified inter-provincial industrial policy can be formulated from the perspective of the industrial chain. In response to the lack of a unified market system, a list of inter-provincial approval items should be established to achieve mutual recognition of certificates and qualifications. In order to improve the convenience of inter-provincial public services, we believe that we can explore mutual recognition of social security and provident funds, unify the enterprise service platform, and hope to establish a cross-region credit information sharing mechanism.

To sum up, first of all, environmental factors are the general factors of industrial relocation; the major factors that affect industrial relocation are location and transportation, industrial clusters, talent advantages, and imbalance in industrial development power. The advantages of core urban agglomerations are obvious.

The suggestions have several focuses: first, developing a coordinated and convenient inter-city transportation network. The Yangtze River Delta high-speed rail network is leading in China, but it cannot completely solve intercity transportation. There should be a more convenient network, including a ticket purchase system. Can one card go through the entire Yangtze River Delta? Ten years ago, we studied the urbanization of Guangzhou and Foshan. Guangzhou and Foshan already have a municipal-level transportation network. A few yuan can travel from Guangzhou to Foshan, which is very convenient. The second is to jointly build an international science and technology innovation center. It is recommended to attract national research institutes in Jiangsu, Zhejiang and Anhui to Shanghai to set up branches. The third is to build a world-class industrial cluster. This is the core competitiveness of Shanghai.

长三角区域协同的现状与未来

张　帆

麦肯锡全球董事合伙人

　　长三角一体化这个话题提出已经很久了,过去我们讲城市圈协同,现在讲一体化。城市圈协同基本上可以分成几个层次。一开始是通基建、通民生,建立公路、高铁网络。但比较难的是"通"后面的几个层次,比如通产业、通制度。通基建比较容易,过去有大量的基建投资,包括民生方面,我们打破一些行政藩篱,马上就能实现。但产业和制度相通则比较难,因为这里面有很多区域的行政藩篱有待打破。同样一个企业,如果在两个地方投资,税收怎么结算,投资额怎么分成? 其实每个城市都有自己的经济发展指标。所以,真正要实现产业的协同一体化相当难。但我们也认为,产业相通是我们真正能实现区域一体化,甚至使得资源要素和市场真正实现自由流通非常关键的一个方面。而且在目前的形势下,这也变得非常必要。我们做了一些初步的宏观形势研究,为什么说区域城市之间的分工非常必要? 可以来看一些数据。

　　过去十几年,尤其是在制造业,产品的全球化流向发生了很重要的变化。当然,贸易摩擦只是一些短期的突发性的因素,从长远看,从过去十年的趋势来看,供应链在变得越来越区域化。也就是说,过去可能是全球分工体系,发展中国家生产、发达国家消费,资金流动有一个传导效应。但现在,在一个固定的或分销半径非常小的区域,比如东北亚,甚至长三角区域,有很多产业80%—90%的供应链都可以在这个区域里完成。这就造成一个结果,城市与城市之间的协同,尤其相邻城市之间的协同变得非常必要。因为在过去,我们都是依靠国际市场需求或成本优势来做,但在未来,很多产业,尤其长三角非常有优势的高新技术产业、技术密集型产业,中间品非常依赖区域内的供应。所以,城市之间的分工合作就变得非常有必要,产业协同就成为下一步推进协同一体化的重要抓手之一。

　　长三角一体化有很好的基础,城市发展能级在全国都是居领先地位的,但长三角不是铁板一块,具体来看,长三角有明显的两极分化的倾向。长三角的北翼——上海、苏南苏北和安徽,南翼——上海沿着 G60 高速公路到浙江的北部,协同状态其实很不一样。

先看北翼,以先进制造业为主。近几年,很多"卡脖子"的高技术产业如生物医药、高端装备制造、电子信息行业,有非常清楚的分工协作的体系——苏北、皖南进行原材料供应和中间品生产,南京、苏南进行高端制造,通过上海的港口和贸易中心枢纽,输出全球,而上海的高端服务业如金融、法务等专业服务,又可以反哺北翼很多制造业基地。这样的分工梯次非常紧密。但浙江不一样,过去是两种模式。一是浙南很多民营经济,以一般的传统加工出口贸易产业为主,通常是围绕一个中小型城市完成供应链,然后通过宁波港或上海输往全球,城市间不需要很多合作,因为这些产业供应链相对比较简单。二是近几年以杭州为首的互联网经济——电商、新经济、数字经济的发展,因为本身更多的是消费或服务业的应用,跟实体制造产业的连接很缺乏。由于这两个趋势,使得南翼城市之间的协同分工与北翼之间有很大的差别。那么未来往前走,怎么弥补南北之间这种区域协同上的不一致?

首先,在政策层面,我们刚刚发布了长三角协同一体化政策,尝试打破行政藩篱,有了一些产业协同的举措,也有一些很好的趋势在发生。两三年前上海就在推动 G60 科创走廊,里面出现了 9 个产业集群,已经探索出了怎样在浙江,比如与嘉兴这些临近上海的城市做高科技产业上的协同,大家共同投资,建一些创新平台。有很多高新技术产业设备研发设施,都是几个城市一起共同承担,然后得出的科研成果或 IP、产业产生的效益,也通过创新利益分享机制在城市之间做平衡。所以,建设 G60 科创走廊这样新的举措,可以推动形成未来南北之间协同的好的趋势。

此外,基础设施资源能不能更好地加以利用?在全国其他区域,比如珠三角、胶东半岛,有很多港口设施实现了整合。上海港、张家港、宁波港的利用效率都不平衡,从国家投资优化效率来说,基础设施能不能加以进一步整合,使得北货南运的措施能够落实?

往前走,从城市管理者或企业投资的角度,长三角协同一体化会有一些新的启示。我们做了一下预测,关于目前几个大的产业门类在长三角的占比,以及未来2025 年的占比及其变化。很多新兴城市或城市圈正在形成,尤其是过去发展相对滞后的安徽,围绕科创中心建设,怎么与上海、北部的制造业形成协同?这里面会出现一些新的机会。还有杭州,最近重提了浙江制造业重新再升值的路径。这些都可以成为未来企业投资的新路径。

从政府管理的角度,承接国家战略,在协同一体化政策的强推上,我们发挥了一定的作用。但未来关键的是要解决区域之间、城市之间的利益分享机制,怎么把

G60 科创走廊当中好的举措进一步放大？比如一家企业在不同地方投资，是不是可以有统一结算、统一经济指标的核算机制？在其他国家，以及中国珠三角，这方面有很多尝试。比如前海的自贸区，其中有很多地方是由澳门管理的。这些好的模式都可以供长三角未来参考，在产业协同上进一步探索与推广。

The Status and Future of Regional Synergy in the Yangtze River Delta

Derek Zhang

Partner at McKinsey & Company

The topic of the integration of the Yangtze River Delta has been discussed for a long time, only we mentioned it as city circles coordination and now integration. Basically, city circles coordination can be divided into several levels. It begins with the connection of infrastructures on traffic and standards of living, such as the construction of highway and high speed railway network. But it becomes more and more difficult when it comes to the connection of the following levels like industry and administrative system. It is obvious that the connection of infrastructures on traffic and living standards are relatively easy to accomplish once we break down some administrative barriers. However, it is difficult for industry and administrative system, because there are many administrative barriers to be broken. If the same enterprise invests in two places, how will the tax be settled and how will the investment be divided? Truth is each city actually has its own economic development index. So it is very difficult to realize the industrial integration.

However, we think that industrial connectivity is a system that is critical for us to really achieve regional integration, and even for the real free flow of resources and markets. And in the current situation, it's becoming necessary. We did some preliminary macro studies on why industry segmentation between regional cities is necessary. Let's look at some of the data.

Over the past decade, there has been an important change in the global flow of products, especially in the manufacturing sector. Of course, trade frictions are only some short-term and sudden factors. In the long run, the trend of the past decade shows that the supply chain is actually becoming more and more regional. In other words, in the past, it may has been a global division of industry system, production in developing countries, consumption in developed countries, capital flows have a transmission effect. But now, there are a lot of industries concentrated in a region with a fixed or very small distribution radius, like northeast Asia, or even the Yangtze River Delta, where 80 to 90 percent of the supply chain can be done. As a result, coordination between cities, especially between neighboring cities, becomes necessary. In the past, we all relied on the international market demand or cost advantage to plan our industry, but in the future, in many industries, especially for those very advantageous high-tech and technology intensive industries in the Yangtze River Delta, intermediate products will highly depend on regional supply. Therefore, the division of labor and cooperation between cities becomes very necessary, and industrial cooperation becomes one of the important factors to promote the collaborative integration in the next step.

The integration of the Yangtze River Delta has a good foundation, the cities' development level are leading the country, but there are still deficiencies. We can easily find that it has an obvious trend of polarization. Synergy condition of the north wing, including Shanghai, Jiangsu and Anhui province is highly different from the south wing, spreading from the high way G60 in Shanghai to the north part of Zhejiang province.

Let's start with the north wing, most of the industries are advanced manufacturing industry, especially in recent years, many China's bottleneck high technology industries, such as biological medicine, high-end equipment manufacturing, electronic information industry, has developed a very clear division of industrial cooperation system, north Jiangsu and south Anhui provide raw materials and intermediates production, Nanjing and south Jiangsu in charge of high-end manufacturing, then export to the global market through ports and trade center in Shanghai, in the mean time, the high-end service industries in Shanghai, such as financial, legal and professional services, can feedback many north wing manufacturing bases. This division of labor chain is very tight. But Zhejiang is very different, there were two models in the past. The first one, there are many private enterprises in southern Zhejiang, which are dominated by traditional industries of processing and export trade, the supply chain is usually completed around a small or medium-sized city and then exported to the world through Ningbo port or Shanghai port. There is no need for much cooperation between cities, because the supply chain of these industries is relatively simple. The other is the Internet economy led by Hangzhou in recent years, the development of e-commerce, new economy and digital economy, because it is more about the application on consumption or service industry, thus lack the connection with physical manufacturing. So these two trends make the synergy system in the south wing very different from that in the north wing. So going forward, how do you make up for this discrepancy in regional synergy between north and south?

First of all, at the policy level, China has just introduced a series of policies regarding the collaborative integration of the Yangtze River Delta, showing good signs on trying to break down administrative barriers and build industrial coordination. The "G60 Science and Innovation Corridor", which Shanghai endeavored to promote no more than three years ago, has cultivated 9 industry clusters and has already explored a good solution on how to realize high-tech industry synergy with the neighboring cities like Jiaxing city in Zhejiang province. They jointly invest and build some innovation platforms, many research and development facilities for high-tech industry are jointly undertaken by several cities. The research achievements or benefits generated by IP and industry can also be balanced among cities through the innovation of interest sharing mechanism. Therefore, such new initiatives as the G60 Science and Innovation Corridor can be a good trend for future north-south wing collaboration.

In addition, can infrastructure resources be better used? In other regions of the country, such as the Pearl River Delta and Jiaodong peninsula, a lot of port facilities are being integrated. In contrast, Shanghai port, Zhangjiagang port and Ningbo port's use efficiency are far from balanced, from the angle of optimization of state investment and efficiency, can the infrastructure resources be further integrated, so as to achieve a smooth channel connecting north and south?

Going forward, from the perspective of city manager or enterprise investor, the Yangtze River Delta collaborative integration will give us some enlightenment. We made a prediction about the current proportion of several major industrial categories in the Yangtze River Delta, and the future proportion and changes in 2025. Many emerging cities or city circles are taking shape, especially in Anhui province, which has a relatively sluggish development in the past. How to form a synergy with the manufacturing industry in Shanghai and the north based on the construction of science and innovation center? There will be new opportunities. Hangzhou also has recently brought up again the reviving route of Zhejiang's manufacturing sector. These can be a new direction for companies to invest in the future.

From the perspective of government management, we have played a certain role in carrying on the national strategy and promoting the collaborative integration policy. But in the future, the key is to solve the benefit sharing mechanism between regions and cities. How to further enlarge the good measures of G60 Science and Innovation Corridor? For example, if an enterprise invests in different places, can there be a unified accounting mechanism for settling accounts and unifying economic indicators? These have been explored a lot in other countries, and the Pearl River Delta in China. The free trade zone in Qianhai, Shenzhen, for example, has much of it managed by Macao. All these good models can be further explored and promoted in the process of Yangtze River Delta industrial collaboration in the future.

加强战略性新兴产业在长三角的发展

吴允燊

仲量联行华东区董事总经理

今天我们想看一下在长三角一体化以及高质量发展的顶层设计上,国家战略目标到底是怎么来诠释的。毫无疑问,我们国家面临着新一轮的国际竞争与合作,我们需要新动能来带动我们国家在全球的新一轮发展以及竞争力。

为什么我们需要强调推动战略性新兴产业发展的重要性,是因为中国经济发展速度放缓了,面对新一轮国际竞争,战略性新兴产业的发展能拉动我们产业的边际效应,实现更高的产业发展,有更多持续发展的可能性,能带来更好的就业质量,能突破产业链上"卡脖子"的环节,提升我们在全球价值链中的地位。

为什么选择长三角一体化作为战略目标? 其实长三角很多城市之间存在不均衡,但相较粤港澳大湾区和京津冀,其实我们是发展相对平衡的一个城市群。国庆节的时候我特地考察了粤港澳大湾区的一些二线城市,从深圳开车过去需要一个半小时到两个小时,那里的一线城市和二三线城市的发展差异非常大,在这样一个内部产业发展差异很大的城市群要推动新兴性战略产业,难度可想而知。另外,我们注意到上海和长三角地区主要城市每年投入的研发经费非常庞大,2018 年是5 900亿元,相当于德国的 70%,《长江三角洲区域一体化发展规划纲要》提出了很宏伟的目标,2025 年长三角城市群的研发投入要占 GDP 的 3%。战略性新兴产业发展的另一个基础,就是区域的经济基础,我们有非常庞大的 GDP 来支持我们的发展。

在区域联动性上,长三角比南北另外两个区域有更好的联动基础,根据仲量联行的内部数据,同时结合外部数据分析可以看到,城市与城市之间的联动,依托更完善的交通网络以及技术产业的扩散效应。上海作为一个核心,能带动周边地区,包括苏州、杭州、宁波、南京等多个城市的发展。

观察大湾区以及京津冀地区,它们确实有很好的龙头城市引领,比如香港、澳门、深圳、北京、天津，但周边其他城市的产业基础相对比较薄弱，能承载战略性新兴产业的可能性也相对较低。

战略性新兴产业的发展与传统产业发展的模式不同，传统产业发展偏向于产业链的整合发展模式，主要发展要素是土地、能源、劳动力。但新兴产业的发展更倾向于产业链、创新链深度融合的模式，依托研发、数据、资本以及人才，战略性新兴产业的发展偏向于产业链的赋能发展模式，需要有重大经济技术突破，形成创意园区、商业销售以及营商生态圈闭环，还要有生产要素的变化，这些要素也是未来长三角需要关注的。在顶层设计上，长三角一体化的管理模式要打破城市与城市之间管理模式的定式，避免恶性竞争政策。我们需要释放市场创新的红利，通过政策调整，更开放的管理，引进更多产业动能以及研发能力。

仲量联行在过去一段时间推动了很多产业入驻长三角地区。在过去六个月，我们也有幸参与了有关长三角一体化示范区一部分的战略研究。在这个过程中，我们对30多家战略性新兴产业企业做了简单的调研。战略性新兴产业对商业办公以及产业选址需求的考虑因素其实有所不同，比如在城市较核心的地方，它们选址主要考虑成本以及交通、楼宇形象；距离市中心较远的地方，考虑更多的是产业集群、优惠政策，以及交房、设备的标准。我们知道，很多新兴产业的发展都非常快，在传统的区域开发计划上，我们往往没有办法满足它们的需求。受访的30多家企业里，有85%的企业在一年内的规模扩张就能超过10%，新兴产业对办公、研发空间的需求以及特点非常明显，再沿用传统的开发模式，可能就无法预留更多的开发空间给它们。我们也看到，这些新兴产业走在前面，已经设立了不动产部门，采用更新型的办公模式（比如联合办公、移动办公），更能吸引全国乃至全球的新生代人才。

最后，我们想针对长三角生态绿色一体化发展示范区提出一些诚恳的建议：一是要加快相关一体化发展政策细则的落地；二是吸引战略性新兴产业市场主体参与。因为这些产业的诉求不一样，我们要让更多的市场力量参与；三是创新城市管理，积极探索大区域的创新管理模式。

Strengthening the Development of Strategic Emerging Industries in the Yangtze River Delta

Eddie Ng

Managing Director for Shanghai and East China at JLL

In today's speech, we want to see how the national strategic goals are interpreted in the top-level design of the integration of the Yangtze River Delta and high-quality development. There is no doubt that our country is facing a new round of international competition and cooperation. We need new kinetic energy to drive our country's new round of development and competitiveness in the worldwide.

We need to emphasize the importance of promoting the development of strategic emerging industries, because China's economic development has slowed down, and in the face of a new round of international competition, the development of strategic emerging industries can drive the marginal effect of our industry and achieve higher industrial development There are more possibilities for sustainable development, which can bring better employment quality, can break through the "stuck neck" link in the industry chain, and enhance our influence in the global value chain.

Why choose the integration of Yangtze River Delta as a strategic goal? In fact, the development of many cities in the Yangtze River Delta are not balanced, but comparing with Guangdong-Hong Kong-Macao Greater Bay Area and Beijing-Tianjin-Hebei, we are actually a relatively more balanced city cluster. During the National Day, I visited some second-tier cities in the Guangdong-Hong Kong-Macao Greater Bay Area. It took about 1.5 to 2 hours to drive from Shenzhen, but the development gap between the first-tier cities and the second-tier and third-tier cities were very big. It is conceivable that it is difficult to promote an strategic emerging industry in a city cluster when internal industry development differs greatly. In addition, we have noticed that the annual R&D expenditure of major cities in Shanghai and the Yangtze River Delta region is very large. In 2018, it is 590 billion RMB, equivalent to 70% of Germany. Urban agglomeration investment in research and development accounts for 3% of GDP. Another foundation for the development of strategic emerging industries is the regional economic foundation. We have a very large GDP to support our development.

In terms of regional linkage, the Yangtze River Delta has a better foundation than the other two regions. From the analysis of Jones Lang LaSalle's internal data combined with external data analysis, it can be seen that the linkage between cities depends on a more comprehensive transportation network. As well as the diffusion effect of the technology industry, Shanghai as a core can drive the development of surrounding areas, including Suzhou, Hangzhou, Ningbo, Nanjing and other cities.

Looking at the Greater Bay Area and the Beijing-Tianjin-Hebei region, they do have very good leading cities, including Hong Kong, Macao, Shenzhen, Beijing, Tianjin, but the industrial bases of other neighboring cities are relatively weak and the possibility to develop the strategic emerging industries is relatively low.

The development pattern of strategic emerging industries is different from that of traditional industries. The development of traditional industries is biased towards the integrated development model of the industrial chain. The main factors are land, energy, and labor. However, the development pattern of strategic emerging industry is more inclined to the deep integration of the industrial chain and the innovation chain. It is an enabling development pattern that relies on R&D, data, capital, and talents, and strategic emerging industries are inclined to the industrial chain. Major economic and technological breakthroughs are needed to form. The closed loop of creative parks, commercial sales, and business ecosystems, as well as changes in production factors, are also factors that need attention in the Yangtze River Delta in the future. In the top-level design, the Yangtze River Delta integrated management pattern, to break the paradigm of the management model between cities, to avoid vicious competition policies, we need to release the dividends of market innovation, through policy adjustments, more open management, the introduction of more multi-industry kinetic energy and R&D capabilities.

Jones Lang LaSalle has driven many industries to settle in the Yangtze River Delta in the past period. In the past six months, we have also been fortunate to participate in the strategic research on part of the Demonstration Area in the Yangtze River Delta. In this process, we make a simple survey of more than 30 emerging strategic industrial companies. Strategic emerging industries have different considerations for commercial office and industrial site selection requirements. For example, in the core areas of cities, their location is mainly considered in terms of cost, transportation, and building image. Most are industrial clusters, preferential policies, and standards for house delivery and equipment. We know that many emerging industry development patterns are very fast. In our traditional regional development plans, we often cannot meet their needs. Of the more than 30 companies surveyed, 85% of them have expanded within a year, and the expansion rate are exceed 10%. The demands and features for office and R&D space in emerging industries are very obvious. There may be no more reserved development space for them, if continue to use the traditional development pattern. We have also seen that these emerging industries are leading the way, they have set up real estate departments, and are also adopting newer office models (such as joint office and mobile office), which can attract new generations of talents nationwide and even globally.

Last but not the least, I would like to make some sincere suggestions for the Demonstration Area in the Yangtze River Delta on Ecologically Friendly Development. First of all, to accelerate the implementation of relevant integration policy. Secondly, to attract market players participating into the strategic emerging industry. Because the demands of strategic emerging industries are different, we must allow more market players to participate. Thirdly, to innovate urban management and actively explore innovative management models in large regions.

跨国企业对长三角一体化的期待

欧　文

美中贸易全国委员会上海首席代表

在中国市场,美中贸易全国委员会有 220 个成员单位,它们涉及不同的行业,而且每个都在长三角区域有自己的企业。在参加这次会议之前,我们对成员企业进行了调研,看看它们认为在长三角有什么样的机会,长三角一体化对它们意味着什么、政策有没有落地,以及营商环境是否得到提高等,帮助它们更好地在长三角发展,并表达它们的意见。

许多公司提到了机会,比如互联互通方面的一体化可以促进企业的发展,高速公路的发展可以帮助它们减少跨省交通时间、降低成本。这是一个非常正面的变化。还有整体上的能源、基建,在上海和浙江之间天然气的互联互通,使得公司能够更好地获得相关原料资源,提升供应链的能力。还有许多一体化的服务,跨区域都能获得,也非常有帮助。所以总体来说,长三角一体化的互联互通,对营商环境是一个正面的推动。我们有很多公司也在继续加强对长三角地区的投入和建设。我们研究发现,长三角一体化中有一系列的机会。同时,美资企业也表示了一些担忧和未来有进一步发展空间的地方。我们想强调几个方面。

在与企业对话的过程中,企业提到了四个方面,一是固体垃圾,二是知识产权,还有产业转移和海关监管。在这四个方面,我们的成员单位希望推动更多的一体化工作,并取得进展,优化营商环境。

首先,固废的处理能力,这是跟环保相关的。生态保护是长三角一体化的重点之一,包括制造业固废处理的能力。以前渠道有限,成本也比较高,在不同的地方如江苏、上海、浙江都是如此,都是紧密相关的。上海固废处理的供需不太匹配,因此成本比较高,而且准入途径也有限。希望今后这方面能在不同行政区之间建立更多的资源分享机制,这样就可以帮助制造业企业发展。这也是过去几年我们经常提到的一点。

第二是知识产权保护。我们有91%的成员单位对知识产权方面的保护仍然比较担心，有1/3认为研发是受此影响的。在整个国家的知识产权保护和执法方面，长三角一直发挥着领头羊的作用。我们希望在各个行政区之间能形成互动和合作。比如跨地区执法中就存在问题。如果企业的注册地和侵权行为发生地不在同一地区，那么维权就会变得非常困难，也不能得到重视，解决问题需要更多的时间和精力。所以需要更多的互动、对话、合作，这样可以改善美资企业在华发展的状况，也可以增加我们对长三角的信心，并且在中国建立更多的研发中心。

第三，关于产业转移政策。在长三角区域，包括上海、浙江、江苏、安徽"三省一市"之间，以及不同城市之间，很多高端制造业企业都希望可以更好地接触当地市场，制定全球的产业政策。我们成员单位经常会提到它们在长三角区域内的战略。为了实现战略，它们可能要重新分配资源或要建新的办公室，它们发现有时候进行产业转移，各个政府在税务和经济上会有不同的看法。如果一些行政区之间无法充分对话，将阻碍它们基于商业的决策，带来一些挑战，也给企业产业转移带来了阻碍。我们认为，这些问题多多沟通就可以解决，在省、市、区各个级别，要有更多沟通，更好地支持在华企业在长三角地区开展更多的商业行为。

第四，有关海关执法以及海关相关政策涉及各个行政区。我们长三角区域的许多成员单位都发现一个问题，就是不同地区的海关执法情况不太一样。希望在这方面可以看到更清晰的政策，有更好的政策。目前情况非常好，这也是为什么我们在长三角会开展很多业务，在安徽、张家港等地有很多数据分享，在我们成员单位看来，这是非常有效的，也希望这方面能做得更多。还有，希望检查流程能更加标准化；申报的数据能在不同的地方得到更新、分享，这样可以节省很多时间，也可以更好地促进全球贸易的发展，做到流程简明。

总体来说，我们认为长三角在跨国企业发展中，一直扮演着领头羊的角色。所以我们很多企业选择和青睐长三角作为它们的基地和重心。但是在刚才说的这四个方面以及其他一些问题上，还需要有更多沟通和合作，尤其在各个行政区之间需要有所整合，这样就能大大帮助在华的美国企业实现更好的发展。

Expectations from Multinational Enterprises in the Integration of the Yangtze River Delta

Owen Haacke

Chief Representative of US-China Business Council Shanghai Office

The US-China Business Council has 220 members in China. They are involved in different industries, and each has its own enterprise in the Yangtze River Delta region. Before this summit, we conducted a member survey about what opportunities they think there are in the Yangtze River Delta, what the Yangtze River Delta's integration means to them, and whether the policies have been implemented and whether the business environment has improved to help them better develop in the Yangtze River Delta and express their opinions.

Many companies have mentioned opportunities, such as the integration of interconnection, which can improve enterprises' development. For example, the development of highways can help reduce the cost and time of inter-provincial transportation. This is a very positive change. The interconnection of overall energy, infrastructure, and natural gas between Shanghai and Zhejiang helps companies better obtain relevant raw material resources and improve the capacity of the supply chain. It's very helpful to have many available integrated services across regions. In general, the integration and interconnection of the Yangtze River Delta is a positive impetus to the business environment. Many companies also continue to strengthen their investment and construction in the Yangtze River Delta region. Our research found that there is a series of opportunities during the process of the Yangtze River Delta's integration. At the same time, US companies also mentioned some concerns and areas for further development in the future. We want to highlight a few points.

During the dialogue with companies for past few weeks, they has mentioned four parts — solid waste, intellectual property, industrial transfer and customs supervision. In these four aspects, our members hope to promote deeper integration to optimize the business environment.

First, the solid waste treatment capacity is related to environmental protection. Ecological protection is one of the key points of the Yangtze River Delta's integration, including the capacity of solid waste treatment in manufacturing. Channels were limited and costs were relatively high in the past, which was very common in different cities, including Jiangsu, Shanghai, and Zhejiang. The supply and demand of solid waste in Shanghai is not well matched, so the cost is relatively high, and the access is also limited. It is hoped that in this regard, more mechanisms of resource sharing can be established across different administrative regions to improve the development of manufacturing enterprises. This is also a point frequently mentioned in the past few years.

The second is protection of intellectual property rights. 91% of our members are still worried about the protection of intellectual property rights, and 1/3 think that R&D is affected by this. The Yangtze River Delta has always been a leader in the protection and enforcement of intellectual property rights, and we hope to form interaction and cooperation among various administrative regions. For example, there are problems in cross-regional law enforcement. If the registration of the company and the infringement don't occur in the same area, rights protection will become very difficult at this time. If not taken seriously, it will take more time and energy to solve the problem. Therefore, more interaction, dialogue, and cooperation are required to improve the development of US-funded companies in China, increase our confidence in the Yangtze River Delta, and establish more R&D centers in China.

Third, the policy on industrial transfer. In the Yangtze River Delta region, including Shanghai, Zhejiang, Jiangsu, and Anhui's "three provinces and one city", as well as among various cities, many high-end manufacturing companies hope to have better access to the local market and formulate global industrial policies. Our members often mention their strategy in the Yangtze River Delta region. In order to achieve the strategy, they may reallocate resources or build new offices. They find that sometimes during the process of industry transfer, each government hold different opinions about taxation and economy. Since some administrative regions cannot fully talk to each other, it will hinder their business-based decision-making, bring some challenges, and hinder the transfer of enterprises. We think more communication can solve these problems. At levels of the province, city, and district, there is more communication and better support for companies to conduct more business activities in the Yangtze River Delta.

Fourth, law enforcement and policies related to customs involves various administrative regions. Many members in the Yangtze River Delta region will find a problem that the customs enforcement of different regions are different. We hope to see clearer and better policies in this area. The current situation is very good, and this is why we have a lot of business in the Yangtze River Delta and a lot of data sharing in Anhui, Zhangjiagang and other places. Our members think they are very effective, and we hope more can be done in this part. In addition, we hope that the inspection process can be more standardized; the declared data can be updated and shared in different places, which can save a lot of time, better improve the development of global trade, make the process more concise.

In general, we believe that the Yangtze River Delta has always played a leading role in the development of multinational enterprises. So many companies prefer the Yangtze River Delta as their base and focus. However, on these four points just mentioned and other areas, more communication and cooperation are required, especially among various administrative regions. The integration can greatly help US companies in China achieve better development.

自贸区在推动长三角一体化中的作用

刘　明

毕马威政府与公共事务、特殊经济区咨询服务合伙人

今天我想从一个比较重要的特殊经济区域，即自贸区入手，把它作为一个视角，对长三角一体化发展情况进行分析。

长三角一体化过程中，自贸区从成立到深化，到走向联动，在整个长三角地区是作为一个引领。从 2013 年 9 月中国第一个自贸区在浦东挂牌，到 2017 年唯一一个由陆域和海洋锚地组成的浙江自贸试验区成立，再到 2019 年 8 月江苏自贸区问世，长三角片区里的自贸区在发展和深化改革方面，一直走在各个区域带头的位置。长三角区域在我国改革开放过程中，一直处于一个引领的地位。2018 年习近平总书记在上海宣布增设自贸区新片区，这对我们是非常利好的信息。一年后，我们自贸区临港新片区挂牌，实现了从投资贸易便利化向投资贸易自由化的大跨度升级。浙江从全国首提建设自贸试验区的联动创新区开始，到探索更大程度发挥自贸试验区在制度创新、产业引领、贸易便利、综合监管方面的优势，也形成了一定的辐射效应。江苏自贸区虽然成立时间比较短，但在精准聚焦、回归初心方面也下了很多功夫，定位是着力打造开放型的经济发展的先行区，实体经济创新发展和产业转型的升级示范区，为实体经济开放转型提供更多重要的制度创新。

我们回顾整个长三角地区的自贸区，从成立到深化，已经经历了这两个非常重要的里程碑，下一步关键在于各个自贸区如何借助长三角一体化实现非常好的联动发展。有关联动发展，我们进行了一些思考。

一是在自贸试验区联动方面，应该构建营商环境、产业协同和区域港口这三个一体化。先来看营商环境一体化的概念。2018 年的论坛我们认真思考过如何优化提升营商环境，当时我们在全球的排名是第 46 位，最新发布的 2019 年报告显示，我们已经上升了 15 位，排在第 31，站到了"三环边"。在这样的情况下，我们认为，刺激和帮助我们成绩大幅度提升的主要原因，在于高位推动和上下协同。也就是说，

来自100项改革政策的创新，以及狠抓落实工作。同时我们希望2019年这个话题更深入一些，探讨如何利用不同区域——长三角区域内不同地区、各个自贸试验区在营商环境方面的建设、发展和创新，形成一套稳定的体制规范，对标国际高水平，构建长三角区域一体化营商环境。

从实践来看，各地都做了很多工作。比如，在共同优化知识产权、营商环境合作意向方面，长三角的上海、江苏、浙江、安徽四地都走在全国前列。上海主要是围绕知识产权做了非常积极的探索，比如成立专利、商标、版权三合一的知识产权局；长三角其他兄弟省份也做了非常多、非常深入的改革和创新。所以，三省一市在未来可以聚焦营商环境中的知识产权，在这个领域做更多、更深化的创新工作。以知识产权作为一个切入点，未来长三角区域在开办企业、登记财产、获得信贷、跨境贸易、合同执行等方面，达成一些统一的营商环境的指标，在长三角三省一市，突出高标准营商环境规则的引领作用。此外，长三角地区在营商环境方面应该率先实现一体化的优化标准。这样一来，各个省市、自贸区，就不再是强调上海的准入负面清单是不是缩减了、浙江"最多跑一次"的登记流程是不是更简便了，而是会关注整个区域的竞争力和营商环境的提升。这是非常重要的一个方面。

二是产业一体化和要素协同领域的流通。基于一体化的营商环境，我们认为下沉到产业发展来讲，各类型的产业要素会实现自然分配，也会变成自发性的、市场性的生长。以纽约湾区为例，它的产业结构是一个好的集群系统，核心城市纽约依托独一无二的地理优势，对内背靠世界最大的消费市场和腹地，对外是美国面向海外的主要港口，再加上全美第一也是最大范围的自贸区，高度自由的国际贸易规则，极具竞争力的关税政策，效率非常高的政府及其审批，使得纽约在工业时代的转型方面具备了非常好的基础。后工业时代里，也正是借助这样的相关优势，实现了第二产业向小型制造业和高科技产业的转型。包括纽约周边湾区，北部波士顿有相关的大学资源、人才要素资源，南部费城作为工业化最早的一个区域，在统一、创新、高效的自贸改革政策引领下，各个城市的要素实现了自然流动和协同，所以打造成了纽约这样一个非常重要的国际标杆区域。基于这个国际案例，我们可以思考，对我们长三角区域来讲，它到底有什么样的示范作用？上海、舟山、杭州、苏州、南京、芜湖等地，到底应该怎样通过产业要素协同和配比实现长三角一体化？

三是以管理创新作为切入口，构建比较有特色的港口运营一体化。长三角地区有16个港口，港口群分布密集，比较有地区特色，吞吐量大的包括上海港、宁波舟山港，各个港口的协调联动已经成为长三角区域促进一体化非常重要的一个抓手。下一步，希望通过对标，比如对标荷兰阿姆斯特丹港、新加坡港，利用信息化、数字化方面的优势，实现长三角区域港口协同一体化发展。

以上是我们针对一体化方面的一些初步思考。对于未来,我提出三个比较重要的建议:第一,要打造一套有自身特色的自贸区发展指标体系,这非常重要。作为长三角一体化发展的指引,《长江三角洲区域一体化发展规划纲要》也发布了,在这样的基础上,我们要促进未来指标体系的构建,实现协同化的可评估、可追溯。第二,产业要素、产业政策、产业相关招商引资,要如何通过政府内部的沟通协调,建立一个非常通畅的交流机制,摒弃过去各地政府在招商引资中的绩效考核导向,实现区域的产业发展、产业协同"一盘棋"? 第三,要让数据跑起来,让信息跑起来,让数字化成为整个长三角一体化的先行抓手。大家知道,地理隔绝是天然形成的,行政区划隔绝是后天形成的,但数据、信息、要素这些东西是挡不住的。所以我们建议,让数字、信息和数字化先在整个长三角片区跑起来。

The Role of Free Trade Zones in Promoting the Integration of the Yangtze River Delta

Liu Ming

Partner of Government & Pubic Sector and Special Economic Zone Service at KPMG China

Today, I want to start with a comparatively important economic zone, namely the free trade zone, as a viewpoint to analyze the development of the integration of the Yangtze River Delta.

From the establishment and deepening of the pilot free trade zones to linkage, the free trade zone has always been a pioneer in the integration of the Yangtze River Delta. China's first pilot free trade zone (FTZ) was established in Shanghai in September 2013; and the Zhejiang Pilot Free Trade Zone, the only FTZ consisting of both land and marine anchorages, was established in 2017; and then the Jiangsu Pilot Free Trade Zone was established in August 2019. The establishment of these FTZs marked a new milestone in the effort to deepen reform and opening-up in the Yangtze River Delta region. At the 2018 China Expo, President Xi Jinping announced the establishment of a new area in the Shanghai Pilot Free Trade Zone. A year later, the Lingang New Area was established. The Lingang New Area represents a historical transition from investment and trade facilitation towards investment and trade liberalization. Zhejiang was the first province in China to propose building an Innovation Linkage Zone in the FTZ, and was also the first to explore ways to make greater use of the radiation effects of a pilot free trade zone in terms of system innovation, industry leadership, trade facilitation, comprehensive supervision, and other areas. The Jiangsu

FTZ has only been established for a short period of time, but it has stayed true to its original goal by focusing on building an opening-up zone for economic development and a model demonstration zone for innovative development of the real economy and industrial transformation and upgrading. In this way, the Jiangsu FTZ aims to better serve the opening-up and transformation of the real economy.

When we look back, we will find that the free trade zone in the Yangtze River Delta region have already crossed the two milestones of establishment and deepening, and the next key step is how to fulfill the linkage of each free trade zone by taking the advantage of the integration of the Yangtze River Delta. Here I have some insights.

First, in terms of the linkage of the free trade zones, we should promote the integrate in the business environment, industrial synergies and regional ports. Let's look at the business environment integration first. We gathered here last year to explore the idea of optimising the business environment in Shanghai. At that time, Shanghai was ranked 46th in the world in this regard in 2018. This year the city's ranking increased 15 places, almost reaching 31st in 2019. This progress was the result of high-level promotion and top-to-bottom coordination, as well as the introduction of 100 reform policies which are being implemented quite effectively. This year we hope to take this topic one step further by exploring how to use the development and innovation experience that has been made in the business environment by the three regions' pilot free trade zones to produce a set of stable institutional norms, benchmark international high level, and finally build a integrated business environment in the Yangtze River Delta.

From the practical perspective, a lot of work has been done in the region. For example, Shanghai, Jiangsu, Zhejiang and Anhui in the Yangtze River Delta are the pionner in the country in terms of cooperation to optimise the business environment for intellectual property rights. Shanghai has extensively explored IPR. As part of its efforts, the FTZ established a three-in-one IPR office for patents, trademarks and copyrights. Other provinces in the Yangtze River Delta have also made many in-depth reforms and innovation practices. Therefore, the three provinces and Shanghai can do more deepening work focusing on the intellectual property in business environment. These IPR initiatives represent a significant step forward for the region. We also recommend that the Yangtze River Delta region cooperate to achieve consistency in areas such as starting a business, property registration, obtaining credit, cross-border trade, contract execution, etc. In this regard, the pilot free trade zones in Shanghai, Zhejiang and Jiangsu should play a leading role. In addition, the Yangtze River Delta should take the lead in achieving a integrative standard in terms of business environment. Under such circumstances, we will focus on the upgrading of the regional competitiveness and business environment, other than to highlight whether the negative list for market access in the Shanghai FTZ has been reduced, or whether the "one-stop application" measure in the Zhejiang FTZ has made the registration process easier. This is a very important point.

The second is the industrial integration and factor circulation. With the support of an integrated business environment, we believe that different industrial factors will achieve natural distribution and will also realize spontaneous and market-oriented growth. Under such conditions, taking the New York Bay Area as an example, its industrial structure is a good cluster system. The core city of New York relies on a unique geographical advantage, internally backed by the world's largest consumer market and hinterland, and externally oriented by the United States to overseas main ports, superimposing the first and largest free trade zone in the United States, highly free international trade rules, highly competitive tariff policies, very efficient government services and approval, makes New York in the transformation of the industrial era, with a very good foundation. New York laid a solid economic foundation during the industrial age and transformed its declining secondary industries into small manufacturing and high-tech industries during the post-industrial age. In the New York Bay Area, many universities and talents resources are located in Boston which lies the north of the Bay Area, whereas south of the Bay Area lies Philadelphia, which was the first region in the country to industrialise.

Under the guidance of a unified, innovative and efficient free trade reform policy, the elements of the city have achieved natural flow and synergy, so it has built New York into a very important international benchmarking area. Based on this international case, we can think about what kind of demonstration role does it have for the Yangtze River Delta? How should Shanghai, Zhoushan, Hangzhou, Suzhou, Nanjing, Wuhu and other places realize the integration of the Yangtze River Delta through the coordination of industrial factors?

The third is to develop integrative port operations with our own characteristic through management innovation. There are 16 ports in the Yangtze River Delta. The entire port group is densely distributed and have regional characteristics. The region's port group includes the Shanghai Port and Ningbo Zhoushan Port, which are the two most important deep-water ports in the country. The coordination of the various ports has become a very important part of the Yangtze River Delta to promote the integration. In the next step, we hope to achieve the coordinated and integrated development of ports in the Yangtze River Delta through benchmarking, such as the ports of Amsterdam and Singapore in the Netherlands in terms of informationization and digitization.

The above are some preliminary thoughts on the integration of the Yangtze River Delta. In the future, I share three important suggestions. First of all, it is very important to build a set of free trade zone development indicator system with its own characteristics. As a guide for the integrated development of the Yangtze River Delta, *the Outline of the Integrated Regional Development of the Yangtze River Delta* has also recently been released. On this basis, we must promote the construction of the future index system to achieve coordinated evaluability and traceability. Secondly, how to establish a very smooth communication mechanism through communication and coordination within the government for industry factors, industrial policies, and industry-related investment attraction? We should abandon the past investment attraction-oriented performance review method, and build a smooth communication mechanism to realize "a chess game" for industrial development and collaboration in the Yangtze River Delta. Last but not the least, let the data run, let the information run, and make digitization the forerunner of the integration of the entire Yangtze River Delta. As everyone knows, geographical isolation is naturally formed, and administrative division isolation is formed the day after tomorrow, but data, information, and factors cannot be isolated. So we suggest that numbers, information and digitization should be run in the entire Yangtze River Delta area first.

中国特大城市群与国际城市群的管理经验

梅柏杰

世界银行社会、城市、农村和灾害风险管理全球发展实践局首席城市专家

今天,我要说的是更宏观的特大城市群,包括长三角在内的特大城市群的发展,还有国际经验的借鉴。这很重要,因为世界银行所有的成员都在问中国这些特大城市群的最新进展。在全球范围,从规模以及发展速度来看,像中国这种特大城市群在世界上是没有先例的。中国在管理其特大城市群方面到底做了哪些工作,这不仅对中国,而且对全球都非常重要。

我们首先统一一下术语。因为中国的规模一向非常大,我们说的"城市区"或"大都市区"指的是单一的经济体,我们也说到"特大城市",像纽约、波士顿和华盛顿特区,都叫"特大城市"。现在还有一个词,叫"特大城市区域",在中国或者叫"城市群",它包括很多大都市区,有统一的功能,这个词以前是没有的。

中国公布了城市群以后,世界银行的成员都希望我们加强研究。我们在研究中国19个城市群后发现,每个城市群中都有100万以上人口规模的特大城市,长三角就有16个特大城市。在世界上,没有哪一个城市群是包括了16个特大城市并且有共同发展的统一愿望的。

再看人口变化,这一点非常重要。根据我们采集的数据,2000—2014年,有13个城市群的人口有所减少,但长三角人口增加了,因为中国的GDP聚集在这些城市群中,占全国GDP的18%之多。特大城市群涉及三个变量:首先是城市规模,都非常大;第二,人口增加也非常多;第三,聚集了全国大量的GDP份额。这意味着特大城市群的管理和治理非常复杂,你的管理方法非常重要。当然,规划、管理说起来简单,要落地是很难的。因此做规划,根据规划管理新型的特大城市群,这对全球来说、对中国来说,都非常重要。

我们先看这些城市群。不是所有的城市群人口都是平均分布的,有的城市群的人口在减少或迁出,还有其他一些地方的人口又聚集了,比如成都、重庆。在长

三角我们可以看到大量的人口聚集，一些城镇、小的区域基本搬空了，有的地方人口聚集很多。这样一些动态的变化需要更好的城市管理。中国有不同规模的融合、协同发展，在长三角有16个特大城市，从2000年到2014年，长三角增加了2400多万人口，占全国GDP的18%（2014年数据）；我们也看到在城市群内，核心城市周边的聚集度是增加的，而边缘地区在减少。所以原有的城市治理方法，只是过去让中国增长的原因，以前地方政府之间还有竞争心态，但现在这些都行不通了，要有协同共事的方法。这一点非常重要，也需要中国建立起不同的城市治理方式。如果没有新的管理思维，就会有负面的人口流动、不好的公共服务，区域之间就会发展不均衡。

国际上的城市群，主要有"美国2050"规划定义的11个特大城市区域，英国的一些大都市圈，包括英国西南大都市圈（伦敦通勤带），"2020新世代东京"计划中的东京大都市圈，法国巴黎2016年规划中提到的巴黎大都市圈等。这些都是大的城市群，在管理机构上，通常设立城市间论坛、大城市管理局，或者是单独的地区政府作为管理机构，负责城市群协作；有的管理机构只负责某一些功能，比如专门负责环境规划，包括固废处理等。还有一些做法是，通过一个研究机构或者规划部门来进行共同的规划和协调。

对我们来说，中国要有新的治理方式，它的结构、管理机构、管理内容、资金来源、灵活性等问题，都非常重要。

在早期，我们都说是比较轻型的管理。然后慢慢地，变到加强版的治理方式。我们是在参照美国、法国、巴西的做法。而到了成熟阶段，当之前的治理方式、小的地方已经铺平做好了，那就可以做比较全面复杂的政府管理。我们认为，长三角作为一个非常重要的试验区，这个前提是非常重要的。从世界银行的角度来看，我们认为这是一个非常积极的发展势头。结构上看，长三角获得了中央政府最高行政级别的支持；管理机构上看，由上海、江苏、浙江、安徽"三省一市"进行合作，发挥联动优势；管理范围上看，包括加强地区发展、促进合作创新、注重基础设施、推进生态环境建设、加强公共服务、扩大对外开放、创建统一市场等方面；同时明确了一个示范区，即长三角生态绿色一体化发展示范区，并设立了由各三省一市副市长、副省长组成的执委会，来促进一体化发展。

所以在现在这样一个时间点，世界银行非常看好长三角的发展，并且借此机会，希望可以进行合作、协作。世界银行也非常愿意像过去四十年一样，与大家共同打造长三角的高质量发展。

China's Megaurban Regions and Lessons from International Experiences for Their Management

Barjor Mehta

Lead Urban Specialist of Social, Rural, Urban & Resilience Global Practice in the World Bank

Today, what I am referring to is Megaurban Regions, and to expound on this macro conception, I shall review and discuss primarily the development of the large cities clusters including the Yangtze River Delta, together with what we can draw from the global experience. This is of paramount importance since all the members of the World Bank are wondering what is the headway that these Chinese large cities clusters have made of late. From a broad global perspective and taking into consideration the scale and the speed of development, Chinese Mega City Cluster is a real rarity, unprecedented in the world. Therefore, our question boils down to this: in so far as management is concerned, what has China done? I believe the answer to this question is meaningful not only to China itself, but also to the world at large.

First things first, we have to clarify our working definitions. We know when it comes to China, an idea or a conception is invariably associated with something big. Likewise, what we mean by "Metropolitan Area" or "City-Region" is a large single economy. We also talk about the "Megalopolis" such as New York, Boston and Washington D. C. They all fall into the category of "Megalopolis". The last is "Megaurban region" or rather what we call "City Cluster" in China. It encompasses multiple "Metropolitan Areas" with a unity of functions. The term has come into use only recently.

Right after China named its "Metropolitan Areas", all the members of the World Bank urged us to double our efforts in probing into them. Our finding is that without exception, each of those 19 "Metropolitan Areas" has within its terrain a city or cities whose population exceeding 1 million, with the Yangtze River Delta Region a much higher concentration of 16. And the fact is that this inclusiveness of 16 Mega cities within one single area sharing a common vision has no counterparts in the rest of world.

Let's take a look at one aspect which matters a lot: population. According to the statistics we have collected, during 2000–2014, a total of 13 Chinese city clusters reported a declining population while the Yangtze River Delta saw a rise in its inhabitants. Considering that 18% of China's GDP is engendered in those Chinese city clusters, that's a huge impact. Generally, there are three variables bearing directly on Mega City Clusters. The first is the city's size. All the Mega City Clusters are exceedingly large in scale; the second is its population growth; the third is the fact that they offer a lion's share of the state's GDP. When the three factors combine, the governance of the Mega City Clusters becomes challenging, making its measures a problem that comes into fore. For sure, the planning and management would be easier said than done. Consequently, how to manage the emerging Mega City Clusters in line with the planning and management is a critical question not only for China but also for the rest of the world.

Let's first take a look at these city clusters. Population is not evenly distributed in all the city clusters. You would lose some population if people out-migrate. Reversely, you would gain some if people come and settle down. And the later is just what has happened in cities like Chengdu and Chongqing. And the case is also true in Yangtze River Delta, where people keep flowing into some small some areas to form a huge population density, leaving behind them some rural or small townships almost empty. This dynamic demographic picture certainly calls for a better urban management. Nowadays, China boasts integrative and synergistic development of different scales. During 2000–2014, the population of the 16 mega cities in Yangtze River Delta have grown by 24 million, representing altogether 18% of

China's GDP as of 2014.

Within the city clusters, we are also seeing an increase in population density around the core city, while a decrease in marginal areas. In the past, the yardstick against which to evaluate the approach to urban governance was whether the economy fared well or not. And to go with it, there used to be a competitive mentality between the local governments. But that doesn't work any more. At present, there has to be a synergistic approach to work together. The current context dictates that China should establish a variety of different approaches to urban governance. Because without fresh management thoughts, there will be negative spillovers, poor public services and unbalanced development between regions.

Internationally, there are mainly 11 Megaurban Regions as defined in the American 2050, referring to a number of UK metropolitan areas in UK, including the Southeast Metropolitan Area (London Commuter Belt), the Tokyo Metropolitan Area specified in the NexTokyo 2020, and Métropole du Grand Paris mentioned in the France's 2016 Plan for Paris, etc. These are large city clusters, which are governed by inter-urban forums, metropolitan authorities or separate regional governments responsible for the coordination between city clusters; others are only responsible for performing certain functions, such as environmental planning, solid waste disposal, etc. There are also practices where common planning and coordination is carried out through a research institute or planning department.

For us, China is in need of a new mode of governance. And it will be determined by its formation, authority, scope, funding, flexibility and other related issues.

In the early stage, we would emphasize a "light" management. It gradually shifted to a bolstered version. What we have learned from America, France and Brazil is that when we have entered into the maturity stage, where a solid foundation has been laid in secondary aspects, we can venture into a more complicated and comprehensive mode of governance. What we believe is that as a pilot zone, Yangtze River Delta plays an important role. That's the point from which we can proceed our work. In the view of the World Bank, the Delta provides a sound momentum for the following reasons. Administratively, Yangtze River Delta is entitled to the highest-level support from the central government. With respect to authority, it is placed jointly under Shanghai municipality and provincial governments of Jiangsu, Zhejiang and Anhui, giving full play to interconnectivity. In terms of its scope of governance, efforts can be made in endeavors such as coordinated regional development, collaborative innovation, infrastructure, ecological environment, public services, opening up to the world and creating a unified market. At the same time, it has specified a model area, namely the Demonstration Area in the Yangtze River Delta on Ecologically Friendly Development, and established an executive committee composed of deputy mayors and vice-governors from each of the three provinces and one municipality to promote integrated development.

In light of the current time line, the World Bank is quite optimistic about what Yangtze River Delta can achieve in the future. And I would like to avail myself of this opportunity to call for more cooperation and concerted efforts. As we have always been during the past forty years, the World Bank is ready to build Yangtze River Delta into a region of high-quality development together with you.

Panel Discussion

互动讨论

主题一:国际区域一体化经验及其对
长三角高质量发展的启示

王宇:大家下午好,我是科尔尼公司的全球合伙人王宇。今天第一个议题是"国际区域一体化经验及其对长三角高质量发展的启示"。在座嘉宾包括野村综研咨询公司副总经理、合伙人朱四明先生,普华永道中国创新城市综合服务合伙人高骏杰先生,日本贸易振兴机构上海代表处副所长船桥宪先生,还有上海财经大学长三角与长江经济带发展研究院执行院长张学良先生,其中两位嘉宾都有日本背景。毫无疑问,在全球城市发展过程中,相对于纽约、伦敦、巴黎等西方城市,亚洲城市在人口的聚集、城市布局、空间形态方面具有相似性。而且在亚洲城市之中,东京无疑在影响力等方面是位居首位的城市。科尔尼在全球城市指数报告里指出,东京连续十年位居全球第四、亚洲第一。这也验证了这一点。

首先,我们请朱四明先生发言。由于时间紧张,请朱先生和各位嘉宾在发言时控制时间。我们留下足够的时间进行互动。谢谢!

朱四明:首先,非常感谢主办方给我们这样一个机会跟大家分享一些我们的心得。我们野村综合研究所是日本的一家咨询公司。作为日本的一个国家智库,我们参与了比较多的与日本相关的产业规划、区域规划和建设,以及非常多的与中国国内相关的区域、产业研究项目,包括上海的很多项目。

关于这个话题,我谈三个观点。首先这里面有两个概念,我们先界定一下,即都市圈和城市群。日本的发展,有好的地方,但是也有很多地方并不尽如人意,离政府当初的设想有很大出入。这对我们上海有很大的借鉴作用,对长三角一体化的借鉴功能更大。第一,整个东京占地面积非常小,只有2 000多平方公里,人口1 000多万人,相当于我们上海核心群。东京圈,包括周边的千叶这些县,占地面积达10 000多平方公里;首都圈,占地30 000多平方公里,包括东京圈外面4个县;最大的是广域都市圈,有80 000多平方公里,5 000多万人口,占了日本差不多40%,但这跟我们长三角的体量相比还是有非常大的差距。第二,日本真正算得上成功的就是东京圈,做了六次相关的规划,希望东京与周边县之间形成差异化发展、区隔定位。但真正发展得比较好的,就是千叶、神奈川、横滨,这些地方和东京之间形成了很好的协同,外面的发展则非常弱。为什么会形成这种情况?主要是政府希望各个产业区域之间有很好的分工,但产业集聚有产业发展自身的特点,尤其是研发。刚才嘉宾讲得非常好。比如,人才在上海的迁入和迁出都起到很大的作用,有的迁出是因为人才,迁入也是因为人才。现在东京具有巨大的虹吸效应,对周边区域是虹吸的。对于高科技研发的相关产业,东京的集聚效应更明显。东京都、东京圈这两个还不错,其他的谈不上成功。第三,从更大的城市群的角度来看,整个日本目前有三个大的都市圈。除东京圈以外,还有大阪、关西、名古屋,这三个特色比较明显。对于这三个城市,日本政府也试图形成一种协同效应。其实把这三个放在一起,和我们长三角的体量比较相当,可能面积没有长三角这么大,但差不多也可以做类比了。但三者的协同,现在最多就是在交通方面先行一步,实现整个产业的协同还比较远。所以我们先做试点,小的区域先行,我们也认为这非常对。先行以后,怎么样把它放大,虹吸效应和分流效应之间如何形成良好的互动,可能还需要花比较多的时间去探索。

王宇:非常感谢。朱四明先生从东京都市圈和日本大城市发展的角度提出了对上海都市圈与长三角城市一体化的展望。下面我们请普华永道的高先生发言。

高骏杰:感谢主持人,感谢大家!非常荣幸有机会在这里讲述我们对一体化城市圈合作的一些观点。围绕分论坛的主题,我就从高质量发展角度简单阐述一下我们的观点。

高质量发展有别于大规模发展或高速度发展,这不只是单单追求经济总量,更多的是要从产业内容、效率、生态和人文的角度,综合地看一个城市的发展水平和效率。接下来我将从大家都熟悉的角度——产、城、人,谈一下我们的观点。

首先,产的角度。对于长三角一体化产业发展,很多专家和领导都提到了经济密度。在一定的技术水平之下经济密度会达到一个上限,之后产业反而会从集聚转向外溢。如何把握住每一波全球技术发展对我们未来长三角地区发展的促进作用,如何找出比较合适的经济密度、合适的各地区的主导产业、合适的科创方向?长三角产业要参与全球竞争,需要力量集中办大事,所以我呼吁,我们需要一个类似智库、协会的机构,这方面有一个比较好的参考。我观察到,纽约、波士顿等地区都有很明确的大纽约、大波士顿地区的产业智库委员会,虽然不一定具有绝对的决策力,但对执行委员会或城市规划委员会都有很强的建议效力,而且每年都会提交相关的专业的产业课题和全球发展趋势报告,所提出建议的被采纳率在很多时候对市长或区域组织人员的绩效考核评分有一定的影响。

第二,从城市角度来说,基础设施建设或者互联互通是非常简单的一个工作。但我在之前的工作生活中发现,城市和城市之间,产业是企业自主选择的,但基建投资属于政府开支。很多时候在一个区域中,重要的基建先建在哪里、谁先建的问题,确实会影响到未来城市和产业发展的潜力。我以前在纽约、波士顿东区工作,那里有一个明确的指标体系,考核未来基础设施投资的优先级。而且指标体系和优先级考核指标是以学术方式呈现,在一定程度上向公众发布,公众也有获取的渠道。城市基础设施或重大项目建设中,我们是不是也可以有一个比较科学的、多方学术或技术方面建议渠道的指标体系?而且这是需要动态更新的,对未来在区域的重大基础设施建设上能起到一个建议作用。这不只是涉及城市基础设施建设,更是创新收益的分享。思路有了,未来制度是怎样的,这是非常重要的一个考量。

最后,讲到人。未来不是只考虑我们这些人或 90 后,更多要考虑 00 后、10 后他们工作和生活的长三角地区一体化是怎样的。我觉得更多的是他们的数字痕迹、信息。刚才毕马威的刘总也提到了,数字经济在长三角一体化中未来的定位,对数据的应用和对未来数字经济的分享。在长三角地区或中国,乃至全球最有竞争力的就是数字经济。因为我们有大量的数字原创和人口,那么是不是该有更专业的制度、标准,甚至更专业的探讨和分享平台呢?这是产、城、人中关于人的角度对高质量发展具有的巨大推动作用。谢谢!

王宇:谢谢,高骏杰先生从产、城、人方面介绍了他的经验,这对长三角一体化发展颇具借鉴意义。下面我们请船桥宪先生发言。

船桥宪:2019 年夏天我刚刚从东京到这里常驻、工作,我想说说东京的经验与借鉴。

长三角是一个非常大的区域,有很多行业、部门都在长三角,这里还有完备的工业体系。但说到东京湾,其实还不是那么完备,大部分是服务业。服务业在东京很大,占到了 80% 以上的国民生产总值。但说到上海,从服务业的增长率来看,2019 年前三季度是 8.9%,总体同比增长率为 6%,服务业经济增长率是快于整体经济增长率的。所以,我们应该更加注重服务业的发展,不一定所有的行业都要在长三角区域存在,我们可以合理地分配角色、进行分工,在上海和其他三个省份中做分配。上海可能更多的是关注服务业发展。东京本身制造业占比较轻,东京周围的城市制造业占比则高很多,所以上海的城市规划在吸引外资时可以更多地倚重服务业的发展,包括通信、零售业以及其他相关行业,这些跟人们生活息息相关的行业,与我们的生活作息、态度有关。而且随着时代发展,未来这块在经济发展中的占比会越来越多。所以,我们应该更加注重和鼓励服务业的发展,促进人们生活方式的多样化。

我想与大家分享一些东京服务业发展的案例。比如快递,我们可以设定具体的配送时间。现在有许多家庭,爸爸妈妈都是双职工,孩子早上要上学。在这样的情况下,家里就没有人收快递了,因此如果可以提前定好送货上门的时间,就不会错过快递员配送快递了。这对传统快递业是很大的改变。同样,比如幼托所,我们现在有 24 小时全营业的,以及日间对婴儿和儿童进行照顾的养育中心,有了这样的设施,家长就可以有更灵活的时间。而且这种新型服务也可以促进新的生活方式和习惯的养成,东京的居民生活就能变得更便捷。

所以,我希望上海能更注重服务业的全面发展,为人们创建更好的生活方式,并且能将其传导到整个长三角一体化的过程中。谢谢!

王宇:感谢船桥宪先生,他从东京服务业的角度谈了一些经验,而且举了非常实际的一些例子。下面我们请张学良先生发言。

张学良:感谢主持人。长三角一体化进入到一个新阶段,受几位的启发,我觉得长三角一体化发展应该有"四个放在"的概念:要放在国际对比中找到我们的方位,放在历史的维度里看我们的方向,也要放在未来的趋势中找到我们未来的前途,当然也要放在党和国家政府对我们的期待上来做一些回应。

首先就是要从国际上的先发地区的经验找到我们对标的方向。我梳理了一下,不管是欧洲两大城市群发展的经验、欧盟一体化的经验、美国大西洋沿岸和太平洋沿岸这两大城市群的经验,还是日本的太平洋沿岸城市群的经验,无外乎几条:第一,市场发挥决定作用。这不是三十年或四十年的市场,可能是上百年的市场的作用。纽约从 1929 年成立地区规划协会,到今天编制了四轮规划,主线就是面对社会需求和市场需求来编制的。但我们要知道,当长三角一体化热起来以后,我们还是要再思考一下市场所起的决定性作用。第二,要发挥龙头城市的作用。龙头城市非常重要,纽约、东京、伦敦都发挥了龙头带动和辐射的作用。第三,龙头城市也要有所为,有所不为。这就涉及城市的核心功能和非核心功能的认识问题。上海的核心功能,传统做法就是"五个中心",核心功能定下来以后,我们要想想非核心功能在什么地方,要跟周边城市进行协同。当然,核心功能也有关键环节、非关键环节。对上海来说,可能要做核心功能的关键环节,非关键环节要跟周边地区做协同。第四,要规划引领。中国是一个市场经济国家,在这个过程中,地方政府和中央政府都发挥了非常重要的作用。纽约都市圈做了四次规划,20世纪20年代、60年代以及21世纪2007年前后和2017年的四次规划,都有规划引领,在不同时期做了不同的规划。长三角地区的规划是2016年城市群的规划,不久前发布了《长江三角洲区域一体化发展规划纲要》,如果算上历史上1982年上海经济区的发展,当时也有一轮规划的话,那么到今天也就三轮规划。对现有的规划来说,可能要发挥规划引领的作用。当然,还可以学习到很多经验。

中国是世界的一部分,长三角也是世界城市群中一个关键的核心。我做了一个比较有趣的研究,研究整个城市群的演变。第一次工业革命从英国开始,形成了英国的城市群,第二次工业革命形成了欧洲的城市群,世界的中心从欧洲转移到美洲,形成了美国的两大城市群。20世纪五六十年代,日本崛起,形成了日本的城市群。如果从历史维度讲,我们今天讲的江南,公元300年前,魏晋南北朝的南朝时期,南京的发展,然后运河发展形成了扬州的崛起,到两宋时期形成了杭州的发展,到明清时期苏州发展,1853年上海开埠以后上海的发展。整个发展阶段,历史维度上如果有城市群或是都市圈的概念,那么中国江南地区,也就是我们所在的长三角,实际在很长一段时间,是世界的城市发展重心。所以,我觉得应该是一个闭环,从长三角到欧洲,到美洲,再回到了长三角。我个人更愿意从这个角度把长三角纳入整个全球城市体系里来思考这个问题,可能故事就能说得很全了。我就分享到这里。

王宇:非常感谢。今天四位嘉宾从不同的角度介绍了国际经验的启示,其中东京是出现频次比较高的一个区域。在几个嘉宾发言的基础之上,我也想谈一谈从东京都市圈里得到的借鉴。

我的发言相对来说比较具体,会结合我们科尔尼公司东京办公室的一个实践经验。根据科尔尼2019年全球城市指数报告,可以看到,在整个长三角的城市排名里,现在已经有6座城市列入全球130个城市榜单,这是2019年的最新报告。这6座城市分别是上海、南京、杭州、苏州、无锡和宁波。正如张主任谈到的,正好这6座城市是GDP过万亿元的。如果仔细看,上海始终是排名第20位左右,南京、杭州、苏州三个城市是2015年进入科尔尼全球城市排行榜的,排名在第85—100名之间。之后,后起之秀宁波和无锡在2018年上榜,排名第116、第124名。由此可以看到,自从科尔尼2008年发表全球城市指数,这也是全球首次五个以上城市出现在同城城市圈中。这也反映出了我们长三角城市群的综合能力、竞争力。究其原因,除了得益于经济发展、商业活动较高能级的竞争力以外,我们也认为,这里面得益于人力资本的关注,就是刚才说的产、城、人。这很重要,尤其是以市民为中心的发展模式创新,意味着未来的城市不仅是宜居城市、公共服务高效便民的城市,更重要的是真正将本地市民纳入区域发展的主体。尤其结合近几年的高质量发展,这样的要求以及治理体系的要求,我们认为包括上海在内的长三角各个主要城市,应该在国际超大城市的治理中做一些探索。

我跟大家分享一下科尔尼公司在东京做的一系列工作。东京在双向城市治理方面有很多经验。比如超大型城市治理方面,包括政府、企业、市民之间如何进行协作,如何形成国际超大城市治理的良好示范。2014 年,科尔尼日本公司总经理提出"新世代东京计划",联合了建筑、城市规划、设计、艺术、体育、媒体以及法律方面的专家,同贤达人士共同以东京 2020 年奥运会为契机发起这样一个计划,在社会各界、政界和媒体方面引起了一系列的关注和讨论。

其中有三个关键的成功要素:第一,建立了一个从上到下的对话机制,它是跨学科多元的意见输入。这也是综合、复合性的知识解答,着眼于城市未来的发展思路。特别是从决策、建设两个层面来看,重视来源于民间的想法,然后引入本地专家,给本地意见领袖很大的发挥空间,形成上传下达的一个途径。这些专家包括来自科技创业的企业家,还有律师,以及很多相关的社会精英,还有原来当地的奥运冠军。第二,推动政策制定和本地立法,促进城市规划有效落地。我们认为这很重要。最终很多事情其实都落位于最后的立法。"新世代东京计划"与东京都政府、日本中央政府建立了密切的沟通和交流机制,向政府的国家特别工作委员会提交了很多议案,包括放开对外来人才的签证,对休闲娱乐时间的经营限制,立法方面都进行了修改。第三,引入"超级项目经理"机制。通过这种机制,能发起介入区域再开发落地的一些项目。有两个案例,一个就是在东京联合英国皇家艺术学院和东京大学的生产技术研究所,成立东京设计实验室,得到了内阁政府的支持,另一个是推动了东京创业园区引入国际知名的孵化器 CIC 孵化机制落地。前文所述的三个方面我们觉得是可以借鉴的。"新世代东京计划"动员本土的精英人才,我们认为这样的治理经验,对我们打造长三角各大城市、打造国际超大型城市的治理结构具有借鉴意义。长三角作为中国乃至全球的人才高地,我们有大批专业能力非常强、商业运作和管理经验非常丰富、有国际视野,并且对当地有本土人文关怀的精英人才。所以我们建议和呼吁,上海、杭州、苏州、南京、无锡、宁波等一系列城市,借鉴打造根植本地、展望全球的本土计划,切实发挥本地企业、学者和专家学者群体的智慧,推进国际化发展。

下面进入问答环节。

现场嘉宾：请问各位专家，针对外资中小型制造企业，在上海由于工业用地紧张以及各方面成本上涨问题，搬迁流失到外地，甚至离开了长三角地区，其中不乏隐形冠军企业，那么在长三角一体化过程中，上海是否会考虑与外地政府对接，在当地为企业提供工业用地，并附加相当于上海水平的政府服务，共同推动产业经济发展？这样一来，不仅可以把技术密集型的企业留在长三角，也能盘活当地工业用地的有效使用。

张学良：首先您提到的这个现象是不是一种趋势，可能要做一些严谨的判断。第一，对于劳动力成本，我个人认为不能简单地从工资水平或土地用地来判断。劳动力成本，它的分子应该是劳动生产率，分母为工资水平的分数。上海工资水平用工成本高，但技术很好，因而单位劳动力成本还是低的。同时区域比较，很多东西具有上海优势，我们的营商环境比较好，政府信誉比较好，劳动力成本、科创环境以及劳动力蓄水池和科技人才比较好。这是很多地方没有办法相比的。所以，我个人认为这不一定是一个趋势，只是一个现象。这个现象在 20 世纪八九十年代都有。第二，讲到"飞地"问题，这是很好的探索。传统的区域合作，比如上海，也有很好的担当，我们在中西部地区有很多扶贫和帮扶，今天我们上海正在探索做一些新的工作，对口合作的工作，上海跟大连有对口合作，跟中西部很多地方也有。新型"飞地"模式可以探讨。现在做得比较好的经验是在广东省汕尾市海丰县，有个深汕特别合作区，是深圳特区的特区。这样合作就比较彻底，它是深圳的一块"飞地"，行政管辖、派出所、公安局都是深圳的。在安徽也有，铜陵在安庆市有"飞地"，在池州也有，邮政编码都是铜陵的。省内的是很好实现的。省域间的探索，则面临挑战，这需要党中央、国务院批准。还有就是税收和 GDP 分成的问题，投入产出后问题，具有很大挑战。今天我们长三角一体化示范区也在做一些尝试，我觉得这是方向，可以做探索，但怎么做，还要考虑各地的顾虑、把预案做好。我们高校智库以及在座各位智库可以在这方面提前做一些研究。

高骏杰：刚才张教授谈了这个现象，包括"飞地"的一些情况，我非常认同。我补充另外一个选择。从企业角度，企业关心更多的是如何享受到相当于上海的高水平的整体服务。这当然也包括了政府服务、园区服务、物业服务以及专业性比较强的平台服务。这当中，除了"飞地"需要很多行政力量、政策资源来进行探讨和介入之外，现在国内还有很多合作产业园区的方式。比如，中兴在苏州的产业园，还有园外园、区外园的方式，还有深圳输出的深哈产业园等。以产业园的方式作为一种补充。虽然不涉及税收、当地行政管理、教育和医疗的设施，但可以在当地相对比较低的服务水平下，直接加进去一些比较先进的好的管理经验、相关的服务资源，带入当地，也能很大程度上提升。因为它是市场化的力量，现在很多产业园区正面临上市的机会，国家也发布了相关的政策，在名单中有 90 家园区管理企业，也有 IPO 的机会，它们在积极寻求市场化的资本运作。所以未来，在市场推动下它们能用市场力量给当地的营商环境、企业服务，甚至在上海服务和品牌输出中起到更大的作用。这是一个很好的补充。

现场嘉宾：我的问题是，作为世界工厂的四十年里，中国的制造及创新能力急速提升，但中国品牌国际化程度较低。未来长三角区域在哪几个方面，能为中国品牌出海以及提升国际化认可度提供支持？

朱四明：品牌出海，出什么？品牌下面一定是有很多产业、产品的，哪些东西出？仅仅通过上海出，还是说出上海的东西、长三角的东西？国家现在处在重化工业化末期，提出七个战略性新兴产业。各国产业发展路径是大同小异的，像亚洲的日本、韩国作为后发国家，从劳动密集型到重化工工业化，到产业升级、国际化，都是这么几个阶段。现在我们在第二、三阶段之间，确实到了产业升级的时候。升级升得好，出去是非常自然的事情，如果不好，前面劳动密集型的东西我们并不一定想出去，也谈不上品牌的概念。所以核心还是：你出什么？

最近二十年，整个日本在消费方面，现在唯一还能在国际上进行全面竞争，大家熟悉的品牌可能就是汽车了。其他耳熟能详的很多东西，都已经退到后台了。像松下这样的公司，80% 的业务是 2B、2C 的。日本有非常多的隐形冠军企业，出口非常大。比如一个做小电容的公司纯利润高达 20%，全世界可能就只有它在做。

上海以前是"四个中心"，现在是建设"五个中心"。我们归纳一下，如果上海仅仅作为一个贸易中心，把中国的东西拿到海外去，甚至低端的东西，这是没有价值的。如果上海这样的地方作为龙头，能引领整个产业的升级，然后出去一些非常有价值的东西，这就是非常有价值的。

王宇：非常感谢朱四明先生。我做一点补充。从品牌的角度来说，应该结合一下产业集群。我们看全球，谈到机械制造，第一个想到的就是德国，谈到皮包，想到的是意大利，谈到高科技、IT，是美国西海岸。其实未来长三角，是不是从政府、企业和产业园区来考虑一下，做品牌的打造？比如上海的集成电路、南京的电力装配、苏州的生命科学。

下面我自己有一个问题想请教两位日本专家。在最近发布的《长江三角洲区域一体化发展规划纲要》中提出五大定位，第一就是全国发展强劲活跃的增长极，这里面提到了创新。东京在科技文创方面，在亚洲地区，甚至在全球都是处于领先地位，请两位日本专家介绍一下，未来在长三角促进创新方面有什么经验可以分享？

船桥宪: 全球化很重要，但要往外推什么，这个也很重要。中国有许多独角兽，都是年轻有为、发展非常迅猛的公司。中国当然也需要做更多创新，更多"走出去"。为什么中国要有这么多独角兽？那就是因为它的本地市场已经足够大了，容量很大，可以容纳这么多独角兽在这里获得长足的发展。这之后，它们才需要讨论全球化。比如我们日本贸易振兴机构，一直想帮助日本的公司、初创企业走到中国，希望进入新的市场。对日本企业和中国企业来说，道理都是一样的，要往外走，这非常重要，这方面可以做创新。

朱四明: 我们的基础设施建设做得非常好，但为什么很多方面的进展不尽如人意呢？有两个原因，第一是机制层面，这个机制分两个方面，软的和硬的，我们没有像日本 NEDO① 那样的一个协调机构，很多事情好像都由部委牵头，有很多企业参与，但没有非常强有力的国家认同的、有足够权威的协调机构协调这个事情。第二就是知识产权，始终不清晰。知识产权分不清，企业就不愿意参与。新能源做不起来，中国做新能源最好的公司，不愿意参与到国家体系里。为什么要参与？知识产权归谁？这也是百度和高德不能合并的原因。基础产权归大家吗？大家一起分享吗？应用产权是归自己所有的吗？如果这件事情搞不定，很多都是空话。当然，上面的机制，有没有一个比较强的跨越各个部委和各个区域真实存在的机构，像 NEDO 这样的协调机构是非常重要的。

王宇: 谢谢各位嘉宾！

---

① 即 The New Energy and Industrial Technology Development Organization(日本新能源产业技术综合开发机构)，是日本最大的公立研究开发管理机构，政产学研一体化的平台机构。

Panel Discussion 1: Experience from International Integrative Regions and Its Enlightenment for High-quality Development of the Yangtze River Delta

Jefferson Wang: Good afternoon everyone! I am Jefferson Wang, Partner-Head of ATK China Government & Economic Development Practice. The first panel discussion is about "Experience from International Integrative Regions and Its Enlightenment for High-quality Development of the Yangtze River Delta". Here are our distinguished guests—Zhu Siming, Deputy General Manager and Partner of NRI (Shanghai), Ken Gao, Partner of Integrated Urban Services at PwC, Ken FUNABASHI, Vice President of Japan Trade Promotion Organization (JETRO) Shanghai and Zhang Xueliang, Executive Dean of the Development Research Institute of the Yangtze River Delta and Yangtze River Economic Belt in Shanghai University of Finance and Economics, two of whom have great knowledge of Japan. There is no doubt that during the development of the global city, Asian cities share the similarity in terms of the concentration of population, the layout of the city and the spatial form of the area when it comes to those of western cities like New York, London and Paris. Then, among all the Asian cities, Tokyo is undoubtedly ranked as the most influential one, which is proved by Kearney's Global Cities Index. Next, let's welcome Zhu Siming to deliver the speech. Given that the time is limited, please, Mr. Zhu and the following speakers should be aware of the length of the speech, which leave us enough time for Q & As.

Zhu Siming: First of all, I appreciate it that the host provides the opportunity for us to share the ideas. NRI is a Japanese think-tank. As a national think-tank for Japanese government, NRI takes part in a lot of industrial planning, regional planning and constructing as well as plenty of domestic industries and fields.

I want to share my viewpoint from three aspects. For starter, it is necessary to make a definition of metropolitan area and mega-city cluster. The process of development of Japan is not perfect when there are a lot of things that are far from satisfaction and failed to meet the expectation of Japan authority. Therefore, Shanghai, during the integration of the Yangtze River Delta could draw the inspiration from Japanese experience. I will illustrate from the following three aspects.

First of all, Tokyo has limited landscape and population, with about 2,000 square kilometers and 10 million population, is equal to central circle of Shanghai. The Tokyo Metropolitan Area, including counties like Chiba, covers more than 10,000 square kilometers. The Capital Circle, including four counties covers 30,000 square kilometers. But the biggest one is "Megaurban Regions", which covers 80,000 square kilometers and has 50 million population, which is about 40% of the whole Japan's population. However, there are the huge discrepancy in acreage and population between the Tokyo Metropolitan Area and the Yangtze River Delta.

Secondly, what can be took as the successful example is none other than the Tokyo Metropolitan Area which after six times' planning amendments, forms the differentiated development and target segments from the surrounding counties. In the meantime, Chiba, Kanagawa and Yokohama build the cooperation with Tokyo and make essential development, but other counties are still at the square one. In essence, the authority hopes that different industries divide the work based on the specification. And the industrialization concentration has its own feature especially in the R&D Department. As the former speaker mentioned, the immigration and migration of talents exert great influence in Shanghai. Nowadays, Tokyo appears the siphonic effect which pushes the Tokyo forward and strengthen the agglomeration effect. Tokyo and the Tokyo Metropolitan Area do make some progress but not the others.

Thirdly, considering that Japan has three metropolitan areas, some put up that Japan should have a bigger city cluster. Besides the Tokyo Metropolitan Area, Osaka, Kansai and Nagoya have their own characteristics which would help to form another Metropolitan Area. The authority manages to produce synergetic effect. In fact, the size of the three metropolitan areas, if put together, is comparable to that of our Yangtze River Delta, while their geographic area is smaller than that of the Delta. Transportation takes the lead in the coordinated development of the three areas, but there is a long way to go for that of the whole industry. So, we believe it is justifiable to pilot in a small area. More time is needed to explore how to materialize and enhance its siphonic effect and form a good interaction between its siphon effect and diversion effect.

Jefferson Wang: Thank you, Mr. Zhu introduces the experience of the development of the Tokyo Metropolitan Area and other Japan's big city as well as makes an outlook of the Yangtze River Delta's integration. Then, let's welcome Mr. Gao from PwC.

Ken Gao: Thank you. It is my honor to deliver a speech in terms of the cooperation of metropolitan region's integration. I will illustrate from the high-quality development to echo with the topic of the panel discussion.

Different from the large-scale development or high-speed development, high-quality development underscores, on the one hand, the volume of economy, on the other hand, the level and efficiency of comprehensive development of city in the aspects of politics, economy, ecology and the culture. I will illustrate from the industry, city and people aspects.

Firstly, from the industry perspective, as mentioned before, the economic density of industry exerts great influence on the Yangtze River Delta's integration. However, under certain level of technology, the industry would transfer from concentration to spillover when the economic density reaches the extreme. But the problems laid in front of us are how to grasp every opportunity of technological revolution, find out the balanced economic density and point out the direction of leading industry. At this juncture, I think it is time to set up Think-tank Association which could provide the suggestions to promote the competitiveness of the Yangtze River Delta in the fierce global competition. It is clear to see that the cities like New York and Boston have their own think-tank committee. Although the committees do not have the decisive power, the City Planning Commission would take their suggestions seriously. Besides, to the city mayors and regional organizers, the adoption rate of the think-tanks' plan related to the industry and global development would influence their performance assessment.

Secondly, from the city aspect, the connectivity of infrastructure between cities is a simple task. According to my observation, the settlement or the location of the factory is decided by company while the government takes the responsibility of the investment of infrastructure. However, within certain region, where to build the infrastructure and who takes the lead would influence the development of the city and industry potential. I used to work in New York and the east zone of Boston, and there has a direct target system, put up in the academic way and launched to the public in some degree, which is aimed to assess the priority of infrastructure investment. Therefore, is it necessary for us to have a scientific, academic and technological target system in urban infrastructure or some important projects? Besides, the system should be dynamic update and adapt to different situation so as to provide efficient plans. Since we have already had a framework, the buildup of the system should be put on the top of the agenda.

Last but not the least, the people. It is of crucial importance to consider the influence of the Yangtze River Delta's integration on the post-90s and Z generation who pays more attention on the data and information. As Mr. Liu from KPMG mentioned before, it is necessary to make out importance of digital economy that weighs in the fields of digital practice and the share of

长三角一体化与高质量发展
Integration of the Yangtze River Delta for High-quality Development

digital economy. There is no deny that digital economy is and will be the most competitiveness industry of the Yangtze River Delta or China, even around the world. As we have a large number of digital creation and e-people, do we need to set up a more professional system and standard, or even build a more specialized discussion and sharing platform? This is from the perspective of people. Thank you!

Jefferson Wang: Thank you. Mr. Gao make a brief introduction from the industry, city and people which is helpful for the development of the Yangtze River Delta. Next, let's welcome Mr. Ken FUNABASHI from JETRO.

Ken FUNABASHI: I have moved to Shanghai since this summer. I would like to share some experience of Tokyo.

Compared to Tokyo Bay, the Yangtze River Delta covers a larger scale, which owns different industry departments and forms a comprehensive industrial system. In Tokyo Bay, the industrial system is not that integrated, and the service industry accounts for the largest share, making up 80% of GNP. As for Shanghai, the growth rate of service industry in the past three quarters reaches 8.9%, 6% year-on-year, which is higher than total increase rate of GDP. Therefore, we should pay more attention on the development of the service industry. Besides, for the Yangtze River Delta, it is not necessary to cover each industry but to promote the efficiency of every department, which could push every sector to better play their own roles. Maybe Shanghai should focus on the development of the service industry, and coordinate with Zhejiang, Jiangsu and Anhui Provinces. For example, the proportion of manufacturing industry takes larger part in cities around Tokyo than in Tokyo itself. So Shanghai could attract more foreign investment to the communication, retail and others service industries which has close connection with people's daily life and will have great influence in the future. And hence more effort should be paid to advance the development of service sector in order to create various ways of lifestyle.

I want to share some specific cases. Mention should be made on Tokyo's express service. Nowadays, more and more families have been perplexed by the situation that both the father and mother have to work at the same time while the children should go to school early in the morning. Under such circumstance, no one would be at home to receive the express package. In order to solve the problem, the express departments of Tokyo launch a new policy that every family could set the time ahead to receive the package, which greatly changes the traditional way of express delivery. Likewise, in Tokyo, there are the 24-hour kindergartens and day-time infant centers which help free parents from daily trivialities. These new types of services can help the cultivation of the new living style and habits, which makes the Japanese's life easier.

Therefore, I hope that Shanghai can pay more attention to the comprehensive development of the service industry, creating a better lifestyle for people and influencing the integration of the Yangtze River Delta. Thank you!

Jefferson Wang: Thanks Mr. Ken FUNABASHI, he introduced the experience of Tokyo and provided some practical suggestions. Then, Let's welcome Mr. Zhang Xueliang from Shanghai University of Finance and Economics.

Zhang Xueliang: Thanks. Inspired by the speakers, I think the integrated development of the Yangtze River Delta should follow four dimensions when the integration has moved into a new stage that we should make out the direction according to the international experience, historical dimension, future trend and the expectation from the party and central government.

Firstly, we should learn from the advanced experience in the global scale. There are the salient features of the city clusters in Europe, European Union, U.S. as well as Japan. For starter, market still plays the decisive role, which means the market only uphold the economy in the past three or four decades but also will push forward the country for centuries. Following the direction of displaying the market in accordance to the demands of society and the market, New York has gone through four rounds of city planning since the founding of Regional Plan Association in 1929. But one point could not bear to be neglected is that the market should still be the pillar of economy when the Yangtze River Delta's integration comes to its summit. Then, the performance of leading cities should be underscored. It is clear to see that cities surrounding New York, Tokyo and London take the advantages of those megalopolis. Next, the leading cities should make a balance between industries, which brings out the distinction of core function and non-core function of cities. For example, Shanghai needs to build "five centers" and form core competitiveness, figures out the non-core functions and makes the cooperation with the surrounding areas afterwards. Also, Shanghai should pay more attention on the key joints while others could be spared to other cities. Lastly, the programmatic documents should be made by local and central governments to direct the development of market-oriented economy. The New York Metropolitan Area has gone through four rounds of planning according to the changes of different periods and external environment, whereas the Yangtze River Delta makes three rounds of planning in 1982, 2016, and 2019 respectively. Recently, *the Outline of the Integrated Regional Development of the Yangtze River Delta* was released. The related documents should still play the leading role in the long run.

China is a part of the world, the Yangtze River Delta is also a part of global city clusters. Out of interests, I study on the evolution of global city clusters and find out that the city clusters in U.K. happens after the world industrialization, city clusters in U.S. starts when the global center transfers from Europe to America while the city clusters in Japan builds up after the rebirth of Japan in the 1950s. From historical dimension, the Jiangnan area, namely the south of the lower reaches of the Yangtze river, which we are talking about today, has gone through a long way to reach its full development. The city of Nanjing came into being in the Northern dynasties (439-589 CE); Yangzhou started to develop thanks to the Grand Canal in the

Sui dynasty (581-618 CE); Hangzhou developed in the Song Dynasty (960-1279), Suzhou in the Ming and Qing Dynasties (1369-1912). and Shanghai after the opening of Shanghai port in 1853. Looking through the history of these major cities, the Jiangnan area, or the Yangtze River Delta, can be regarded as early metropolitan areas or urban agglomerations, and has actually been the center of urban development in the world for a long time. Therefore, I personally prefer to think about this issue by incorporating the Yangtze River Delta into the entire global urban system. A closed loop that stans from the Yangtze River Delta to Europe, to the Americas, and then back to the Yangtze River Delta, may as well fully explain the whole story. This is all I want to share.

Jefferson Wang: Thank you all. Four guests introduce the international experience from four aspects. I notice that Tokyo has been mentioned from time to time. Therefore, I would like to share some points of the Tokyo Metropolitan Area on the basis of former discussion.

My speech is more concise and compact which is the result of the practical research of A.T. Kearney Tokyo Office. According to the Global Cities Index of A.T. Kearney, 2019, six cities of the Yangtze River Delta are enlisted on the top 130 world cities including Shanghai, Nanjing, Hangzhou, Suzhou, Wuxi and Ningbo whose GDP has reached trillion yuan. Shanghai ranks the top 20. Nanjing, Hangzhou and Suzhou stand between 85th~100th after 2015 while Ningbo and Wuxi are enlisted in the last year, ranking 116th and 124th. It is the first time that more than five cities of the same city cluster are nominated in the Global Cities Index since 2008, which reflects the comprehensive competitiveness of the Yangtze River Delta. After serious research, we think that the human capital is of crucial importance to the economy in spite of the business activities and the competitiveness. It means that the innovative citizen-oriented development model would embrace locals as the entity of the regional development so as to build a more comfortable, efficient and convenient city. In consideration of the high-quality development in recent years, we believe cities in the Yangtze River Delta especially Shanghai should take up the responsibility to make some exploration in the field of the renewed governance of global mega-city.

I am willing to share with you some research of A.T. Kearney Tokyo Office. Tokyo has made some progress in two-way governance which is worth mentioning. Authority, corporations and citizens make great effort to set good example of the management of megalopolis. In 2014, manager of A.T. Kearney Tokyo Office launches the NexTokyo program, which combines the experts in the areas of construction, city planning, design, art, sports, media and law so as to catch up with the opportunity of 2020 Tokyo Olympic Games. The plan raises the heated discussion in every corner of the country.

The following three points make the plan come in to being. Firstly, the founding of the up-bottom dialogue mechanism encourages the import of interdisciplinary proposal. To think in a bigger picture, it helps to take in the academic suggestions without ignoring the citizens' opinions, which gives the local authorities ample leeway to perform. The experts are composed of the start-up entrepreneurs, lawyers and the former Olympic champions. Secondly, the enforcement of city planning is ensured by the politics and acts. The committee of "NexTokyo" has a close connection with Tokyo government and Japan central government. The committee hands in several proposals concerning the adaption of the visa towards foreign talents and the limit of the entertainment activities. Thirdly, the import of mechanism of "Super Project Manager" helps the re-exploitation of some projects in interventional region. There are two cases. One is the settlement of the Tokyo Design Lab, endorsed by the cabinet and founded by the bilateral effort of Royal College of Art and the Institute of Industrial Science, the University of Tokyo. And the other is the import of the renowned CIC incubation mechanism in Tokyo innovation center. The point that "NexTokyo" activates the local elites in an all-around way, which can also be applied in the Yangtze River Delta. Given that the Yangtze River Delta standing at the high ground and embraces global talents, there are bunches of intellects who are able and skilled in the commercial management.

Therefore, I think cities like Shanghai, Hangzhou, Suzhou, Nanjing, Wuxi and Ningbo should make the plan according to their own characteristics, the future development together with the suggestions of local companies and experts.

Then, let's start the Q & A section.

Audience: I have a question to the experts in terms of the development of the foreign small to medium-sized manufacturing enterprises. It is known that the reduction of the industrial use of land and the soaring labor cost press the enterprises including some invisible champions to move out of Shanghai or even the Yangtze River Delta. Then, during the process of the integration of the Yangtze River Delta, it is possible for Shanghai to cooperate with other local goverments, which means local governments provide the industrial use of land while Shanghai provides the standard government services, to mutually promote the industrial and economic development. In this way can the technologically-intensive enterprises stay within the Yangtze River Delta as well as activate the use of the local industrial land.

Zhang Xueliang: The conclusion that whether the phenomenon as you mentioned before can transfer to the trend will be made on the basis of the detailed researches. First, in my view, the labor cost which is the rate of productivity and wage cannot be seen as the individual factor. True, the average salary level of Shanghai is relatively high compared to other areas. But the advanced technology, good government credit, positive innovation environment and the big pool of talent reduce the unit labor costs, which is the unique advantage of Shanghai. Then, I prefer to name it as the phenomenon rather than the trend for this question appears as early as the 1980s. Second, it will be practical to explore in the field of "enclaves". In the past, Shanghai takes good responsibility to help the central and western regions in China uproot the poverty in an all-around way, which is the traditional territorial cooperation. But, today, Shanghai is trying to make the breakthrough in form of the one-on-one cooperation like the bilateral cooperation with Dalian and western China. The new development pattern of "enclaves" leaves us large room to discuss. The practice of the Shenzhen-Shanwei Special Cooperation Zone, which located in Haifeng county of Shan Wei City in Guangdong Province while serve as a special area in Shenzhen, provides a relative throughout example since the local authority, police and security bureau are all under the management of the government of Shenzhen. The same pattern is also applied in Anhui province, such as the Tongling-Anqing and Tongling-Chizhou enclaves, which share the same ZIP code with Tongling. The enclave model is easier to fulfill within the province, while the cross-administrative exploration is faced with more challenges and needs the approval from the central government. And there are also big challenges in taxation, distribution of GDP, input and output. Recently, the Demonstration Area in the Yangtze River Delta has made some steps in this field, which I think is the future trend that needs exploration. But the full preparation and the implementation are necessary before the proposal comes into being. Both the university think tanks and the international think tanks can do some researches in advance.

Ken Gao: I agree with Prof. Zhang when it comes to the trend and the "enclaves". But there is another option. From the enterprise perspective, what they care is whether they can enjoy the same high-quality overall services that equals to Shanghai. This includes the government service, industrial park service, property service as well as the platform service with relative strong professionalism. The exploration of the enclave model needs much support from the administrative forces and policy resources, so besides this model, there are models like different cooperate industrial parks. For example, there are Suzhou Industrial Park which attracts ZTE to locate, Shenha Industrial Park in Shenzhen and some other forms of the Park Outside Industrial Park or the District Outside the Industrial Park are in fact promote the development. The Industrial Park, as the supplement of development pattern, is free from the bondage of taxation, local administrative management and the construction of education and health infrastructure. Besides, the introduction of the Industrial Park could directly bring in the advanced management system and related service resources, which could speed up the regional development. Then, the Industrial Parks, born out of the market, are striving to get listed. Given that the national government has launched relative policies, there are 90 industrial park management enterprises in list who are seeking IPO opportunities to function in a capitalized way so as to tap into the bigger market. Therefore, in the future, the industrial park, benefiting from the commercial environment and convenient service, could stand as the pillar during the process of national brand output.

Audience: China has been labeled as the world factory for about 40 years. But the crux is that the advancement of the innovative technology and the manufacturing techniques cannot get the worldwide recognition, which means Chinese brands are not yet internationalized. Here is my question. How can the Yangtze River Delta driven up the process to promote the Chinese products to go overseas and help the national brand to get global recognition in the future.

Zhu Siming: What is the core of "going overseas"? There are various industries and products under a brand, so what kind of things should we choose to "go overseas"? We should make clear on the concept between "Products from Shanghai or Yangtze River Delta to go overseas" and "the products shipping overseas by Shanghai port". Now, China is in the end of the industrialization, and brings forward seven strategic emerging industries. Countries experience the same process to transform from the primary to advanced stage like Japan and Korea, as the backward countries, going through the phases from labor intensive industry, heavy industry, industrial upgrading and the product internationalization. Now China stands at the end of the second stage and tries to step into the third stage, and the industrial upgrade is a must. The smooth and successful upgrading could sharp the pace of internationalization of domestic products while the failure of upgrading would disturb the structure of established labor-intensive industry, not to mention the export of national brand. And the core of the question is what kind of things you intend to export?

In recent 20 years, for the consumer side, the only Japanese brand that can compete internationally may be the car, while some other things that people are familiar with have been replaced. Some enterprises like Panasonic focus on 2B and 2C the order of which take up 80% of one company. There are a lot of invisible champions in Japan, and they export a lot. For example, a company that focuses on ECQV may has a profit up to 20%, and it may be the only company in this field.

The development strategy of Shanghai has transformed from the "Four Centers" to "Five Centers". Therefore, if Shanghai only acts as the transfer station to sell the low-end products overseas rather than the powerful engine to lead the upgrading of all industry, the transformation from the second to the third stage would be shaky. It is worthwhile for Shanghai to serve as a pioneer in leading the industry upgrade and export something valuable.

Jefferson Wang: Thank you, Mr. Zhu. And I will make some implementation. The development of one brand cannot live without the industrial clusters. Globally, once we talk about the machinery manufacturing, purse or IT, we would associate it with the brand of German, Italy and the west coast of America respectively. Therefore, the brand of the Yangtze River Delta could be developed under the cooperation among the government, enterprise and the industrial park. Such as the integrated circuit of Shanghai, power system equipment of Nanjing and bioscience of Suzhou.

Besides, I have questions for two Japanese experts. The *Outline of the Integrated Regional Development of the Yangtze River Delta* was release recently, which highlights the importance of five positions. One of the most important aspects is to make the Yangtze River Delta grow into the powerful engine and take the lead in the field of innovation. It is universally known that Tokyo is in the lead in terms of the technological and cultural innovation. Can the experts share something with us?

Ken FUNABASHI: Globalization is very important, but people should make clear that what kind of product can be launched into international market before we talk about the globalization. China has the largest and most stable market which could embrace the vigorous and ambitious unicorn companies. But what becomes the core competitiveness of the unicorn companies is innovation. Only when the company is mature enough in certain field can it talk about the globalization. In Japan, there is the JETRO which aims to helping Japanese enterprises and startups to get the foothold in Chinese or other markets. The approach can also be applied in China. The spirit of innovation is always the trump card.

Zhu Siming: We should consider a question. Why Chinese industry in some filed cannot come to the expectation though we already have the sound infrastructure system. The reasons behind the phenomenon are as followed. Firstly, the mechanism should be processed. In Japan, there is an coordinating institution named NEDO① to coordinate different parties. But, in China, the projects or the programs are proposed by ministries and commissions, with a lot of companies joining in, lacking a coordinating institution that empowered by national recognition and authorization. Secondly, the boundary of intellectual property rights(IPR) is ambiguous, which hinder the market participation of enterprises. For example, the best new energy company in China does not want to join the national system, and China does not do very well in this field for this reason. Why should we participate? Who the intellectual property belongs to? And this is also the reason that leads to the unsuccessful mergence between Baidu and AotuNavi. Does the basic IPR belong to everyone? Does everyone share it together? Does the applied IPR belong to oneself? Therefore, it is important to make

---

① NEDO, which is short for New Energy and Industrial Technology Development Organization, is the biggest public research and development management institution in Japan, and the integrated platform institution that involves Government-Industry-Academia-Research cooperation.

clear the above questions including the ownership and sharing mechanism of the IPR, otherwise the innovation will be a castle-in-the-air. Of course, it also worth thinking whether the cross-ministries or cross-region institution like NEDO can come into being or not.

Jefferson Wang: Thank you for your sharing.

主题二:长三角一体化与营商环境共建

杨洁:各位嘉宾,非常荣幸能主持第二个论坛,我是毕马威中国合伙人杨洁。在这里我先介绍一下我们第二个圆桌论坛的嘉宾,他们分别是:凯捷咨询(中国)有限公司的首席执行官余煌超先生,高风咨询创始人兼董事长谢祖墀先生,安永中国管理咨询总监、区域经济业务合伙人周亮先生,印度工业联合会中国代表处首席代表马德武先生以及上海社科院副院长王振先生。现在第二个圆桌论坛讨论的主题是"长三角一体化与营商环境共建"。

余煌超:凯捷咨询是一家法国上市公司,在全球有 26 万名员工,进入中国超过25 年了,约有 3 500 名员工。我想提供一个思路,就是大家都在谈长三角的发展、一体化的重要性,比较城市群的规划,大家何不谈谈国土级的规划? 大家知道,长三角整体的 GDP 现在在竞争全世界第五的位置,这个竞争对手不是一个国家,而是美国的一个地区,就是加州。来做个简单的比较:长三角面积 35.8 万平方公里,GDP 达到 3 亿多美元,人口特别多,有 1.5 亿人口;德国面积为 35.7 万平方公里,只比我们少 1 000 平方公里,GDP 为 4 亿多美元,人口是 8 200 多万人;加州面积 42.3万平方公里,GDP 接近 3 亿美元,人口 3 950 万人;日本东京城市群只有 37.8 万平方公里,GDP 有 5 亿美元,人口 1.3 亿人;法国本土面积是 55 万平方公里,GDP 为2.8 亿美元,人口 6 500 万人。从这个角度,大家可以知道,其实整个长三角应该有的规划,不只是单一城市的规划,也不只是一个城市群的规划,而应该是一个国土级的规划。未来我们面向的是德国、日本这样的竞争,有点类似"国中之国"的一个竞争。从这个角度看,就知道我们到底整个地区要发展到什么样。

我常常去德国,因为凯捷汽车咨询做得非常好。我发现,德国整个国家的 GDP差不多 4 亿美元,但全国只有 4 个超过 100 万人口的大都市,汉堡 180 万人,柏林

350 万人,慕尼黑 150 万人,不莱梅 100 万人,斯图加特只有五六十万人。这样的城市群,竟然可以创造出这么大的 GDP。

所以我想强调一件事情,因为凯捷是从法国来的,法国常常强调人文:如果我们要把长三角做好,除了刚才谈的科技、发展、品牌、政府政策、国家支持战略,我只问一件事情——莫忘世上庶民多,我们 1.5 亿名老百姓,怎么给他更多稳稳的幸福?谢谢!

杨洁:谢谢,余总给我们提供了一个全新的视角。以前我们一直在对标纽约、东京、伦敦,我们可能还要再找一些其他的对标。尤其提到一个新的点,我们在做城市群的时候,人文也是我们必须要重视的一个因素。

谢祖墀:过去一段时间,我们针对粤港澳大湾区有很多讨论,粤港澳大湾区是中国发展的一个重要湾区,现在又看到长三角城市群的出现,这也是国家重要政策之一。这是很好的,代表我们已经意识到了未来的竞争不仅仅是城市与城市的竞争,更多的是城市群跟市群的竞争。我们思考这些问题的时候,要把各个地方放在全国的角度来看。我们研究了粤港澳大湾区,其实大湾区的规模不小,人口、GDP、很多方面都达到了国家级。我们的发展不单是国家整体层面的发展,这是中国发展过程中很特别的一个现象。从经济发展角度看,可以分成几个大的区域,在这几个大的区域发展过程中,把政策、战略做好,可以让我们中国的发展下一步走向更高的台阶。

我的工作是做战略咨询,回国已经接近三十年,任职过几家大型咨询公司,六年前我成立了自己的咨询公司——高风咨询公司。我的客户几乎都是跟科技创新相关的,客户需求反映了客户在中国的发展,无论外企、国企还是民企,都是朝着科技创新、商业创新在发展。

我想从另外一个角度讨论一下,我们从未来看中国的创新,会有什么发展?我个人觉得,我们将进入一个新时代。2007 年,苹果公司的乔布斯在美国宣布 iPhone 上市,iPhone 代表着移动互联网时代的来临,过去 12 年,中国很多企业都好好地利用了移动互联网时代,也产生了很多的创新、卓越的科技和互联网公司,有一部分做到了世界级。这 12 年,我个人觉得只是创新时代的一个热身,是中国人的热身,还没有进入真正的创新时代。我们现在要进入一个新的时代,因为我们面临几个巨大的颠覆性的科技,就是 AI(人工智能)、5G。中国在 5G 商业应用方面肯定是走在世界前列的。IoT 物联网,还有区块链,这几个科技都有极大的颠覆性作用。还有,中国已经累积了大量的数据,在未来,大数据还会变成更大的数据,这个大数据是我们的竞争优势。人工智能其实不是很智能,是很傻,因为没有数据、算法,它就没有办法研究问题,有数据的话,给它输入,它很快就可以通过算法研究新的智能的打法。这是中国的优势。

我们面临新的创新时代,长三角一体化能给予我们一个很大的试验田,引领我们进行新的尝试。目前,好多城市都在做大数据,已经建立了很多智能的基建,收集了很多部门的数据。长三角很多城市都在试验,比如无人驾驶汽车,但每个城市智能基建的基本条件、标准是不一样的。想象一下,我有一辆无人驾驶汽车,这辆车在上海、无锡、杭州、南京,可能因为各地硬件不一样,要怎么配合它?自动驾驶、互联互通的智能汽车,让它更规模化地发展,我们肯定要在大数据方面把整个区域打通,要标准化,让汽车行业、出行行业有足够的条件来发展。区块链也是一样。区块链的发展,需要去中心化,需要有一些实验室来试验新的产品。我觉得长三角是一个很好的地方,能开展很多实验。还有就是物流方面,它有不同的标准,不同的做法,不同的公司。我们要把长三角里基本的做法、标准做得更规范,在物流方面也配合科技的创新发展。

总而言之,我们思考问题的时候,把过去的发展历程搞清楚是对的,国际对标也是对的,但我们未来几年,马上会进入一个"无人区",这个"无人区"是没有对标的,那我们该怎么去尝试,怎么在这些标准不太一致的方面尽量把标准做好?谢谢!

杨洁:谢总提炼了一个关键词,就是新时代,也是中共十九大习总书记讲得更多的一个词。下面有请安永周亮总。

周亮:我们这么多年来一直服务中国,包括长三角地区,最近在做"一带一路"的一些工作以及具体项目,根据我们观察到的现象和提出的一些建议,跟大家做个探讨和交流。

长三角这么多年来一直处于全国领先地位。当前面临的几个核心问题,毋庸讳言:

第一,就是长三角大中小城市齐头并进,我们有 6 个 GDP 超万亿元的城市,上海是中国唯一一个 GDP 超 3 万亿元的城市,也有昆山、江阴、常熟这样的中小城市,它们的 GDP 规模都超过了一些内陆省份。但产业发展过程中,城市与城市之间的产业结构存在着严重的同质化问题。上海在大力发展新能源汽车、高端装备制造、新一代电子信息,无锡、苏州乃至南京也提出要建设同样的产业。甚至在同一个城市的不同区域,对同一个项目也在进行竞争。比如,某区竞争一家集成电路企业,最终这家企业选择落户在交通相对偏远但政府给予补贴多的某个地方。企业家说每天往返于工作地与居住地,路上堵2个小时,这对社会资源是极大的浪费,对企业来说也是很大的浪费。第二,自主创新能力。刚才我们说对标大湾区、太平洋沿岸城市群、东京湾,其实在自主创新能力方面,长三角与珠三角相比已经落后了。我印象非常深,2018年去广东,当时广东的干部跟我探讨,为什么这几年广东尤其是深圳的增速超过了上海?为什么深圳的创新企业超过了上海?有一个直观数据,就是获得A轮融资之前风投融资笔数和金额,上海大大落后于深圳,整个长三角落后于珠三角地区。这体现了自主创新活力的差距,更不用说我们缺少像华为、大疆这样的在全世界范围内领先的创新企业。究其原因,可能多种多样,但事实是在和珠三角的竞争中,我们落后了。2015年广东提出要学习长三角,当时他们考察了张江、苏州工业园,把同样的政策复制回了广东,而且加码,我们奖励3 000万元,他们奖励6 000万元,鼓励创新,于是抓住了企业迭代创新驱动的先机。所以在发展的长跑中,我们现在处在了一个跟跑、落后的位置。

我们在考虑未来如何发展的时候,不仅仅要考虑过去世界领先城市群是怎么发展的,我们一定要考虑,每个时代有每个时代的特征,好的战略一定是顺势而为的,在新时代之下,如何打造长三角一体化,实现高质量发展,就一定要理解现在新的时代特征:首先,国际形势方面。中美贸易战的核心是什么?其实就是美国要阻止中国科技产业的崛起,掌握下一代产业的话语权。所以竞争过程中,美国和一些欧洲发达国家把国门关闭了,而中国通过"一带一路"政策鼓励企业尤其是创新企业,参与到全球产业链竞争和全球产业价值链的环节中进行共享发展。这非常重要,这是当前时代最主要的一个特征。我们长三角一定要考虑这一点。第二,当今世界,科技创新是一个非常重要的推动力。在科技创新之下,产业形态其实也发生了变化,出现了新产业、新模式,现在制造业也是服务业,很多服务业也在做制造业,产业边界在模糊、产业之间的界限在融合,所以我们要抓新兴产业新的特征,有针对性地发展、打造产业生态圈。第三,2019年中央经济工作会议第五次会议提出,我们要改变发展思路,从原先提的大城市发展到中小城市发展,到现在又要提出城市群的发展,其背后的用意,就是在新的人口形势下、新的劳动力要素成本之下,我们反过来要提升经济密度。过去我们说大城市太拥挤,有大城市病,但其实经济密度相比东京、德国还是低的。所以,应该如何利用城市群来提高我们的经济密度,提升产业发展效率?

这是全新的发展形势和思路。面对这样的形势和思路,长三角在下一步的发展中,要发挥市场的主导作用,让市场有效配置资源。同时,政府要进行有效的资源配置,优化资源配置,形成不同地区的差异化产业资源竞争和名片。比如上海,应该专注于中国企业"走出去"、对外开放和高端外资企业"引进来",服务于中国的市场和中国的产业链,提供更好的平台服务,知识产权、商务服务,还包括法务等诸多方面。而各个地区应该根据自身的产业先发优势、资源禀赋,进行资源优化和配置,形成各具特色的产业高地和产业生态圈,最终降低我们整个区域的创新成本,适应下一个时代产业迭代的诉求。

杨洁:周总的关键词是顺势而为,要顺应时代特征,谋划以后的战略。接下来有请马首席和我们分享他的见解。

马德武:谢谢,我代表印度工业联合会这个组织,我们任务是帮助印度的公司更好地在国内投资,同时在国外投资。

我们对中国企业和印度企业做了一些调查,我向大家介绍一些基本情况:72%的在华投资的印度企业主要分布在上海、江苏、浙江;超过50%的印度在华企业大约十年前就已经进入中国;将近1/3的印度在华企业在长三角地区注册了新的业务,其中48%是服务业,剩下的是其他行业;超过50%的受访企业一开始会建设一个代表处,熟悉市场以后会进一步扩张,40%多的企业会从代表处扩展到在中国设立公司、雇佣员工,98%的印度在华企业计划在2020年新增投资。我们访问了三家企业,它们表现出在长三角增加投资的兴趣,60%多的投资者都感到非常有信心,认为未来五年可以实现盈利,80%的制造业、物流业、消费品企业也这样认为。但是,也有一些挑战。74%的公司认为找到合适的人才并留住人才是关键,同时,获得许可、环境保护等政策变化是关键问题。还有,对于雇佣外国员工,目前政府的要求很多,这也是很大的障碍。那么长三角如何应用技术来精简流程,让外国投资商可以真正关注到长三角,让他们在长三角安居乐业?

我们收到了一些反馈,有一些关键的观点我要跟大家分享,和人力资源非常相关。首先是人才,比如为企业提供服务的时候,要如何帮助企业招聘人才?本土公司为期三四个月的短期项目能招到人才,但外资企业招不到,怎么解决?第二是流动性上受到限制。服务业,比如通信、IT行业,有些公司的项目周期非常短,在国外,公司可以在各个城市之间调人,但在中国做不到。如果想在不同地区、不同城市开展业务,就必须在各地注册,然后在当地招人。这很麻烦。如果不在当地注册分公司,就不能把上海的人才调到其他城市,否则要向外管局、中国政府再次申请工作许可、外国人居留许可,这很麻烦。有时候一些企业不注册就没办法在不同城市开展新业务。比如有一家印度企业是做IT教育的,但企业不得不在很多城市都注册分公司,在行政上简直是匪夷所思。同时,设立那么多代表处,自己的合规、监管方面也会变得很困难。

这些政策、流程怎样精简？短期雇佣如何改进？如何确保公司可以只注册一个代表处，然后在有短期项目的时候可以在各个地区、各个城市之间调派人才？这些都是企业共同面临和希望解决的问题。希望能有一个超级商会一样的组织来帮助它们。如果外国企业想在中国开展业务，希望有这样的机构可以进行合作。

杨洁：马德武先生向我们介绍了印度在华企业所面临的挑战，包括短期招工、设立地区办事处等。这些挑战都需要我们从中国方面寻求解决方案，尤其在长三角一体化过程中，需要解决这些问题。下面我们请上海社科院副院长王振先生跟我们分享。

王振：我谈两个方面的想法。

第一，关于长三角地区营商环境的共建，到底共建什么？因为这个地区很大，有36万平方公里，这么多人这么多城市。我觉得三个方面要共建：一是标准。世界银行现在有评价体系，各个地方特别是上海，要对标国际上最好水平、最高标准来优化营商环境。除了国际对标，也要在地区内部进行对标，在长三角地区，上海各方面是做得好的，但不是说样样都做得好，也有个别地方存在一些不足。周边地区，如杭州、苏州，在营商环境某些方面可能走在上海的前面，它们灵活、往前冲，它们的标准肯定比我们高。比如注册，动作比我们快，处理特别的事情也会快一点。长三角地区发展到今天，各个地方营商环境的标准不一样，今天既然谈一体化，首先要对标国际，对标最高标准。还有，我们有的标准不一定比国际水平低，我们就要把自己作为标杆，形成自己的标杆。这样形成共识以后，我们就知道要怎么把标准统一。二是规则。标准有了，但是达到这个标准的程序、处理原则，实际上各个地方还是不一样的，而且细致梳理，规则上更不一样。长三角一体化过程中，如何围绕各地共同的标准把规则理顺呢？就像马德武先生刚才讲到的注册代表处，在上海还可以，到有些地方可能就很难，因为涉及外资背景。这关系到我们国家的开放、整个规则上的一些东西。三是管理体系。对于现在的管理体系，特别是区域一体化框架下，我们经常碰到问题，上海已经认定的，到其他地方需要重新认定。比如，开办食品连锁店、加工厂，总部设在上海，到各个地方开分工厂，就像不断开分行、办事处一样，都要从头开始、从头准备资料。包括外资银行，在上海已经设立银行了，到各地区设支行要重新开始，据说要准备两三年，在全国开下来要花几十年。这里面就是管理系统的问题。我们能不能有一个统筹？当然，这涉及方方面面，包括现在推行的"一网通办"、异地办理，现在提出来了，在做试点，但推进过程也不是那么容易。由于行政区经济、行政区板块很多是分割的，各地形成了一些自有的标准、规则、体系,所以在今后的大格局中,特别是面向世界级城市群,我们要努力开展营商环境共建。当然,这涉及各个领域,可以做的有很多。

第二,怎么共建? 营商环境更主要是有关城市,这么多城市,怎么共建? 我们可以做的一个事情,就是要有个"指挥棒"。我受世界银行的启发,世界银行每年公布各个国家营商环境排名,我们高度关注,进步了很高兴,下降了压力很大,说明这个指挥棒很灵。那我们可不可以有个机构,或者联合起来,在长三角这个地方公布一个营商环境指数,我们自己创造一个体系,然后评估,通过这个指挥棒发挥作用。现在各地的重点是对标上海,把上海作为标杆,那上海就作为标杆,发布指数,让各地不断向你靠。这样可以让大家共同进步,这就是共建。政府各个相关部门应该借助这个一体化,从各个方面建立一个联合体,或是一个联盟,或是通过第三方机构,不断在专业领域里共同把规则标准建立起来,然后做一个共同的平台。这样才能把运转体系共同建起来。现在从国家规划来说,中央已经对长三角提出了要求,就是这方面是可以先行的,应该走在全国前面。而且我们对标,就是对标最高的国际标准。我想,今后可以把智库力量、第三方的作用发挥出来,政府各条线也发挥作用,包括各个行业部门,把大家都调动起来,然后推动我们营商环境的共建。

杨洁:谢谢王院长,讲了共建什么、怎么共建。其中也有几个关键词,一是中国标杆,二是要有中国的指挥棒,提出了营商环境指数,让世界跟着我们走,可能是更好的一个想法。圆桌论坛各位嘉宾都分享了他们的见解,这次长三角地区政府驻上海代表处都有同事过来参会,现场我们进行一下互动,看看有没有观众向在场的嘉宾提问?

现场嘉宾:感谢嘉宾和主持人的分享! 众所周知,欧盟标准、欧盟认证得到了全球认可,并且是一种品质保证。各位嘉宾认为长三角区域如何在认证和标准上与国际接轨,且打造受全球认可的中国标准和中国认证? 谢谢。

余煌超:首先,认证是一种双方相互信任的过程。第二,标准的认证,到底是买家认证还是卖家认证? 长三角有 1.5 亿名消费者,我们其实有能力做某种程度的认证。我们外商客户80%—90%的业务都在做中国数字化,而不是强力让中国去适应他们。相反,他们想适应中国,因为中国消费者的数字化程度很高。有一种认证,就是消费者都已经这样做了,我们都用微信了、支付宝了,他们就必须跟着我们走。但有一种认证——实物认证如药品认证,他们比我们先进,我们就要学习。但我们有 5G、高铁,是走在前面的。我们不可能依附别人的认证,大就是美,必须把消费者的力量表现出来。谢谢!

马德武: 每个国家的认证过程和体系都不一样。标准在国内是不是统一,是不是大家都了解?落地的时候大家的理解是不是一样?比如进出口,是不是知道这些标准在城市之间有所区分?这一点是非常关键的,是要着力把握的。

王振: 就像汽车排放一样,最早我们是对欧标,但标准认定上,目前中国包括上海在内,还刚刚起步,时间不长。所以我们要对标国际先进,先模仿、学习。特别是企业"走出去",面向全球,还是非常需要用欧盟的这些标准认证。但现在开始,我们要做另一手准备了,中国已经迈向治理现代化了,所以要学习,然后逐步创造条件,形成我们的标准,形成我们的权威认证。上海应该成为全国标准、全国认证的一个中心,服务业认证的一个中心。我觉得上海是有条件的。

周亮: 我简单补充几句。行业话语权决定了谁制定标准或用谁的标准。很多传统产业,确实是欧美走在我们前面。所以我们需要把中国标准跟欧美主动对接、衔接,减少跨国企业进入中国市场的壁垒和烦恼。但新兴产业中,确实我们要主动争夺话语权。比如,3D打印产业,现在全球范围内没有一个标准,如果我们是世界最大的产业应用国家,我们就有责任制定这个标准。长三角作为中国对外开放的窗口,确实也需要走在前面,需要进一步加快速度。这也是政府需要思考的一个问题。

杨洁: 考虑到时间,只能再提一个问题了。

现场嘉宾: 谢谢,今天听了一下午的演讲,有很多体会。我想问在座的几位,特别是王院长。刚才余总提出了一个问题,就是长三角一体化建设中有一个规划和市场的问题,这本身就是一对矛盾,市场和规划怎么进行结合?这是一个老问题。但至少现在在政策上,已经有了很好的说法,怎样处理好市场和规划的问题、市场和计划的问题。现在王院长又提出一个问题,那是不是还有个标杆的问题?世界上有各种城市群的建设标杆,刚才余总也介绍了德国城市是怎么建的,法国城市是怎么建的。如果把标杆提出来,把营商环境作为一个标杆,那是不是它属于规划和市场以外的第三种方法?我们不是每年都做规划,一般五年、十年做一次规划。对于标杆,每年世界银行都会出一份营商环境报告,每年都会有个新的标杆出来。首先我们对标哪种标杆?世界银行的营商环境是一种标杆,城市群方面,我们对标的是德国的城市群、美国城市群,还是东京的城市群的标杆?这个标杆怎么确立?确立这个标杆有什么标准?我们用什么方法确立这个标杆?当然,这可以说有历史原因、地理原因等,请问这和国家战略有什么关系?

王振:首先,长三角的标杆是什么?上一场很多专家都谈到了东京,因为我们上海有很多专家都是到东京去考察的。上海跟东京城市群比较相近,而且都是东亚文化。我认为上海现在对标的就是东京城市群,这是比较清晰的,而且仔细观察,我们和东京在很多方面差距还比较大,比如我们的农业、农村。对标东京,这是毫无疑问的,包括城市管理在内。营商环境,这只是一个排名,反正排在我们前面的,都是标杆,然后我们一步步往前走。

杨洁:非常感谢现场观众的互动,以及圆桌嘉宾的真知灼见!

Panel Discussion 2: Integration of the Yangtze River Delta and Co-construction of Doing-business Environment

Tracy Yang: Dear guests, I am very honored to host the second panel discussion. My name is Tracy Yang, Partner of KPMG China. Here I'd like to introduce our distinguished guests. They are Mr. Cliff Yu, CEO of Capgemini Consulting (China); Mr. Edward Tse, Founder and CEO of Gao Feng Advisory Company; Mr. Bryant Zhou, Director of Business Advisory Services in Ernst & Young, Partner of Regional Economic Business; Mr. Madhav Sharma, Head-Greater China & Chief Representative of the Confederation of Indian Industry China (CII); and Mr. Wang Zhen, Vice President of the Shanghai Academy of Social Sciences.

The topic of our second panel is the "Integration of the Yangtze River Delta and Co-construction of Doing-business Environment".

Cliff Yu: Capgemini Consulting is a French-listed company. We have 260,000 employees worldwide and have been in China for more than 25 years, with about 3,500 employees in China. Since Capgemini is a European company, I want to share an idea from the national plan standpoint. As you know, the Yangtze River Delta now competes with a place for the fifth place in the world. This place is not a country but California, a city in the United States. For a simple comparison, the Yangtze River Delta has a population of 358,000 square kilometers, a GDP over 3 trillion US dollars, and a large population of 150 million. Germany is with 357,000 square kilometers, only 1,000 square kilometers less than the YRD, with a GDP over 4 trillion US dollars and a population of more than 820 million. California has 423,000 square kilometers, with a GDP of nearly 3 trillion US dollars and a population of 39.5 million. The Tokyo Metropolitan Area, with only 378,000 square kilometers, has a GDP of 5 trillion US dollars, and a population of 130 million. France has 550,000 square kilometers, a GDP of 2.8 trillion US dollars and a population of 65 million. From this perspective, the planning we should have in the YRD is not just a single city plan, but also a city cluster plan. In fact, the entire Yangtze River Delta plan should be a national level plan. In the future, we will be facing competitors like Germany and Japan, and it's a bit like a "state within a country" competition. From this point of view, we know exactly how our entire region will look like.

I often go to Germany because Capgemini does very well in the field of the car. I find that the GDP of the entire Germany is almost 4 trillion US dollars, but there are only 4 cities in the national metropolis with more than 1 million people, 1.8 million in Hamburg, 3.5 million in Berlin, and 1.5 million in Muni, 1 million in Bremen, and the remaining Stuttgart, with only five or six hundred thousand. However, this city cluster can create such a large GDP.

So I want to emphasize one thing. Capgemini is based on France, a country that underscores humanity. But when we talk about Shanghai, we mention technology, development, branding, government policy, and state support strategies except humanity. I want to ask one question, thus if we do a good job in the Yangtze River Delta, how can we give more steady happiness to our 150 million people? Do not forget that there are many common people in the world.

Tracy Yang: Thank you, Mr. Yu has provided us with a new perspective. Before that, we have been making benchmark with New York, Tokyo, and London. Now, we may have to find some other benchmarks. In particular, when we mention a city cluster, humanity is also a factor that we must pay attention to.

Edward Tse: In the past, we have a lot of discussions about the Guangdong-Hong Kong-Macao Greater Bay Area, which is an important bay area for China's development. Now we have seen the emergence of the Yangtze River Delta and it is also one of the important national policies. This is very good, because it means that we have realized the future competition is not only the competition among cities, but also the competition among city clusters. When we think about these issues, we should view each place from the perspective of a country. We have also studied the Greater Bay Area, and in fact, the size of the Greater Bay Area is not small, and its population, GDP, and many other aspects have reached the national level. This is a very special phenomenon in China's development. Our development is not just the development of a country. From economic development perspective, it can be divided into several big regions. In the development of these regions, good policies and strategies are needed. It can take China's development to the next step.

My job is to do strategic consulting. It has been nearly 30 years since I returned to China. After going through several large consulting companies, I set up my own consulting company, Gaofeng Consulting Company six years ago. Our customers are almost all related to technological innovation. The needs of our customers reflect their development in China. Whether foreign companies, state-owned enterprises or private enterprises, they are all developing towards technological innovation and business innovation.

I would like to comment from another angle. Let's have a look at the future. What will be the development of China's innovation in the future? I personally feel that we will enter a new era. In 2007, Steve Jobs of Apple announced the launch of iPhone in the United States. The iPhone represents the advent of the mobile Internet era. In the past 12 years, many Chinese companies have made good use of the mobile Internet era, and also produced many innovative and outstanding technology companies. Some of Internet companies are world-class. In the past 12 years, I personally feel that it is just a warm-up for our era of innovation, a warm-up for the Chinese, and has not yet entered the era of true innovation. We are now entering a new era, because we are facing several huge disruptive technologies, namely AI (artificial intelligence), 5G. China is certainly in the forefront of 5G commercial applications all over the world. All these technologies, such as IoT (Internet of Things) and block chain have great disruptive effects. In addition, China has accumulated a large amount of data. In the future, this big data will become larger data. This big data is our competitive advantage, because artificial intelligence is actually not very intelligent but very stupid. Because there is no data, there is no way for the algorithm to study the problem. If there is data, input it, and it can quickly research new intelligent play through the algorithm, which is China's advantage.

We are facing a new era of innovation, and the integration of the Yangtze River Delta can give us a large test field and lead us to a new attempt to innovate. At present, many cities are doing big data, and many smart infrastructures have been established, and many departments have collected data. Many cities in the Yangtze River Delta are experimenting, such as driverless cars. However, the basic conditions and standards of smart infrastructure in each city are different. Imagine I have a self-driving car. The hardware of cars in Shanghai, Wuxi, Hangzhou, Nanjing maybe different, and how can I cooperate with it? To develop the autonomous driving, interconnected and intelligent cars to a larger scale, we should definitely connect the entire region in terms of big data, standardize it, and give the automotive industry and the travel industry sufficient conditions to develop. So does the development of block chain. The development of block chain requires decentralization, and some laboratories are needed to test new products. I think the Yangtze River Delta is a very good place to conduct many experiments. And logistics has different standards, different modes, and different companies. We should make the basic modes and standards in the Yangtze River Delta more formal, and make logistics cooperate with technological innovation.

All in all, when we think about problems, it is right to clarify the past development process and make international benchmarking, but in the next few years we will soon enter a "no man zone" without benchmarking. How can we try to improve the standards that are not consistent with each other as much as possible?

Tracy Yang: Mr. Tse has refined a key word, that is, the new era, and also a word spoken by President Xi on the 19th CPC National Congress. Next, let's welcome Mr. Bryant Zhou.

Bryant Zhou: Based on the work we have done in the Yangtze River Delta for many years, including in China and the recent work about the "Belt and Road" and the observations and suggestions in specific projects, I want to exchange my ideas with you.

The development of the Yangtze River Delta in these years has been leading the country.We are facing several core issues.

First, the large, medium and small cities in the Yangtze River Delta go hand in hand. We have six cities with GDP exceeding one trillion RMB in the YRD. Shanghai is the only city with GDP exceeding three trillion yuan in China. We have small and medium cities such as Kunshan, Jiangyin, and Changshu, GDP of which exceed some of inland provinces. However, in the process of industrial development, there are serious problems of homogeneity in the industrial structure between cities since Shanghai puts emphasis on new energy vehicles, high-end equipment manufacturing and new-generation electronic information, and Wuxi, Suzhou and even Nanjing have mentioned the same industries. Even in different areas of the same city, there is still competition in the same project. Like the competition of electronic integrated circuit companies in the same district, the project will finally locate in the place where is relatively remote in transportation but the government offers a lot of subsidies. Entrepreneurs said that two-hour traffic jam each day and commuting between work and residence is a huge waste both for social resources and for enterprises.

Second, the capabilities of self-independent innovation. We just talked about the benchmarking of the Greater Bay Area, the Pacific Coast City Cluster, and the Tokyo Bay, but in fact, the Yangtze River Delta has fallen behind in self-independent innovation when compared with the Pearl River Delta. I was very impressed that when I went to Guangdong last year, Guangdong officials discussed with me about reasons why Guangdong, especially Shenzhen, has grown faster than Shanghai and why the number of Shenzhen's innovative companies exceed Shanghai's in recent years. An intuitive data shows that in terms of the number and amount of venture capital financing before obtaining the Series-A financing, Shanghai lags behind Shenzhen and the entire Yangtze River Delta lags behind the Pearl River Delta. This reflects the vitality of self-independent innovation, not to mention that we lack leading innovative companies worldwide such as Huawei and DJI. The reasons may be various, but the fact is that we lag behind in the competition with the Pearl River Delta. Guangdong proposed to study the Yangtze River Delta in 2015. At that time, the officials of Guangdong inspected Zhangjiang and Suzhou Industrial Park, copied the same policy to Guangdong, and overweight. We reward 30 million RMB, and they reward 60 million RMB to encourage innovation, which seized enterprises' opportunity of iterative innovation driving force. Therefore, during the development process, we can see that in the long-distance development, we are now in a following and backward position.

For the future, when we consider how to develop, we should not only consider how the world's leading city clusters developed in the past, but also each era's own characteristics. A good strategy is to take advantage of the current situation. Besides, in the new era, the integrated and high-quality development of the Yangtze River Delta is based on the understanding of the new era's characteristics. First, we should understand the international situation. What is the core of the Sino-US trade war? In fact, it aims to stop the rise of China's industry of science and technology and master the discourse power of the next-generation industries. Therefore, in the process of competition, the United States, including some developed European countries, closed its doors, while China encouraged enterprises, especially innovative companies, to participate in the global industry chain competition and the global industry chain and value chain through the "Belt and Road" initiative for shared development, which is very important. This is the most important feature of the current era. In terms of Yangtze River Delta's development, we should take this into consideration. Second, we should understand that technological innovation is a very important driving force nowadays. Under technological innovation, the industry has actually changed its form into new industries and new models. Now the manufacturing industry is also a service industry, and many service industries have manufacturing function. The industry boundaries are blurred and the boundaries between industries are merging. Therefore, we must grasp the new characteristics of emerging industries, carry out targeted development, and build an industrial ecosystem. Third, the fifth meeting of the Central Economic Work Conference proposed this year that we must change our development mode, from the development of the large cities to the small and medium cities, and step forward to consider the development of city cluster. The intention behind is that under the new demographic situation and the cost of new labor factors, we must increase the economic density in turn. We used to talk about big cities' crowding and illness, but in fact our economic density is still lower than Tokyo or Germany. So, how to make full use of the city clusters to increase our economic density and improve the efficiency of industrial development?

This is a new development situation and idea. Facing such situation and idea, the Yangtze River Delta will play a leading role in the following development, and make the use of market to effectively allocate resources. At the same time, the government must carry out effective resource allocation, optimize resource allocation, and form differentiated industrial resource competition and business cards in different regions. For example, Shanghai should focus on the "going abroad" of Chinese companies, opening up and "bringing in" high-end foreign companies, serving the Chinese market and China's industrial chain, providing better platform for the service industry, such as intellectual property rights, business services, legal affairs and many other aspects. Each region should optimize and allocate resources, form distinctive industrial highlands and industrial ecosystems, and ultimately reduce the innovation cost of our entire region and adapt to the industrial iteration appeal of the next era according to its own industry's first-mover advantage and resource endowment.

Tracy Yang: The core of Mr. Zhou's speech is to take advantage of the trend, to adapt to the characteristics of the times, and to do the future strategies. Next, let us invite Mr. Madhav Sharma to share his insights.

Madhav Sharma: Thank you. I am from the Confederation of Indian Industry. As an organization representing India, our mission is to help Indian companies better invest in China and beyond.

Based on the surveys we have done on Chinese and Indian companies, 72% of the Indian companies which have investment in China are mainly located in Shanghai, Jiangsu and Zhejiang. Over 50% of Indian companies in China entered China's market about ten years ago. Nearly one-third of Indian companies in China register new businesses in the Yangtze River Delta region, and 48% of them are in the service industry, the rest being in other industries. More than 50% of the companies surveyed start up an office and further expand their business when they are more familiar with Chinese market. Above 40% later set up companies and hire employees based on their previous offices. 98% of Indian companies in China have plans to increase investment in 2020. We visited three companies and they showed interest in increasing investment in the Yangtze River Delta. More than 60% of investors feel very confident that they will make profits in the next five years. 80% of enterprises in the manufacturing, logistics, and consumer goods industries hold the same opinion. But there are also some challenges. 74% of companies consider it a key issue to find and keep talented people. The same is true of obtaining permits when policies on environmental protection change. In addition, the government has many requirements on hiring foreign employees, causing great obstacles to them. So what can the Yangtze River Delta do to streamline some processes technologically to attract the real attention of foreign investors to this region and let them live and work well here?

We have received some feedbacks, and I'd like to share with you some of the key issues highly relevant to human resources. The first one is about recruiting talented people, for example, how to help foreign companies hire the people they need. It is easy for Chinese companies to find people they need for short-term projects lasting 3 or 4 months, but difficult for foreign companies. How to solve this problem? The second is related to the restriction on mobility. Some companies in the service industry like ICT and IT can mobilize their staff from other cities in their own country for projects lasting a very short period. But they cannot do so in China. They need to register in different cities and then hire people locally if their business covers many locations, and this procedure is rather troublesome. Without a local branch office, they are unable to transfer talents in Shanghai to other cities, or they have to go through the cumbersome procedures to apply once more for work permits and residence permits for foreign workers. It occurs to some companies to register a new company to start a new business in different cities. For example, an Indian company in IT education registers many branches in different cities, which is administratively ridiculous. Meanwhile, it causes great difficulty in regulating and supervising so many branches and offices.

How to streamline these policies and procedures? How to improve the short-term employment? How to make sure companies can do business and allocate talents in different regions or cities by setting up only one office? These are the problems that enterprises face together and hope to solve. They hope an organization like the Super Chamber of Commerce to help them. Such an organization will also be of help for foreign companies who want to operate in China.

Tracy Yang: Mr. Madhav Sharma just talked about the challenges faced by Indian companies in China, including short-term recruitment and local offices. All of these challenges require solutions from us, especially for the integrated development of the Yangtze River Delta. Now, let's welcome Mr. Wang Zhen, Vice President of the Shanghai Academy of Social Sciences, to speak something.

Wang Zhen: I'd like to say two things. First of all, what will we co-construct for the business environment in the Yangtze River Delta? With an area of 360,000 square kilometers, this region is home to so many people covering so many cities. I think we can work together in three areas.

The first one is on the standard. The World Bank has now set its evaluating system for doing-business environment. Cities in the YRD region, especially Shanghai, should benchmark against the most advanced and highest international standards. Besides international standards, cities in this region can learn from each other in providing a more favorable business environment. Shanghai takes a lead in all aspects, but still has its shortcomings in certain areas. Neighboring Hangzhou and Suzhou may do better in some aspects as they are more flexible and run faster in setting higher standards for the business environment. For example, their registration procedure is shorter than Shanghai, and faster for special issues. Until today, standards of doing-business environment in the Yangtze River Delta vary from place to place. Since we are talking about integration today, we must first benchmark against international standards and the highest standards. As our standards are not necessarily lower than the international ones, there is a need to improve and form our own benchmark. Based on this consensus, we know how to raise our standards to the same level.

The second is about the rules. Though we have a unified standard, different cities will design a variety of detailed rules and regulations in operating procedures and principles to achieve this standard. In the integration of the Yangtze River Delta, how to straighten out the rules around the common standards of all regions? As Mr. Madhav Sharma has just said, it is easy for foreign companies to register an office in Shanghai, but may be difficult in other places because of its foreign investment background. This has something to do with the whole rule in the opening of our country.

The third is related to the management system. We often encounter problems in our current system, especially under the framework of regional integration. What Shanghai has already approved needs to be re-approved elsewhere. For example, a Shanghai-based food chain and processing factory must start from scratch and prepare materials from the beginning to open branch plants in other places, facing similar encounter in opening branches and offices. Foreign banks which have been established in Shanghai have to start over if they intend to set up branch offices beyond Shanghai, the preparation of which is said to take two to three years, and it will take decades to open branches all over the country. This is caused by the drawback of the management system. Can we have an overall plan? Of course, this involves efforts from all parties, including the government portal website for off-site processing. It has now been proposed and is being piloted, but its advocacy is not that easy. Due to the separation of economic administration from many other administrative areas, local governments have their own standards, rules and systems. Therefore, we must strive to jointly build a better business environment in the future, especially for world-class city clusters. Obviously, there are many things that can be done in various fields.

Secondly, how do we co-construct a favorable doing business environment? It calls for endeavors at city levels. How can we organize so many cities in our joint efforts? One thing we can do is to have an orchestral "baton". We follow closely the annual doing-business report released by the World Bank. We are very happy to see the rise of our ranking and feel great pressure if our ranking falls down. This "baton" works well. Inspired by this, it is plausible to have an organization, or work together, to publish a doing-business environment index in the Yangtze River Delta. We can create a system ourselves, and make evaluations through this "baton". Now other local governments are striving to keep up with Shanghai. So we can count on Shanghai as a benchmark to release an index, encouraging other cities to follow suit. In this way, we can make progress together. This is co-construction. Relevant government departments should take advantage of this integration to form a union, or an alliance, or through third-party agencies, to establish and develop rules and standards in the professional field and then make a common platform. Only in this way can the operating system be built together. In terms of national planning, the central government has already put forward requirements for the Yangtze River Delta, that is, to go ahead and even take the lead in this regard. So our benchmarking should be the highest international standards. I think, in the future, we will bring into play the role of think tanks and third parties, and work with government departments and agencies at all levels and various industrial sectors, to motivate everyone to take part in the co-construction of our doing-business environment.

Tracy Yang: Thanks Mr. Wang, he talked about what and how to build together. He mentioned some keywords. One is Chinese benchmark, and the other is to have a China baton. He put forward a doing-business environment index. Asking the world to follow us may be a good idea. All the guests at the roundtable have shared their opinions. We have colleagues from the Yangtze River Delta Regional Government Office in Shanghai here. Please allow me to give the floor to them. Do you have questions for them?

Audience: I'd like to thank all the guests and host for your sharing. As we all know, EU standards and EU certifications are globally recognized as a guarantee of quality. Distinguished guests, how does the Yangtze River Delta region meet international standards in terms of certification and standards, and build a globally recognized Chinese standard and Chinese certification? Thank you.

Cliff Yu: First, certification is a process of mutual trust. Second, we need to decide who set the standard and make the certification, the buyers or the sellers. We actually have the ability to do some certification with a consumer base of 150 million in the Yangtze River Delta. 80% or 90% of our foreign customers are digitalizing their business in China rather than forcing China to adapt to them. Instead, they want to follow China's practice because Chinese consumers are highly digitalized. As for certification, Chinese consumers have already accustomed to use WeChat and Alipay, and they need to take our way. But for certification of physical goods and drugs, they are more advanced than us, so we will learn from them. As we take the lead in 5G technology and high-speed train, it is impossible for us to rely on others' certification. Greatness is the power and consumers have the say. Thank you.

Madhav Sharma: Different countries have different processes and systems of certification. Is there a unified set of standards in China? Do we have the same understanding when carrying out these standards? Taking import and export as an example, do these standards differ among cities? This is very critical and we must pay attention to it.

Wang Zhen: Just like automobile emissions, we first benchmark the European standards, but in terms of certification, China, including Shanghai, has just on the way for a short time. Therefore, we must benchmark international standards, follow their practices and learn from them at the beginning. Companies still need to use these European standards for certification when they go out and enter the global market. But now, we have to make another preparation. China has already moved towards modernization of governance, so we first learn, and then gradually form our own standards and turn our certifications authoritative. Moreover, Shanghai should become a center for national standards and certification, especially for the service industry. I believe Shanghai has such potential.

Bryant Zhou: I simple add a few words. The right to speak in the industry determines who sets standards and whose standards are used. In many traditional industries, Europe and the United States are indeed ahead of us. Therefore, we need to actively connect and integrate Chinese standards with European and American ones to reduce barriers and troubles for multinational companies to enter the Chinese market. However, in emerging industries, we do have to take the initiative to fight for the right to speak. For example, the 3D printing industry hasn't had a global standard yet. As we have the world's largest 3D printing industry, we have the duty to formulate a standard for this sector. As the window of China's opening up, the Yangtze River Delta really needs to be ahead and further accelerates its progress. This is also an issue that the government needs to think about.

Tracy Yang: As time is limited, the last question, pleases.

Audience: Thank you. After listening to all the speeches this whole afternoon, I have a lot of feelings. I'd like to ask some of you here, especially Mr. Wang. Just now, Mr. Yu raised a question on how to combine the contradictory pair of market and guidelines in the integrated development of the Yangtze River Delta. This is an old question. But at least now, in terms of policy, it turns into how to properly handle the relationship between market and guidelines, and that between market and planning. Now Mr. Wang raised the issue of benchmarking. There are good illustrations in the world in the construction of various city clusters. Just now Mr. Yu also introduced how German and French cities were built. If business environment is proposed as a benchmark, can we regard it as the third factor besides guidelines and the market? We usually do not make plans every year but every five or ten years. Each year the World Bank will release a doing-business environment report, which gives a benchmark to refer to. First of all, which city cluster should we refer to? The Doing-business Report from the World Bank can be used as a bencbmark. Then, from the city cluster perspective, who should we learn from? Is the German, the US or the Tokyo city cluster? We also need to know how this benchmark is established. What are the criteria for establishing this benchmark? How to establish this benchmark? Of course, it can be explained by historical, geographical or other reasons, but what is their relationship with national strategy?

Wang Zhen: First, what's the benchmark of the Yangtze River Delta? Many experts talked about Tokyo in the early discussions. This year many experts from Shanghai government chose to visit Tokyo, rather than New York. Shanghai is relatively similar to Tokyo, as both are located in East Asian and have a cultural affinity. I think it is clear that we are now taking the Tokyo city cluster as a benchmark, and a close look will find great gap between Shanghai and Tokyo in many aspects such as in the agricultural and rural areas. We are undoubtedly benchmarking Tokyo in terms of city management. Doing-business environment is just a ranking. We are now learning from those in front of us and moving our ranks step by step.

Tracy Yang: Thank you very much for interaction and insights from the guests!

Concluding
Speech

总结发言

杨 洁 Tracy Yang

毕马威中国董事合伙人

Partner of KPMG China Board Member

有一句古诗云:潮平两岸阔,风正一帆悬。我认为,把它用在今天这场论坛上非常合适。它寓意着,长三角一体化未来的道路是一方坦途,前行的航向已经明确,高质量发展的进程已然开启。

随着《长江三角洲区域一体化发展规划纲要》的发布,长三角迎来了一体化当前和未来发展的根本遵循。目标已定,具体怎么干? 今天的论坛上,各位来自国际各大机构的智囊们纷纷贡献了真知灼见。这半天下来,我学到很多,收获很多。

我一边听,一边在脑海中记录着、梳理着。在我看来,今天的大会总的议题是长三角一体化,但实际上,又分为四个小议题,分别是高质量的一体化、更好的营商环境、未来产业布局和城市群借鉴。

比如,说到长三角一体化,我们总是在说要高质量的一体化。波士顿咨询的朱晖总告诉我们,重点要在哪些方面高质量。比如,体制机制上,需要长久有效的跨省协调机制从根本上推动长三角产业与发展的深度融合。产业协同上,缺少全域覆盖的产业布局来明晰产业分工,应消除各区域当前由于发展程度差异所带来的融合发展壁垒。人才流动上,区域内城市品质与公共服务差距阻碍人才流动。

众所周知,在我国,城市群建设也不仅仅是长三角一家。包括粤港澳大湾区、京津冀等在内,大家都在探索更好的发展道路,也拥有各自的发展引擎。那么,对比其他城市群,长三角一体化的优势和特点在哪里? 来自我公司的刘明总点出了上海自贸试验区的作用。作为全国第一家自贸区,其率先积累、引领全国的经验,正是长三角一体化高质量发展的重要引擎和抓手。通过发挥上海自贸区效应,长三角地区要构建营商环境、产业协同、区域港口三个一体化,再通过全面开放、深度参与国际分工与全球竞争,打造引领全国、辐射全球的世界级开放城市群。

当然,随着长三角一体化发展,越来越多的企业和机构会选择长三角。我们达成的共识是,长三角内各地方政府绝不能过度依靠外部政策拉拢企业导致恶性竞争形成。那要靠什么？靠营商环境来竞争。比如，戴德梁行的黎庆文总就建议，区域之间资源要充分共享，要建立有利于长三角一体化健康发展的统一管理制度、健全长三角地区争议协调机制。政策要基于公共服务均等化引导全要素公平合理流动。

站在市场的角度，美中贸易全国委员会上海首席代表欧文先生则替企业发声。他呼吁，为了帮助外资企业更好地融入长三角一体化发展环境，企业对于长三角区域内跨省知识产权保护、环境保护、产业转移和海关监管，一共四个方面的具体关切与期待值得被政策制定相关部门纳入考量范畴。

有了高质量发展的基调，有了好的营商环境、大环境的支持，那么具体问题就来了，我们该如何布局产业？当然，合理的产业布局，也会进一步促进高质量的发展和更好的营商环境的形成。

习近平总书记在2019年11月进博会前在上海考察时特别强调，要强化科技创新策源功能，努力实现科学新发现、技术新发明、产业新方向、发展新理念从无到有的跨越，形成一批基础研究和应用基础研究的原创性成果，突破一批"卡脖子"的关键核心技术。

那么，现在长三角这一块做得怎样呢？今天，德勤的刘明华总为我们带来了他们对长三角主要城市创新环境与潜力的分析。德勤认为，目前长三角城市在规范创新产业方面已显示出"各有侧重"的可喜迹象。例如，根据沪、杭两地发布的政策文件，上海旨在对标全球先进，杭州则对标全国领先；上海重在提供创新资源（金融、技术），杭州重在创新应用。为了摸清长三角创新产业分布及各自优势，建议委托相关机构制定"长三角创新产业地图"，在此基础上推进各地创新产业规划对接。

尽管目前这样一张直观的地图还没问世，但我们已经可以感受到。当然，长三角地区的资源分布存在着不均衡。为此，罗兰贝格的许季刚总给出的解决方案是：超级产业集群战略。我的理解是，超级产业集群是一种资源配置的组织构架，通过建立产业集群的评价体系、长三角地区经济地图与创新地图等方式，以技术产业化为主轴，让跨三省一市产业集群中的教育、科研、企业、资本等要素进行有效沟通，增强它们之间的互信，从而让任意集群中的要素在进入其他集群时，都能迅速融入并且产生黏性。

麦肯锡的张帆总也认为只有做好产业发展才是区域协同的第一驱动力。他提出，从城市管理者的角度来看，未来产城发展必须从"一极独大"的单城市配置走向"多极并驱"的城市群平衡，积极打破行政壁垒、融入区域分工协同、拥抱一体化发展，这是占据新时代发展高地的关键；对企业管理者而言，把握区域变革须从等待机遇到来的"红利追逐者"走向前瞻宏观趋势的"先机创造者"，转换思路，从被动接受变革到积极影响变革,这是打造新时代价值高地的关键。

此外,仲量联行的吴允燊总也提醒我们,随着产业能级的提升、产业方向的更新,城市在土地、物业规划方面要及时做好策略调整,以应对源源不断的人才输入,成为战略性新兴产业等保持持续活力和国际竞争力的动能。

遥望 2035 年,到那一年,"长三角一体化发展达到较高水平""成为最具影响力和带动力的强劲活跃增长极"。要达到这一目标,我们可以说是摸着石头过河,但也可以说很有底气。因为,我们不是在黑夜中前行,我们的前方已有不少借鉴。不论是以纽约为首的美国东北部城市群,以伦敦为首的英格兰城市群,以巴黎为首的西欧城市群,还是和我们在同一时区,距离也最近的,以东京为首的日本太平洋沿岸城市群,它们都已经走过了很长的路,都有许多我们可以学习、借鉴的地方。结合它们的经验,再融入自身情况和优势,我们能少走很多弯路。

我想到了将近 10 年前,上海举办世博会时的口号:城市,让生活更美好。今天,有嘉宾也谈到了,打造更高质量的一体化城市群,归根结底,成功与否还要体现在微观层面居民幸福度的提升。两者可谓不谋而合。从国际超大城市治理实践来看,政府、企业、市民之间如何充分协作,结合自上而下的统筹规划和自下而上的市民多元参与,是超大城市治理的一个关键,也是衡量一个城市群建设成功与否的重要考核。尤其是,这个城市群能不能在机制上充分动员、保障和鼓励城市群中本土的精英贤达人士对城市发展的热情与设想。

以上是我在今天论坛上获得的一些收获,希望对大家有所帮助。现在,我宣布今天的论坛圆满落幕,谢谢各位!

An ancient Chinese poem says, "The distance from shore to shore seems wide at high tide, and a single sail is being lifted by a fair wind." I think this verse is very suitable for today's summit. The implication is that the future integrated development of the Yangtze River Delta will go smoothly; the course ahead is clear; and the process for achieving high-quality development has begun.

At present, *the Outline of the Integrated Regional Development of the Yangtze River Delta* has been reviewed at the central level. The fundamental principles for the current and future integrated development of the Yangtze River Delta have been established, and the goals have been set. How will they be accomplished? At today's summit, think tanks from various international institutions have contributed their insights. I learned a lot at this half-day session.

While listening, I was steadily thinking and making mental notes. The general topic of today's summit is the integration of the Yangtze River Delta; but in fact, I think the conference can be divided into four smaller topics: high-quality integration, improved business environment, future industrial framework, and experience from city clusters.

When it comes to the integration of the Yangtze River Delta, we are always talking about high-quality integration, but what does that mean? Mr. Zhu Hui of Boston Consulting Group explained what aspects we need to focus on for high-quality integration. For example, in terms of systems and mechanisms, he said that a long-term and effective inter-provincial coordination mechanism is needed to fundamentally promote the deep integration of the Yangtze River Delta's industries and overall development. In terms of industrial synergy, he explained that there is no comprehensive industrial framework to clarify the division of labour and to eliminate the current barriers to integration and development that have arisen due to differences in development levels in the various regions. Finally, in terms of talent flows, the gap between different areas of the region in terms of urban quality and public services is hindering the mobility of talented people.

As we all know, in our country, the construction of a city cluster is not just taking place in the Yangtze River Delta. There is also the Guangdong-Hong Kong-Macao Greater Bay Area, the Beijing-Tianjin-Hebei region, and other areas. Every region is exploring an enhanced developmental path, and each has its own development engine. So, compared with the other city clusters, what are the advantages and characteristics of the Yangtze River Delta's integration? In this regard, Mr. Liu Ming from KPMG made note of the role played by the Shanghai Pilot Free Trade Zone. As the nation's first free trade zone, it has served as an important engine for the country's development. In addition, it is playing an important role in the high-quality development of the Yangtze River Delta. By taking advantage of the Shanghai Free Trade Zone, the Yangtze River Delta region can integrate its business environment, industrial synergies, and regional ports. Through full opening-up, deep participation in the international division of labour, and global competition, Mr. Liu said that we can create a world-class city cluster that leads the country and serves as a beacon to the world.

Of course, as the integrated development of the Yangtze River Delta progresses, more and more companies and institutions will choose to set up and stay in the Yangtze River Delta. The consensus we reached is that local governments in the Yangtze River Delta must not rely too much on external policies to attract enterprises because this may result in vicious competition. So, what should these local governments rely on? They should focus on creating a favourable business environment in which enterprises can compete. For example, Mr.Kelvin Li of Cushman & Wakefield suggested that resources be fully shared between regions and that a unified management system that is conducive to the healthy and integrated development of the Yangtze River Delta. He also recommended that the coordination mechanism for disputes in the Yangtze River Delta be improved. Overall, policies should guide the fair flow of all factors and be based on the equal offering of public services.

From a market perspective, Mr.Owen Haacke, the chief representative of the US-China Business Council in Shanghai, spoke on behalf of businesses. He said that in order to help foreign-funded enterprises better integrate into the integrated development of the Yangtze River Delta, the relevant policy-making departments should take into consideration enterprises' specific concerns and expectations in the following four aspects: inter-provincial protection of intellectual property rights, environmental protection, industrial tranfer and the customs supervision.

The goal of achieving high-quality development and a good business environment have been set, so how should we arrange the industrial structure? Of course, a reasonable industrial framework will also further promote high-quality development and the formation of a better business environment.

During his inspection in Shanghai before the China International Import Expo in November 2019, President Xi Jinping emphasised that the original function of science and technology innovation should be strengthened and that efforts should be made to generate new scientific discoveries, inventions and directions in industry, as well as new ideas for development. In this way, he said that the country can achieve a number of innovations in both basic research and applied basic research, resulting in breakthroughs in key core technologies.

So, how is the Yangtze River Delta doing in this regard? Today, Ms. Dora Liu of Deloitte presented the firm's analysis of the innovation environment and innovation potential of the major cities in the Yangtze River Delta. Deloitte believes that at present, the cities in the Yangtze River Delta have shown promising signs as they "each have their own priorities" in the regulation of innovation industries. For example, according to the policy documents issued by Shanghai and Hangzhou, Shanghai aims to serve as a global benchmark for best practices, while Hangzhou aims to serve as a national benchmark for best practices. Shanghai is focusing on providing innovative resources (finance and technology), and Hangzhou is focusing on innovative applications. In order to determine the distribution of innovation industries in the Yangtze River Delta and their respective advantages, Deloitte recommends entrusting relevant agencies with developing a Yangtze River Delta Innovation Industry Map. With such a map, the region can promote the establishment of innovation industries in different areas.

Although an intuitive map like this has not yet been released, we can roughly envision one in spite of the uneven distribution of resources in the Yangtze River Delta region. To this end, Mr. Alex Xu of Roland Berger recommended a solution consisting of a super-industry cluster strategy. As I understand it, a super industrial cluster is an organisational structure for resource allocation. Such a structure would guide different factors, such as education, scientific research, enterprises, capital, etc., so that they flow effectively into the industrial clusters across the three provinces and one municipality. This structure would also strengthen mutual trust between these areas by establishing an industrial cluster evaluation system, economic maps and innovation maps for the Yangtze River Delta, with technology industrialisation as the focus. This would allow factors in any cluster to quickly integrate and merge together when entering other clusters.

Mr. Derek Zhang of McKinsey also believes that industrial development is the primary driving force for regional synergy. From a city management perspective, he said that the future development of industrial cities must shift from a single city configuration in which one city dominates exclusively to a balance between city clusters in which all the cities contribute to drive development. Actively breaking administrative barriers, integrating the regional division of labour, improving coordination between the regions, and embracing integrated development are the keys to achieving high-quality development in the new era. Mr. Zhang suggested that enterprise managers should effect change in the region by shifting from "chasing dividends" and waiting for opportunity to "preemptively creating opportunity" by considering future macro trends. Overall, Mr. Zhang said that changing mindsets and shifting from passively accepting change to positively influencing change is the key to building value in the new era.

In addition, Mr. Eddie Ng of JLL reminded us that with the upgrading of industries and the renewal of industrial direction, cities should make timely strategic adjustments in terms of land and property planning in order to handle the continuous inflow of talent. He also said that cities should aim to become a driving force for strategic emerging industries in order to maintain their vitality and international competitiveness.

By 2035, "the Yangtze River Delta will be deeply integrated," and the region will "be the most influential and vigorous force for growth" in the country. To achieve these goals, we might say that we are crossing the river by feeling the stones, but we can also say that we are very confident. We are confident because we are not operating in the dark; there are many references available to us. The Northeastern U.S.'s city cluster led by New York, England's city cluster led by London, the Western European city cluster led by Paris, and the Japanese Pacific Coastal city cluster led by Tokyo — which is closest to us and in the same time zone — have all come a long way, so there are many places we can learn from. By considering their experience and taking into account our own circumstances and advantages, we can avoid a lot of mistakes.

I recently thought of the slogan from the Shanghai World Expo that was held almost 10 years ago: "Better City, Better Life." Today, a speaker also talked about creating a higher-quality city cluster. Ultimately, success in this regard is reflected in the improvement of residents' happiness at the individual level. The two coincide with each other. From the perspective of international megacity governance practices, how the government, enterprises, and citizens can fully cooperate — combined with top-down overall planning and bottom-up citizen participation — is key to megacity governance. These elements are also an important part of assessing the success of city cluster. In particular, success depends on whether this city cluster can fully mobilise, guarantee and encourage the passion and vision of local elites for urban development.

These are some of the insights I gained from today's summit. I hope the summary I have provided will be helpful to everyone. Now I will announce the successful conclusion of today's summit. Thank you all.

Conference
Review

会议综述

科技赋能高质量发展，协同提升一体化水平

——2019年上海国际智库高峰论坛会议综述

一、论坛形成的主要观点

（一）上海要在标准制定、制度创新和统一的产业营商环境方面发挥引领作用

高风咨询、波士顿咨询强调，产业的集聚辐射主要是市场作用的结果，在当前不打破行政隶属的情况下，上海要打破行政边界发挥产业对外辐射作用，但更重要的是在标准制定、政策创新、政府服务等方面发挥"核心城市"的引领作用。一是牵头制定统一的产业标准和产业政策。例如，牵头数据管理一体化和降低区域物流成本，尤其是根据长三角地区不同产业的发展现状，制定统一的产业营商环境标准。二是上海要在创新探索和技术测试等方面发挥先行先试的作用。比如，上海要对标美国加州无人驾驶路测开放政策，带头推进长三角跨省市道路"无人驾驶"路测权限开放。三是发挥好核心城市功能，有效配置长三角资源。上海要在长三角地区有效配置人才、科技、信息、资本等资源，让科技与产业在长三角地区发挥有效互动。

（二）通过科技创新拓展企业市场范围，降低企业成本，实现高质量发展

德勤认为，要通过科技创新赋能企业，实现长三角高质量一体化发展。一是通过核心节点城市的研发成果孵化等外溢作用，推动缩小其所在城市的经济差距。二是借助大数据共享和科技创新券，为企业提供专业化、精准化服务，赋能各细分产业环节，实现要素的高效集聚与配置。三是通过技术创新拓展企业市场范围，优化区域内的产业生态，推动人工智能、无人驾驶和先进制造等重点领域的科技创新

成果快速商业化。四是利用现代技术手段优化制度环境,降低企业制度交易成本。

(三)长三角三省一市要以政府服务竞争,取代不同行政区域的市场同质竞争

专家们普遍认为,长三角一体化并非一样化,长三角各地内部发展水平不一,公共服务需求差异较大,如果把一体化错误地理解为一样化,不仅不利于高质量发展,反而会阻碍市场发挥决定性作用,降低市场效率。麦肯锡等专家提出,在交通互联互通及公共服务便利化的基础上,应该将产业协同作为核心动力,推进长三角一体化发展,特别是要以政府服务竞争取代不同行政区划的市场同质竞争。

二、长三角高质量一体化推进中应该注重的问题

国际智库专家认为,长三角三省一市在体制、创新、产业和营商环境层面上,仍面临着挑战,需要重点探索。

(一)注重形成跨省市协调的长效机制以及统一的市场体系

戴德梁行、罗兰贝格提出,一方面,当前长三角一体化协调仍停留在专题层面,三省一市各单位、各部门分头推进、单点支持,信息不一、资源分散,还有待建立覆盖全域的立法、监管体系等顶层制度设计;另一方面,受经济考核指标限制,长三角各地政府促进产业输出转移的意愿低,缺乏普惠性政策,要注重破除制度壁垒,打破行政边界,促进统一大市场的建设。

(二)注重数字技术在推进长三角一体化中的作用

凯捷和高风咨询的专家认为,未来数字技术等新兴科技在新旧动能转换、促进一体化方面将发挥重要作用。目前,长三角各地对数据采集、数据开放和调取标准各异,上海要牵头建立长三角数据管理中心,优化数字资源配置效率,深化重点领域的智慧应用和区域联动。

(三)注重从区域和产业两个角度促进实现产业协同发展

麦肯锡专家指出,从区域层面看,当前长三角南北动能不一,区域分化明显。比如,受产业类型和动能影响,南翼的轻工制造未能形成合力,城市间缺少互动。从产业层面看,仲量联行等提出,长三角产业协同存在恶性竞争、重复建设、产业空间纵深度不足等现象,部分中小城市产业跟风发展、缺乏主线。罗兰贝格认为,传

统的招商引资和产业园区发展模式不能承载长三角地区高质量一体化发展的战略重任,未来长三角要注重从区域和产业两个角度同时发力,破解产业间的恶性竞争,促进产业协同发展。

(四)注重形成统一的长三角营商环境

毕马威提出,不同产业对营商环境有不同需求,长三角一体化推进过程中,应根据不同产业发展规律,形成有特色的产业营商环境。戴德梁行反映,长三角各地政策法规各异,地方政府执法标准不一,甚至选择性执法,不仅增加了企业成本,而且形成了人为的市场分割。

三、值得长三角借鉴的国际经验和做法

世界银行、波士顿咨询、毕马威、普华永道和野村综研结合国际经验,为长三角高质量一体化发展提供了思路。

(一)设立跨区域协调组织和专业管理机构,打破融合发展的机制壁垒

世界银行、普华永道等专家提出,长三角可以参照里尔城市群经验成立跨区域"大都市局",或参照跨区域管理的纽约和新泽西以及阿姆斯特丹港务局的做法,推进长三角一体化发展。一是成立跨地区合作组织,突破传统管控模式。里尔城市群设立跨区域的"大都市局",由三方市长组成领导小组,一改传统的"中央、行政省、行政市"管控模式,形成"欧盟、跨境合作区、都市区、邻里社区"的城市群创新协同机制,由"大都市局"对市议会直接监管,监控城市群协同政策与举措的落地效果。二是中央政府高度授权,成立专业领域的统一管理机构。纽约和新泽西港务局是具有法人资格的公共机构,管理大纽约地区的港务和运输。在财务上自给自足,通过港口和机场设施服务收费,没有地方财政税收支持。港务局管理委员会负责规划和运营,但两州州长对委员会的决议有否决权,形成权力制衡。阿姆斯特丹港务局实行的是"港区合一,高度授权"机制,负责管理和协调阿姆斯特丹港及内部自由贸易区的整体事务,投资建设必要的基础设施,并且有权审批项目立项①。

---

① 特别是着眼于自由贸易区与城市功能的相互促进,在金融、保险、商贸、中介等第三产业发展上成效显著。而跨市港口的管理由港务局下属的中央航运管辖中心负责,并获得中央政府和当地市政的统一授权,各个港口设立港务办公室,执行管辖中心的规定,负责港口畅通、安全、发展。

（二）借鉴欧洲超级产业集群的成功经验，促进长三角地区产业协同发展

欧洲通过超级产业集群，有效地促进了区域产业一体化，形成了区域产业核心竞争力。其打造的超级产业群有三种模式：一是龙头企业协调模式。这是空客的航空产业发展的模式，以飞机机型为龙头，拉动各国航空产业链上下游产业集群的协同发展，为整个产业生态带来溢出效应，增强企业合作。二是联盟协调模式。这是欧洲健康中轴线（Health Axis Europe）发展模式，由在生命健康领域最领先的比利时鲁汶、德国海德堡、荷兰马斯特里赫特以及丹麦哥本哈根的生命产业集群组成战略联盟，成果进行跨地区转化，拓展科技网络。三是超国家协调模式。由欧盟设立创新与科技研究所，围绕8大产业形成超级产业集群，提供合作的公共资源，以欧盟教育科研一体化项目和高科技战略为核心形成地平线（Horizon 2020）研发共同体。

以空客的航空航天超级产业集群为例，欧洲形成了以空客法国总部图卢兹为主的组装产业，德国汉堡、慕尼黑和腓特烈港为主的航空内饰、直升机和航空叶片产业，英国的航空发动机产业，以及意大利和西班牙的航天相关产业，各大产业基地通过建立应用型研究中心、公共研发平台、职业教育培训中心，提高了区域研发能力和劳动者技能。以飞机机型为龙头，空客项目拉动了欧洲各国航空产业链上下游产业集群的协同发展，为整个产业生态带来溢出效应，增强企业合作。

（三）在产业差异化的基础上，以产学研协同组织和创新服务平台为抓手，实现产业协同

美国波士华①城市群产业梯级布局合理，各地区优势差异明显。单一产业内，通过组建跨区域产学研协同组织，破除区域行政壁垒，进行全产业链深入布局。以生物医药为例，麻省生物技术委员会是该区域生物技术企业成员的贸易联合机构，它联合包括政府、学校和药企在内的多方参与主体，为区域84个产业园区评级，并为不同级别的园区制定差异化发展策略。同时，该委员会为生态圈搭建人才促进、资金对接、行业交流、技术服务和大数据共享平台，实现产业要素的集聚和配置，形成了剑桥研发为主导，长木发展医疗服务，莱克星顿、沃尔瑟姆及其他区域负责产业化制造的梯级布局，使其建成为美国乃至世界最前沿、产值最大、最领先的生物医药集群。

---

① 即美国东北部城市群，北起波士顿、南至华盛顿，是美国人口密度最高的地区、美国最大的商业贸易中心、国际金融中心和创新中心。

（四）借鉴东京都市圈"多心多核"空间布局经验,促进区域协同发展

野村综研和日本贸易振兴协会指出,东京都市圈经历六轮规划,从"一极集中"向"多心多核"的空间发展格局转变,实现区域内的"对流"。前期,政府规划推动东京湾区区域间、城市间实现差异化发展,逐渐形成了以东京为"雁首"的"雁形模式"①城市分工体系。后期,东京都市圈在东京都内建设了多个副都心,在东京周边还大力发展"业务核都市",让中小城市成为具有产业韧性的节点城市。例如,川崎成为产业创新节点,宇都宫市成为核心制造节点。通过平衡大都市圈中核心城市与周边城市的"虹吸效应"与"分流效应",让周边城市充分发展其"个性",形成差异化错位发展,在一定程度上避免了此消彼长的无效竞争,促进了区域协同发展。

四、对长三角一体化与高质量发展的对策建议

与会智库专家建议推进长三角高质量一体化发展,应"大处着眼、小处着手",从以下三个方面切入。

（一）在自贸区制度创新基础上,推动区域港务管理创新,实现长三角港口群运营一体化

安永、毕马威、美中贸易全国委员会等智库提出,港口经济是长三角的特色和优势。当前长三角区域的港口一体化已经在进行探索,但相对零散,在高层级的管理机构和协调机制上没有实质性突破,而江浙沪自贸区有最适合进行机制创新的土壤,可以学习借鉴纽约新泽西和阿姆斯特丹港务局的经验,通过建立中央授权的统一管理机构,实现区域内港务运营的高度协调,推动港口一体化发展。同时,港口运营一体化也可以为长三角区域内其他的机制和管理创新提供范本。

（二）促进"创新链+产业链+价值链"深度融合,优化长三角产业协同布局

穆迪、德勤、罗兰贝格等智库表示,产业协同是长三角高质量一体化发展的核心动力。一是要制定"长三角创新产业地图"和"城市经济地图",加强资源可视化。要尽早梳理出三省一市各自的资源禀赋、发展优势与短板,形成体现差异化、梯度显著的区域产业地图,辅以案例资料,指导全域未来产业发展方向,形成纵深链状

---

① 雁形模式指处于"雁首"地位的城市具备经济和科学技术等方面的核心地位,其通过资金和技术供应、市场吸收及产业转移等,带动周边地区的经济发展。

协同。二是发起跨长三角的旗舰型科研项目,促进技术外溢。例如,围绕跨界水系治理,制定龙头研发项目,针对水质传感器等开展科研攻关,同时拉动相关设备制造和人工智能初创企业发展,实现生态可持续。航空产业更是可以围绕南京、上海的科研资源以及无锡、宁波的产业资源建立协同项目,同时拉动邻省江西的航空产业资源。三是组建跨区产业协同组织和科创资源共享平台,推动优势产业的高质量发展落地。在关键领域,组建跨区域产学研协同组织,为业界搭建人才促进、资金对接、行业交流、技术服务和大数据共享平台,增强产业要素集聚与互动,推动研发成果跨地区转化。

(三)发挥长三角创新生态"合力",形成自下而上和多元参与的良好科创环境

科尔尼、仲量联行等建议,一是鼓励区域内科创人才流动。积极探索并逐步放开科创人员居住证积分、专业技术职称等关键领域的跨区互认机制,从根本上消除阻碍人才跨区域流动的障碍。二是降低上海科技创新的商务成本。进一步落实上海科创企业或跨国研发中心在用地、房租、人才公寓方面的优惠与补贴政策。三是建立自下而上、多元参与的智库咨询机制。长三角三省一市要注重建立包括企业、高校、研究院等更多社会主体参与的专家智库委员会,为长三角一体化示范区产业导入和发展模式建言献策;自上而下地充分听取具有不同学科背景和专业知识认识的意见,以复合知识解答长三角高质量一体化发展中面临的问题。

The Empowering Role of Science and Technology in High-quality Development, and the Boosting Effect of Collaboration on the Integration Level of the Yangtze River Delta

—Summary of the 2019 Shanghai International Think Tank Summit

Ⅰ. Main ideas formed on the Summit

1. Shanghai shall play a leading role in standards formulation, institutional innovation, and a unified industrial and business environment

Gao Feng Advisory Company and Boston Consulting Group emphasized that both industrial agglomeration and radiation result from market effects. Shanghai should transcend administrative boundaries without changing the current administrative affiliation and play not only a radiating role in the development of regional industry, but also a leading role as core city in various aspects such as standards formulation, policy innovation, government services, and so on.

First, Shanghai should play a leading role in developing unified industrial standards and policies. For example, Shanghai should take the lead in integrating data management, reducing regional logistics costs, and, particularly, developing unified standards on industrial and business environment in accordance with the current development of different industries in the Yangtze River Delta Region.

Second, Shanghai should play a pioneering role in aspects such as innovative exploration and technical tests. For instance, Shanghai should benchmark the California Autonomous Vehicle Testing Regulations and lead in allowing the testing of autonomous vehicles on inter-provincial roadways in the Yangtze River Delta.

Third, Shanghai should maximize the role of core city in effectively allocating resources in the Yangtze River Delta Region, such as talents, science and technology, information, capital, and so on, promoting an effective interaction between science and technology and industry.

2. Enterprises shall expand market scope and reduce costs through sci-tech innovation for high-quality development

Deloitte said that it is necessary to empower enterprises through scientific and technological innovation for high-quality integrated development of the Yangtze River Delta.

First, it is necessary to narrow the economic gap in robust node cites through spilling effects of R&D achievements incubation among others.

Second, it is necessary to offer enterprises specialized and targeted services, to empower each link in all industry segments, and to facilitate the capacity to gather and allocate factors through big data sharing and scientific and technological innovation coupon.

Third, it is necessary to expand enterprise market scope, to upgrade regional industrial ecology, and to rapidly commercialize scientific and technological innovation achievements in key fields such as artificial intelligence, autonomous vehicle, advanced manufacturing, and so on through technological innovation.

Fourth, it is necessary to upgrade institutional environment and to reduce institutional transaction costs for enterprises through modern technologies and methods.

3. The three provinces and one municipality shall substitute government service competition for market homogeneous competition between administrative regions

Experts generally agreed that to integrate the Yangtze River Delta is not to homogenize it. The level of development in the Yangtze River Delta varies from area to area, which results in a largely differentiated demand for public services. If integration is mistaken for homogenization, not only will high-quality development be hampered, but the decisive role of market will also be significantly weakened, reducing the market efficiency.

Experts from McKinsey and other think tanks proposed that industrial coordination should be taken as the core driver for the integrated development of the Yangtze River Delta on the basis of transport connectivity and the facilitation of public services. It is also of profound importance to substitute government service competition for market homogeneous competition between administrative regions.

II. Key issues the Yangtze River Delta should focus on advancing the high-quality integration

Experts from international think tanks said that the Yangtze River Delta, which encompasses the three provinces of Jiangsu, Zhejiang, Anhui and the municipality of Shanghai, should still focus on challenges in mechanism, institution, innovation, industry, and business environment.

1. To form a long-term mechanism and a unified market system coordinated by multiple provinces and cities

Cushman & Wakefield, Roland Berger made its proposition from two perspectives.

On the one hand, the coordinated integration of the Yangtze River Delta still remains at the policy level. All units and departments in the three provinces and one municipality are now promoting development respectively and have to rely on themselves due to the lack of unified information and the dispersion of resources. Therefore, it is a must to establish top-level institutional design, including legislative and regulatory systems, that covers the entire region.

On the other hand, subject to the restrictions of economy assessment indicators, governments in the Yangtze River Delta do not have a strong wish to facilitate the export and relocation of industries or to formulate inclusive and convenient policies. Accordingly, they should then focus on removing institutional barriers, transcending administrative boundaries, and advancing the construction of a unified large market.

2. To promote the role of digital technology in the integration of the Yangtze River Delta

Experts from Capgemini and Gao Feng Advisory Company said that in the future, emerging science and technology such as digitalization will play an important role in shifting from old to new momentum and in facilitating integration.

To date, the standards in data collection, openness, and obtainment vary from one area to another in the Yangtze River Delta. Shanghai should take the lead in building the Yangtze River Delta Data Management Center, so as to optimize the allocation of digital resources, and further promote smart applications and regional interaction in key fields.

3. To achieve coordinated development of industries from regional and industrious perspectives

From the perspective of regional development, expert from McKinsey pointed out that with the north and the south diverging in momentum, the Yangtze River Delta is now confronting obvious regional differentiation. For example, influenced by the types of industries and driving forces, light manufacturing industry in the south wing fails to form a joint force, while cities do not have enough interaction.

From the perspective of industrial development, JLL and others proposed that vicious competitions, duplicated constructions, insufficient spatial depth of industries, and other phenomena are posing challenges to the industrial coordination of the Yangtze River Delta.

Roland Berger said that the traditional pattern of investment attraction and industrial parks development are not capable of carrying the strategic task to fulfill high-quality integrated development of the Yangtze River Delta Region. In the future, the Yangtze River Delta should focus on solving the problem of vicious competitions between enterprises and advancing the coordinated development of industries from the perspective of both regional and industrial development.

4. To form a unified business environment in the Yangtze River Delta

KPMG said that the Yangtze River Delta should be aware of different demands on business environment from different industries, and form a characteristic business environment for industries according to the development rules of different industries.

Cushman & Wakefield indicated that policies and regulations vary from area to area in the Yangtze River Delta, while the law is enforced under separate standards or even selectively by local governments. This not only increases costs for enterprises, but also results in a man-made market segmentation.

III. International experiences and practices beneficial for the Yangtze River Delta

World Bank, Boston Consulting Group, KPMG, PwC, and NRI put forward ideas for high-quality integration of the Yangtze River Delta in light of international experiences.

1. Setting up inter-regional coordinating organizations and specialized administrative institutions so as to remove the mechanism barrier for integrated development

Experts from World Bank, PwC, and other think tanks suggested that the Yangtze River Delta can set up a cross-regional "Bureau of Metropolitan" referring to the experience of European Metropolis of Lille, or promote the integrated development with reference to the Port Authority of New York and New Jersey, the Port of Amsterdam, and their cross-regional management.

Firstly, cross-regional cooperative organizations shall be established and breakthroughs shall be made in traditional mode of management and control. Set up by the European Metropolis of Lille, the "bureau de la Métropole" is conducted under the leading group composed of mayors from the three sub-regions. Instead of the traditional mode of management and control that includes central government, administrative provinces, and administrative cities, the bureau has innovated a coordinated mechanism for city clusters, involving the European Union, cross-border cooperation zones, metropolitan areas, and neighborhoods and communities. This enables the bureau to directly supervise city councils, as well as observe and control the actual effects of coordinated policies and measures for the city cluster.

Secondly, unified administrative institutions for specialized fields shall be established with high-level authorization from the central government. As a public institution with legal person status, the Port Authority of New York and New Jersey manages the port and transportation in the Greater New York area. It is financially self-sufficient with charges for facility services in harbors and airports, thus free of local tax and revenue. While the Board of Commissioners is responsible for planning and operation, the governors of the two states retain the right to veto the resolutions of the Board, forming a scientific mechanism with balance of power.

As for the Port of Amsterdam, adhering to the mechanism of "port integration under high-level authorization," it is responsible for the overall management and coordination of the port of Amsterdam and the internal free trade area, as well as the investment and construction of necessary infrastructures; besides, it is authorized to approve projects.[1]

2. Drawing on successful experience of super industrial clusters in Europe so as to promote coordinated development of industries in the Yangtze River Delta Region

Europe has effectively promoted the integration of its regional industries by means of super industrial clusters, enhancing their core competitiveness. There are three coordination modes applied in building those super industrial clusters.

First, leading enterprise oriented mode, in which Airbus develops the aviation industry. New designs of aircrafts as its leading force, Airbus stimulates the coordinated development between upstream and downstream industrial clusters of the aviation industry chain in multiple countries,

---

[1] The Port of Amsterdam particularly highlights the mutual promotion between the free trade area and municipal functions, and has scored significant achievements in tertiary industry such as finance, insurance, trade, intermediary and so on. Ports covering multiple cities are administrated by the Central Nautical Management, which is mandated by both the central government and local municipalities. To implement the Management's rules, Harbor Master's Office is set up in each port for sake of its safety, smoothness, and development.

exerting the spillover effect on the industrial ecology along with strengthening cooperation between enterprises.

Second, alliance oriented mode, the development mode of Health Axis Europe, a strategic alliance between the leading life-science clusters Leuven (Belgium), Heidelberg (Germany), Maastricht (Netherland) and Copenhagen (Denmark) in order to accelerate cross-regional transformation of outcomes and expand the science and technology network.

Third, supernational organization oriented mode. Created by the European Union, the European Institute of Innovation and Technology, with high-tech strategies and integration of the European Union for education and scientific research at the core, is a R&D community as a part of Horizon 2020. It builds super industrial clusters around eight major industries and provides public resources for cooperation.

To take the aerospace super industry clusters of Airbus as an example, Europe has produced the assembly industry led by Toulouse (France), home to Airbus headquarters, the cabin interior, helicopter, and aero-engine blade industry led by Hamburg, Munich, and Friedrichshafen (German), aero-engine industry in Britain, and other aircraft related industries in Italy and Spain. Major industrial bases have improved regional R&D capacity and workers' skills by establishing applied research centers, public R&D platforms, and vocational education and training centers.

To conclude, new designs of aircrafts as its leading force, Airbus programs stimulate the coordinated development between upstream and downstream industry clusters of the aviation industry chain in European countries, exerting the spillover effect on the industrial ecology along with strengthening cooperation between enterprises.

3. Leveraging innovation service platforms and organizations integrating industries, universities, and research institutes so as to achieve industrial coordination on the basis of industrial differentiation

BosWash Megalopolis[①] in the United States has a reasonable cascaded

---

① BosWash Megalopolis, the Northeast megalopolis in the United States, running north to south from Boston to Washington, D.C., is the most densely populated region and the largest commercial and trade center in the United States; it is also an international financial center and innovative center.

layout of industry, which demonstrates vast differentiation in advantages between various regions. For a given industry, cross-regional organizations integrating industries, universities, and research institutes are constructed to remove regional administrative barriers, and deepen the layout of the whole industry chain.

To take biomedical industry as an example, Massachusetts Biotechnology Council is a trade association whose membership is open to biotechnology enterprises in the area. It associates multiple participants including government, universities, and pharmaceutical companies to rank 84 industrial parks in the region and develop differentiated development strategies on the grounds of ranks.

Meanwhile, the council erects platforms for the ecosphere in terms of talent promotion, financing connection, industry exchange, technical service, and big data sharing, well facilitating the capacity to gather and allocate industrial factors.

With the leading role of Cambridge in research and development, Longwood developing medical service, Lexington, Waltham, and other areas working on cascaded layout of industrial production, BosWash has built the most advanced biomedical cluster, also the one with the largest output value, both in the United States and all around the world.

4. Drawing on Tokyo Metropolitan Area's experience and spatial layout of "Multiple Sub-centers" so as to promote regional coordinated development

NRI and JETRO pointed out that after six round of planning, Tokyo Metropolitan Area has changed its spatial development pattern from "one polar concentration" to "multiple sub-centers". At the early stage, the government planned to promote differentiated development between regions and cities in the Tokyo Bay Area, by which the urban division system named "flying geese model"[1] gradually took shape with Tokyo as the "leading goose." Later, Tokyo Metropolitan Area constructed several sub-centers

---

[1] The flying geese model is a model in which the city in the position of the "leading goose" plays a central role in economy, science and technology, and other aspects, and gives rise to the economic development of surrounding areas through investment, technical supply, market absorption, relocation of industries, etc.

within the Prefecture of Tokyo, vigorously developed core business cities around Tokyo small and medium-sized cities into node cities with resilient industries. For instance, Kawasaki has become the node of industrial innovation, and Utsunomiya has become the node of core manufacturing.

The balance between core cities in the metropolitan area and the "siphonic effect" and "diversion effect" of surrounding cities ensure a full and differential development of their characteristics. To some degree, this avoids constant ineffective competitions and promotes regional coordinated development.

IV. Countermeasures and suggestions on the integration of the Yangtze River Delta for high-quality development

Experts from multiple think tanks suggested that to enhance high-quality integrated development of the Yangtze River Delta, we should "start small, but think big" with an eye on three aspects.

1. Administrative innovation for regional ports should be promoted on the basis of Free Trade Zone's institutional innovation in order to achieve integrated operation of the port clusters in the Yangtze River Delta

Ernst & Young, KPMG, USCBC and other think tanks said that port economy is the characteristic and advantage of the Yangtze River Delta. Exploration has been started on the port integration of the Yangtze River Delta Region, but there is neither enough systematical research, nor any substantive breakthroughs in coordinated mechanism or high-level administrative institutions.

In fact, free trade zones in Jiangsu, Zhejiang, and Shanghai provide the most appropriate conditions for mechanism innovation. By learning from the experience of the Port Authority of New York and New Jersey and the Port of Amsterdam, they can promote an integrated development and highly coordinated operation of regional ports through unified administrative institutions with authorization from the central government. In turn, the integrated operation of regional ports can also set an example for the

Yangtze River Delta in regards to mechanism and administration innovation in other fields.

2. Deep integration of "innovation chain ＋ industry chain ＋ value chain" should be advanced in order to upgrade the coordination of industrial layout in the Yangtze River Delta

Moody, Deloitte, Roland Berger and other think tanks indicated that industrial coordination is the core driver of high-quality integrated development in the Yangtze River Delta.

First, mapping the innovative industries in the Yangtze River Delta and the economic powers of cities in order to make resources more visible. It is necessary to sort out the resource endowment, development advantages, and weakness of the three provinces and one municipality as soon as possible, visualizing a regional industrial map that clearly shows differences and cascade. On this basis, chain coordination shall be intensified while the future of regional industrial development shall be directed with the help of practical cases and data.

Second, launching flagship scientific research projects covering the whole Yangtze River Delta Region in order to accelerate technology spillover. As an example, leading R&D projects shall be initiated revolving the restoration of water system, while key problems shall be tackled and scientific researches shall be carried on over water quality sensors and other technologies; in the meantime, the manufacturing of related equipment and development of startup AI enterprises shall be stimulated to build a sustainable ecology.

As for the aviation industry, coordinated programs shall be established with scientific research resources in Nanjing and Shanghai, and industrial resources in Wuxi and Ningbo, pulling aviation industry resources in neighboring Jiangxi province.

Third, setting up cross-regional organizations coordinating industries as well as platforms sharing scientific and innovation resources in order to facilitate the high-quality development of competitive industries. Organizations integrating industries, universities, and research institutes shall be set up in key fields as platforms for market participants in terms of talent promotion, financing connection, industry exchange, technical service, and big data sharing, improving the agglomeration of and interaction between industrial factors with further cross-regional transformation of R&D outcomes.

3. "Joint strength" of the Yangtze River Delta innovation ecology should be exploited in order to form a favorable bottom-up sci-tech innovation environment involving multiple parities

ATK, JLL and other think tanks made the following proposals.

The first is to encourage regional movement of scientific innovation talents.It is important to actively explore and gradually relax cross-regional mutual recognition in key fields such as the residential permit points and professional and technical titles for scientific innovation workers, eliminating obstacles that hinder cross-regional movement of talents.

The second is to reduce the business cost of sci-tech innovation for Shanghai. It is important to further implement preferential and subsidy policies for scientific innovation enterprises or multinational R&D centers in Shanghai from various aspects such as land, rent, and talent apartment.

The third is to build a bottom-up think tank consulting mechanism involving multiple parties. The three provinces and one municipality in the Yangtze River Delta should lay emphasis on building committees of experts and think tanks, which consist of more social subjects from enterprises, universities, to research institutes, and others. These committees aim at contributing ideas for industrial import and development pattern of the demonstration zone for the integration of the Yangtze River Delta, while provincial and municipal governments should conquer challenges in the high-quality integrated development of the Yangtze River Delta with professional and compound knowledge by fully listening to opinions from different disciplines.

APPENDIX

附　录

2019 年上海国际智库高峰论坛办会参会单位简介

1. 主办单位

上海市人民政府发展研究中心

上海市人民政府发展研究中心(前身是上海经济研究中心)于 1980 年 12 月 26 日正式成立,于 1995 年 12 月 22 日根据市政府决定,更名为上海市人民政府发展研究中心。上海市人民政府发展研究中心是为市政府决策服务,承担本市决策咨询的研究、组织、协调、管理、服务的市政府决策咨询研究机构。

主要职责:

(1) 研究本市经济、社会发展和改革开放中具有全局性、综合性、战略性的问题。

(2) 了解动态、分析矛盾、研究对策、预测前景,及时向市委、市政府提出决策建议和咨询意见。

(3) 负责本市两年一度的市决策咨询研究成果奖的评奖工作。

(4) 组织、协调市政府系统的决策咨询研究工作。

(5) 负责本市决策咨询系统建议库信息管理和维护工作。

(6) 受市政府委托,管理有关组织和事业机构。

(7) 编辑出版《上海经济年鉴》和《科学发展》杂志。

(8) 承办市领导交办的其他事项。

2. 支持单位

长三角区域合作办公室

2018 年 1 月,沪苏浙皖三省一市共同组建长三角区域合作办公室,在上海联合集中办公,主任由上海市发改委主任兼任,工作人员由三省一市统一选派。长三角区域合作办公室是长三角高质量一体化发展的服务平台和推进机构,负责组织研究长三角一体化发展的重大问题,牵头编制有关规划、计划,统筹协调和督促检查重点领域合作事项,完成长三角地区主要领导座谈会和长三角地区合作与发展联席会议交办事项等,在跨省信息沟通、工作联动、资源统筹等方面发挥重要作用。

东方网·东方智库

东方网成立于 2000 年 5 月 28 日,是全国重点新闻网站,上海市新型主流媒体集团。东方网拥有中、英、日三个语种版本,通过 PC 端、"翱翔"和"东方头条"新闻客户端、微博微信等移动产品构建全媒体传播体系,实现影响力的覆盖。

2012 年 3 月,东方网完成转企改制,由上海市国有资产监督管理委员会控股,注册资本 9.97 亿元。2015 年 12 月,东方网正式在全国中小企业股转系统挂牌。东方网成立以来,所有财务年度均实现盈利,做到了社会效益和经济效益兼顾。

在中央、上海两级主管部门的指导下,东方网围绕建设"以科技创新为引领的新闻＋政务＋服务的新型主流媒体集团"的发展目标,坚持专业化、市场化、资本化的发展原则,努力建设成为全国最具影响力的新型主流网络媒体集团之一和互联网文化上市公司。

东方智库由上海新型主流媒体集团——东方网主办,于 2018 年成立,是上海首个研究阐释、分享交流国际议题的平台化媒体型智库。东方智库以"构建具有兼容性、公信力、多元化的国际议题朋友圈"为宗旨,以"围绕时事热点,立足中央口径,阐释来龙去脉,评析事件本质"为定位,被喻为上海国际议题智库领域的"发声器"和"会客厅"。

东方智库立足上海,以全球化的国际视野和融媒体的传播渠道,汇聚国内外国际问题领域的意见领袖、政商精英和学界翘楚,聚焦中外关系与中国外交政策、国际政治局势与经济形势,全球治理与国别研究,公共外交与"一带一路"等热点,建成兼具社会型决策参考、融合型观点传播、产学研社群联动的复合式平台,以提升国际议题阐释传播的质量和透明度,并推动多元而畅通的全球观点碰撞和观念交流。

东方智库专家委员会由新华社原副社长周锡生领衔,汇聚中央外办、外交部、中联部,新华社,中共中央党校、上海社科院、上海国际问题研究院,复旦大学、东南大学、上海外国语大学等数十位专家学者和意见领袖。同时,东方智库也与上海国际问题研究院、上海社科院国际问题研究所、上海市政府发展研究中心、上海市对外文化交流协会、上海全球治理与区域国别研究院形成了常态化的联动合作机制。

3. 承办单位

上海国际智库交流中心

2010年,按照时任上海市市长韩正同志关于进一步拓展上海市决策咨询研究工作,汇集国内外专家学者智慧服务上海市委、市政府的科学决策、民主决策,不断扩大中心的国际影响力的指示要求,上海市人民政府发展研究中心联合埃森哲、凯捷、德勤、IBM 等在沪国际智库牵头成立了"上海国际智库交流中心"。2011年,上海国际智库交流中心召开成立大会并举办首届"上海智慧论坛"。时任市长韩正市长发来贺信,时任市政府秘书长姜平出席会议,宣读了韩正的贺信,致贺词并揭牌。

自2014年起,在原"上海智慧论坛"基础上,上海市发展研究中心将论坛提升为"上海国际智库峰会",进一步提升了上海市政府发展研究中心整合国际智库的功能,拓展了上海与国际智库间的友好交往。2014年,围绕上海建设具有全球影响力的科技创新中心战略,上海国际智库交流中心举办了以"问策全球科技创新中心"为主题的第一届上海国际智库峰会,国际智库、委办局和高校学者近100人参会,时任上海市政府秘书长李逸平出席会议并致辞。2015年,召开了以"2050年的上海:愿景与挑战"为主题的第二届上海国际智库峰会,时任上海市政府常务副市长屠光绍、市政府秘书长李逸平出席会议并致闭幕词。2016年,第三届上海国际智库峰会如期举办,国内外专家学者围绕"如何提升上海投资贸易便利化水平"进行了深入的研讨和交流,为上海投资贸易发展献计献策。2017年,第四届上海国际智库高峰论坛以"如何发挥上海在'一带一路'中的桥头堡作用"为主题,时任市政府秘书长肖贵玉出席论坛并作开幕致辞。2018年,上海市人民政府发展研究中心与轮值主席世界银行驻华办事处,联合20余家驻沪国际知名智库举办了第五届上海国际智库高峰论坛,主题是"如何进一步优化上海营商环境",时任市政府秘书长汤志平出席论坛并致辞。

上海国际智库交流中心的主要职责是:

(1) 开展政府决策咨询研究。

(2) 服务企业发展开展应用研究、企业规划、管理咨询。

(3) 开展双边和多边国际合作研讨。

(4) 承担国际合作课题研究。

(5) 提供专业人才培养、培训与信息服务。

毕马威

毕马威是专业服务领域的领先机构。毕马威的成员所遍布全球 153 个国家和地区,拥有专业人员 207 000 名,提供审计、税务和咨询等专业服务。毕马威独立成员所网络中的成员与瑞士实体——毕马威国际合作组织("毕马威国际")相关联。毕马威各成员所在法律上均属独立及分设的法人。我们的网络是一个由符合资格专业人士组成的强大联盟。毕马威拥有将环球经验和当地/地区知识相结合的专业团队,通过团结协作、相互了解,迅速解决棘手问题。

毕马威早在 1945 年开始在中国香港特别行政区提供专业服务。1992 年,毕马威在中国内地成为首家获准合资开业的国际会计师事务所。2012 年 8 月 1 日,毕马威成为四大会计师事务所之中,首家从中外合作制转为特殊普通合伙的事务所。至 2019 年 9 月底,毕马威中国已在 21 个城市设立办公室,并拥有 12 000 多名合伙人及员工。

毕马威始终与国际知名企业的中国管理层,以及新兴企业和新创公司紧密合作。我们致力为客户提升业务价值,让客户从中获得裨益。我们通过整合跨职能工作小组,为客户提供优质完善的服务。具体来说,毕马威不同服务范畴(审计、税务、咨询)的专业人员会紧密合作,我们的专业人员通常拥有丰富的行业和市场知识,他们可协助我们的客户解决行业热点问题并妥善管理风险。

我们凭借崇高的信誉和优质的服务,成为中国最大的集审计、税务和咨询于一体的会计师事务所之一。毕马威办公室所在地与客户邻近,而且毕马威以统一的经营方式来管理中国内地、香港和澳门的业务。这能确保我们能够高效和迅速地调动各方面的资源,为客户提供高质量的服务。

上海发展研究基金会

上海发展研究基金会成立于 1993 年,是利用自然人、法人或者其他组织捐赠的财产,以从事公益事业为目的,按照国家有关规定的公募基金会、非营利性法人。

上海发展研究基金会以促进对发展问题的研究、推进决策咨询事业为宗旨;以募集、运作资金,研究、交流、资助、奖励经济、社会、城市发展决策咨询项目为业务范围。

二十几年来,基金会大力支持上海市决策咨询研究工作,资助了许多研究项目,并资助开展了上海市决策咨询研究成果奖评奖工作。同时,基金会也组织研究团队,完成了自行设立的或从其他单位承接的一系列研究项目。

近年来,基金会为实现其宗旨而积极探索。基金会每月举办一次"上海发展沙龙",邀请国内外知名专家、学者就当前的热点或敏感问题作演讲,并与参会者进行互动讨论;每年举办两到三次高层次的研讨会,邀请多位海内外专家与政、商、学界人士共聚一堂,就全球经济和中国经济的形势进行讨论和交流;举办"中国经济未来"系列小型研讨会,针对中国经济发展中一些深层次问题进行深入的讨论。基金会还通过资助的方式,与大学和研究机构合作举办了各种形式的研讨活动。基金会把各种研讨活动中的精彩内容,不定期地编撰出版内部资料《研讨实录》和《研究简报》,在更大的范围内推广对发展问题的研究和讨论成果。

自 2008 年开始,基金会与上海市人民政府发展研究中心共同设立了"上海发展研究奖学金"项目,每年资助上海市高校的数名博士或硕士研究生,为决策咨询研究队伍培养后备力量。

上海发展研究基金会现由原上海市副市长、原上海市人大常委会副主任胡延照任会长;原上海市政协副主席王荣华、原上海社会科学院院长王战、原上海国盛(集团)有限公司董事长张立平任副会长;乔依德任副会长兼秘书长。

4. 参会单位(按单位名称拼音排序)

安永

安永致力于建设一个更美好的商业世界,因为安永坚信这个信念将会带来庞大的正面影响:让企业之间有更多的信任,以支持企业可持续发展,同时可以培育出各种形式的人才,并鼓励更多、更大程度的互相协作。安永希望能通过自身的行动以及让志同道合的机构和个人参与,共同建设更美好的商业世界。这是我们的宗旨,也是安永作为一家专业服务机构存在的原因。全球化正重塑我们身处的世界。随着贸易、科技及投资等把全球各国和企业更紧密联系起来,人与产品的流动以及信息与理念传播,都缩短得更快、距离更短,全球化不断把边界扩大。为了确保提供更快速有效的服务,安永把全球 26 个区域的业务都综合起来,将分布在全球逾 150 个国家或地区的 700 多个办事处分为三个业务地区进行管理,分别为:美洲区;欧洲、中东、印度和非洲区(EMEIA),以及亚太区。经过理顺后的结构,让安永可迅速做出决策,并促进战略的执行力,有助于我们向在世界各地发展的客户提供卓越的客户服务。其中,大中华业务更是安永亚太区业务的一个重要部分。

安永的大中华业务覆盖中国"内地、香港、澳门、台湾"及蒙古,让我们的专业服务网络高度整合起来。与此同时,安永也是大中华规模最大的专业服务机构之一,在区内提供专业服务 50 年。这段期间,安永取得多项具有里程碑意义的发展:安永的前身雅特杨会计师事务所(Arthur Young)于 1968 年在香港成立首个成员办事处;1981 年安永成为首批获准在中国内地开展业务的国际专业服务机构之一。

安永大中华区通过 27 个成员办事处为客户提供服务,办事处地点包括:北京、香港、上海、广州、澳门、深圳、成都、杭州、南京、沈阳、苏州、天津、武汉、西安、长沙、大连、青岛、厦门、郑州和海口。在台湾,安永的办事处设于台北、桃园、新竹、台中、台南和高雄,而蒙古业务的办事处则设在乌兰巴托。

安永在大中华区的员工达 16 000 名,致力在适当时候,在适当地点配置适当人员,向客户提供所需的无缝衔接及优质服务。这就是安永在行业中独树一帜之处。

贝恩公司

贝恩公司是一家全球性咨询公司,致力于帮助世界各地有雄心、以变革为导向的商业领袖共同定义未来。

自 1973 年成立以来,我们根据客户的业绩来衡量自己的成功。我们在业内享有良好的客户拥护度,贝恩客户的业绩相较同期股票市场的表现高出四倍。

贝恩公司在全球设有 58 个分公司,我们与客户并肩工作,拥有共同的目标:取得超越对手的非凡业绩,重新定义客户所在的行业。凭借度身定做的整合性专业能力,配以精心打造的数字创新生态系统,我们为客户提供更好、更快和更持久的业绩结果。

波士顿咨询公司

波士顿咨询公司(BCG)与商界以及社会领袖携手并肩,帮助他们在应对最严峻挑战的同时,把握千载难逢的绝佳机遇。自 1963 年成立伊始,BCG 便成为商业战略的开拓者和引领者。如今,BCG 致力于帮助客户启动和落实整体转型——推动变革、赋能组织、打造优势、提升业绩。

组织卓越要求有效整合数字化能力和人才。BCG 复合多样的国际化团队能够为客户提供深厚的行业知识、职能专长和深刻洞察,激发组织变革。BCG 基于最前沿的技术和构思,结合企业数字化创新实践,为客户量身打造符合其商业目标的解决方案。BCG 创立的独特合作模式,与客户组织的各个层面紧密协作,帮助客户实现卓越发展。

戴德梁行

戴德梁行是享誉全球的房地产服务和咨询顾问公司,通过兼具本土洞察与全球视野的房地产解决方案为客户创造卓越价值。

戴德梁行的业务遍布全球 70 多个国家,设有 400 多个办公室,拥有 51 000 名专业员工。在大中华区,我们的 22 家分公司合力引领市场发展,并于 2017 年和

2018 年连续两年蝉联《欧洲货币》综合实力、租赁及销售代理、评估、研究四项中国区年度大奖。2018 年公司营业收入达 82 亿美元,核心业务涵盖物业管理、设施管理、项目管理、租赁代理、资本市场及顾问服务等。

德国阿登纳基金会

阿登纳基金会是亲德国现执政党——基督教民主联盟(简称基民盟或 CDU)的机构。首任德国联邦总理康拉德·阿登纳(Konrad Adenauer,1876—1967)作为基民盟的创建者之一,始终秉承保守、社会和自由的传统。提到阿登纳的名字,人们一定会想到德国战后重建、德国在国际一体化中的外交政策、欧洲联盟倡议和德国的社会市场经济定位等重大问题。由此,其卓越功勋可见一斑。阿登纳基金会的主要合作伙伴有政府机构、政党、民间组织以及各界社会精英等。在基金会目标体系和世界观框架内,基金会不仅致力于推进地区性的和全球化的发展与合作,而且还试图与合作伙伴一道,共同创建一个使每个国家独立自主发展的良性国际秩序。

为更好地促进中德双边关系对话,德国阿登纳基金会于 1996 年和 2001 年在北京和上海分别设立办公室。阿登纳基金会在中国的指导思想是增进中德伙伴之间的理解、推动中欧双边关系对话、促进中德两国之间在学术、经济、科技和社会领域等诸多方面的交流,并期望在中国可持续的改革和融入国际社会的进程中发挥积极作用。阿登纳基金会在由中国和德国政府共同资助的许多项目中扮演着积极的角色。具体而言,阿登纳基金会支持的领域有:

(1) 中德、中欧双边关系对话。

(2) 中德在国际经济事务中的交流与合作。

(3) 介绍德国老龄化社会以及社会保障体系的研究成果并加强中德学者间的学术交流。

(4) 以市场为导向的经济准则的推广。

(5) 城镇化进程中的可持续发展。

(6) 区域间合作与全球化研究。

(7) "一带一路"的研究与展望。

(8) 气候变化与能源研究。

(9) 介绍德国环保的经验与教训。

德国工商大会大中华区

德国工商大会大中华区是德国工商大会分设在全球 92 个国家、140 个海外代表处的一部分。早在 1981 年,德国工商大会大中华区就在台北开设了第一个代表处。设立在大中华区和德国的 5 个主要办公室及 7 个办事处长期致力于中德两国间的投资及经贸往来,并通过商务与投资及会员渠道为 3 100 家会员企业提供全方位的服务。

通过"DEinternational"这个服务品牌,我们不仅成为"引进来"的德国企业以及"走出去"的中国企业的首选合作伙伴,同时还在各个方面为客户提供量身定制的咨询和服务。

德国工商大会有三个组成部分:

(1) 顶层主导——官方代表

分设在北京、上海、广州三地的德国工商大会各代表处,设在香港的德国工商会有限公司以及设在台湾的德国经济办事处是德国工商大会(DIHK)设在大中华区的官方代表。德国工商大会大中华区是一个非政府,不涉及政治利益的公共组织,并代表着德国经济的整体利益。

(2) 会员组织——中国德国商会

设在中国大陆和香港地区的中国德国商会为旗下的 2 900 家会员企业服务。在为会员提供服务与促进双边经贸合作的同时,还代表着其旗下会员企业的利益。

(3) 服务提供——德中工商技术咨询服务有限公司

德中工商技术咨询服务(太仓)有限公司、香港德中工商技术咨询服务有限公司、台湾德国经济办事处是德国商会全球网络在大中华区的服务机构。通过"DEinternational"这个品牌,德中工商技术咨询服务有限公司为德国及中国企业提供广泛的支持和服务。

德勤

德勤是全球最大的专业服务机构之一,拥有超过 170 年的历史。德勤全球的服务网络遍及逾 150 个国家与地区,拥有约 312 000 名专业人士,致力于为客户提供审计及鉴证、管理咨询、风险咨询、财务咨询、税务与商务咨询等领域的全方位专业服务。2019 财年,德勤成员所全球总收入达到 462 亿美元。全球总收入在"四大"中连续多年位居全球第一。自 1917 年进入中国以来,德勤凭借卓越的专业服务,在中国市场建立了独树一帜的品牌形象。德勤中国目前已在中国大陆、香港、澳门等 22 个主要城市设有办公室,有近 16 000 名专业人士,为各行业的客户提供高质量的专业服务。依托至精至善的专业服务和至深至广的行业经验,德勤协助客户把握宝贵商机,应对复杂的商业挑战。我们以专业服务为本,秉持"因我不同"的德勤宗旨,着力打造超越商业需求的更高价值,助力客户、企业、社会成就不凡。

高风咨询公司

高风咨询公司是一家全球专业的战略和管理咨询公司,植根于中国,同时拥有全球视野、能力以及广泛的资源网络。我们为客户解决他们最棘手的问题,亦即在当前快速变化、复杂且不确定性的经营环境之中所出现的战略、组织和管理问题。我们将客户的利益放在最根本和最重要的位置。我们是客观的,我们致力于与客户建立长期的合作关系,而不是单独的项目。我们不仅为我们的客户"构建"问题解决方案,同时亦协助方案的执行与落地,与客户携手合作。我们从最基层到最高级的顾问,都以帮助客户解决难题和并肩合作提升价值为信条。

IBM

IBM 是一家全球整合的信息技术、咨询服务和业务解决方案公司。IBM 公司业务遍及 170 多个国家,运用最先进的信息科技,助力各行各业的客户创造商业价值。同时,IBM 吸引并拥有全球最优秀的人才,助力对客户及整个社会至关重要的事业,致力于让世界更美好。

IBM 的业务涵盖技术与商业领域,始终寻求高价值创新,推动持续改造与转型自身的业务。通过从行业领先的大数据、云、社交移动与认知计算技术、企业级系统和软件、咨询和 IT 服务中形成的产品与整合业务解决方案,为客户创造价值。同时,所有这些方案都汲取着全球最领先的 IBM 研究机构的创新支持。

目前,IBM 致力于推进三大战略——利用大数据推动行业转型、打造竞争优势;利用云计算,重塑企业 IT 架构,推动业务模式变革;以及利用移动和社交技术并依托安全能力构建企业互动参与体系。我们正在为现代 IT 骨干创建一个专注于开放创新的全新系统基础架构,以满足新计算时代前所未有、日新月异的需求。IBM 员工与客户通力合作,利用公司的业务咨询、技术和研发能力构建稳健的系统,以创造动态高效的组织、更便捷的交通、更安全的空气、食品、更清洁的水源和更健康的生活。

2018 年,据财报显示,IBM 的持续运营收入达 796 亿美元。IBM 在美国共申请 9 100 项专利,连续 26 年位居全球排名第一。

凭借在中国超过 30 年的丰富经验,IBM 一直提供领先的技术、卓越的管理和独特的解决方案及服务,帮助推动中国 IT 行业及金融、电信、能源、制造、零售等众多行业的中国企业的创新、转型与发展。

秉承"成就客户""创新为要"和"诚信负责"的核心价值观,IBM 中国的员工致力于将公司打造为行业客户与社会有价值的合作伙伴。

经济学人智库

经济学人智库(EIU)是世界领先的经济和商业研究、预测、分析资源库。EIU成立于 1946 年,为全球各地的企业、政府机构、金融机构和学术组织提供准确、全面的信息。经济学人智库的产品包括旗舰产品"国别报告"服务,提供 195 个国家的政治经济分析,以及供订阅的数据和预测服务组合。并且,该公司还可以根据个别的市场和商业领域来定制研究和分析项目。

EIU 总部设在英国伦敦,在 40 多个城市设有办公室,在全球拥有约 650 名国家专家和分析师。它作为经济学人集团的企业对企业分支独立运作。

凯捷咨询（中国）有限公司

作为咨询、技术服务和数字化转型的全球领先企业,凯捷始终处于创新前沿,在不断发展的云计算、数字化和平台领域,助力所有客户把握机遇、提升竞争力。依托长达 50 余载的丰富行业经验和深厚的专业知识,凯捷通过从战略到运营等一系列服务,助力企业实现伟略。凯捷始终坚信的发展理念是:技术的商业价值源于人,并由人来实现。凯捷是一家具有深厚多元文化底蕴的公司,拥有来自 40 多个国家和地区的超过 211 000 名团队成员。2018 年,集团全球营业收入为 132 亿欧元。

科尔尼公司

科尔尼公司即将成为"百年老店"。科尔尼是一家注册于英国的全球领先的国际管理咨询控股有限公司,始建于 1926 年,拥有近 100 年的历史。目前,科尔尼在全球 40 多个国家的主要商业城市设有 61 个办事处,共有约 4 000 名员工。

科尔尼是最早在大中华区开展业务的咨询公司之一,是中国管理咨询行业的引领者。科尔尼在中国最早的项目可追溯到 20 世纪 80 年代,曾帮助中国外经贸部开展研究项目。1992 年,科尔尼正式建立了在中国的第一个分支机构,并在过去的二十几年中不断扩大在中国的业务布局,广泛的客户群体包括政府机构、跨国企业、国有企业、国内私营企业、投资基金等。目前科尔尼在香港、北京、上海和台北设有办公室。

科尔尼擅长将全球经验与本地知识深度融合。科尔尼的优势在于能够将战略和运营建议付诸有效的实践,是世界上屈指可数的能够提供战略、组织有效性、营运、技术以及实施的综合性咨询服务的公司,擅长整合全球范围内的职能专长和行业经验,从而为客户提供全方位战略及管理咨询服务。重点行业包括政府、汽车、消费品和零售、交通运输、化工、能源/公用事业、经济开发和金融机构等。

科尔尼在区域经济和城市发展领域具有全球洞察力和世界级影响力。科尔尼于 1992 年设立了专业智囊机构"全球商业政策委员会"(GBPC),其成员包含全球政商领袖,提供全球经济发展的地缘政治洞察。GBPC每年都会权威发布全球城市指数(GCI)、外商直接投资信心指数(FDI Index)以及全球化指数(GI)等出版物,被全球主流媒体广泛报道并对企业和组织产生了深远影响。其中,GCI是全球最权威、认可度最高的城市竞争力指数,每年的全球城市指数都会由科尔尼的资深合伙人组织编纂;FDI Index针对外商直接投资目标市场为投资者提供最具前瞻性的视角;GI提供最全面的不同国家全球化程度的比较和评估洞见。

此外,科尔尼拥有超过40年作为世界经济论坛(达沃斯论坛)战略合作伙伴的经验,为全世界最重要的经济议题提出洞见。科尔尼也有幸受到中国政府邀请,成为2016年杭州G20/B20二十国峰会的核心智库。

罗兰贝格管理咨询公司

罗兰贝格管理咨询公司于1967年在欧洲大陆成立,现为全球顶级战略管理咨询公司之一,在全球35个国家设有52家分支机构,拥有2400余名员工,并在国际各大主要市场成功运作。

罗兰贝格是一家由230名合伙人共有的独立咨询机构,为跨国企业、非营利组织和公共机构提供全面的管理解决方案和咨询服务,包括建立战略联盟、引进新的商业模式和流程、构建组织结构和制定信息战略等。

罗兰贝格在全球分别设立了不同的行业中心和功能中心,我们通过有效整合各个功能中心的资源,兼容并蓄来自不同行业的专家能力,为客户量身定制优秀的管理解决方案。

罗兰贝格协同客户一起创制个性化的发展战略。我们认为,在实施阶段为客户提供强有力的支持是非常关键的,它能为客户创造宝贵的价值。因此,我们的工作方式立足于每位咨询顾问的企业家精神和行业专长。罗兰贝格的员工始终秉承公司的三个核心价值理念:创业之基、卓越之范与共赢之道。

罗兰贝格一直把中国视为公司国际化道路中最重要的市场之一。自从1983年在中国开展第一个项目以来,罗兰贝格已经先后在上海、北京、香港、台北和广州开设了办事处,拥有数百名咨询顾问。在长期的发展中,罗兰贝格已经与众多跨国企业及中国企业建立起战略性的合作伙伴关系。

作为全球5大顶级战略管理咨询公司中唯一一家源于欧洲的成员,罗兰贝格咨询的专业性建立在它50余年来与各式各样的客户在复杂商业案例运作中取得的丰富经验之上。卓越的战略分析及在方案实施上的深厚功底是罗兰贝格咨询服务的优势所在。以自己多元化的欧洲背景和丰富的本土经验为依托,罗兰贝格将会运用这种优势,帮助我们的客户在中国应对挑战,取得成功。

麦肯锡公司

麦肯锡是一家全球领先的管理咨询公司,1926年创立于美国,致力于为企业和公共机构提供有关战略、组织、运营和技术方面的咨询,足迹遍布全球60多个国家和地区的120多座城市。麦肯锡在全球范围内的客户包括最知名的企业及机构,占据《财富》全球500强公司排行榜的80%。来到中国内地三十余年来,麦肯锡一直致力于帮助本土领先企业改善管理技能和提升全球竞争力,并为寻求在本地区扩大业务的跨国企业提供咨询,同时也积极参与中国公共政策咨询和公共事业建设。麦肯锡的客户遍及22个行业,包括国家级、地区级及省市级的政府及机构。目前麦肯锡在中国区开设了北京、上海、深圳、香港、台北及成都等六家分公司,共有70名合伙人,500名咨询顾问,还有150名研究员及350名专业人员。

美中贸易全国委员会

美中贸易全国委员会(USCBC)是非政府、无党派的,非营利性机构,拥有200多家在华经营的美国会员公司。自1973年成立以来的四十多年中,美中贸易全国委员会为会员公司提供了大量的信息以及咨询、倡导等服务,并举办了多项活动。通过设在华盛顿的总部以及北京和上海的办事处,美中贸易全国委员会以其独特的定位优势在美、中两地为会员提供服务。

美中贸易全国委员会的使命是扩大美中商务联系,为在华的美资企业提供服务,帮助其发展在华业务,并支持中国的改革开放和经济发展。我们提倡与中国进行建设性的商务联系——共同致力于消除贸易投资壁垒,并为双方营造一个规范、可预测的、透明的商务环境。

在美中贸易全国委员会的会员公司中,既有诸多知名的大型企业,也有相当比例的小型企业和服务业公司。美中贸易全国委员会董事会是委员会的管理机构,由杰出的企业领导人组成。本届董事会主席由安达集团(CHUBB)的董事长兼首席执行官埃文·格林伯格(Evan G. Greenberg)担任。自2018年7月以来,克雷格·艾伦(Craig Allen)任美中贸易全国委员会会长。

长期以来,美中贸易全国委员会接待了中美两国政府诸多的高级官员。近几年来,委员会接待了中国共产党中央委员会总书记、中华人民共和国国家主席习近平,国务院总理李克强,时任国务院副总理王岐山,时任国务院副总理汪洋,以及其他来自中央及地方政府的重要官员。

美中贸易全国委员会在美国和中国多次成功举办会员公司与美国政要的会晤,包括美国前副总统乔·拜登(Joe Biden)、前国务卿希拉里·克林顿(Hillary Clinton)、商务部长威尔伯·罗斯(Wilbur Ross)、前商务部长佩尼·普利茨克

(Penny Pritzker)、财政部长史蒂芬·姆努钦(Steven Mnuchin)、前财政部长蒂莫西·盖特纳(Timothy Geithner)和前财政部长雅各布·卢(Jack Lew)、美国驻华大使特里·布兰斯塔德(Terry Branstad)等重要官员,有影响力的美国国会议员以及众多美国政府行政机构和智库的美中事务专家。

穆迪公司

穆迪是全球资本市场不可或缺的一部分,提供信用评级、研究报告、研究工具及分析,为金融市场的透明度和整体性作出了积极贡献。穆迪公司是穆迪投资者服务公司(MIS)和穆迪分析(Moody's Analytics, MA)的母公司。穆迪投资者服务公司提供债务工具和证券的信用评级与研究报告,穆迪分析则针对信用与经济分析及金融风险管理提供先进的软件、咨询服务和研究报告。穆迪公司 2018 年收入为 44 亿美元,全球员工约 13 100 人,在 42 个国家或地区设有办事处。

普华永道

普华永道拥有全球领先的专业服务网络,最早在英国伦敦成立,历经 160 多年的辉煌历史。如今,普华永道各成员机构组成的网络遍及 157 个国家和地区,有超过 27 万名员工,致力于在审计、税务及咨询领域提供高质量的服务。2018 财年普华永道全球网络收入达到 413 亿美元,基于固定汇率计算,普华永道全球收入增长了 7%。主要市场及各业务条线,受到来自品牌、创新、科技和新兴业务领域投资驱动的影响增长强劲。全球《财富》500 强企业中超过 84% 的企业是普华永道的服务客户。

日本贸易振兴机构

日本贸易振兴机构(JETRO)是促进日本与海外国家和地区间贸易与投资的政府机构。前身"日本贸易振兴会"成立于 1958 年,当时以"振兴出口"为工作重心。进入 21 世纪,工作重心已转向吸引海外国家对日本直接投资以及支持中小企业最大限度地开拓全球市场。2003 年由日本经济产业省的下属特殊法人变更成为独立行政法人日本贸易振兴机构。现在,拥有东京和大阪总部,亚洲经济研究所和 47 个国内事务所,在海外 54 个国家和地区拥有 74 个事务所。现在主要的业务如下:吸引海外企业对日投资;协助日本农林水产品和食品对外出口;协助日本中小和中坚企业开拓海外市场;通过信息提供及调查研究为企业提供商业活动及通商政策。JETRO 在中国的上海、北京、广州、成都、武汉、大连、青岛、香港分别设有代表处。

JETRO 特别支援日本的中坚和中小企业开拓海外市场。根据企业的不同需求，在向企业提供从出口到向海外投资的"全程支援"的同时，为协助海外企业快速解决所面临的问题，在海外具有现地律师、会计等专家提供咨询服务的体制。此外，JETRO还与当地政府协同合作保护知识产权及活用知识产权的商业服务。

深化吸引外国对日本直接投资（FDI）并促进跨境商务合作，FDI带来先进技术、经验及知识产权，这对于复兴日本经济至关重要。JETRO作为国外企业投资日本的最初窗口，也致力于研发及雇用能力充足的行业对日本的投资。针对已进入日本市场的外资企业，也向它们提供扩大地区投资的服务。

JETRO向海外投资的日本企业所面临的商业环境的改善提供意见和建议，通过对海外两国或多国间的经济合作协定（EPA）的形成开展调查研究，为政府间的通商贸易做出贡献。亚洲经济研究所作为国际性的发达国家及发展中国家的研究基地，通过其研究所创造出的高附加值的研究成果，为国内外政策的建言献策贡献力量。

上海美国商会

上海美国商会被称为在华"美国商业之声"，是亚太地区规模最大的美国商会之一。商会成立于1915年，是第三家设立于美国境外的美国商会。上海美国商会致力于自由贸易政策、市场开放、私有企业和信息的自由流通。

上海美国商会的使命是努力通过提供高质量的商务信息与服务，政策游说支持及丰富的商业联系与交流，为会员的成功经营以及美中商贸关系的增进提供支持与帮助。

世界银行

世界银行集团有189个成员国，员工来自170多个国家，在130多个地方设有办事处。世界银行集团是一个独特的全球性合作伙伴，所属五家机构共同致力于寻求在发展中国家减少贫困和建立共享繁荣的可持续之道。

IBRD和IDA共同构成世界银行，向发展中国家政府提供资金、政策咨询和技术援助。IDA的重点是援助世界最贫困国家，IBRD援助中等收入国家和资信良好的较贫困国家。IFC、MIGA和ICSID的重点是加强发展中国家的私营部门。世界银行集团通过这三家机构向私营企业，包括金融机构，提供资金、技术援助、政治风险担保和争端调解服务。

中国与世界银行的合作开始于1980年改革开放之初。中国初期是作为世界银行面向最贫困国家的国际开发协会的受援国，1999年中国从国际开发协会"毕业"，2007年成为国际开发协会的捐款国。2010年，中国在与世界银行合作30周年之际完成增资，成为世行第三大股东国。

30 多年来,为满足中国快速变化的需求,世界银行在华工作的性质也不断做出调整。在早期阶段,世界银行提供技术援助,引进经济改革的基本理念、先进的项目管理方法和新技术。后来,世界银行的工作重点逐渐转向制度建设和知识转让。目前,世界银行主张知识分享,帮助其他国家学习中国的经验。

印度工业联合会

印度工业联合会(CII)致力于通过咨询和顾问服务,联合产业界、政府部门和社会团体的共同力量,创建和维持一个有利于印度工业发展的理想环境。

印度工业联合会是一个非政府、非营利性的行业领导机构,由印度工业界自主领导和管理,对于印度经济的繁荣和发展起到了积极的推进作用。印度工业联合会成立于 1895 年,是目前印度最重要的商业协会。它拥有超过 9 100 家的直属成员机构,涵盖国有及私有性质的各大中小型企业和跨国公司。此外,通过 291 个全国性和地区性的行业协会,联合会更是与 300 000 多家间接会员保持着紧密联系。

长期以来,印度工业联合会始终与政府部门保持紧密协作,共同探讨政策事宜,并通过一系列的专业服务及遍布全球的战略合作网络,帮助印度产业界对话思想领袖、改善绩效、提升竞争力、拓展商业契机,以此来推进创新与变革。与此同时,它还为印度产业界提供了一个有利于构建行业共识和拓展业务网络的高效平台。

印度工业联合会始终强调树立企业的正面形象,并积极协助各个工业企业制定和执行企业形象战略规划。它与民间社会机构建立了战略伙伴关系,共同推进印度在平权法案、医疗保健、教育、民生、多元化管理、技能发展、妇女权益和水资源等各项领域的一体化、综合性发展。

印度工业联合会在印度设有 68 个办事处,其中包括 9 家卓越中心(Centers of Excellence)。此外,印度工业联合会还拥有 11 家海外办事处,分别位于澳大利亚、中国、埃及、法国、德国、印度尼西亚、新加坡、南非、阿联酋、英国和美国,以及遍布 133 个国家的 394 家合作机构。今天,它已成为印度产业界与国际商业界之间重要的枢纽机构。

株式会社野村综合研究所

株式会社野村综合研究所(NRI)是起源于亚洲规模最大的智库之一,成立于 1965 年,1988 年成为全球首家集智库、咨询和系统集成功能为一体的企业,2001 年在东京证券交易所主板上市。目前,NRI 集团拥有 10 000 多名专业人员,年营业额超过 35 亿美元,是亚洲最大的咨询集团。

NRI 研究领域覆盖各主要产业,每年持续向各国政府及大型企业提供全方位的服务,迄今已在超过 5 000 个对象领域(产业×课题)上,执行了累计超过 2 万个项目。

NRI 在大中华地区的上海、北京、大连、香港和台北设有独立的业务公司,拥有 1 000 多名专业人员。NRI 自 1989 年开始在中国大陆开展面向中国政府和中国企业的研究及咨询业务,于 2002 年在上海成立野村综研(上海)咨询有限公司(NRI 上海),2009 年设立北京分公司。目前 NRI 上海是 NRI 在中国大陆的咨询业务总部,业务涵盖面向中国各级政府机构的公共发展战略咨询、面向全球企业及中国企业的管理咨询。

NRI 秉持集"调查研究、经营顾问、运营管理"为一体的企业发展理念,以踏实的工作作风和对亚洲文化的深刻理解著称,在日本本土和中国大陆都享有很好的口碑。

中国欧盟商会上海分会

中国欧盟商会由 51 家会员企业于 2000 年成立,代表欧盟不同行业在华企业的共同声音。中国欧盟商会是一个在会员指导下开展工作的,独立的非营利性机构,其核心结构是代表欧盟在华企业的 31 个工作组和论坛。欧盟商会作为在华欧洲企业的独立官方代言机构,得到了欧盟委员会和中国政府的一致认可。

中国欧盟商会上海分会成立于 2002 年,在会员企业数量上是目前欧盟商会最大的分会。上海分会现有 21 个活跃的工作组,三个论坛以及三个行业项目,如独立(汽车)售后市场工作组,欧洲供热子工作组等。上海分会与地方政府各个部门都有紧密联系,包括与上海市发改委、上海市商务委员会、上海海关的定期深层对话。

仲量联行

仲量联行(JLL)是全球领先的房地产专业服务和投资管理公司。我们始终致力于房地产领域的持续创新;不断创造机遇,打造理想空间,实现价值回报以成就商业及个人愿景,从而为我们的客户、员工和社会创建一个更美好的明天。仲量联行是《财富》500 强企业,截至 2019 年 6 月 30 日,仲量联行业务遍及全球 80 多个国家,员工总数超过 92 000 人, 2018 财政年度收入达 163 亿美元。JLL 是仲量联行的品牌名称以及注册商标。

仲量联行在亚太地区开展业务超过 50 年。公司目前在亚太地区的 16 个国家拥有 82 个分公司,员工总数超过 41 400 人。在"2018 年国际物业奖"评选中,仲量联行荣膺"全球最佳房地产咨询公司"和"亚太区最佳房地产咨询公司"。

在大中华区,仲量联行目前拥有超过 2 580 名专业人员及 17 930 名驻场员工,所提供的专业房地产服务遍及全国 80 多个城市。在"2018 年国际物业奖"评选中,仲量联行再度荣膺"中国最佳房地产咨询公司",连续八年获此殊荣。

Organizers and Participants of the 2019 Shanghai International Think Tank Summit

---

1. Host

The Development Research Centre of Shanghai Municipal People's Government

The Development Research Centre of Shanghai Municipal People's Government (SDRC) was formerly known as Shanghai Center for Economic Research (SCER) which was founded on Dec. 26th, 1980, and was renamed by SDRC on Dec. 22nd, 1995. SDRC is a decision-making research institution led by Shanghai Municipal People's Government, providing comprehensive consulting services with the functions of organizing, coordinating and managing the government research projects.

Main functions:

(1) Study on the overall and strategic issues concerning Shanghai economy, social development, reform and opening-up.

(2) Trace the dynamic trends, analyze the inconsistency, study the countermeasures and forecast the prospects, submit decision-making proposals and consulting advices to the CPC Shanghai Committee and the Shanghai Municipal People's Government in due course.

(3) Organize the assessment of the decision-making and consulting research results as well as the appraisal of the distinguished research achievements once every two years.

(4) Organize and coordinate the decision-making and consulting research work within the government system.

(5) Conduct the information maintenance work of the Shanghai Decision-making and Consulting Proposals System.

(6) Administrate the related organizations and institutions entrusted by the Shanghai Municipal People's Government.

(7) Compile and publish *Shanghai Economy Almanac* and *Journal of Scientific Development*.

(8) Undertake other missions assigned by the leaders of the Shanghai Municipality.

2. Supporters

Yangtze River Delta Regional Cooperation Office

The Yangtze River Delta Regional Cooperation Office was established jointly by Shanghai Municipality, and Jiangsu, Zhejiang, Anhui provinces with its office in Shanghai in January 2018. Director of the Office is concurrently Director of Shanghai Development and Reform Commission and the staff is selected within the municipality and three provinces. The Yangtze River Delta Regional Cooperation Office serves as a platform and enforcement institute in promoting high-quality integration of the Delta Region, which is responsible for the organization and research of major issues regarding the integrated development of the Yangtze River Delta. Also, it takes the lead in programming, planning, coordination, supervision and inspection of cooperation in key areas as well as in the holding of major leaders' symposiums and joint conferences on cooperation and development of the Yangtze River Delta. The Yangtze River Delta Regional Cooperation Office plays an important role in such aspects as trans-provincial-level information communication, joint operation and resource coordination.

Eastday · Oriental Think Tank

Founded on May 28, 2000, Eastday is one of the national key news websites and a new mainstream media company in Shanghai which offers three versions in Chinese, English and Japanese. Through PC and mobile platforms such as news apps (eg: Aoxiang and Dongfang Toutiao), Weibo and Wechat, Eastday has constructed an all-media communication system and has become increasingly influential.

After being restructured in March 2012, Eastday is now held by the Shanghai Municipal State-owned Assets Supervision and Administration Commission with a registered capital of 997 million yuan. In December 2015, it was officially listed on the NEEQ (National Equities Exchange and Quotations). Since its establishment, Eastday has made profits in all financial years, achieving both social and economic benefits.

With the guidance of the central government and the municipal administrative authorities, Eastday is now ramping up its effort to achieve the goal of establishing "a new mainstream media company with the business mode of news + government affairs + service led by sci-tech innovation" under the development principles of specialization, marketization and capitalization, so as to build itself into one of China's most influential mainstream Internet-based media companies with modern communication characteristics and a publicly listed Internet culture company.

Established in 2018, Oriental Think Tank, sponsored by Eastday —a new mainstream media company in Shanghai, is the city's first media-based think tank that serves as a platform to study, interpret, share and exchange opinions towards international issues. With the purpose of "building a compatible, credible and diversified friend circle on international issues" and the orientation of "focusing on current issues, basing itself upon the central standard, explaining the ins and outs and evaluating the essence of events", Oriental Think Tank is described as the "voice generator" and "reception hall" in the field of think tank on international issues in Shanghai.

Based on Shanghai's condition, Oriental Think Tank gathers together opinion leaders, political and business elites and eminent scholars in the field of international issues at home and abroad, focusing on such hotspot issues as Sino-foreign relations and China's foreign policy, international political and economical situations, global governance and country studies, public diplomacy and Belt and Road Initiative from the perspective of globalization and through the communication channel of media convergence. Oriental Think Tank has built up a combined platform of references for societal decision-making, dissemination of integrated opinions and cooperation of production, teaching and research in communities with a view to improving quality and transparency of the interpretation and communication of international issues as well as promoting diversified and smooth exchange of global opinions and ideas.

The expert committee of Oriental Think Tank is led by Zhou Xisheng, former Vice President of Xinhua News Agency, which brings together dozens of experts, scholars and opinion leaders from the Central Foreign Affairs Office, the Ministry of Foreign Affairs, the International Department Central Committee of CPC, Xinhua News agency, the Party School of the CPC Central Committee, Shanghai Academy of Social Sciences, Shanghai Institutes for International Studies, Fudan University, Southeast University and Shanghai International Studies University. At the same time, Oriental Think Tank has also formed a regular linkage and cooperation mechanism with Shanghai Institutes for International Studies, Institute of International Relations, SASS, the Development Research Center of Shanghai Municipal People's Government, Shanghai International Cultural Association and Shanghai Academy for Global Governance and Area Studies.

3. Organizers

Shanghai International Think Tank Exchange Center

Shanghai International Think Tank Exchange Center is one of the open and public decision-making and consulting research platforms, set up by the Development Research Center of Shanghai Municipal People's Government

(SDRC). In 2010, SDRC, as required by the then Mayor Han Zheng proactively made contact with thirteen world-renowned think tanks in Shanghai like Accenture, Capgemini, Deloitte and IBM, aiming to further Shanghai's decision making and consulting research by drawing on the wisdom of experts and scholars from home and abroad to enable the CPC Shanghai Committee and Shanghai Municipal People's Government to do decision-making in a more democratic and scientific way and constantly expand the influence of SDRC in the world. In January, 2011, the center was established and the first "Shanghai Intelligent Forum" with the theme "Innovation, Transformation and Development". Mr. Han Zheng, the then Shanghai Mayor, sent his message of congratulation and Mr. Jiang Ping, the then Secretary General of Shanghai Municipal People's Government, attended the forum and delivered an address.

The main responsibilities for the Shanghai International Think Tank Exchange Center are as follows:

(1) To conduct decision-making research for the government.

(2) To provide application research, business planning, managerial consulting services for enterprises.

(3) To organize international bilateral and multilateral corporation seminar.

(4) To study international cooperation and exchanges subjects.

(5) To provide development, training and information services for professionals.

For the past few years, the Shanghai International Think Tank Exchange Center has conducted plenty of international cooperation researches with focus on the economic and social development of Shanghai by taking advantage of talents, resources and information, jointly with the public decision-making consulting research platforms of experts, workshops, social surveys, research projects and college forums. Until now, the Shanghai International Think Tank Exchanges Center has held bilateral forums for 18 times, "Shanghai Intelligent Forum" for 5 times and fifth "Shanghai International Think Tank Summit", which effectively improves the function and role of the Development Research Center of Shanghai Municipal People's Government in integrating the think tank resources at the national level, and provides lots of advices and suggestions to the CPC Shanghai Committee and the Shanghai Municipal People's Government from leading think tanks at home and abroad.

KPMG

KPMG is a leading firm in our business. KPMG has 207,000 professionals in 153 countries and regions, providing audit, tax and consulting services. Our network is a strong alliance of qualified professionals. The independent member firms of the KPMG network are associated with the Swiss entity KPMG International Cooperation ("KPMG international"). KPMG member firms are legally independent and separate legal entities. KPMG has a unified team with global experience and local/regional knowledge. Through working together and knowing each other, we resolve complex issues quickly.

Our Hong Kong office can trace its origins to 1945. In 1992, KPMG became the first international accounting network to be granted a joint venture license in Chinese mainland. As of 1 August 2012, KPMG China was the first among the Big Four in Chinese mainland to convert from a joint venture to a special general partnership. By the end of September 2019, KPMG China set up 23 offices in 21 cities, and has more than 12,000 partners and staff.

KPMG teams work with local Chinese management of global leaders and the management of emerging companies and start-ups. We aim to add more business value for the benefit of our clients. Integration is key to delivering leading services to our clients. Specifically speaking, our professionals from different service lines, i.e. Audit, Tax, and Advisory are working together. They have intimate industry/sector knowledge. They are able to help our clients tackle industry issues and risks.

Our excellent reputation and quality service has helped to establish KPMG as one of the largest audit, tax and advisory firm in China. KPMG offices are located close to our clients. KPMG benefits from a single management structure across Chinese mainland, Hong Kong and Macau. This enables efficient and rapid deployment of resources wherever the client is located and allows us to effectively serve companies across the country.

Shanghai Development Research Foundation (SDRF)

SDRF was established in 1993 as a non-profit organization, aiming at development research and decision-making consultations. Over the past decades, we have gained high recognitions in academic circles, by establishing high-level platforms for exchanges of views, conducting deep research on development issues and providing constructive decision-making consultations to Chinese governments.

SDRF Newsletter will constantly compile the essential contents of our conferences and research work into brief reports. We wish to further spread the achievements of research and discussion on the development issues, and look forward your feedbacks.

The activities we hold as platforms:

(1) Monthly "Shanghai Development Salon"

Well-known experts are invited to make speeches on hotspot topics, and participants from various circles are encouraged to share their opinions. Over the past 10 years from 2005, the salon has obtained great popularity and reputation.

(2) Yearly forums on World and Chinese Economy

Forums on World and Chinese Economy are held twice a year. They are organized to make a real-time analysis of the economic performances in China and the world in the year, as well as to predict the economic trends of the coming year.

(3) High-level International symposiums

Several high-level symposiums are held every year, which invite honored scholars from home and abroad to present their views around some important of macro-economy and international finance, such as global financial governance, international financial architecture, and global economic growth, etc.

The Research work we devote to:

Our research focuses on the issues of macro-economy and international finance, such as the reform of international monetary system, RMB internationalization, the regulation of cross-border capital flows, and further enhancing the role of SDR, etc. Several books and pamphlets on these have been published.

The main board members of SDRF are Mr. Hu Yanzhao (Chairman of SDRF and the Former Deputy Mayor of Shanghai), Mr. Wang Ronghua (Deputy Chairman of SDRF and the Former Deputy Chairman of Shanghai CPPCC), and Mr. Zhan Wang (Deputy Chairman of SDRF and the President of Shanghai Academy of Social Sciences), Mr. Zhang Liping (Deputy Chairman of SDRF and Former Chairman of Shanghai Guosheng (Group) Co., Ltd), and Mr. Qiao Yide (Deputy Chairman and Secretary General of SDRF).

4. Participants (in alphabetical order)

EY

At EY, we are committed to building a better working world-with increased trust and confidence in business, sustainable growth, the development of talent in all its forms, and greater collaboration. EY wants to build a better working world through actions and by engaging with like-minded organizations and individuals. This is our purpose-and why EY exists as an organization. Globalization is shaping our world: it is expanding horizons as trade, technology and investment increasingly connect countries and companies around the globe; and it is compressing time and distance as people and products move-and ideas spread-faster than ever before. To ensure we are efficient and effective, the EY network is organized into 26 business units, called Regions, in terms of both people and revenues. EY, with over 700 office locations in over 150 countries rigions are grouped under three geographic areas: Americas; Europe, Middle East, India and Africa

(EMEIA); and Asia-Pacific. This structure is streamlined-it allows EY to make decisions quickly, and promotes the execution of EY strategy and the provision of exceptional client service wherever in the world EY clients do business.

In the Greater China Region, the EY network brings together practices in China (Chinese mainland, Hong Kong, Macau, Taiwan) and also Mongolia, making EY an integrated professional services network. Meanwhile, EY, one of the largest professional services organizations in Greater China, has been present in the region for 50 years and in that time EY has achieved many major milestones: opening the first Hong Kong member firm office in 1968 as Arthur Young and in 1981, being one of the first international organizations to establish operations in Chinese mainland.

EY is able to support you through the member firms' 27 offices in EY Greater China Region: Beijing, Hong Kong, Shanghai, Guangzhou, Macau, Shenzhen, Chengdu, Hangzhou, Nanjing, Shenyang, Suzhou, Tianjin, Wuhan, Xi'an, Changsha, Dalian, Qingdao, Xiamen, Zhengzhou and Haikou. In Taiwan, EY offices are located in Taipei, Taoyuan, Hsinchu, Taichung, Tainan and Kaohsiung-and in Mongolia the EY member firm's office is located in Ulaanbaatar.

With 16,000 professionals in Greater China, EY is committed to bringing together the right people, at the right time, and in the right place to give you the seamless, high-quality service you need. That is how we make a difference.

Bain & Company

We're a global consultancy that helps the world's most ambitious change makers define the future. Across 58 offices in the world, we work alongside our clients as one team with a shared ambition to achieve extraordinary results, outperform the competition and redefine industries. We complement our tailored, integrated expertise with a vibrant ecosystem of digital innovators to deliver better, faster and more enduring outcomes.

Boston Consulting Group

Boston Consulting Group partners with leaders in business and society to tackle their most important challenges and capture their greatest opportunities. BCG was the pioneer in business strategy when it was founded in 1963. Today, we help clients with total transformation — inspiring complex change, enabling organizations to grow, building competitive advantage, and driving bottom-line impact.

To succeed, organizations must blend digital and human capabilities. Our diverse, global teams bring deep industry and functional expertise and a range of perspectives to spark change. BCG delivers solutions through leading-edge management consulting along with technology and design, corporate and digital ventures—and business purpose. We work in a uniquely collaborative model across the firm and throughout all levels of the client organization, generating results that allow our clients to thrive.

Cushman & Wakefield

Cushman & Wakefield is a leading global real estate services firm that delivers exceptional value for real estate occupiers and owners.

Cushman & Wakefield is among the largest real estate services firms with 51,000 employees in approximately 400 offices and 70 countries. Across Greater China, there are 22 offices servicing the local market. The company won four of the top awards in the Euromoney Survey 2017 and 2018 in the categories of Overall, Agency Letting/Sales, Valuation and Research in China. In 2018, the firm had revenue of $8.2 billion across core services of property, facilities and project management, leasing, capital markets, valuation and other services.

Konrad-Adenauer-Stiftung

The Konrad-Adenauer-Stiftung (KAS) is a political foundation, closely associated with the Christian Democratic Union of Germany (CDU). As co-founder of the CDU and the first Chancellor of the Federal Republic of Germany, Konrad Adenauer (1876–1967) united Christian-social, conservative and liberal traditions. We cooperate with governmental institutions, political parties, civil society organizations and handpicked elites, building strong partnerships along the way. In particular we seek to intensify political cooperation in the area of development cooperation at the national and international levels on the foundations of our objectives and values. Together with our partners we make a contribution to the creation of an international order that enables every country to develop under its own responsibility.

In order to better promote the Sino-German bilateral dialogue, the Konrad Adenauer Foundation established Representative offices in Beijing and Shanghai in 1996 and 2001. The Adenauer Foundation's guiding ideology in China is to enhance understanding between Chinese and German partners, promote dialogue between China and the EU on bilateral relations, and promote exchanges between China and Germany in the academic, economic, scientific, and social fields. China plays an active role in the process of sustainable reform and integration into the international community. The Adenauer Foundation plays an active role in many projects co-financed by the Chinese and German governments. Specifically, the areas we support are:

- Intensifying the dialogue between Germany/ Europe and China
- Integrating China into the global economy
- Introducing the research results of the German aging society and social security system and strengthening the academic exchanges between Chinese and German scholars
- Promotion of market-oriented economic criteria
- Sustainable development in the process of urbanization
- Interregional cooperation and globalization research
- Research and Prospects of the Belt and Road Initiative
- Climate Change and Energy Research
- Introducing German environmental protection experiences.

AHK Greater China

AHK Greater China is part of the German Chambers of Commerce Worldwide Network (AHK) which includes 140 offices in 92 countries. The AHK's history in Greater China stretches back to 1981, when the first office was opened in Taipei. With our five main offices and seven supporting offices in Greater China and Germany, we focus on trade and investment between these two regions. We also support our 3,100 members' business interests through the comprehensive services provided by our business and investment, and membership platforms.

Under the brand DEinternational, our organization is not only the first contact point for German companies deciding to enter the Chinese market and for Chinese companies entering the German market, but also a provider of a wide range of customized advice and services.

Three Branches:

1. Umbrella Organisation-Official Representation-The Delegation of German Industry & Commerce

The Delegations of German Industry & Commerce in Beijing, Shanghai and Guangzhou, German Industry & Commerce Ltd. in Hong Kong, and German Trade Office Taipei officially represent the Association of German Chambers of Industry & Commerce in Greater China. The Association is a non-governmental, non-politically affiliated association with a public mandate to represent the overall economic interests of Germany in its host countries.

2. The Member Organization- The German Chamber of Commerce in China

The German Chambers in Chinese Mainland and Hong Kong cater to the needs of over 2,900 members. They represent the interests of their members, provide services, and work to promote bilateral economic cooperation.

3. The Service Provider-German Industry & Commerce

German Industry & Commerce (Taicang) Ltd. for Chinese Mainland, German Industry & Commerce Ltd. for Hong Kong and DEinternational Taiwan Ltd. are the service branches of the German Chamber Network in

Greater China. Under the brand DEinternational, German Industry & Commerce (GIC) offers a wide range of services to German and local companies to support their businesses.

Deloitte

Deloitte is one of the largest professional services firm globally with a history of more than 170 years. Deloitte employs approximately 312,000 professionals in more than 150 countries and territories, providing a full range of professional services including audit & assurance, consulting, risk advisory, financial advisory, and tax & business advisory. Our aggregate member firm revenue was USD 46.2 billion in FY2019, maintaining first place among the "Big Four" for several consecutive years. Since the inception of our China firm in 1917, Deloitte's professional services practice has established its reputation as a force to reckon with in the China market. With 22 offices and approximately 16,000 professionals across the Chinese Mainland, Hong Kong and Macau, Deloitte China network provides high quality professional services for clients spanning multiple industries. Deloitte is committed to helping clients navigate business opportunities and complex challenges with best-in-class professional services and extensive industry expertise. By leveraging professional services offerings, we seek to create value beyond clients' business needs and make an impact that matters for clients, businesses and the society.

Gao Feng Advisory Company

Gao Feng Advisory Company is a professional strategy and management consulting firm with roots in China coupled with global vision, capabilities, and a broad resources network. We help our clients address and solve their toughest business and management issues-issues that arise in the current fast-changing, complicated and ambiguous operating environment.

We commit to putting our clients' interest first and foremost. We are objective and we view our client engagements as long-term relationships rather than one-off projects. We not only help our clients "formulate" the solutions but also assist in implementation, often hand-in-hand. We believe in teaming and working together to add value and contribute to problem solving for our clients, from the most junior to the most senior.

IBM

IBM is a globally integrated technology and consulting company headquartered in Armonk, New York. With operations in more than 170 countries, IBM attracts and retains some of the world's most talented people to help solve problems and provide an edge for businesses, governments and non-profits.

Innovation is at the core of IBM's strategy. The company develops and sells software and systems hardware and a broad range of infrastructure, cloud and consulting services.

Today, IBM is focused on four growth initiatives-business analytics, cloud computing, growth markets and Smarter Planet.IBMers are working with customers around the world to apply the company's business consulting, technology and R&D expertise to build systems that enable dynamic and efficient organizations, better transportation, safer food, cleaner water and healthier populations.

Our values as IBMers shape everything we do, every choice we make on behalf of this company. Having a shared set of values helps us make decisions and, in the process, makes our company great. But their real influence occurs when we apply these values to our personal work and our interactions with one another and the wider world. IBMers determined that our actions will be driven by these values:

— Dedication to every client's success;

— Innovation that matters, for our company and for the world;

— Trust and personal responsibility in all relationships.

IBM is unique. It is the only company in our industry that has reinvented itself through multiple technology eras and economic cycles. We do so for one reason: to create differentiating value for our clients and for you, our owners.

We are doing so again, in an IT industry that is fundamentally reordering at an unprecedented pace.

In important ways, our industry is unrecognizable from what it looked like just a few years ago. So is your company. Today, IBM is much more than a "hardware, software, services" company. IBM is now emerging as a cognitive solutions and cloud platform company.

Economist Intelligence Unit

The Economist Intelligence Unit (The EIU) is the world's leading resource for economic and business research, forecasting and analysis. It provides accurate and impartial intelligence for companies, government agencies, financial institutions and academic organisations around the globe, inspiring business leaders to act with confidence since 1946. The EIU products include its flagship Country Reports service, providing political and economic analysis for 195 countries, and a portfolio of subscription-based data and forecasting services. The company also undertakes bespoke research and analysis projects on individual markets and business sectors.

The EIU is headquartered in London, UK, with offices in more than 40 cities and a network of some 650 country experts and analysts worldwide. It operates independently as the business-to-business arm of The Economist Group.

Capgemini

A global leader in consulting, technology services and digital transformation, Capgemini is at the forefront of innovation to address the entire breadth of clients' opportunities in the evolving world of cloud, digital and platforms. Building on its strong 50-year heritage and deep industry-specific expertise, Capgemini enables organizations to realize their business ambitions through an array of services from strategy to operations. Capgemini is driven by the conviction that the business value of technology comes from and through people. It is a multicultural company of over 211,000 team members in more than 40 countries. The Group reported 2018 global revenues of EUR 13.2 billion.

A.T. Kearney

A. T. Kearney is a leading global management consulting company registered in UK. It was founded in 1926 and has a history of nearly 100 years. Currently, A.T. Kearney has 61 offices in major commercial cities in more than 40 countries around the world, with approximately 4, 000 employees.

A. T. Kearney is one of the first consulting companies to conduct business in Greater China and is a leader in China's management consulting industry. A.T. Kearney's earliest projects in China date back to the 1980s and helped the Ministry of Foreign Trade and Economics to carry out research projects. In 1992, A. T. Kearney officially established its first branch in China, and has expanded its business presence in China over the past two decades. The broad customer base includes government agencies, multinational corporations, state-owned enterprises, and domestic private enterprises, investment funds, etc. Currently A.T. Kearney has offices in Hong Kong, Beijing, Shanghai and Taipei.

A. T. Kearney is good at integrating global experience with local knowledge. A.T. Kearney's strength lies in its ability to put strategic and operational advice into effective practice. It is one of the world's leading companies that provides comprehensive consulting services for strategy, organizational effectiveness, operations, technology and implementation. A. T. Kearney has extensive functional expertise and industry experience worldwide to provide clients with a full range of strategic and management consulting services. Key industries include government, automotive, consumer goods and retail, transportation, chemicals, energy/utilities, economic development and financial institutions.

A.T. Kearney has global insight and world-class influence in regional economics and urban development. In 1992, A.T. Kearney established the Global Business Policy Committee (GBPC), a professional think-tank, whose members include global political and business leaders and provides geopolitical insights into global economic development. Every year, GBPC publishes publications such as the Global Cities Index (GCI), the Foreign Direct Investment Confidence Index (FDI Index), and the Globalization Index (GI). Among them, GCI is the most authoritative and recognized city competitiveness index in the world. The annual Global Cities Index is compiled by A.T. Kearney's senior partners; FDI Index provides investors with the most forward-looking perspectives for foreign direct investment target market; GI provides the most comprehensive comparison and assessment insights on the degree of globalization in different countries.

In addition, A.T. Kearney has more than 40 years of experience as a Strategic Partner of the World Economic Forum (Davos Forum), providing insights on the world's most important economic issues. A.T. Kearney was also fortunate to be invited by the Chinese government to become the core think tank of the 2016 G20/B20 Hangzhou Summit.

Roland Berger

Roland Berger, founded in 1967, is one of the world's leading strategy consultancies. With 52 offices in 35 countries and over 2,400 employees, the company has successful operations in all major international markets. The strategy consultancy is an independent partnership exclusively owned by about 230 Partners.

Roland Berger supports leading international corporations, non-profit organizations and public institutions in all management issues - ranging from strategic alignment and introducing new business models and processes to organizational structures and IT strategy. Roland Berger is based on global Competence Centers that are organized along functional and industry lines. This allows us to offer tailor-made solutions devised by our interdisciplinary teams of experts drawn from different Competence Centers.

At Roland Berger we develop customized, creative strategies together with our clients. Providing support in the implementation phase is particularly important to us. In so doing, we create value for our clients. That's why our approach is based on the entrepreneurial character and individuality of our consultants. All employees at Roland Berger strive to adhere to our three core values: entrepreneurship, excellence and empathy.

The Chinese market is a key pillar of Roland Berger's international expansion. Since our first project in China in 1983, the consultancy has grown rapidly: The five Chinese offices (Shanghai, Beijing, Hong Kong, Taipei and Guangzhou) now have hundreds of consultants dedicated to working extensively with both leading Chinese and international companies.

As the only consulting firm of European origin among the global Top 5, Roland Berger has built its expertise on its extensive experience working with clients on complex business cases for over 50 years. Outstanding strategic analysis and in-depth knowledge on implementation measures are the strengths of the company's consulting approach. Roland Berger consultants combine their analytical and strategic know-how within a diverse company setting to help clients in Greater China successfully master their unique challenges.

McKinsey & Company

McKinsey & Company is the leading global management consulting firm and by far the largest global management consulting firm in Greater China. Globally, we are the trusted advisor and counselor to many of the most influential businesses and institutions in the world. We serve more than 80 percent of Fortune magazine's list of the Most Admired Companies. In Greater China, we advise clients in over 22 different industry sectors, and work with dozens of government agencies and institutions at the national, regional and municipal levels. Our primary mission is to help our clients achieve substantial and enduring impact by tackling their biggest issues concerning strategy, operations, organization, technology and finance. Today we have more than 500 consultants and over 70 Partners located across four locations in Greater China region: Beijing, Shanghai, Hong Kong, Taipei and Chengdu. They are supported by more than 150 research professionals, and over 350 professional support staff.

US-China Business Council

The US-China Business Council (USCBC) is a private, nonpartisan, nonprofit organization of approximately 200 American companies that do business with China. Founded in 1973, USCBC has provided unmatched information, advisory, advocacy, and program services to its members for over four decades. Through its offices in Washington, DC, Beijing, and Shanghai, USCBC is uniquely positioned to serve its members' interests in the United States and China.

USCBC's mission is to expand the US-China commercial relationship to the benefit of its membership and, more broadly, the US economy. It favors constructive, results-oriented engagement with China to eliminate trade and investment barriers and develop a rules-based commercial environment that is predictable and transparent to all parties.

Among USCBC's members are many large and well-known US corporations, but smaller companies and professional services firms make up a substantial portion of the overall membership. USCBC is governed by a board of directors composed of distinguished corporate leaders; the current chair is Evan Greenberg, chairman and CEO of Chubb. Craig Allen has been USCBC's president since July of 2018.

In recent years, USCBC has been honored to host events for Chinese Communist Party (CCP) General Secretary and President Xi Jinping, Premier Li Keqiang, then-Vice President Wang Qishan, then-Vice Premier Wang Yang, ministers and other distinguished guests from central and provincial Chinese government entities.

USCBC has organized events and meetings featuring: former Vice President Joe Biden, Secretary of State Hillary Clinton, Treasury Secretaries Timothy Geithner, Jacob Lew, and Steven Mnuchin, Commerce Secretaries Penny Pritzker and Wilbur Ross, Chinese Ambassador to the US Cui Tiankai, US Ambassador to China Terry Branstad, the former Prime Minister of Australia Kevin Rudd, and other senior officials. In addition, USCBC also regularly meets with key members of Congress and numerous specialists on US-China affairs from various agencies of the executive branch of government and the think tank community.

Moody's

Moody's is an essential component of the global capital markets, providing credit ratings, research, tools and analysis that contribute to transparent and integrated financial markets. Moody's Corporation is the parent company of Moody's Investors Service, which provides credit ratings and research covering debt instruments and securities, and Moody's Analytics, which offers leading-edge software, advisory services and research for credit and economic analysis and financial risk management. The Corporation, which reported revenue of $4.4 billion in 2018, employs approximately 13,100 people worldwide and maintains a presence in 42 countries.

PwC

At PwC, our purpose is to build trust in society and solve important problems. We're a network of firms in 157 countries with more than 27,000 people who are committed to delivering quality in assurance, advisory and tax services. In fiscal year 2018, PwC global network revenue reached $41.3 billion that grew by 7%. The major markets and business lines are strongly driven by investment from brand, innovation, technology and emerging business sectors. Over 84% of the Fortune 500 companies in the world are PwC's clients.

We provide organizations with the professional service they need, wherever they may be located. Our highly qualified, experienced professionals listen to different points of view to help organizations solve their business issues and identify and maximize the opportunities they seek. Our industry specialization allows us to help co-create solutions with our clients for their sector of interest.

JETRO

The Japan External Trade Organization (JETRO) is a government-related organization that works to promote mutual trade and investment between Japan and the rest of the world. Originally established in 1958 to promote Japanese exports abroad, JETRO's core focus in the 21st century has shifted toward promoting foreign direct investment into Japan and helping small to medium size Japanese firms maximize their global export potential. JETRO has 74 overseas offices in 54 countries worldwide, as well as 8 offices in China, including Shanghai, Beijing, Guangzhou, Chengdu, Wuhan, Dalian, Qingdao and Hong Kong, 47 offices in Japan, including Tokyo and Osaka headquarters.

Helping Japanese firms, especially SMEs, expand business overseas. To help businesses enter or expand into overseas markets, JETRO provides a wealth of support and services, from advice on legal and tax matters to helping firms understand relevant economic partnership agreements (EPAs). JETRO also helps firms with business-related difficulties in these foreign markets, including working with local governments to seek improved intellectual property protection for their products.

Working to further boost foreign direct investment (FDI) in Japan and promote cross-border business tie-ups. FDI, which brings with it advanced technologies, know-how and intellectual assets, has become increasingly important to Japan, helping revitalize the country's economy and keeping Japan at the forefront of the global economy. Facilitating international business and technology partnerships between Japanese and foreign firms in high-tech fields is another important activity for us.

JETRO also continues to carry out economic research overseas and collect extensive information for dissemination to business circles. IDE conducts extensive studies of developing economies. JETRO provides a variety of other valuable services and support as well, including the organization of exhibitions and trade fairs and the dispatch of international trade and investment missions. Through these efforts, JETRO hopes to do its part in helping Japan maintain its role as a reliable member of the global economy.

AmCham Shanghai

The American Chamber of Commerce in Shanghai (AmCham Shanghai), known as the "Voice of American Business" in China, is one of the largest American Chambers in the Asia Pacific region. Founded in 1915, AmCham Shanghai was the third American Chamber established outside the United States. As a non-profit, non-partisan business organization, AmCham Shanghai is committed to the principles of free trade, open markets, private enterprise and the unrestricted flow of information.

AmCham Shanghai's mission is to enable the success of its members and strengthen U.S.-China commercial ties through its role as a not-for-profit service provider of high quality business resources and support, policy advocacy, and relationship-building opportunities.

The World Bank

With 189 member countries, staff from more than 170 countries and offices in over 130 locations, the World Bank Group is a unique global partnership: five institutions working for sustainable solutions that reduce poverty and build shared prosperity in developing countries.

Together, IBRD and IDA form the World Bank, which provides financing, policy advice, and technical assistance to governments of developing countries. IDA focuses on the world's poorest countries, while IBRD assists middle-income and creditworthy poorer countries. IFC, MIGA, and ICSID focus on strengthening the private sector in developing countries. Through these institutions, the World Bank Group provides financing, technical assistance, political risk insurance, and settlement of disputes to private enterprises, including financial institutions.

China began its partnership with the World Bank in 1980, just as it embarked on its reforms. Starting as a recipient of support from the International Development Association (IDA), the World Bank's fund for the poorest, China graduated from IDA in 1999 and became a contributor in 2007. It became the third largest shareholder in the World Bank upon completion of the capital increase approved in 2010, the 30th anniversary year of its partnership.

Throughout this time, the nature of the World Bank's activities in China changed to meet the country's rapidly evolving needs. Initially, the World Bank provided technical assistance to introduce basic economic reforms, modern project management methodologies, and new technologies. Later, the focus shifted to institutional strengthening and knowledge transfer. The World Bank now encourages knowledge sharing to enable the rest of the world to learn from China's experience.

Confederation of Indian Industry

The Confederation of Indian Industry (CII) works to create and sustain an environment conducive to the development of India, partnering industry, Government, and civil society, through advisory and consultative processes.

CII is a non-government, not-for-profit, industry-led and industry-managed organization, playing a proactive role in India's development process. Founded in 1895, India's premier business association has over 9,100 members, from the private as well as public sectors, including SMEs and MNCs, and an indirect membership of over 300,000 enterprises from around 291 national and regional sectoral industry bodies.

CII charts change by working closely with Government on policy issues, interfacing with thought leaders, and enhancing efficiency, competitiveness and business opportunities for industry through a range of specialized services and strategic global linkages. It also provides a platform for consensus-building and networking on key issues.

Extending its agenda beyond business, CII assists industry to identify and execute corporate citizenship programmes. Partnerships with civil society organizations carry forward corporate initiatives for integrated and inclusive development across diverse domains including affirmative action, healthcare, education, livelihood, diversity management, skill development, empowerment of women, and water, to name a few.

With 68 offices, including 9 Centres of Excellence, in India, and 11 overseas offices in Australia, China, Egypt, France, Germany, Indonesia,

Singapore, South Africa, UAE, UK, and USA, as well as institutional partnerships with 394 counterpart organizations in 133 countries, CII serves as a reference point for Indian industry and the international business community.

Nomura Research Institute

Nomura Research Institute (NRI), the largest think tank in Asia, was founded in 1965 and became the world's first think tank, consulting and system integration enterprise in 1988. It was listed on the main board of the Tokyo stock exchange in 2001. With more than 10,000 professionals and an annual turnover of over $3.5 billion, NRI group is the largest consulting group in Asia.

NRI research covers all major industries and continues to provide comprehensive services to governments and large enterprises every year. Up to now, more than 20,000 projects have been executed in more than 5,000 target areas (industry $\times$ subject).

NRI has more than 1,000 professionals with independent operations in greater China in Shanghai, Beijing, Dalian, Hong Kong and Taipei. Since 1989, NRI has been conducting research and consulting business for Chinese government and enterprises in Chinese mainland. In 2002, it established Nomura integrated research in Shanghai, and in 2009, it established Beijing branch. Currently, NRI Shanghai is the consulting business headquarters of NRI in Chinese mainland, covering public development strategy consulting for Chinese government agencies at all levels, management consulting for global enterprises and Chinese enterprises.

NRI adheres to the corporate development concept of "research, management consulting, operation management", and is known for its steadfast work style and profound understanding of Asian culture, and enjoys a good reputation in Japan and China.

European Chamber, Shanghai Chapter

The European Union Chamber of Commerce in China (European

Chamber) was founded in 2000 by 51 member companies that shared a goal of establishing a common voice for the various business sectors of the European Union and European businesses operating in China. It is a members-driven, non-profit, fee-based organisation with a core structure of 31 working groups and for a representing European business in China. The European Chamber is recognised by the European Commission and the Chinese authorities as the official voice of European business in China.

The Shanghai Chapter of the European Union Chamber of Commerce in China was opened in 2002 and is currently the largest chapter in terms of number of member companies. It hosts over 21 active Working Groups and three Forums, as well as the China Desks for a number of European industry associations, such as the Independent (Auto) Aftermarket (AM) Desk, and the European Heating Industry (EHI). The chapter has strong relations with various branches of the local government including regular strategic dialogues with the Shanghai Development and Reform Commission (SDRC), the Shanghai Municipal Commission of Commerce (SCOFCOM), and the Shanghai Customs Bureau.

JLL

JLL is a leading professional services firm that specializes in real estate and investment management. Our vision is to reimagine the world of real estate, creating rewarding opportunities and amazing spaces where people can achieve their ambitions. In doing so, we will build a better tomorrow for our clients, our people and our communities. JLL is a Fortune 500 company with annual revenue of $16.3 billion, operations in over 80 countries and a global workforce of nearly 92,000 as of June 30, 2019. JLL is the brand name, and a registered trademark, of Jones Lang LaSalle Incorporated.

JLL has over 50 years of experience in Asia Pacific, with over 41,400 employees operating in 82 offices in 16 countries across the region. The firm won the "World's Best" and "Best in Asia Pacific" International Property Consultancy at the International Property Awards in 2018.

In Greater China, the firm was named "Best Property Consultancy in

China" at the International Property Awards Asia Pacific 2018, and has more than 2,580 professionals and 17,930 on-site staff providing quality real estate advice and services in over 80 cities across the country.

POSTSCRIPT

后　记

　　根据上海市人民政府发展研究中心主要从事战略性、前瞻性和综合性研究的职能定位，结合上海市委、市政府年度重点工作和国际智库选题建议，上海市人民政府发展研究中心通过举办以"长三角一体化与高质量发展"为主题的"2019年上海国际智库高峰论坛"，组织国际智库开展了长三角一体化相关研究。

　　本次论坛由上海市人民政府发展研究中心主办，毕马威华振会计师事务所担任轮值主席单位，并首次邀请长三角区域合作办公室和东方网・东方智库作为论坛支持单位，上海市人民政府发展研究中心国际合作交流办公室、毕马威和上海发展研究基金会组成论坛筹备组具体开展会务组织和策划工作。为做好相关研究和会议筹备工作，2019年4—5月，上海市人民政府发展研究中心向22家上海国际智库交流中心成员单位发放《2019年上海国际智库高峰论坛意见征询表》，广泛听取各智库成员单位对上海国际智库高峰论坛2019年选题、组织形式和改进创新的意见与建议；6月，与轮值主席毕马威中国组成筹备团队，商讨论坛初步筹备方案；7月，正式确定了本届论坛主题——"长三角一体化与高质量发展"，组织国际智库启动相关研究；8月，在上海书展期间，东方网・东方智库联合上海远东出版社、普华永道、毕马威等智库，开展了2019年上海国际智库高峰论坛预热活动；9—10月，筹备组召集20余家上海国际智库交流中心成员单位召开高峰论坛筹办预备会议，并走访了29家驻沪国际智库，启动演讲嘉宾邀请、演讲主题角度的选择等工作；11月，围绕论坛主题公开征集了本市高校和国际智库相关研究报告。同时，围绕论坛主题，筹备组拜会了日本贸易振兴机构和戴德梁行等智库机构，在调研基础上完成了三篇"长三角一体化发展"系列研究报告，报上海市领导决策参考。

　　本次高峰论坛得到了上海市政府办公厅、市外办、市台办等方面的大力支持和指导，尤其是获得了世界银行驻华代表处吴晶女士、波士顿咨询公司梁瑜女士、麦肯锡公司罗至诚女士、罗兰贝格公司夏一正先生、科尔尼公司周鹏远先生、普华永道张艳女士、德勤滕婧静女士、毕马威高虹女士、安永袁霖女士、野村综研黄思华先生、凯捷咨询曹艳女士、高风咨询林君倩女士、戴德梁行胡桐女士、仲量联行王沛先生、美中贸易全国委员会上海代表处许子兰女士、日本贸易振兴机构刘元森先生、印度工业联合会杨春兰女士等上海国际智库交流中心成员单位联络人员的鼎力支持和积极配合。

本书的出版得到了各位与会国际智库和专家学者以及上海世纪出版集团上海远东出版社的大力支持,上海外国语大学肖维青教授团队承担了大量的译校工作,上海市人民政府发展研究中心国合办负责主要编辑工作,信息处和科研处的同仁也给予了积极协助,在此一并表示感谢!

上海市人民政府发展研究中心国合办

上海国际智库交流中心

2020 年 5 月 18 日

Drawing on its main functional positioning engaged in strategic, forward-looking and comprehensive research, the Development Research Center of Shanghai Municipal People's Government (SDRC) has organized international think tanks to carry out research on the integration of the Yangtze River Delta and held the "2019 Shanghai International Think Tank Summit" themed on "Integration of the Yangtze River Delta for High-quality Development" according to annual priorities of the CPC Shanghai Committee and the Shanghai Municipal People's Government and the topics advised by international think tanks.

This Summit is hosted by the SDRC and the chairman-in-office this year is KPMG China, and supported by the Yangtze River Delta Regional Cooperation Office and Eastday·Oriental Think Tank. The Preparatory Group includes the International Cooperation & Exchange Office of the SDRC, KPMG China and the Shanghai Development Research Foundation. The Group is responsible for detailed summit organization and planning. In order to make relevant research and preparation, the SDRC issued questionnaires to 22 members of the Shanghai International Think Tank Exchange Center from April to May in 2019 for extensive opinions and suggestions on the topic selection, organization form, work improvement and innovation; in June, a preparatory team was formed and it worked with the chairman-in-office KPMG China to discuss the preliminary preparation plan for the summit; in July, the theme of this year was officially decided as "Integration of the Yangtze River Delta for High-quality Development", and relevant research was initiated by some international think tanks; in September, during the Shanghai Book Fair, Eastday · Oriental Think Tank cooperated with Shanghai Far East Publishers, PwC and KPMG to organize warming-up activities for the summit; from September to October, the preparatory group convened more than 20 members of the Shanghai International Think Tank Exchange Center to hold a preparatory meeting, and visited 29 international think tanks in Shanghai to start works including presenter invitation and speech topic selection, etc.; in November, open call was made for theme-related research reports from universities and international think tanks in Shanghai. At the same time, the preparatory group also visited think tanks such as JETRO and Cushman & Wakefield to complete three survey reports on "Integration of the Yangtze River Delta for High-quality Development" and submitted them to the municipal leaders for decision-making.

This Summit has received much support and guidance from the General Office, Foreign Affairs Office and Taiwan Affairs Office of Shanghai Municipal People's Government. Special thanks are due to all of the contacts of the Shanghai International Think Tank Exchange Center members who have lent their support and coordination, including Ms. Wu Xiao from the World Bank Beijing Office, Ms. Liang Yu from Boston Consulting Group, Ms. Luo Zhicheng from McKinsey & Company, Mr. Xia Yizheng from Roland Berger, Mr. Zhou Pengyuan from A.T. Kearney, Ms. Zhang Yan from PwC, Ms. Teng Jingjing from Deloitte, Ms. Gao Hong from KPMG, Ms. Yuan Lin from Ernst & Young, Mr. Huang Sihua from NRI, Ms. Cao Yan from Capgemini, Ms. Lin Junqian from Gao Feng Advisory Company,

Ms. Hu Tong from Cushman & Wakefield, Mr. Wang Pei from JLL, Ms. Xu Zilan from US-China Business Council, Mr. Liu Yuansen from Japan External Trade Organization, and Ms. Yang Chunlan from Confederation of Indian Industry.

This book has been published with the generous support from all participating international think tanks, experts and scholars and Shanghai Far East Publishers. The team lead by Professor Xiao Weiqing of Shanghai International Studies University undertook the translation and proofreading of the book. International Cooperation & Exchange Office of the SDRC was in charge of editing the book; and colleagues from Information Division and Academic Cooperation Division also lent active assistance. We therefore would like to take this opportunity to publicly thank all of those involved!

International Cooperation & Exchange Office of the SDRC

Shanghai International Think Tank Exchange Center

May 18, 2020

图书在版编目(CIP)数据

长三角一体化与高质量发展:2019年上海国际智库
咨询研究报告:汉文、英文 / 上海市人民政府发展研究
中心编. —上海:上海远东出版社,2020
(上海市人民政府发展研究中心系列报告)
ISBN 978 - 7 - 5476 - 1608 - 6

Ⅰ. ①长… Ⅱ. ①上… Ⅲ. ①长江三角洲—区域经济一
体化—区域经济发展—研究报告—2019 Ⅳ. ①F127.5

中国版本图书馆 CIP 数据核字(2020)第 106252 号

责任编辑 程云琦
封面设计 李 廉

长三角一体化与高质量发展
　　——2019 年上海国际智库咨询研究报告

上海市人民政府发展研究中心 编

出　　版 **上海远东出版社**
　　　　　(200235 中国上海市钦州南路 81 号)
发　　行 上海人民出版社发行中心
印　　刷 江苏凤凰数码印务有限公司
开　　本 787×1092 1/16
印　　张 27.75
字　　数 513,000
插　　页 10
版　　次 2020 年 8 月第 1 版
印　　次 2021 年 7 月第 2 次印刷
ISBN 978 - 7 - 5476 - 1608 - 6/F · 660
定　　价 148.00 元